WOMEN'S HEALTH

WOMEN'S HEALTH

PROFESSOR PETER ABRAHAMS

amber
BOOKS

This edition first published in 2010

Published by
Amber Books Ltd
Bradley's Close
74–77 White Lion Street
London N1 9PF
United Kingdom
www.amberbooks.co.uk

ISBN: 978-1-906626-76-1

Project Editor: Sarah Uttridge
Additional Design: Hawes Design
Jacket Design: Keren Harragan

Printed in Thailand

Contents

Introduction

Women's health is more complex and more varied than men's
health, notably because of our reproductive system, our biological
clock, pregnancy and the menopause

This book simplifies this huge, complex subject by breaking it down into several substantial sections:

■ Medical briefing that explains the structure or anatomy of the female body

■ Female reproductive system from the start of the menstrual cycle, through pregnancy and childbirth, to the menopause and HRT

■ Sexual health including contraception, pelvic pain, vaginal pain, vulval itching and infections

■ Female cancers – of which breast cancer, rare in men, is by far the most common cancer in women – with a strong focus on preventative health through regular screening

■ Skin disorders – including acne and disorders of the scalp

■ Mental health, including, for example, depression, obsessive compulsive disorder and bulimia and anorexia, all of which are more common in women than men

■ Complementary medicine – a selection of therapies to strengthen the immune system, increase your vitality, promote

Left: A female patient is examined by a doctor. It is vital to consult a doctor if you are concerned about health issues.

relaxation and, above all, alleviate depression and anxiety

Each large section comprises a number of topics, listed on the contents page, each of which is described in detail and clearly illustrated.

YOUR VITALITY AND WELL BEING

Feeling good, living your life to the full, rests with good health – and this in turn depends on you making your health your top priority. If you need a test of any sort, don't delay. If you are called, for example, for a cervical smear or mammogram, take the appointment – don't put it off. These apparently routine appointments play a vital role in detecting any early signs of disease or disorder.

MAMMOGRAMS

While mammograms are momentarily uncomfortable, rather than painful, they are important in picking up abnormalities that could signal early signs of breast cancer, the most common female cancer in women under the age of 35. The likelihood of breast cancer increases with age, with the greatest rate of increase seen prior to the menopause. The lifetime risk of being diagnosed with breast cancer in women in

1 is 9.5. Early detection often leads to a good outcome: breast cancer is no longer the killer it once was. The chances of surviving breast cancer for more than five years are now over 75 per cent.

Self-examination is equally important: many cases of breast cancer are detected initially by the woman herself noticing a lump or change in shape of the breast and/or nipple.

GIVING UP SMOKING

This is the single biggest step you can take to improve your health and now is the time to do it. Giving up smoking in your forties or fifties is much more difficult than in your twenties or thirties. Smoking adversely affects every part of the body – every system, every organ. It greatly increases the chances of breast cancer and other cancers. It is largely responsible for lung cancer, which in non-smokers is rare. Bronchitis and emphysema are far more common in smokers.

BLOOD PRESSURE CHECKS AND CHOLESTEROL TESTING

These are a vital element in your preventative health care. Stroke is the currently our third biggest killer and is the biggest cause of disability in our middle years.

It is important to monitor blood pressure as high pressure can lead to strokes and heart attack.

Regular exercise not only helps the body to stay healthy, it also increases energy levels and benefits the mind.

Stroke is less likely in women who are taking blood pressure and cholesterol lowering drugs and who do not smoke. Simple lifestyle changes such as eating healthily and exercising regularly are important in warding off heart disease and stroke.

GOLDEN RULES FOR YOUR QUALITY OF LIFE

■ If it hurts, check it out. Pain is always a symptom of something. It is not a disorder in itself.

■ You can be ill as well as pregnant: beware of attributing every ache and pain during pregnancy to your pregnancy.

■ If you feel "just not right", "not myself", consult your family doctor. You may be depressed or suffering the early signs of other illness.

■ Exercise three to five times a week and eat well in order to build a good base for your later years: poor diet and inactivity are the real killers in old age.

■ Have a dental check every six months.

■ Get an optical check every year or two. Disorders such as diabetes, easily treatable, are frequently observed first during an eye examination.

■ Never put off a visit to the family doctor or the hospital. Make your health, and health screening, your priority.

Female reproductive system

The role of the female reproductive tract is twofold.
The ovaries produce eggs for fertilization, and the uterus nurtures
and protects any resulting fetus for its nine-month gestation.

The female reproductive tract is composed of the internal genitalia – the ovaries, uterine (Fallopian) tubes, uterus and vagina – and the external genitalia (the vulva).

INTERNAL GENITALIA

The almond-shaped ovaries lie on either side of the uterus, suspended by ligaments. Above the ovaries are the paired uterine tubes, each of which provides a site for fertilization of the oocyte (egg), which then travels down the tube to the uterus.

The uterus lies within the pelvic cavity and rises into the lower abdominal cavity as a pregnancy progresses. The vagina, which connects the cervix to the vulva, can be distended greatly, as occurs during childbirth when it forms much of the birth canal.

EXTERNAL GENITALIA

The female external genitalia, or vulva, is where the reproductive tract opens to the exterior. The vaginal opening lies behind the opening of the urethra in an area known as the vestibule. This is covered by two folds of skin on each side, the labia minora and labia majora, in front of which lies the raised clitoris.

The female reproductive system is composed of internal and external organs. The internal genitalia are T-shaped and lie within the pelvic cavity.

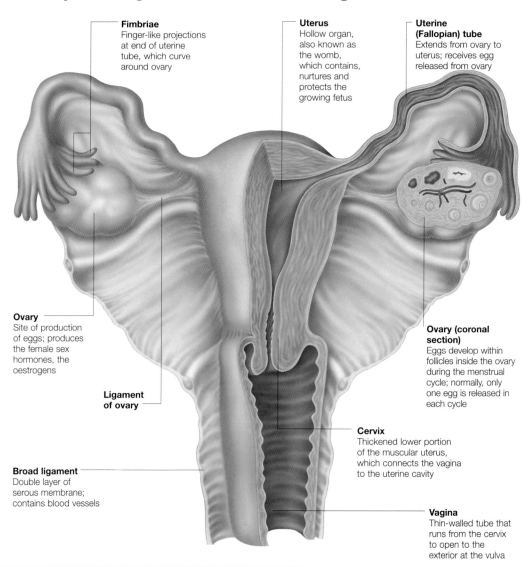

Fimbriae
Finger-like projections at end of uterine tube, which curve around ovary

Uterus
Hollow organ, also known as the womb, which contains, nurtures and protects the growing fetus

Uterine (Fallopian) tube
Extends from ovary to uterus; receives egg released from ovary

Ovary
Site of production of eggs; produces the female sex hormones, the oestrogens

Ligament of ovary

Broad ligament
Double layer of serous membrane; contains blood vessels

Ovary (coronal section)
Eggs develop within follicles inside the ovary during the menstrual cycle; normally, only one egg is released in each cycle

Cervix
Thickened lower portion of the muscular uterus, which connects the vagina to the uterine cavity

Vagina
Thin-walled tube that runs from the cervix to open to the exterior at the vulva

Position of the female reproductive tract

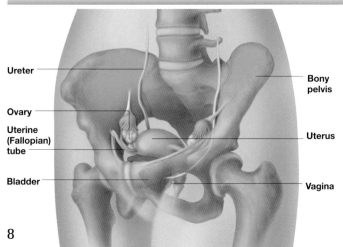

Ureter

Ovary

Uterine (Fallopian) tube

Bladder

Bony pelvis

Uterus

Vagina

The position of the internal genitalia (which, apart from the ovaries, are basically tubular in structure) changes at puberty. In adult women, they are located deep within the pelvic cavity. They are thus protected by the presence of the circle of bone that makes up the pelvis.

The internal reproductive organs in adult women are positioned deep within the pelvic cavity. They are therefore protected by the bony pelvis.

This is in contrast to the pelvic cavity of young children, which is relatively shallow. A girl's uterus, like the bladder behind which it sits, is located within the lower abdomen.

BROAD LIGAMENTS

The upper surface of the uterus and ovaries is draped in a 'tent' of peritoneum, the thin lining of the abdominal and pelvic cavities, forming the broad ligament which helps to keep the uterus in its position.

Blood supply of the internal genitalia

The female reproductive tract receives a rich blood supply via an interconnecting network of arteries. Venous blood is drained by a network of veins.

The four principal arteries of the female genitalia are:

■ **Ovarian artery** – this runs from the abdominal aorta to the ovary.

Branches from the ovarian artery on each side pass through the mesovarium, the fold of peritoneum in which the ovary lies, to supply the ovary and uterine (Fallopian) tubes. The ovarian artery in the tissue of the mesovarium connects with the uterine artery

■ **Uterine artery** – this is a branch of the large internal iliac artery of the pelvis. The uterine artery approaches the uterus at the level of the cervix, which is anchored in place by cervical ligaments.

The uterine artery connects with the ovarian artery above, while a branch connects with the arteries below to supply the cervix and vagina

■ **Vaginal artery** – this is also a branch of the internal iliac artery. Together with blood from the uterine artery, its branches supply blood to the vaginal walls

■ **Internal pudendal artery** – this contributes to the blood supply of the lower third of the vagina and anus.

VEINS

A plexus, or network, of small veins lies within the walls of the uterus and vagina. Blood received into these vessels drains into the internal iliac veins via the uterine vein.

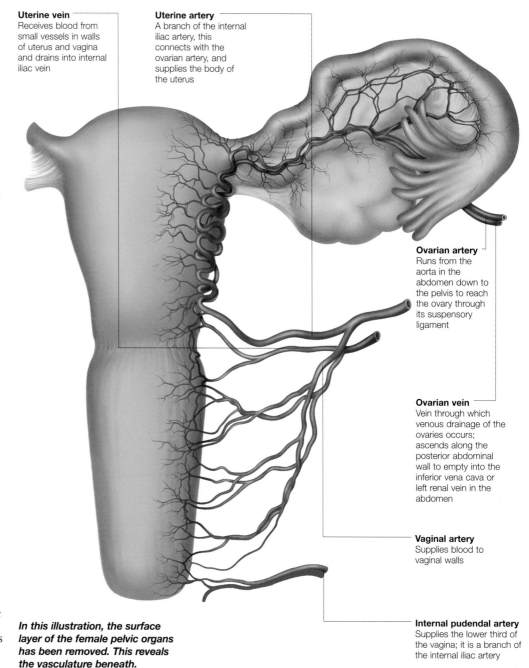

Uterine vein
Receives blood from small vessels in walls of uterus and vagina and drains into internal iliac vein

Uterine artery
A branch of the internal iliac artery, this connects with the ovarian artery, and supplies the body of the uterus

Ovarian artery
Runs from the aorta in the abdomen down to the pelvis to reach the ovary through its suspensory ligament

Ovarian vein
Vein through which venous drainage of the ovaries occurs; ascends along the posterior abdominal wall to empty into the inferior vena cava or left renal vein in the abdomen

Vaginal artery
Supplies blood to vaginal walls

Internal pudendal artery
Supplies the lower third of the vagina; it is a branch of the internal iliac artery

In this illustration, the surface layer of the female pelvic organs has been removed. This reveals the vasculature beneath.

Visualizing the female reproductive tract

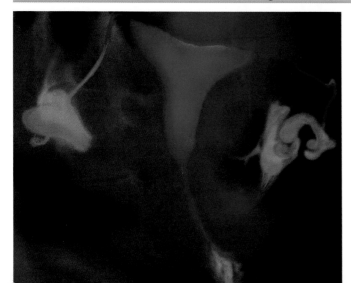

The tubal or hollow parts of the female reproductive tract can be outlined by performing a hysterosalpingogram.

In this procedure, a special radio-opaque dye is passed up into the uterus through the cervix, while X-ray pictures of the area are taken. The dye fills the uterine cavity, and enters

This hysterosalpingogram shows the uterine cavity (centre) filled with dye. Dye is also seen in the uterine tubes and emerging into the peritoneal cavity.

the uterine tubes. It then runs along their length until it flows into the peritoneal cavity at their far end.

ASSESSING TUBES

A hysterosalpingogram is sometimes carried out in the investigation of infertility to determine whether the uterine tubes are still patent (unobstructed). If the tubes have been blocked, as may happen after an infection, the dye will not be able to travel along their full length.

Uterus

The uterus, or womb, is the part of the female reproductive
tract that nurtures and protects the fetus during pregnancy. It lies
within the pelvic cavity and is a hollow, muscular organ.

During a woman's reproductive years, in the non-pregnant state, the uterus is about 7.5cm (3in) long and 5cm (2in) across at its widest point. However, it can expand to accommodate the fetus during pregnancy.

STRUCTURE
The uterus is said to be made up of two parts:
■ The body, forming the upper part of the uterus – this is fairly mobile, as it must expand during pregnancy. The central triangular space, or cavity, of the body receives the openings of the paired uterine (Fallopian) tubes
■ The cervix, the lower part of the uterus – this is a thick, muscular canal, which is anchored to the surrounding pelvic structures for stability.

UTERINE WALLS
The main part of the uterus, the body, has a thick wall which is composed of three layers:
■ Perimetrium – the thin outer coat, which is continuous with the pelvic peritoneum
■ Myometrium – forming the great bulk of the uterine wall
■ Endometrium – the delicate lining, which is specialized to allow implantation of an embryo should fertilization occur.

The uterus resembles an inverted pear in shape. It is suspended in the pelvic cavity by peritoneal folds or ligaments.

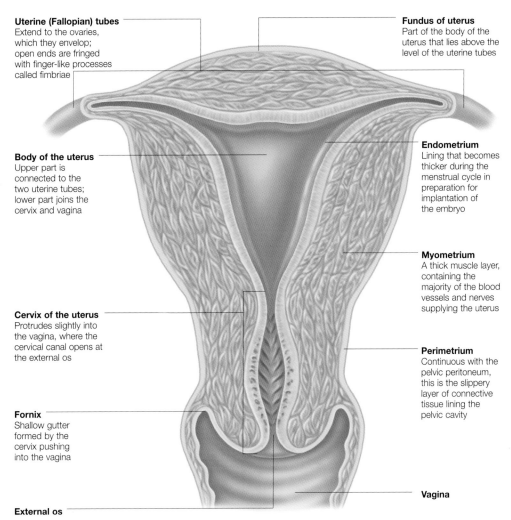

Uterine (Fallopian) tubes
Extend to the ovaries, which they envelop; open ends are fringed with finger-like processes called fimbriae

Body of the uterus
Upper part is connected to the two uterine tubes; lower part joins the cervix and vagina

Cervix of the uterus
Protrudes slightly into the vagina, where the cervical canal opens at the external os

Fornix
Shallow gutter formed by the cervix pushing into the vagina

External os

Fundus of uterus
Part of the body of the uterus that lies above the level of the uterine tubes

Endometrium
Lining that becomes thicker during the menstrual cycle in preparation for implantation of the embryo

Myometrium
A thick muscle layer, containing the majority of the blood vessels and nerves supplying the uterus

Perimetrium
Continuous with the pelvic peritoneum, this is the slippery layer of connective tissue lining the pelvic cavity

Vagina

Position of the uterus

Normal position of the uterus

Bladder

Vagina

Uterus in extreme retroverted position

Rectum

The uterus lies in the pelvis between the bladder and the rectum. However, its position changes with the stage of filling of these two structures and with different postures.

NORMAL POSITION
Normally the long axis of the uterus forms an angle of 90° to the long axis of the vagina, and the uterus lies forward on top of the bladder. This usual position is known as anteversion.

In most women the uterus lies on the bladder, moving backwards as the bladder fills. However, it may lie in any position between the two extremes shown.

ANTEFLEXION
In some women, the uterus lies in the normal position, but may curve forwards slightly between the cervix and fundus. This is termed anteflexion.

RETROFLEXION
In some cases, however, the uterus bends not forwards but backwards, the fundus coming to lie next to the rectum. This is known as a retroverted uterus.
  Regardless of the uterine position, it will normally bend forwards as it expands in pregnancy. A pregnant retroverted uterus, however, may take longer to reach the pelvic brim, at which point it becomes palpable abdominally.

The uterus in pregnancy

In pregnancy, the uterus must enlarge to hold the growing fetus. From being a small pelvic organ, it increases in size to take up much of the space of the abdominal cavity.

Pressure of the enlarged uterus on the abdominal organs pushes them up against the diaphragm, encroaching on the thoracic cavity and causing the ribs to flare out to compensate. Organs such as the stomach and bladder are compressed to such an extent in late pregnancy that their capacity is greatly diminished and they become full sooner.

After pregnancy, the uterus will rapidly decrease in size again, although it will always remain slightly larger than one which has never been pregnant.

HEIGHT OF FUNDUS
During pregnancy, the enlarging uterus can be accommodated within the pelvis for the first 12 weeks, at which time the uppermost part, the fundus, can just be palpated in the lower abdomen. By 20 weeks, the fundus will have reached the region of the umbilicus, and by late pregnancy it may have reached the xiphisternum, the lowest part of the breastbone.

WEIGHT OF UTERUS
In the final stages of pregnancy the uterus will have increased in weight from a pre-pregnant 45g (1 ½oz) to around 900g (32oz). The myometrium (muscle layer) grows as the individual fibres increase in size (hypertrophy). In addition, the fibres increase in number (hyperplasia).

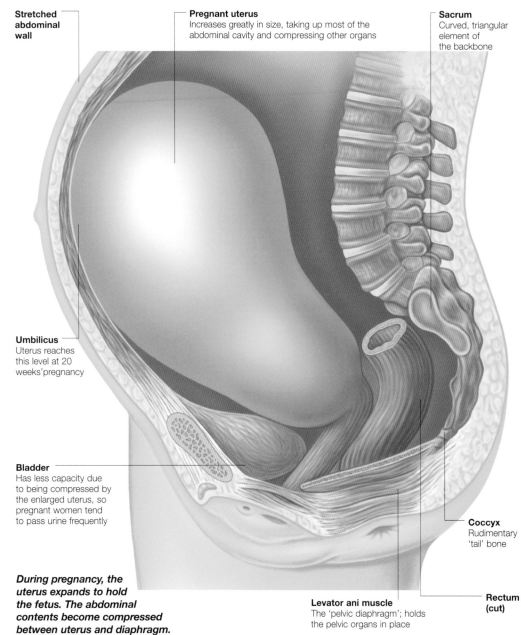

Stretched abdominal wall

Pregnant uterus
Increases greatly in size, taking up most of the abdominal cavity and compressing other organs

Sacrum
Curved, triangular element of the backbone

Umbilicus
Uterus reaches this level at 20 weeks'pregnancy

Bladder
Has less capacity due to being compressed by the enlarged uterus, so pregnant women tend to pass urine frequently

Coccyx
Rudimentary 'tail' bone

Rectum (cut)

Levator ani muscle
The 'pelvic diaphragm'; holds the pelvic organs in place

During pregnancy, the uterus expands to hold the fetus. The abdominal contents become compressed between uterus and diaphragm.

Lining of the uterus

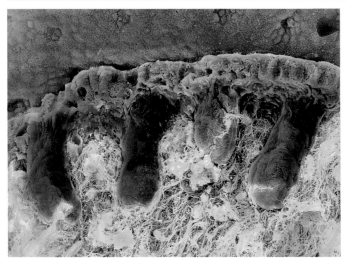

The endometrium is the name given to the lining of the uterus. It consists of a simple surface layer, or epithelium, overlying a thicker layer of highly cellular connective tissue, the lamina propria. Numerous tubular glands are also present within the endometrium.

MENSTRUAL CYCLE
Under the influence of sex hormones, the endometrium undergoes changes during the

This enlarged section through the endometrium of the uterus shows the layer of epithelial cells (blue). Three tubular glands are also clearly visible.

monthly menstrual cycle, which prepare it for the possible implantation of an embryo. It varies in thickness from 1mm to 5mm (up to ¼ in) before being shed at menstruation.

BLOOD SUPPLY
Arteries within the myometrium, the underlying muscle layer, send numerous small branches into the endometrium. There are two types: straight arteries, which supply the lower, permanent layer; and tortuous (twisted) spiral arteries, which supply the upper layer shed during menstruation. The tortuosity of the spiral arteries prevents excess bleeding during menstruation.

Vagina and cervix

The vagina is the thin-walled muscular tube that extends from the cervix of the uterus to the external genitalia. The vagina is closed at rest but is designed to stretch during intercourse or childbirth.

The vagina is approximately 8cm (3 ¼ in) in length and lies between the bladder and the rectum. It forms the main part of the birth canal and receives the penis during sexual intercourse.

STRUCTURE OF THE VAGINA

The front and back walls of the vagina normally lie in contact with one another, closing the lumen (central space), although the vagina can expand greatly, as occurs in childbirth.

The cervix, the lower end of the uterus, projects down into the lumen of the vagina at its upper end. Where the vagina arches up to meet the cervix, it forms recesses known as the vaginal fornices. These are divided into anterior, posterior, right and left fornices, although they form a complete ring.

The thin wall of the vagina has three layers:
■ Adventitia – outer layer composed of fibroelastic connective tissue, which allows distension when necessary
■ Muscularis – the central muscular layer of the vaginal wall
■ Mucosa – the inner layer of the vagina; this is thrown into many rugae (deep folds), and has a layered, stratified squamous (skinlike) epithelium (cell lining), which helps to resist abrasion during intercourse.

The vagina is a muscular, tubular organ designed to expand during sexual intercourse and childbirth. It is approximately 8cm (3.2) long.

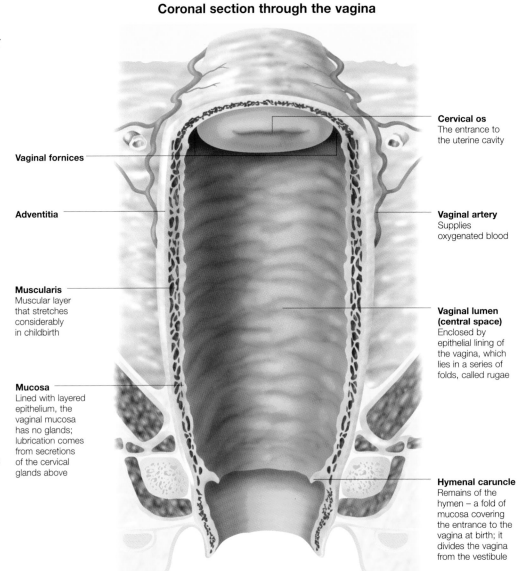

Coronal section through the vagina

Vaginal fornices

Adventitia

Muscularis
Muscular layer that stretches considerably in childbirth

Mucosa
Lined with layered epithelium, the vaginal mucosa has no glands; lubrication comes from secretions of the cervical glands above

Cervical os
The entrance to the uterine cavity

Vaginal artery
Supplies oxygenated blood

Vaginal lumen (central space)
Enclosed by epithelial lining of the vagina, which lies in a series of folds, called rugae

Hymenal caruncle
Remains of the hymen – a fold of mucosa covering the entrance to the vagina at birth; it divides the vagina from the vestibule

External genitalia

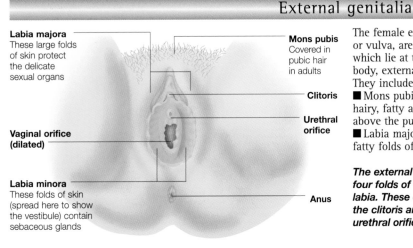

Labia majora
These large folds of skin protect the delicate sexual organs

Mons pubis
Covered in pubic hair in adults

Clitoris

Urethral orifice

Vaginal orifice (dilated)

Labia minora
These folds of skin (spread here to show the vestibule) contain sebaceous glands

Anus

The female external genitalia, or vulva, are those parts which lie at the surface of the body, external to the vagina. They include:
■ Mons pubis – the rounded, hairy, fatty area which lies above the pubic bone
■ Labia majora – the two outer fatty folds of skin, which lie

The external genitalia include four folds of skin, known as the labia. These cover and protect the clitoris and the vaginal and urethral orifices.

across the vulval opening
■ Labia minora – the two smaller folds of skin which lie inside the cleft of the vulva
■ Vestibule – area into which the urethra and vagina open
■ Clitoris – a structure composed of erectile tissue and containing a rich sensory nerve supply; it is analogous to the penis in males.

The vulval opening is partially closed off by a fold of mucosa, the hymen; this may rupture at first intercourse, with tampon use or during a pelvic examination.

The cervix

The cervix, or neck of the uterus, is the narrowed, lower part of the uterus which projects down into the upper vagina.

The cervix is fixed in position by the cervical ligaments, and so anchors the relatively mobile uterine body above.

CERVICAL STRUCTURE

The cervix has a narrow canal, which is approximately 2.5cm (1in) long in adult women. The walls of the cervix are tough, containing much fibrous tissue as well as muscle, unlike the body of the uterus, which is mainly muscular.

The central canal of the cervix is the downwards continuation of the uterine cavity, which opens at its lower end, the external os, into the vagina. The canal is widest at its central point, constricting slightly at the internal os at the upper end and the external os below.

LINING OF THE CERVIX

The epithelium, or lining, of the cervix is of two types:
- Endocervix – this is the lining of the cervical canal, inside the cervix. The epithelium is a simple, single layer of columnar cells, which overlies a surface thrown into many folds containing glands.
- Ectocervix – this covers the portion of the cervix which projects down into the vagina; it is composed of squamous epithelium and has many layers.

The cervix is located at the lower end of the uterus. It contains less muscle tissue than the uterus and is lined with two different types of epithelial cell.

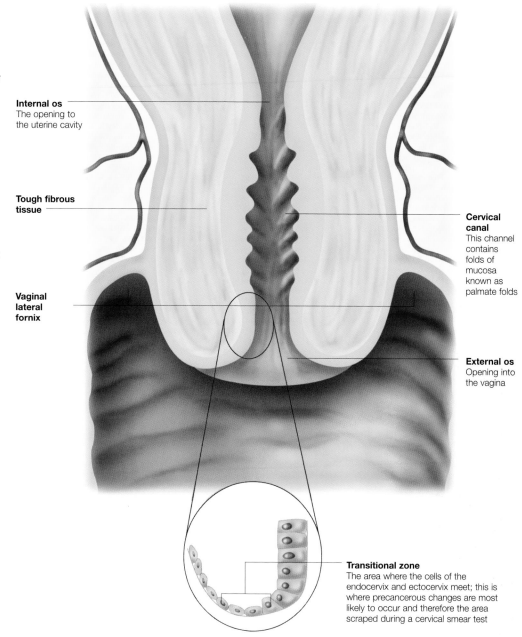

Internal os
The opening to the uterine cavity

Tough fibrous tissue

Vaginal lateral fornix

Cervical canal
This channel contains folds of mucosa known as palmate folds

External os
Opening into the vagina

Transitional zone
The area where the cells of the endocervix and ectocervix meet; this is where precancerous changes are most likely to occur and therefore the area scraped during a cervical smear test

---

Cervical os

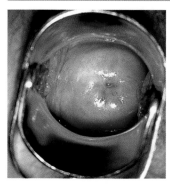

This healthy cervix is viewed through a metal speculum. The deeper pink lining of the inside of the cervix can be seen at the external cervical os.

The opening of the cervical canal into the upper vagina is known as the cervical os.

It may be necessary to look more closely at this area if, for example, some abnormal cells have been seen under the microscope during a routine cervical smear test. In this case a colposcope, a type of low-powered microscope, is used.

COLPOSCOPY

During colposcopy, the cervix is coated with a staining fluid that shows up any abnormal cells. A biopsy may be taken of any suspicious areas; further treatment may then be needed.

Nulliparous cervix

In a woman who has never given birth (nulliparous), the cervical os appears round in shape. The canal is also more tightly closed before childbirth.

Parous cervix

After childbirth, the os becomes slitlike in appearance. The cervical canal is slightly looser, following the passage of the fetus.

Ovaries and uterine tubes

The ovaries are the site of production of oocytes, or eggs, which are fertilized by sperm to produce embryos. The uterine (or Fallopian) tubes conduct the oocytes from the ovaries to the uterus.

The paired ovaries are situated in the lower abdomen and lie on either side of the uterus. Their position may be variable, especially after childbirth, when the supporting ligaments have been stretched.

Each ovary consists of:
■ Tunica albuginea – a protective layer of fibrous tissue
■ Medulla – a central region with blood vessels and nerves
■ Cortex – within which the oocytes develop
■ Surface layer – smooth before puberty but becoming more pitted in the reproductive years.

BLOOD SUPPLY
The arterial supply to the ovaries comes via the ovarian arteries, which arise from the abdominal aorta. After supplying the uterine tubes also, the ovarian arteries overlap with the uterine arteries.

Blood from the ovaries enters a network of tiny veins, the pampiniform plexus, within the broad ligament, from which it enters the right and left ovarian veins. These ascend into the abdomen to drain ultimately into the large inferior vena cava and the renal vein respectively.

This cross-section shows the follicles situated in the cortex of the ovary. Each follicle contains an oocyte at a different stage of development.

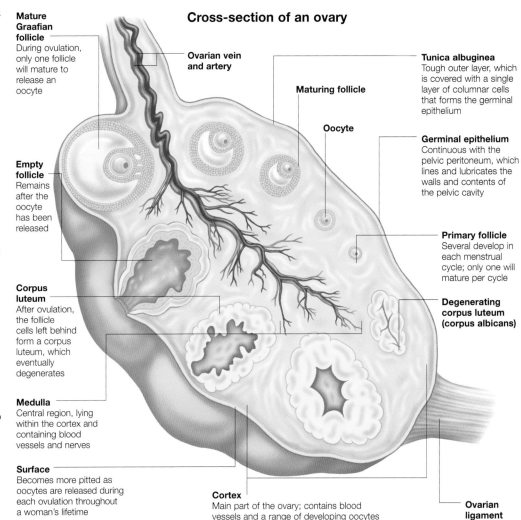

Cross-section of an ovary

Mature Graafian follicle
During ovulation, only one follicle will mature to release an oocyte

Empty follicle
Remains after the oocyte has been released

Corpus luteum
After ovulation, the follicle cells left behind form a corpus luteum, which eventually degenerates

Medulla
Central region, lying within the cortex and containing blood vessels and nerves

Surface
Becomes more pitted as oocytes are released during each ovulation throughout a woman's lifetime

Ovarian vein and artery

Maturing follicle

Oocyte

Cortex
Main part of the ovary; contains blood vessels and a range of developing oocytes

Tunica albuginea
Tough outer layer, which is covered with a single layer of columnar cells that forms the germinal epithelium

Germinal epithelium
Continuous with the pelvic peritoneum, which lines and lubricates the walls and contents of the pelvic cavity

Primary follicle
Several develop in each menstrual cycle; only one will mature per cycle

Degenerating corpus luteum (corpus albicans)

Ovarian ligament

Supporting ligaments

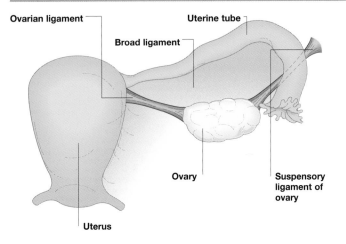

Ovarian ligament

Uterine tube

Broad ligament

Ovary

Suspensory ligament of ovary

Uterus

Each ovary is held in its position relative to the uterus and uterine tubes by several ligaments.

MAIN LIGAMENTS
These ligaments include the following:
■ Broad ligament – the tentlike fold of pelvic peritoneum, which hangs down on either side of the uterus, enclosing the uterine tubes and ovaries

Each ovary is suspended by several ligaments to hold it in position. However, the position varies, especially if the ligaments have stretched.

■ Suspensory ligament of the ovary – that part of the broad ligament which anchors the ovary to the side wall of the pelvis and carries the ovarian vessels and lymphatics
■ Mesovarium – the fold of the broad ligament within which the ovary lies.
■ Ovarian ligament – attaches the ovary to the uterus and runs within the broad ligament.

These ligaments may become stretched in women following childbirth, which in many cases means that the position of the ovary may be more variable than before pregnancy.

The uterine tubes

The uterine, or Fallopian, tubes collect the oocytes released from the ovaries and transport them to the uterus. They also provide a site for fertilization of the oocyte by a sperm to take place.

Each uterine tube is about 10cm (4in) long and extends outwards from the upper part of the body of the uterus towards the lateral wall of the pelvic cavity.

The tubes run within the upper edge of the broad ligament and open into the peritoneal cavity in the region of the ovary.

STRUCTURE
The tubes are divided anatomically into four parts which, from outer to inner, are:

■ Infundibulum – the funnel-shaped outer end of the uterine tubes which opens into the peritoneal cavity
■ Ampulla – the longest and widest part and the most usual site for fertilization of the oocyte
■ Isthmus – a constricted region with thick walls
■ Uterine part – this is the shortest part of the tube.

BLOOD SUPPLY
The uterine tubes have a very rich blood supply, which comes from both the ovarian and the uterine arteries; these overlap to form an arterial arcade.

Venous blood drains from the tubes in a pattern that mirrors the arterial supply.

Major parts of a uterine tube

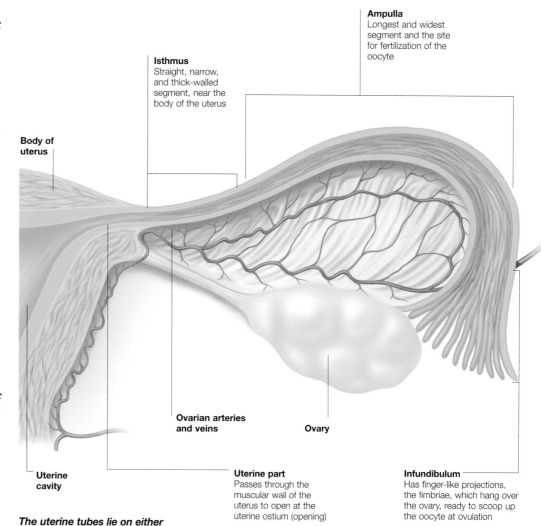

Isthmus
Straight, narrow, and thick-walled segment, near the body of the uterus

Ampulla
Longest and widest segment and the site for fertilization of the oocyte

Body of uterus

Ovarian arteries and veins

Ovary

Uterine cavity

Uterine part
Passes through the muscular wall of the uterus to open at the uterine ostium (opening)

Infundibulum
Has finger-like projections, the fimbriae, which hang over the ovary, ready to scoop up the oocyte at ovulation

The uterine tubes lie on either side of the body. The outer part of each tube lies near the ovary, its end opening there into the abdominal cavity.

Wall of a uterine tube

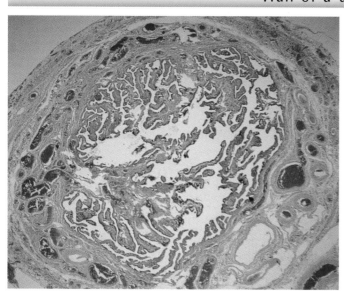

The structure of the wall of a uterine tube shows features that have developed to assist in the task of maintaining the oocyte and carrying it safely to the uterus for implantation:

■ A layer of smooth muscle fibres within the walls allows the uterine tubes to contract rhythmically, the waves of contraction passing towards the uterus.

■ The walls are lined with cells which bear cilia, tiny brushlike

The uterine tube wall is lined with two types of cell: mucus-secreting and ciliated. These act to nourish and propel the oocyte along the length of the tube.

projections that beat to 'sweep' the oocyte inwards towards the uterus.

■ Non-ciliated cells in deep crypts in the lining of the uterine tubes produce secretions that keep the oocyte, and any sperm which may be present, nourished during their journey along the tube.

OVARIAN HORMONES
The lining of the uterine tubes is influenced by ovarian hormones, and so may vary in its activity according to the phase of the menstrual cycle. The hormone progesterone, for instance, increases the amount of mucous secretions that are produced.

Female breast

The breast undergoes structural changes throughout the life of a woman. The most obvious changes occur during pregnancy as the breast prepares for its function as the source of milk for the baby.

Men and women both have breast tissue, but the breast is normally a well-developed structure only in women. The two female breasts are roughly hemispherical and are composed of fat and glandular tissue that overlie the muscle layer of the front of the chest wall on either side of the sternum (breastbone).

BREAST STRUCTURE

The base of the breast is roughly circular in shape and extends from the level of the second rib above to the sixth rib below. In addition, there may be an extension of breast tissue towards the axilla (armpit), known as the 'axillary tail'.

Breast size varies greatly between women; this is mainly due to the amount of fatty tissue present, as there is generally the same amount of glandular tissue in every breast.

The mammary glands consist of 15 to 20 lobules – clusters of secretory tissue from which milk is produced. Milk is carried to the surface of the breast from each lobule by a tube known as a 'lactiferous duct', which has its opening at the nipple.

The nipple is a protruding structure surrounded by a circular, pigmented area, called the areola. The skin of the nipple is very thin and delicate and has no hair follicles or sweat glands.

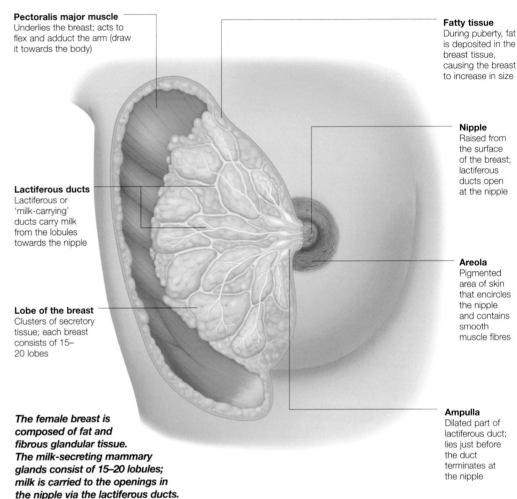

Pectoralis major muscle
Underlies the breast; acts to flex and adduct the arm (draw it towards the body)

Lactiferous ducts
Lactiferous or 'milk-carrying' ducts carry milk from the lobules towards the nipple

Lobe of the breast
Clusters of secretory tissue; each breast consists of 15–20 lobes

The female breast is composed of fat and fibrous glandular tissue. The milk-secreting mammary glands consist of 15–20 lobules; milk is carried to the openings in the nipple via the lactiferous ducts.

Fatty tissue
During puberty, fat is deposited in the breast tissue, causing the breast to increase in size

Nipple
Raised from the surface of the breast; lactiferous ducts open at the nipple

Areola
Pigmented area of skin that encircles the nipple and contains smooth muscle fibres

Ampulla
Dilated part of lactiferous duct; lies just before the duct terminates at the nipple

Blood vessels of the breast

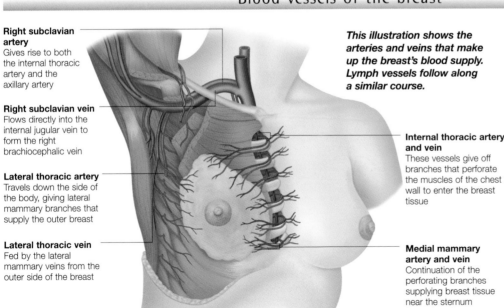

Right subclavian artery
Gives rise to both the internal thoracic artery and the axillary artery

Right subclavian vein
Flows directly into the internal jugular vein to form the right brachiocephalic vein

Lateral thoracic artery
Travels down the side of the body, giving lateral mammary branches that supply the outer breast

Lateral thoracic vein
Fed by the lateral mammary veins from the outer side of the breast

This illustration shows the arteries and veins that make up the breast's blood supply. Lymph vessels follow along a similar course.

Internal thoracic artery and vein
These vessels give off branches that perforate the muscles of the chest wall to enter the breast tissue

Medial mammary artery and vein
Continuation of the perforating branches supplying breast tissue near the sternum (breastbone)

The blood supply to the breast comes from a number of sources; these include the internal thoracic artery, which runs down the length of the front of the chest, and the lateral thoracic artery, which supplies the outer part of the breast and some of the posterior intercostal arteries.

A network of superficial veins underlies the skin of the breast, especially in the region of the areola, and these veins may become very prominent during pregnancy.

The blood collected in these veins drains in various directions, following a similar pattern to the arterial supply, travelling via the internal thoracic veins, the lateral thoracic veins and the posterior intercostal veins to the large veins that return blood to the heart.

Lymphatic drainage of the breast

Lymph, the fluid which leaks out of blood vessels into the spaces between cells, is returned to the blood circulation by the lymphatic system. Lymph passes through a series of lymph nodes, which act as filters to remove bacteria, cells and other particles.

Tiny lymphatic vessels arise from the tissue spaces and converge to form larger vessels, which carry the (usually) clear lymph away from the tissues and into the venous system.

Lymph drains from the nipple, areola and mammary gland lobules into a network of small lymphatic vessels, the 'subareolar lymphatic plexus'. From this plexus the lymph may be carried in several different directions.

PATTERN OF DRAINAGE

About 75 per cent of the lymph from the subareolar plexus drains to the lymph nodes of the armpit, mostly from the outer quadrants of the breast. The lymph passes through a series of nodes in the region of the armpit draining into the subclavian lymph trunk, and ultimately into the right lymphatic trunk, which returns the lymph to the veins above the heart.

Most of the remaining lymph, mainly from the inner quadrants of the breast, is carried to the 'parasternal' lymph nodes, which lie towards the mid-line of the front of the chest. A small percentage of lymphatic vessels from the breast take another route and travel to the posterior intercostal nodes.

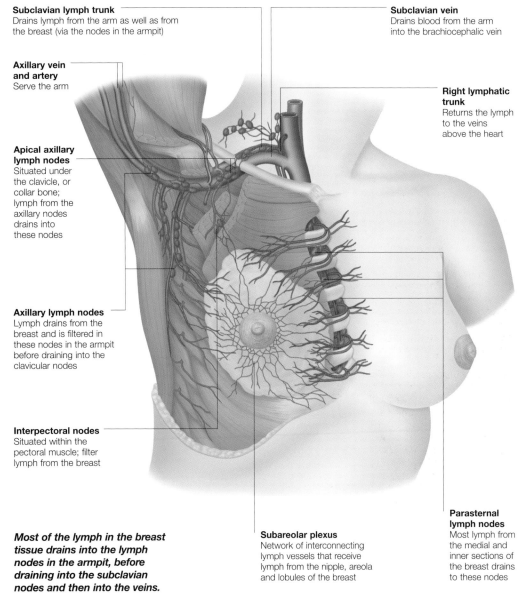

Subclavian lymph trunk
Drains lymph from the arm as well as from the breast (via the nodes in the armpit)

Axillary vein and artery
Serve the arm

Apical axillary lymph nodes
Situated under the clavicle, or collar bone; lymph from the axillary nodes drains into these nodes

Axillary lymph nodes
Lymph drains from the breast and is filtered in these nodes in the armpit before draining into the clavicular nodes

Interpectoral nodes
Situated within the pectoral muscle; filter lymph from the breast

Subclavian vein
Drains blood from the arm into the brachiocephalic vein

Right lymphatic trunk
Returns the lymph to the veins above the heart

Parasternal lymph nodes
Most lymph from the medial and inner sections of the breast drains to these nodes

Subareolar plexus
Network of interconnecting lymph vessels that receive lymph from the nipple, areola and lobules of the breast

Most of the lymph in the breast tissue drains into the lymph nodes in the armpit, before draining into the subclavian nodes and then into the veins.

Lymphatic drainage and breast cancer

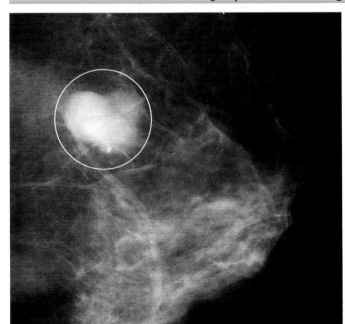

This mammogram shows a malignant tumour in the breast. The tumour is apparent as the dense area (circled) within the breast tissue.

Lymph fluid often contains particles such as cells, which it has cleared from the tissue spaces. If the lymph has come from an area that contains a growing cancer, it may contain cells which have broken off from that tumour. These cells will be filtered out by the lymph nodes, where they may lodge and grow to form a secondary tumour, or 'metastasis'.

Knowledge of the pattern of lymph drainage of each area of

the body, and especially of an area as prone to cancer as the breast, is therefore important to doctors. If a breast lump is found, it is important for the doctor to check the associated lymph nodes for secondary spread of cancer cells.

MAMMOGRAPHY

As well as examination of the breast by the doctor or the woman herself, mammography (X-ray examination of the breasts), can be used to check for breast cancer. Mammograms help to detect the presence of cancer of the breast at an early, and therefore more easily treatable, stage.

Bones of the pelvis

The basin-like pelvis is formed by the hip bones, sacrum and coccyx. The pelvic bones provide sites of attachment for many important muscles, and also help to protect the vital pelvic organs.

The bones of the pelvis form a ring that connects the spine to the lower limbs and protects the pelvic contents, including the reproductive organs and bladder.

The pelvic bones, to which many powerful muscles are attached, allow the weight of the body to be transferred to the legs with great stability.

STRUCTURE OF THE PELVIS

The basin-like pelvis consists of the innominate (hip) bones, the sacrum and the coccyx. The innominate bones meet at the pubic symphysis anteriorly. Posteriorly, these two bones are joined to the sacrum. Extending down from the sacrum at the back of the pelvis is the coccyx.

FALSE AND TRUE PELVIS

The pelvis can be said to be divided into two parts by an imaginary plane passing through the sacral promontory and the pubic symphysis:
■ Above the sacral promontory, the false pelvis flares out and supports the lower abdominal contents
■ Below this plane lies the true pelvis lies; in females, it forms the constricted birth canal through which the baby passes.

The bony structure of the pelvis is formed by the hip bones, sacrum and coccyx. The adult female pelvis, shown here, is adapted for childbirth.

Adult female pelvis from the front

Sacroiliac joint
Broad, flat joint between the sacrum and the wing of the ilium

Sacral promontory

Sacrum

Right innominate bone

Left innominate bone

Coccyx
The vestigial tail bones and lowest part of the backbone; helps to form the back wall of the pelvic ring

Pubic symphysis
Area of the pelvis where two bones of the pubis (the pubes) meet at the front

Ischial tuberosity
Large projection of the ischium, which bears the body's weight when a person is seated

Pubic arch
Angle under the pubic bones at the front of the pelvis; it is wider in females than in males

Differences between male and female pelvis

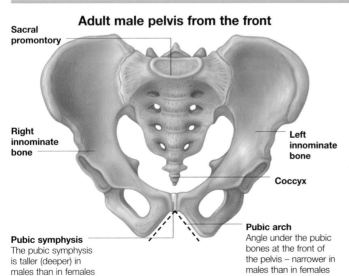

Adult male pelvis from the front

Sacral promontory

Right innominate bone

Left innominate bone

Coccyx

Pubic symphysis
The pubic symphysis is taller (deeper) in males than in females

Pubic arch
Angle under the pubic bones at the front of the pelvis – narrower in males than in females

The skeletons of men and women differ in a number of places, but nowhere is this more marked than in the pelvis.

PHYSICAL VARIATIONS

The differences between the male and female pelvis can be attributed to two factors: the requirements of childbirth and the fact that, in general, men are heavier and more muscular than women.

Some of the more obvious differences are:

The male pelvis differs from the female pelvis in being heavier, with thicker bones. The pubic arch is narrower and the pubic symphysis deeper in males.

■ General structure – the male pelvis is heavier, with thicker bones
■ Pelvic inlet – the 'way into' the true pelvis is a wide oval in females but narrower and heart-shaped in males
■ Pelvic canal – the 'way through' the true pelvis is roughly cylindrical in females, whereas in males it tapers
■ Pubic arch – the angle under the pubic bones at the front of the pelvis is wider in females (100˚ or more) than in males (90˚ or less).

These differences – and other, more subtle, measurements – are used by forensic pathologists and anthropologists to determine the sex of a skeleton.

The hip bone

The two hip bones are fused together at the front and join with the sacrum at the back. They each consist of three bones – the ilium, ischium and pubis.

The two innominate (hip) bones constitute the greater part of the pelvis, joining with each other at the front and with the sacrum at the back.

STRUCTURE

The hip bone is large and strong, due to its function of transmitting the forces between the legs and the spine. As with most bones, it has areas that are raised or roughened by the attachments of muscle or ligaments.

The hip bone is formed by the fusion of three separate bones: the ilium, the ischium and the pubis. In children, these three bones are joined only by cartilage. At puberty, they fuse to form the single innominate, or hip, bone on each side.

FEATURES

The upper margin of the hip bone is formed by the widened iliac crest. Further down the hip bone is the ischial tuberosity, a projection of the ischium.

The obturator foramen lies below and slightly in front of the acetabulum, the latter receiving the head of the femur (thigh bone).

This lateral view of the hip bone clearly shows its constituent parts of ilium, ischium and pubis. These three bones fuse together at puberty.

Right hip bone, lateral view

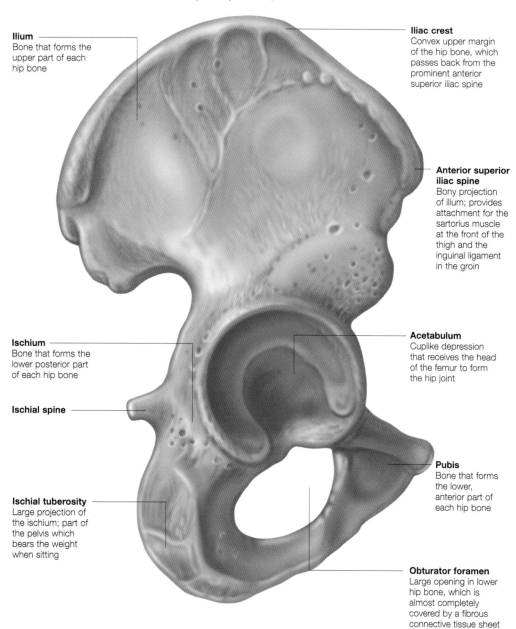

Ilium
Bone that forms the upper part of each hip bone

Iliac crest
Convex upper margin of the hip bone, which passes back from the prominent anterior superior iliac spine

Anterior superior iliac spine
Bony projection of ilium; provides attachment for the sartorius muscle at the front of the thigh and the inguinal ligament in the groin

Ischium
Bone that forms the lower posterior part of each hip bone

Ischial spine

Acetabulum
Cuplike depression that receives the head of the femur to form the hip joint

Pubis
Bone that forms the lower, anterior part of each hip bone

Ischial tuberosity
Large projection of the ischium; part of the pelvis which bears the weight when sitting

Obturator foramen
Large opening in lower hip bone, which is almost completely covered by a fibrous connective tissue sheet

The female pelvic canal

Lateral view of right pelvis

Sacral promontory

Plane of pelvic inlet

Pubic symphysis
Front area of pelvis

Plane of pelvic outlet

In childbirth, the baby passes down into the pelvic canal, through the pelvic inlet and out through the pelvic outlet. The dimensions of the pelvic canal in women are therefore vital.

TRIANGULAR SHAPE

The pelvic canal is almost triangular in section, the short front wall being formed by the pubic symphysis. The much longer back wall is formed by the sacrum and coccyx.

The pelvic canal is defined by the pubic symphysis at the front, and the sacrum and coccyx at the back. The coccyx moves back out of the way in childbirth.

From front to back, the pelvic inlet usually has a diameter of about 11cm (4 ¼in), known as the obstetric conjugate. The inlet is slightly wider from side to side owing to its oval shape.

CHANGES IN CHILDBIRTH

The pelvic outlet is normally slightly larger than the inlet, especially at the end of pregnancy when the ligaments holding the pelvic bones together can stretch under the influence of hormones.

The joint between the coccyx and the sacrum also becomes looser, allowing the coccyx to move back out of the way during childbirth.

Pelvic floor muscles

The muscles of the pelvic floor play a vital role in supporting the abdominal and pelvic organs. They also help to regulate the processes of defecation and urination.

The pelvic floor muscles play an important role in supporting the abdominal and pelvic organs. In pregnancy, these muscles help to carry the growing weight of the uterus, and in childbirth they support the baby's head as the cervix dilates.

MUSCLES

The muscles of the pelvic floor are attached to the inside of the ring of bone that makes up the pelvic skeleton, and slope downwards to form a rough funnel shape.

The levator ani is the largest muscle of the pelvic floor. It is a wide, thin sheet made up of three parts:
■ Pubococcygeus – the main part of the levator ani muscle
■ Puborectalis – joins with its counterpart on the other side to form a U-shaped sling around the rectum
■ Iliococcygeus – the posterior fibres of the levator ani.

A second muscle, the coccygeus (or ischiococcygeus), lies behind the levator ani.

PELVIC WALLS

The pelvic cavity is described as having an anterior, a posterior and two lateral walls.

The anterior wall is formed by the pubic bones and their connection, the pubic symphysis. The posterior wall is formed by the sacrum and coccyx and the neighbouring parts of the iliac bones. The two lateral walls are formed by the obturator internus muscles overlying the hip bones.

Female pelvic diaphragm from above

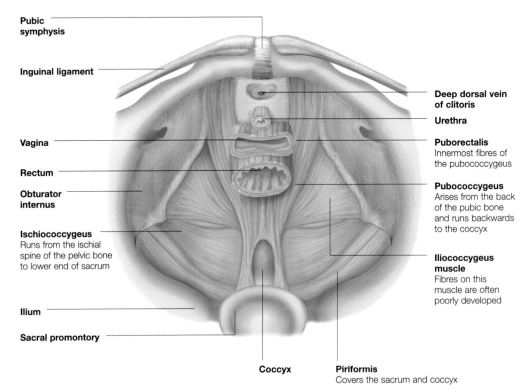

Pubic symphysis

Inguinal ligament

Vagina

Rectum

Obturator internus

Ischiococcygeus
Runs from the ischial spine of the pelvic bone to lower end of sacrum

Ilium

Sacral promontory

Deep dorsal vein of clitoris

Urethra

Puborectalis
Innermost fibres of the pubococcygeus

Pubococcygeus
Arises from the back of the pubic bone and runs backwards to the coccyx

Iliococcygeus muscle
Fibres on this muscle are often poorly developed

Coccyx

Piriformis
Covers the sacrum and coccyx

The pelvic floor muscles are known as the pelvic diaphragm. The levator ani is the most important muscle and is named for its action in lifting the anus.

Perineal body

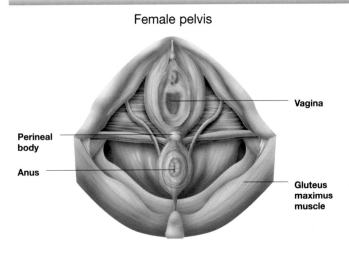

Female pelvis

Perineal body

Anus

Vagina

Gluteus maximus muscle

The perineal body is a small mass of fibrous tissue that lies within the pelvic floor, just in front of the anal canal. This structure provides a site for the attachment of many of the pelvic floor and perineal muscles, so allowing paired muscles to pull against each other, normally one of the functions of bone. It also provides support for the internal organs of the pelvis.

Although the perineal body is small and tucked away, it is a very important structure. It supports the organs of the pelvis which lie above it.

EPISIOTOMY

The perineal body may become damaged during childbirth, either by stretching or tearing as the baby's head passes through the pelvic floor. The loss of the perineal body's support of the posterior vaginal wall may eventually lead to vaginal prolapse.

To prevent damage to the perineal body during childbirth, an obstetrician may perform an episiotomy. This deliberate incision into the muscle behind the vaginal opening enlarges this opening and avoids damage to the perineal body.

Openings of the pelvic floor

The pelvic floor resembles the diaphragm in the chest in that it forms a nearly continuous sheet, but does have openings to allow important structures to pass through it. There are two important openings situated in the pelvic floor region.

From below, the pelvic floor can be seen to assume a funnel shape. The muscles of the pelvic floor are so arranged that there are two main openings:

■ Anorectal hiatus – this opening, or hiatus, allows the rectum and anal canal to pass through the sheet of pelvic floor muscles to reach the anus beneath. The U-shaped fibres of the puborectalis muscle form the posterior edge of this hiatus

■ Urogenital hiatus – lying in front of the anorectal hiatus, there is an opening in the pelvic floor for the urethra, which carries urine from the bladder out of the body. In females, the vagina also passes through the pelvic diaphragm within this opening, just behind the urethra.

FUNCTIONS OF THE PELVIC FLOOR MUSCLES

The functions of the pelvic floor include:

■ Supporting the internal organs of the abdomen and pelvis
■ Helping to resist rises in pressure within the abdomen, such as during coughing and sneezing, which would otherwise cause the bladder/bowel to empty
■ Assisting in the control of defecation and urination
■ Helping to fix and brace the trunk during forceful movements of the upper limbs, such as weight-lifting.

Male pelvic diaphragm from below

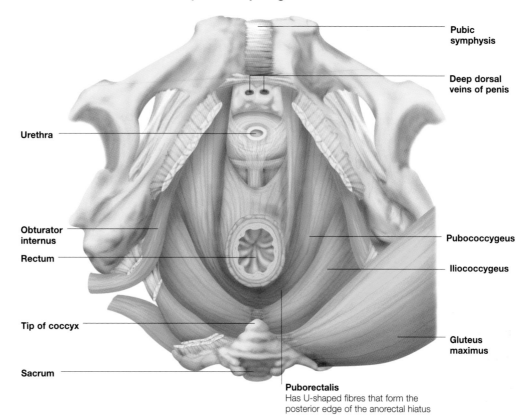

Pubic symphysis

Deep dorsal veins of penis

Urethra

Obturator internus

Rectum

Pubococcygeus

Iliococcygeus

Tip of coccyx

Sacrum

Gluteus maximus

Puborectalis
Has U-shaped fibres that form the posterior edge of the anorectal hiatus

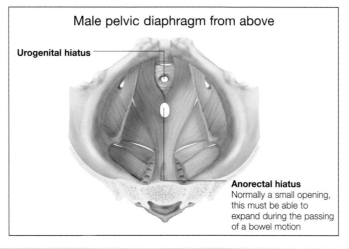

Male pelvic diaphragm from above

Urogenital hiatus

Anorectal hiatus
Normally a small opening, this must be able to expand during the passing of a bowel motion

The pelvic floor muscles play a vital supporting role. Without them, the internal organs of the abdomen and pelvis would sink through the bony pelvic ring.

Ischioanal fossae

Coronal section through pelvis

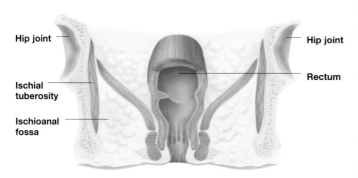

Hip joint

Hip joint

Ischial tuberosity

Rectum

Ischioanal fossa

The ischioanal, or ischiorectal, fossae are spaces formed between the outside of the pelvic diaphragm and the skin around the anus.

The ischioanal fossae are filled with fat. This fat is divided into sections and supported by bands of connective tissue. The fat in the ischioanal fossae acts as a

The ischioanal fossae are wedge-shaped, being narrowest at the top and widest at the bottom. The fossae are filled with sections of fat.

soft packing material, which accommodates changes in the size and position of the anus during a bowel movement.

INFECTION

Ischioanal fossae can become infected (ischioanal/ischiorectal abscess). Any area of the body with a poor blood supply is susceptible to infection and this is certainly the case with the fat within the ischioanal fossae. Infection may spread to the other side and infected areas may need to be surgically drained.

Menstrual cycle

The menstrual cycle is the regular process by which an egg is released from an ovary in preparation for pregnancy. This occurs approximately every four weeks from the time of a woman's first period right up to the menopause.

The menstrual cycle is characterized by the periodic maturation of oocytes (cells that develop into eggs) in the ovaries and associated physical changes in the uterus. Reproductive maturity occurs after a sudden increase in the secretion of hormones during puberty, usually between the ages of 11 and 15.

CYCLE ONSET

The time of the first period, which occurs at about the age of 12, is called the menarche. After this, a reproductive cycle begins, averaging 28 days. This length of time may be longer, shorter or variable, depending on the individual. The cycle is continuous, apart from during pregnancy. However, women suffering from anorexia nervosa or athletes who train intensively may cease to menstruate.

MENSTRUATION

Each month, if conception does not occur, oestrogen and progesterone levels fall and the blood-rich lining of the uterus is shed at menstruation (menses). This takes place every 28 days or so, but the time can range from 19 to 36 days.

Menstruation lasts for about five days. Around 50ml/ ⅜fl oz (about an eggcup) of blood, uterine tissues and fluid is lost, but again this volume varies. Some women lose only 10ml of blood, while others lose 110ml (¹⁄₁₆ –¾ fl oz).

Excessive menstrual bleeding is known as menorrhagia; temporary cessation of menstruation – such as during pregnancy – is called amenorrhoea. The menopause is the complete cessation of the menstrual cycle, and usually occurs between 45 and 55.

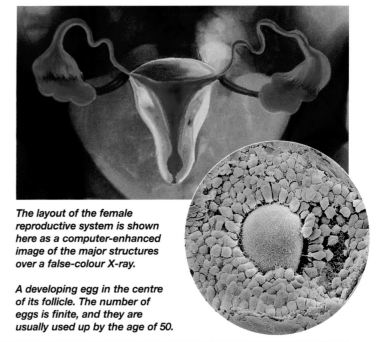

The layout of the female reproductive system is shown here as a computer-enhanced image of the major structures over a false-colour X-ray.

A developing egg in the centre of its follicle. The number of eggs is finite, and they are usually used up by the age of 50.

Monthly physiological changes

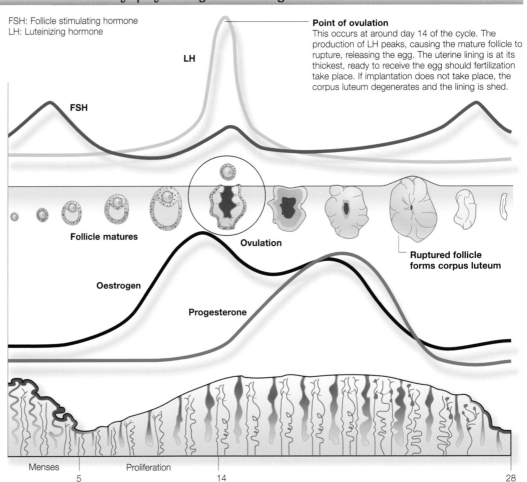

This diagram illustrates the ongoing changes during the cycle. Between days one and five, the lining is discharged, while another follicle is developing. The uterine lining thickens, and around day 14, the egg is released, at the point called ovulation.

Gonadotrophic hormones
Released by the pituitary gland to promote the production of the egg and of sex hormones in the gonads (ovaries)

Ovarian activity
Each month, one follicle develops to maturity, then releases an egg at ovulation; the surviving tissue in the ovary forms the corpus luteum, a temporary hormone-producing gland

Ovarian hormones
Secreted by the ovary to encourage the lining to grow; extra progesterone is produced by the corpus luteum after ovulation to prepare the uterus for pregnancy

Lining of uterus
Progressively thickens to receive the fertilized egg; if the egg does not implant, the lining is shed (menses) during the first five days of the cycle

FSH: Follicle stimulating hormone
LH: Luteinizing hormone

LH

FSH

Point of ovulation
This occurs at around day 14 of the cycle. The production of LH peaks, causing the mature follicle to rupture, releasing the egg. The uterine lining is at its thickest, ready to receive the egg should fertilization take place. If implantation does not take place, the corpus luteum degenerates and the lining is shed.

Follicle matures

Ovulation

Ruptured follicle forms corpus luteum

Oestrogen

Progesterone

Menses   Proliferation
5   14   28

Egg development

The process of developing a healthy egg for release at ovulation takes around six months. It occurs throughout life until the stock of oocytes is exhausted.

Two million eggs (oogonia) are present at birth, distributed between the two ovaries, and 400,000 are left by the time of the first period. During each menstrual cycle, only one egg – from a pool of around 20 potential eggs – develops and is released. By the time menopause is reached, the process of atresia (cell degeneration) in the ovaries is complete and no eggs remain.

Eggs develop within cavity-forming secretory structures called follicles. The first stage of follicle development occurs when an oogonium becomes surrounded by a single layer of granulosa cells and is called a primordial (primary) follicle. The genetic material within the egg at this stage remains undisturbed – but susceptible to alteration –

until ovulation of that egg occurs, up to 45 years after it first developed. This helps to explain the increase in abnormal chromosomes in eggs and offspring of women who conceive later in life.

Primordial follicles develop into secondary follicles by meiotic (reductive) division and then into tertiary (or antral, meaning 'with a cavity') follicles. As many as 20 primary follicles will begin to mature, although 19 will eventually regress. If more than one follicle develops to maturity, twins or triplets may be conceived.

The follicles are located in the cortex of the ovary. This micrograph shows the follicle separated by connective tissue.

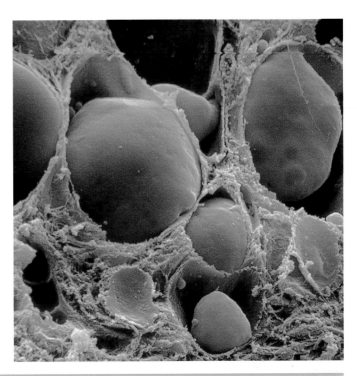

Ovulation

The final 14 day period of follicular development takes place during the first half of the menstrual cycle and depends on the precise hormonal interplay between the ovary, pituitary gland and the hypothalamus.

The trigger for selecting a healthy egg for development at

the start of each cycle is a rise in the secretion of follicle stimulating hormone (FSH) by the pituitary gland. This occurs in response to a fall in the hormones oestrogen and progesterone during the luteal phase (second 14 days) of the previous cycle if conception has not occurred.

EGG SELECTION
At the time of the FSH signal, there are about 20 secondary follicles, 2–5mm ($\frac{1}{16}$–$\frac{1}{4}$in) in diameter, distributed between the two ovaries. A single follicle is selected from this pool, while the others undergo atresia. Once a follicle is selected, the development of further follicles is prevented. A typical 5mm ($\frac{1}{4}$in) secondary follicle will then require 10–12 days of sustained stimulation by FSH to grow to a diameter of 20mm ($\frac{3}{4}$in) before rupturing, releasing the egg into

Under a light microscope, a secondary oocyte (mature egg) can be seen surrounded by the cells of the corona radiata that support it during development.

the uterine (Fallopian) tube. As the follicle enlarges, there is a steady rise in oestrogen production, triggering a mid-cycle rise in luteinizing hormone (LH) by the pituitary, which in causes release and maturation of the egg. The interval between the LH peak and ovulation is relatively constant (about 36 hours). The ruptured follicle (corpus luteum) that remains after ovulation becomes a very important endocrine gland, secreting oestrogen and progesterone.

HORMONE REGULATION
Progesterone levels rise to a peak about seven days after ovulation. If fertilization takes place, the corpus luteum maintains the pregnancy until the placenta takes over at about three months' gestation. If no conception takes place, the gland has a lifespan of 14 days, and oestrogen and progesterone levels decline in anticipation of the next cycle.

In the first half of the cycle, oestrogen secreted by the developing follicle (stage before corpus luteum) enables the lining of the uterus (endometrium) to proliferate and increase in thickness, ready to nourish the egg should it become fertilized. Once the corpus luteum is formed, progesterone converts the endometrium to a more compact layer in anticipation of an embryo implanting.

The fully developed egg is surrounded by a protein coating called the zona pellucida. This serves to trap and bind a single sperm during the process of fertilization.

Menstrual disorders

Heavy or irregular periods can make many women's lives
a misery, affecting family and working life considerably. However,
there are many treatments that will improve the condition.

Period problems are a common reason for women seeing their GP. Heavy or irregular periods can lead to anaemia, as well as contribute to depression or relationship problems.

THE NORMAL CYCLE

Most women have a cycle lasting around 28 days, with three to six days' menstrual flow per cycle.

■ Egg cells (ova) mature within follicles in the ovary; at four-

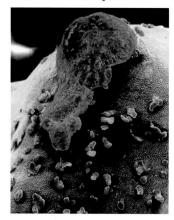

weekly intervals, they burst from the follicle and travel along the Fallopian tube to the uterus

■ A temporary endocrine gland (corpus luteum) develops in the ruptured follicle, and secretes the hormone progesterone

■ This thickens the endometrium (lining of the uterus) with blood in preparation for pregnancy

■ If the ovum is not fertilized, the corpus luteum shrivels away and the fall in progesterone is accompanied by a menstrual bleed.

If ovulation does not take place in a particular cycle, the normal hormonal rise and fall does not occur and this may lead to irregular and heavy bleeding.

Ovulation is the process of the release of an egg from the ovary, which takes place about 14 days before the next period.

Many women suffer from severe period pains. When they visit their GP, they will always receive support and informed advice.

Patient history and examination

When a patient visits her doctor with period problems, she will be asked about her general health, the menstrual cycle experienced and other matters that might point to a cause. Age is a factor, as irregular periods are common during the teenage years and after the age of 45, when many cycles do not result in egg release.

With increasing age, other conditions increase in frequency,

such as fibroids, adenomyosis, and endometrial polyps.

SPOTTING

Painful periods are more common in teenagers, and spotting between periods or after sex can result from a polyp on the cervix. The GP will check that cervical smear tests are up to date and may enquire about any discomfort experienced during intercourse.

A speculum examination will reveal whether a polyp has developed on the cervix. Polyps often cause bleeding between periods or after intercourse.

PHYSICAL EXAMINATION

It is particularly important that a woman has a check-up if she suspects that she may be pregnant. Lower abdominal pain and/or vaginal discharge, particularly if offensive-smelling, can suggest infection.

On examining the abdomen, the doctor may feel an enlarged uterus if fibroids are present. A speculum examination is important to check that the cervix looks normal and, if infection is suspected, swabs can be taken.

A consultation with a doctor for menstrual problems will normally involve an internal examination. A cervical smear may also be performed.

A bimanual examination will reveal how large the woman's uterus is, or if there is any enlargement or tenderness of the ovaries. Many women will need only a standard vaginal examination to determine the cause of the problem.

A blood sample will be taken to check for anaemia or thyroid problems if these are suspected as causes of menstrual problems. Often, a course of tablets is all that is then required.

Investigations

Often, gynaecological investigations need to be undertaken in a hospital or clinic in order to trace problems in the female reproductive system.

Menstrual disorders may be investigated in a number of ways:

■ **Ultrasound** – is a method of body imaging based on the reflectivity of sound, and can be used to look at the pelvic organs. An abdominal scan requires the woman to have a full bladder. A transvaginal scan involves the insertion of a small ultrasound probe just inside the vagina; it is not usually uncomfortable and gives a much clearer view.

■ **Endometrial biopsy** – this is done in a clinic and feels much like a smear test. A fine plastic tube is passed through the cervix and a tiny biopsy of the endometrium taken.

■ **Hysteroscopy** – a small illuminating optical device, called an endoscope, is passed into the uterus to visualize the interior. This can detect endometrial polyps, fibroids or other uterine pathology. The procedure can be performed under local or general anaesthetic. It is often combined with a D and C (dilatation and curettage), which is used to collect a sample of endometrium (uterine lining) for examination.

Ultrasound may be used in the diagnosis of menstrual problems. This scan shows the presence of an intrauterine contraceptive device (IUCD) in the uterus.

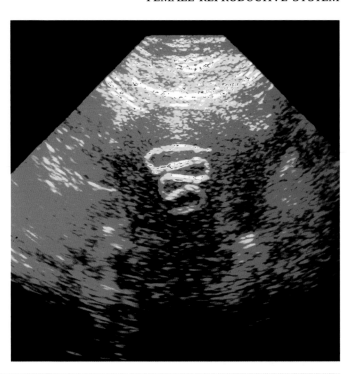

Treatment options

■ **Medical treatment**
Drugs can be used to reduce the heaviness of flow, such as ibuprofen, mefenamic acid or tranexamic acid. These are non-hormonal and taken only at the time of the period.

Means of inducing regularity as well as reducing blood flow include use of the combined contraceptive pill or cyclical progesterone-type hormones, such as Provera and norethisterone respectively.

Mirena IUS is a hormonal-based intrauterine device, much like a contraceptive 'coil', but not associated with side effects such as heavy bleeding or infections. In the clinic it is easily inserted and provides effective contraception, while reducing blood loss at menstruation by 95 per cent.

A range of contraceptive pills can effectively alter the heaviness of menstrual flow and provide cyclical regularity.

Fibroids are often multiple. The growths may become very large, and sustained growth without treatment can cause infertility.

■ **Surgical treatment**
One common and minor surgical procedure is the removal of endometrial or cervical polyps.

Another operation is the transcervical resection of the endometrium (TCRE), in which the endometrial lining is stripped back to the muscle, leading to greatly reduced blood flow each month. It is not always effective and may need to be repeated, but it is a day-case surgical procedure with minimal risk. It can also treat fibroids growing into the uterine cavity

■ **Hysterectomy**
This is a final option for women with significant problems, such as large fibroids, or when other treatments are unsuccessful. Removal of the fibroids, leaving the uterus (myomectomy), is an option for women wishing further pregnancies.

■ **Future treatments**
Other conservative treatments are being investigated, including blocking the blood supply to fibroids to shrink them (arterial embolization) and other ways of removing the endometrial lining using microwave ablation or hot balloon devices.

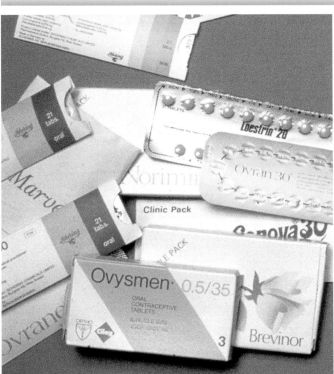

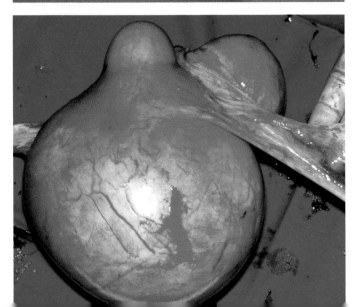

Common conditions

A range of conditions can result in menstrual problems, including:

■ **Fibroids** – benign overgrowths of normal uterine muscle. They are very common after age 40 and can lead to heavy periods. These are sometimes restricted to the body of the uterus, but can grow into the uterine cavity.

■ **Polyps** – growths on the cervix or endometrium. They are common cause of intermenstrual bleeding.

■ **Adenomyosis** – when the endometrium buries itself into the muscular wall of the uterus, causing heavy and often painful periods.

Premenstrual syndrome

At some point during the fertile years, most women experience some physical and psychological symptoms before menstruation; these are referred to collectively as premenstrual syndrome, or PMS.

Premenstrual syndrome (PMS) is a collection of physical and emotional symptoms suffered to some degree by up to 80 per cent of women of childbearing age.

For most women, PMS symptoms – which occur in the second half of the menstrual cycle – are minor and tolerable. However, in about five per cent of cases, the physical and emotional changes that accompany the approaching period are severe enough to interfere with daily life, even to the point of almost complete disability.

MEDICAL RECOGNITION

PMS has been recognized as a genuine medical condition only in the last few decades, and a considerable increase in its incidence has been seen during this time. Many researchers believe that this may be due to the effects of our modern lifestyle and diet. Another theory is that in previous times, women tended to be pregnant for a large proportion of their fertile years, PMS thus not being recognized as a distinct condition.

INCIDENCE OF PMS

PMS occurs only in women who are ovulating and menstruating; these processes involve the release of an egg from the ovary every month followed, about two weeks later, by the menstrual period. PMS will not, therefore, occur before puberty, after the menopause or during pregnancy.

PMS seems to be most common in women in their late 30s, although it can occur at any time from adolescence to middle age. It is more likely to be experienced by women who have:

- A family history of PMS
- Recently had a child
- Recently had a miscarriage
- Just started taking the contraceptive pill
- Just stopped taking the contraceptive pill
- Suffered from post-natal depression.

Headaches are a common feature of premenstrual syndrome. Some women find that the condition has a major effect on their lives every month.

Causes and symptoms of PMS

PMS symptoms occur in the second half of the menstrual cycle. Two common symptoms are back pain and difficulty in concentrating.

Post-natal depression is thought to be a risk factor for the development of severe premenstrual syndrome.

Over the years, much research has been undertaken to find out the cause of PMS, but there are as yet no clear answers. As the symptoms are linked with the menstrual cycle, it is likely that the changing levels of hormones are responsible in some way.

POSSIBLE CAUSES

Suggested hormonal causes include the following:

- Imbalance of the reproductive hormones oestrogen and progesterone
- An excess of the hormone prolactin (which helps to regulate reproductive hormones)
- A deficiency in serotonin,

causing an abnormal sensitivity to changing hormone levels.

Dietary deficiencies, an unhealthy diet and very little exercise may also be factors. However, it is likely that PMS is caused by a combination of all these factors, although this may be different for each woman.

SYMPTOMS

There are believed to be over 150 physical and emotional symptoms of PMS. The most common physical symptoms are:

- Breast tenderness
- Headaches
- Swelling and bloatedness
- Constipation or diarrhoea
- Change in appetite
- Backache
- Skin problems, such as acne.

The emotional symptoms of PMS may be more distressing. These include:

- Tearfulness and depression
- Irritability and mood swings
- Low self-esteem
- Tiredness
- Lack of concentration.

Diagnosing and treating PMS

The symptoms of PMS can be so varied that diagnosis depends on their timing; that is, onset during the second half of the menstrual cycle. If the symptoms do not cease with the start of the woman's next period, then PMS is unlikely to be the cause.

There are no specific examinations or laboratory tests that can be carried out to diagnose PMS. However, further examination or investigations may be undertaken to rule out other causes for PMS symptoms, such as hormonal disorders.

Self-help measures include joining a support group to meet other PMS sufferers. Sharing experiences of PMS may help sufferers cope with the condition.

Women may find that regular exercise helps to relieve the symptoms of PMS. Exercise has been shown to improve mood.

DIAGNOSING PMS
Diagnosis of PMS depends on the woman filling in a menstrual chart, which records the timing of symptoms in relation to the menstrual cycle. This can be filled in by the woman herself over a period of three to four months and shown to the doctor, or used as a basis for self-help.

There is no known 'cure' for PMS, but the symptoms can be relieved and life made more bearable for sufferers.

SELF-HELP
Not all women who suffer from PMS will need medical help; many find that their symptoms can be relieved or controlled by simple self-help measures. These include:
■ Changing to a healthy low-fat, high-fibre diet, similar to that recommended for a healthy heart and body.
■ Eating at three-hourly intervals; a regular intake of

starchy foods has been demonstrated to help control symptoms of PMS.
■ Taking regular exercise to lift one's mood. Other ways of relaxing, such as yoga and t'ai chi chu'an, have also been found to be very helpful.
■ Reducing caffeine and alcohol consumption.
■ Taking vitamin and mineral supplements. Although still

somewhat controversial, evening primrose oil and vitamin B_6 have both been taken to alleviate the symptoms of PMS, with good results reported in some cases; supplements of magnesium, calcium and zinc have also been advocated.
■ Joining a support group, such as those organized by the National Association for Premenstrual Syndrome (NAPS).

Medical treatment of PMS

There is no single effective treatment for PMS. If dietary and lifestyle changes bring no relief or the symptoms are very severe, there are various drugs which may be of some use for sufferers. These include:

■ Progesterone – as a rectal or vaginal pessary, this hormone may help to reduce irritability, anxiety and breast tenderness.
■ Oral contraceptive pill – given to suppress ovulation; however, in some cases it can make

the condition worse.
■ Oestrogen skin patches – some progestogen is given at the same time, to protect the lining of the uterus.
■ Antidepressants – especially those such as Prozac (fluoxetine),

Oestrogen skin patches have been prescribed to treat PMS, but their effectiveness has not been definitively proven.

which work in a way that makes them particularly suitable for the treatment of the emotional symptoms of PMS.
■ Diuretics – may be useful if water retention is a troublesome symptom.
■ Danazol and bromocriptine – these drugs are sometimes used for the specific treatment of breast tenderness in PMS.

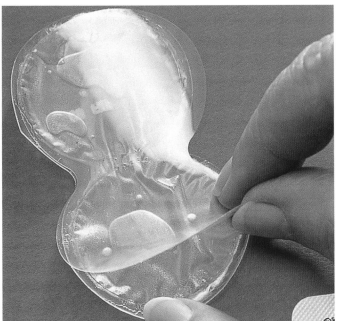

Complementary therapies

Non-medical complementary therapies – including homeopathy, acupuncture, reflexology, aromatherapy and herbalism – have all been offered as treatments for PMS. Some women have been attracted to these therapies because they feel that they have received insufficient help or understanding from their doctors.

Another advantage of consulting complementary therapists is that they tend to have more time to listen to their patients than the average doctor.

Oil of evening primrose is a natural remedy that is believed to be beneficial in a range of medical complaints, including premenstrual syndrome.

How ovulation occurs

The total supply of eggs for a woman's reproductive years is determined before she is born. The immature eggs are stored in the ovary until puberty, after which one is released every month.

An ovum (egg) is the female gamete, or sex cell, which unites with a sperm to form a new individual. Eggs are produced and stored in the ovaries, two walnut-sized organs connected to the uterus via the uterine (Fallopian) tubes.

THE OVARY
Each ovary is covered by a protective layer of peritoneum (abdominal lining). Immediately below this layer is a dense fibrous capsule, the tunica albuginea. The ovary itself consists of a dense outer region, called the cortex, and a less dense inner region, the medulla.

GAMETE PRODUCTION
In females, the supply of eggs is determined at birth. Egg-forming cells degenerate from birth to puberty and the timespan during which a woman can release mature eggs is limited from puberty until menopause. The process by which ova are produced is known as oogenesis,

which literally means 'the beginning of an egg'. Germ cells in the fetus produce many oogonia cells. These divide to form primary oocytes which are enclosed in groups of follicle cells (support cells).

GENETIC DIVISION
The primary oocytes begin to divide by meiosis (a specialized nuclear division), but this process is interrupted in its first phase and is not completed until after puberty. At birth, a lifetime's supply of primary oocytes, numbering between 700,000 and two million, will have been formed. These specialized cells will lie dormant in the cortical region of the immature ovary and slowly degenerate, so that by puberty only 40,000 remain.

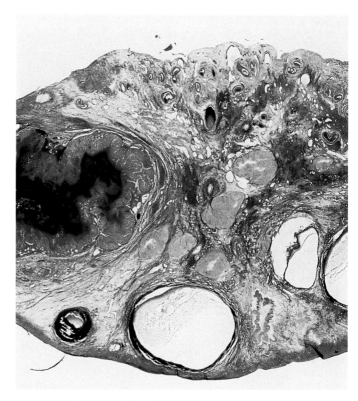

This micrograph shows an ovary with several large follicles (white). During ovulation, up to 20 follicles begin to develop, but only one matures to release an egg.

Egg development

How an egg develops

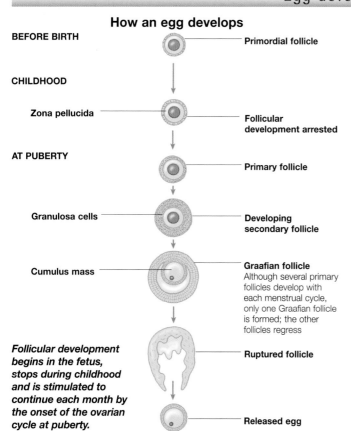

BEFORE BIRTH — Primordial follicle

CHILDHOOD

Zona pellucida — Follicular development arrested

AT PUBERTY — Primary follicle

Granulosa cells — Developing secondary follicle

Cumulus mass — **Graafian follicle**
Although several primary follicles develop with each menstrual cycle, only one Graafian follicle is formed; the other follicles regress

— Ruptured follicle

Follicular development begins in the fetus, stops during childhood and is stimulated to continue each month by the onset of the ovarian cycle at puberty.

— Released egg

Before puberty, the primary oocyte is surrounded by a layer of cells (the granulosa cells), forming a primary follicle.

PUBERTY
With the onset of puberty, some of the primary follicles are stimulated each month by hormones to continue development and become secondary follicles:
■ A layer of clear viscous fluid, the zona pellucida, is deposited on the surface of the oocyte.
■ The granulosa cells multiply and form an increasing number of layers around the oocyte.
■ The centre of the follicle becomes a chamber (the antrum), which fills with fluid secreted by the granulosa cells.
■ The oocyte is pushed to one side of the follicle, and lies in a mass of follicular cells called the cumulus mass.

A mature secondary follicle is called a Graafian follicle.

Meiosis

The first meiotic division produces two cells of unequal size – the secondary oocyte and the first polar body. The secondary oocyte contains nearly all the cytoplasm of the primary oocyte. Both cells begin a second division; however, this process is halted, and is not completed until the oocyte is fertilized by a sperm.

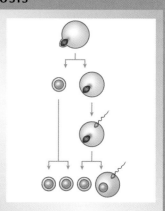

Meiosis, a specialized nuclear division, occurs in the ovaries, giving rise to a female sex cell and three polar bodies.

Egg release

Ovulation occurs when a follicle ruptures, releasing a mature oocyte into the uterine tube. It is at this stage in the menstrual cycle that fertilization may occur.

As the Graafian follicle continues to swell, it can be seen on the surface of the ovary as a blister-like structure.

HORMONAL CHANGES
In response to hormonal changes, the follicular cells surrounding the oocyte begin to secrete a thinner fluid at an increased rate, so that the follicle rapidly swells. As a result, the follicular wall becomes very thin over the area exposed to the ovarian surface, and the follicle eventually ruptures.

OVULATION
A small amount of blood and follicular fluid is forced out of the vesicle, and the secondary oocyte, surrounded by the cumulus mass and zona pellucida, is expelled from the follicle into the peritoneal cavity – the process of ovulation.

Women are generally unaware of this phenomenon, although some experience a twinge of pain in the lower abdomen. This is caused by the intense stretching of the ovarian wall.

FERTILE PERIOD
Ovulation occurs around the 14th day of a woman's menstrual cycle, and it is at this time that a woman is at her most fertile. As sperm can survive in the uterus for up to five days, there is a period of about a week when fertilization can occur.

In the event that the secondary oocyte is penetrated by a sperm cell and pregnancy ensues, the final stages of meiotic division will be triggered. If, however, the egg is not fertilized, the second stage of meiosis will not be completed and the secondary oocyte will simply degenerate.

The ruptured follicle forms a gland called the corpus luteum that secretes progesterone. This hormone prepares the uterine lining to receive an embryo.

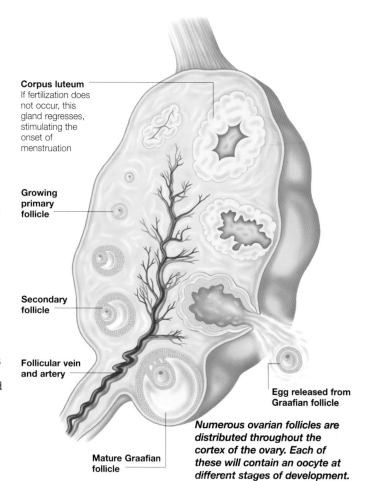

Corpus luteum
If fertilization does not occur, this gland regresses, stimulating the onset of menstruation

Growing primary follicle

Secondary follicle

Follicular vein and artery

Mature Graafian follicle

Egg released from Graafian follicle

Numerous ovarian follicles are distributed throughout the cortex of the ovary. Each of these will contain an oocyte at different stages of development.

The menstrual cycle

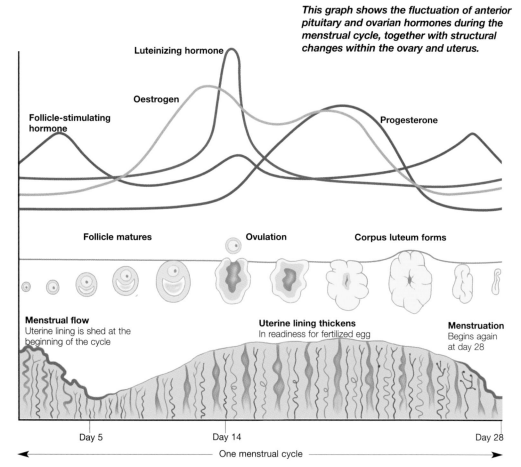

This graph shows the fluctuation of anterior pituitary and ovarian hormones during the menstrual cycle, together with structural changes within the ovary and uterus.

Luteinizing hormone

Oestrogen

Follicle-stimulating hormone

Progesterone

Follicle matures

Ovulation

Corpus luteum forms

Menstrual flow
Uterine lining is shed at the beginning of the cycle

Uterine lining thickens
In readiness for fertilized egg

Menstruation
Begins again at day 28

Day 5

Day 14

Day 28

One menstrual cycle

The oestrus, or menstrual cycle, refers to the cyclical changes which take place in the female reproductive system during the production of eggs.

These changes are controlled by hormones released by the pituitary gland and ovaries: oestrogen, progesterone, luteinizing hormone and follicle-stimulating hormone.

UTERINE CHANGES
Following menstruation, the endometrium thickens and becomes more vascular under the influence of oestrogen and follicle-stimulating hormone.

During the first 14 days of the menstrual cycle, a Graafian follicle matures. Ovulation occurs around day 14 when the secondary oocyte is expelled and swept into the uterine tube.

The ruptured follicle becomes a hormone-secreting body called the corpus luteum. This secretes progesterone, stimulating further thickening of the uterine lining (endometrium) in which the fertilized ovum will implant.

If fertilization does not occur, the levels of progesterone and oestrogen decrease. This causes the endometrium to break down and be excreted into the menstrual flow.

How conception occurs

Millions of sperm cells travel up the female reproductive tract in search of the oocyte (egg). It takes hundreds of sperm to break down the outer coating of the oocyte, but only one will fertilize it.

Fertilization occurs when a single male gamete (sperm cell) and a female gamete (egg or oocyte) are united following sexual intercourse. Fusion of the two cells occurs and a new life is conceived.

SPERM

Following sexual intercourse, the sperm contained in the man's semen travel up through the uterus. Along the way, they are nourished by the alkaline mucus of the cervical canal. From the uterus, the sperm continue their journey into the uterine (Fallopian) tube.

Although the distance involved is only around 20cm (8in), the journey can take up to two hours, since in relation to the size of the sperm the distance is considerable.

SURVIVAL

Although an average ejaculation contains around 300 million sperm cells, only a fraction of these (around 10,000) will manage to reach the uterine tube where the oocyte is located. Even fewer will actually reach the oocyte. This is because many sperm will be destroyed by the hostile vaginal environment, or become lost in other areas of the reproductive tract.

Sperm do not become capable of fertilizing an oocyte until they have spent some time in

the woman's body. Fluids in the reproductive tract activate the sperm, so that the whiplash motion of their tails becomes more powerful.

The sperm are also helped on their way by contractions of the uterus, which force them upwards into the body. The contractions are stimulated by prostaglandins contained in the semen, and which are also produced during female orgasm.

THE OOCYTE

Once it has been ejected from the follicle (during ovulation), the oocyte is pushed towards the uterus by the wavelike motion of the cells lining the uterine tube. The oocyte is usually united with the sperm about two hours after sexual intercourse in the outer part of the uterine tube.

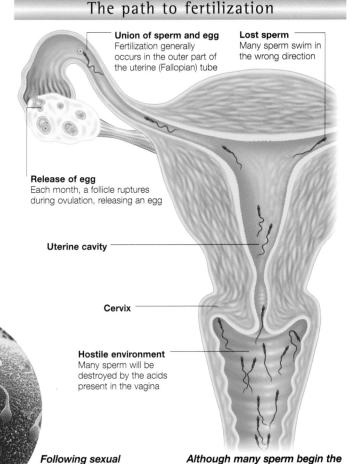

Union of sperm and egg
Fertilization generally occurs in the outer part of the uterine (Fallopian) tube

Lost sperm
Many sperm swim in the wrong direction

Release of egg
Each month, a follicle ruptures during ovulation, releasing an egg

Uterine cavity

Cervix

Hostile environment
Many sperm will be destroyed by the acids present in the vagina

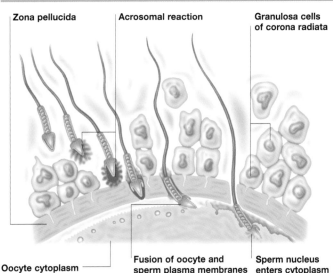

Following sexual intercourse, millions of sperm cells make their way up the reproductive tract in search of the oocyte.

Although many sperm begin the journey towards the oocyte, only a fraction reach the uterine tube. The majority are destroyed or become lost on the way.

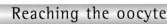

Zona pellucida

Acrosomal reaction

Granulosa cells of corona radiata

Oocyte cytoplasm

Fusion of oocyte and sperm plasma membranes

Sperm nucleus enters cytoplasm

On the journey towards the oocyte, secretions present in the female reproductive tract deplete the sperm cells' cholesterol, thus weakening their acrosomal membranes. This process is known as capacitation, and without it fertilization could not occur.

Once in the vicinity of the oocyte, the sperm are chemically attracted to it. When the sperm cells finally come in to contact with the oocyte, their acrosomal membranes are completely

When sperm cells reach the oocyte, they release enzymes. These enzymes break down the protective outer layers of the ovum, allowing a sperm to enter.

stripped away, so that the contents of each acrosome (the enzyme-containing compartment of the sperm) are released.

PENETRATION

The enzymes released by the sperm cells cause the breakdown of the cumulus mass cells and the zona pellucida, the protective outer layers of the oocyte. It takes at least 100 acrosomes to rupture in order for a path to be digested through these layers for a single sperm to enter.

In this way, the sperm cells that reach the oocyte first sacrifice themselves, to allow penetration of the cytoplasm of the oocyte by another sperm.

Fertilization

When a single sperm has entered the oocyte, the genetic material from each cell fuses. A zygote is formed, which divides to form an embryo.

Once a sperm has penetrated the oocyte, a chemical reaction takes place within the oocyte, making it impossible for another sperm to enter.

MEIOSIS II
Entry of the sperm nucleus into the oocyte triggers the completion of nuclear division (meiosis II) begun during ovulation. A haploid oocyte and the second polar body (which degenerates) are formed.

Almost immediately, the nuclei of the sperm and oocyte fuse to produce a diploid zygote, containing genetic material from both the mother and father.

DETERMINATION OF SEX
It is at the point of fertilization that sex is determined. It is the sperm, and therefore the father, that dictates what sex the offspring will be.

Sex is determined by a combination of the two sex chromosomes, the X and the Y. The female will contribute an X chromosome, while a male may contribute either an X or a Y. Fertilization of the oocyte (X), will either be by a sperm containing an X or a Y to give a female (XX) or a male (XY).

CELL DIVISION
Several hours after fertilization the zygote undergoes a series of mitotic divisions to produce a cluster of cells known as a morula. The morula cells divide every 12 to 15 hours, producing a blastocyst comprised of around 100 cells.

The blastocyst secretes the hormone human chorionic gonadotrophin. This prevents the corpus luteum from being broken down, thus maintaining progesterone secretion.

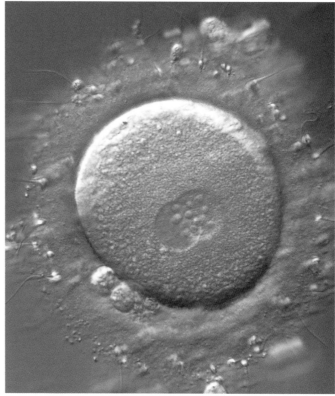

Once a sperm has penetrated the oocyte, the nuclei of both cells fuse. A diploid zygote forms, containing both the mother's and father's genes.

Implantation and development

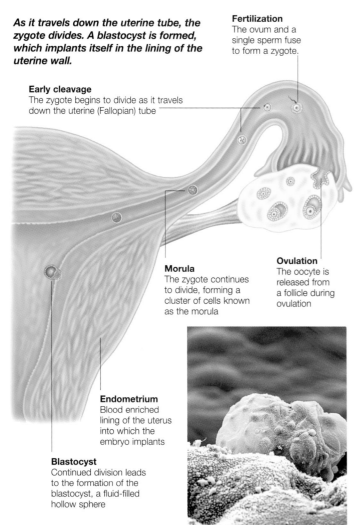

As it travels down the uterine tube, the zygote divides. A blastocyst is formed, which implants itself in the lining of the uterine wall.

Early cleavage
The zygote begins to divide as it travels down the uterine (Fallopian) tube

Fertilization
The ovum and a single sperm fuse to form a zygote.

Morula
The zygote continues to divide, forming a cluster of cells known as the morula

Ovulation
The oocyte is released from a follicle during ovulation

Endometrium
Blood enriched lining of the uterus into which the embryo implants

Blastocyst
Continued division leads to the formation of the blastocyst, a fluid-filled hollow sphere

When the zygote reaches the uterus, it will adhere to the endometrium. Nourished by the rich blood supply, it begins to develop.

Around three days after fertilization, the blastocyst will begin its journey from the uterine (Fallopian) tube to the uterus.

Normally the blastocyst would be unable to pass through the sphincter muscle in the uterine tube. However, the increasing levels of progesterone triggered by fertilization cause the muscle to relax, allowing the blastocyst to continue its journey to the uterus.

A damaged or blocked uterine tube preventing the blastocyst from passing at this stage would result in an ectopic pregnancy, in which the embryo begins to develop within the uterine tube.

MULTIPLE BIRTHS
In most cases, a woman will release one oocyte every month from alternate ovaries.

Occasionally, however, a woman may produce an oocyte from each ovary both of which are fertilized by separate sperm, resulting in the development of non-identical twins. In this case, each fetus will be nourished by its own placenta.

Very occasionally, a fertilized oocyte may split spontaneously in two to produce two embryos. This will result in identical twins that share exactly the same genes, and even the same placenta.

Siamese twins occur when there is an incomplete split of the oocyte several hours after fertilization.

IMPLANTATION
Once it has reached the uterus, the blastocyst will implant itself in the thickened lining of the uterine wall.

Hormones released from the blastocyst mean that it is not identified as a foreign body and expelled. Once the blastocyst is safely implanted, gestation will begin.

IMPERFECTIONS
About one third of fertilized oocytes fail to implant in the uterus and are lost.

Of those that do implant, many embryos contain imperfections in their genetic material, such as bearing an extra chromosome.

Many of these imperfections will cause the embryo to be lost soon after implantation. This can occur even before the first missed period, so that a woman will not even have known that she was pregnant.

How childbirth occurs

Towards the end of pregnancy, physiological changes occur in both mother and fetus. Hormonal triggers cause the muscles in the uterine wall to contract, expelling the baby and placenta.

Parturition – meaning 'bringing forth the young' – is the final stage of pregnancy. It usually occurs 280 days (40 weeks) from the last menstrual period.

The series of physiological events that lead to the baby being delivered from the mother's body are referred to collectively as labour.

INITIATION OF LABOUR

The precise signal that triggers labour is not known, but many factors which play a role in its initiation have been identified.

Before parturition, levels of progesterone secreted by the placenta into the mother's circulation reach a peak. Progesterone is the hormone responsible for maintaining the uterine lining during pregnancy and has an inhibitory effect on the smooth muscle of the uterus.

HORMONAL TRIGGERS

Towards the end of the pregnancy, there is increasingly limited space in the uterus and the fetus' limited oxygen supply becomes increasingly restricted (resulting from a more rapid increase in the size of the fetus than in the size of the placenta). This causes an increased level of adrenocorticotropic hormone (ACTH) to be secreted from the anterior lobe of the fetus' pituitary.

Consequently, the fetus' adrenal cortex is triggered to produce chemical messengers (glucocorticoids) which inhibit

Hormonal changes before delivery

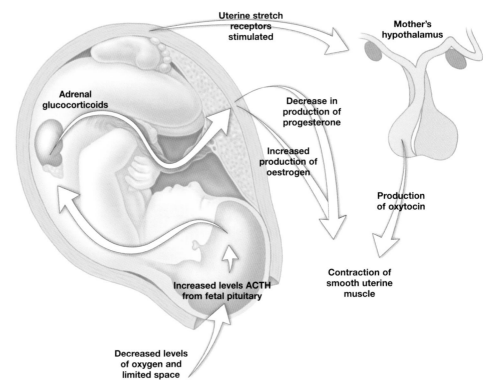

Uterine stretch receptors stimulated

Mother's hypothalamus

Adrenal glucocorticoids

Decrease in production of progesterone

Increased production of oestrogen

Production of oxytocin

Increased levels ACTH from fetal pituitary

Contraction of smooth uterine muscle

Decreased levels of oxygen and limited space

progesterone secretion from the placenta.

Meanwhile, the levels of the hormone oestrogen released by the placenta into the mother's circulation reach a peak. This causes the myometrial cells of the uterus to form an increased number of oxytocin receptors (making the uterus more sensitive to oxytocin).

CONTRACTIONS

Eventually the inhibitory influence of progesterone on the smooth muscle cells of the uterus is overcome by the stimulatory effect of oestrogen.

The inner lining of the uterus (myometrium) weakens, and the uterus begins to contract irregularly. These contractions, known as Braxton Hicks

As the pregnancy reaches full term, a number of hormonal changes occur. These cause the lining of the uterus to weaken and contractions to commence.

contractions, help to soften the cervix in preparation for the birth and are often mistaken by pregnant mothers for the onset of labour.

Onset of labour

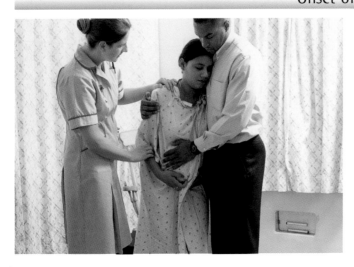

As the pregnancy reaches full term, stretch receptors in the uterine cervix activate the mother's hypothalamus (a region of the brain) to stimulate her posterior pituitary gland in order to release the hormone oxytocin. Certain cells of the fetus also begin to release this hormone.

Elevated levels of oxytocin trigger the placenta to release prostaglandins and together they stimulate the uterus to contract.

Oxytocin triggers uterine contractions that push the fetus against the cervix. Further stretch of the cervix stimulates more oxytocin to be released.

INTENSIFICATION OF CONTRACTIONS

As the uterus is weakened due to suppressed levels of progesterone and is more sensitive to oxytocin, the contractions become stronger and more frequent, and the rhythmic contractions of labour begin.

A 'positive feedback' mechanism is activated whereby the greater the intensity of the contractions, the more oxytocin is released, which in turn causes the contractions to become more intense. The chain is broken when the cervix is no longer stretched after delivery and oxytocin levels drop.

Stages of labour

The birth can be divided in to three distinct stages: dilatation of the cervix, expulsion of the fetus and delivery of the placenta.

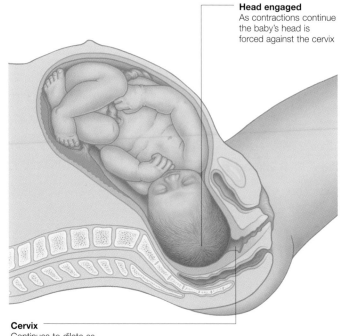

Head engaged
As contractions continue the baby's head is forced against the cervix

Cervix
Continues to dilate as contractions progress

DILATION

In order for the baby's head to pass through the birth canal, the cervix and vagina must dilate to around 10cm (4in) in diameter. As labour commences, weak but regular contractions begin in the upper part of the uterus.

These initial contractions are 15–30 minutes apart and last around 10–30 seconds. As the labour progresses, the contractions become faster and more intense, and the lower part of the uterus begins to contract as well.

The baby's head is forced against the cervix with each contraction, causing the cervix to soften, and gradually dilate.

Eventually the amniotic sac, which has protected the baby for the duration of the pregnancy, ruptures, and the amniotic fluid is released.

ENGAGEMENT

The dilatation stage is the longest part of labour and can last from 8 to 24 hours.

During this phase, the baby begins to descend through the birth canal, rotating as it does so, until the head engages, entering the pelvis.

Dilatation is the longest stage of labour. It can take up to 24 hours for the cervix to dilate sufficiently to allow delivery.

Expulsion

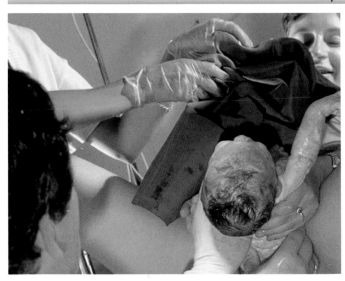

The second stage of labour, expulsion, lasts from full dilation to the actual delivery of the child.

Usually by the time the cervix is fully dilated, strong contractions occur every 2–3 minutes and each lasts around a minute.

URGE TO PUSH

At this point, the mother will have an overwhelming urge to push or bear down with the abdominal muscles.

Once the cervix is fully dilated the baby is ready to be delivered. The mother will feel a strong urge to push, expelling the baby through the cervix.

This phase can take as long as two hours, but is generally much quicker in subsequent births.

DELIVERY

Crowning takes place when the largest part of the baby's head reaches the vagina. In many cases, the vagina will distend to such an extent that it tears.

Once the baby's head has exited, the rest of the body is delivered much more easily.

When the baby emerges head first, the skull (at its widest diameter) acts as a wedge to dilate the cervix. This head-first presentation allows the baby to breathe even before it is completely delivered from the mother.

Delivery of the placenta

The final stage of labour, when the placenta is delivered, can take place up to 30 minutes after the birth.

After the baby has been delivered, the rhythmical uterine contractions continue. These act to compress the uterine blood vessels thus limiting bleeding. The contractions also cause the placenta to break away from the wall of the uterus.

AFTERBIRTH

The placenta and attached fetal membranes (the afterbirth) are then easily removed by pulling gently on the umbilical cord. All placental fragments must be removed to prevent continued uterine bleeding and infection after birth.

The number of vessels in the severed umbilical cord will be counted, as the absence of an umbilical artery is often associated with cardiovascular disorders in the baby.

HORMONE LEVELS

Blood levels of oestrogen and progesterone fall dramatically once their source, the placenta, has been delivered. During the four or five weeks after parturition, the uterus becomes much smaller but remains larger than it was before pregnancy.

Contractions continue after the birth. This causes the placenta to detach from the uterine wall, and it can be removed with a gentle tug of the umbilical cord.

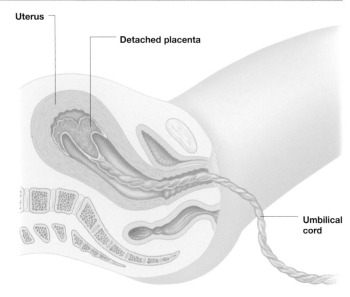

Uterus

Detached placenta

Umbilical cord

Causes of female infertility

Infertility is common and affects one in six couples at some time.
As part of an ongoing analysis, there are several procedures that can
be performed to investigate why a woman cannot conceive.

Although women often wait up to a year after failing to conceive before seeing their doctor, women over 35 should consider being investigated sooner. This is because egg quality declines with age, and success rates, particularly with IVF treatment, are much lower as women approach 40.

A woman usually sees her GP first for simple hormone tests, and her partner will be asked to provide sperm for analysis. The woman is then referred to a gynaecologist for further investigations and treatment.

OVULATION FAILURE

Each month, a healthy egg needs to be released from the ovary (ovulation). One of the first tests the doctor will arrange is a blood test seven days before the period is due, to measure the level of progesterone produced by the corpus luteum formed in the ovary after the egg is released.

The commonest cause of infertility, and the easiest to treat, is failure of ovulation (anovulation) and is typically found when the cycle length varies more than five days from one month to the next.

POLYCYSTIC OVARIES

Many women with anovulation have polycystic ovaries (PCO) and these can be identified on a pelvic ultrasound scan. Although some women with polycystic ovaries have regular cycles and ovulate, most have irregular periods or no periods at all. Other symptoms include increased body and facial hair or hair loss and weight gain. A hormone test may show a raised level of luteinizing hormone (LH) and of the male hormone testosterone.

Being stressed or over- or underweight can also disrupt the cycle and cause anovulation.

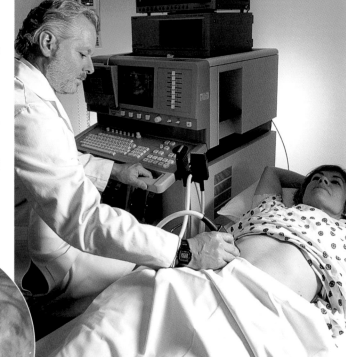

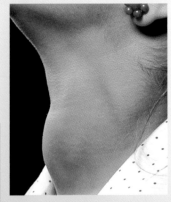

Polycystic ovary syndrome (PCOS-) is a hormonal disorder whereby ovulation fails to occur. Without ovulation, conception can not occur.

The ultrasound probe is passed over the lower abdomen or through the vagina. Both methods allow visualization of the reproductive organs.

Hormonal reasons for infertility

As a woman gets older, her egg quality and numbers start to fall. This is reflected in a rise in FSH (follicle stimulating hormone) levels in the blood. Ideally, this should be measured in the first few days after the period starts, as FSH levels in the early part of the cycle reflect a woman's 'body clock'. Even if ovulation is taking place, high FSH levels imply a reduced number of eggs and poor egg quality and hence a low chance of conceiving.

Premature menopause is when periods cease completely before the age of 40, indicating that the egg supply in the ovary is exhausted. Women so affected can become pregnant only using donated eggs from another woman under an IVF programme.

Another cause of infrequent periods and anovulation is excessive secretion of prolactin by a benign tumour of the pituitary gland. Excessive prolactin interferes with the production of FSH, which is the hormone signal that drives the ovary to make an egg each month. Over- or underactivity of the thyroid gland can also disrupt the cycle and lead to infertility. Both conditions are easily treatable and thyroid hormone and prolactin levels are routinely checked if a woman's cycle has become irregular.

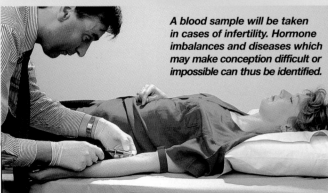

A blood sample will be taken in cases of infertility. Hormone imbalances and diseases which may make conception difficult or impossible can thus be identified.

This goitre (swelling) is caused by an overactive thyroid gland. This condition can disrupt the normal production of eggs.

Investigating female infertility

Several tests can be performed to investigate infertility. Some require invasive surgery, while others use X-ray or ultrasound technology.

LAPAROSCOPY

One method to assess whether the uterine (Fallopian) tubes are working properly is to perform a laparoscopic investigation. This is a minor operation often carried out as a day case.

The patient is given a local, regional or general anaesthetic, and the surgeon makes a small incision near the navel. The peritoneal cavity (which lines

Laparoscopy allows direct visualization of the reproductive organs. The laparoscope is introduced through an incision in the abdomen.

the inside of the abdomen) is then inflated with carbon dioxide gas to 'separate' the internal organs to enable better visualization of the various structures.

A special endoscope called a laparoscope is passed through the incision, and the uterus, Fallopian tubes and ovaries are visualized. Dye is then passed through the neck of the womb into the tubes, via a uterine cannula, to check that they are not blocked or constricted.

The surgeon will be able to see abnormal growths or other problems – occasionally these

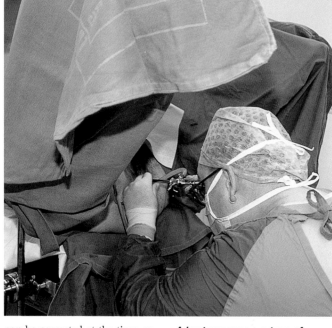

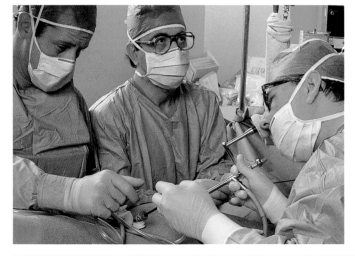

can be corrected at the time, or a biopsy (tissue sample) can be obtained, which will be analyzed. This can then be used to decide on further surgery or investigations.

HYSTEROSCOPY

A hysteroscopic investigation is similar to laparoscopy, except that no incision is made and the investigation is carried out as an outpatient procedure, but still using anaesthesia. The technique is increasingly used to investigate causes of infertility.

A hysteroscope – a type of endoscope – is passed into the uterine cavity via the vagina. This can provide accurate diagnosis of infertility problems.

The hysteroscope – a type of endoscope – is introduced through the neck of the womb into the uterus to check the uterine cavity is of normal shape. This method allows more accurate diagnosis of intrauterine adhesions (such as scar tissue, for example) than other investigative methods.

Other methods of investigating infertility

HYSTEROSALPINGOGRAPHY

An alternative to laparoscopy is X-ray hysterosalpingography (HSG). This provides an image (called a hysterosalpingogram) of the uterine tubes and uterus. It is an X-ray technique that employs a contrast (radio-opaque) medium injected into the uterus to outline the reproductive organs. This allows detailed visualization of possible blockages in the uterine tubes,

which are a potential cause of female infertility.

The test is carried out at an early point of a woman's menstrual cycle (usually in the first 10 days) when she is least likely to be pregnant. This is because X-ray radiation can damage a developing fetus. The dye flows along the tubes, and blockages can be seen. This visualization method identifies 75 per cent of tubal blockages.

The passage of the dye through the reproductive organs can sometimes aid pregnancy by 'flushing' the uterus and uterine tubes. However, disadvantages include pelvic discomfort, allergy to the dye and the danger of radiation exposure.

HYSTEROSALPINGO-CONTRAST SONOGRAPHY

Another related method for investigating infertility is hysterosalpingo-contrast sonography (HyCoSy). This involves a contrast medium injected in to the neck of the womb. A transvaginal ultrasound scan (TVS) is then performed, whereby a probe is introduced into the vagina. The

contrast medium and ultrasound probe allows for detailed visualization of the internal organs, offering minimal discomfort or side effects to the patient.

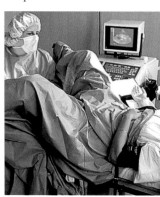

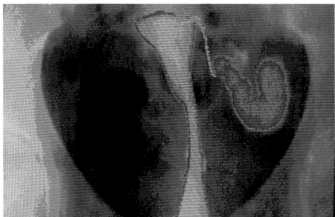

In this false-colour hystero-salpingogram, the blue contrast medium has failed to flow into the right (left on image) uterine tube, indicating a blockage.

Transvaginal ultrasonography uses a higher frequency than abdominal ultrasound. This means that clearer resolution of the pelvic anatomy is possible.

Egg donation

Some couples may be unable to achieve conception due to the woman's failure to produce healthy eggs. *In vitro* fertilization using donated eggs offers these couples the chance to have children.

Some women are unable to conceive naturally because they are unable to produce eggs. This may occur if the ovaries are not properly developed, if a woman has undergone premature menopause, or if surgery or chemotherapy have rendered her sterile.

GENETIC REASONS
Some fertile women opt to use donor eggs if they are carriers of genetic disorders, such as haemophilia, which could be passed on to the child. Rather than risk giving birth to a child who may suffer greatly and die young, egg donation offers the chance of a healthy child.

DONORS
Egg donors should be fit and healthy and preferably already have a family of their own.

Their medical histories are assessed in a similar way to those of sperm donors. Doctors look for any evidence of genetic disorders and diseases that could be transmitted to the recipient or the offspring.

COUNSELLING
Donors also receive counselling to make sure that they fully understand the process of egg donation and any implications to them or their family.

Egg donation is a far more complicated and expensive procedure than sperm donation. This is due to the combination of the egg retrieval procedure and the donor's need to take stimulatory drugs.

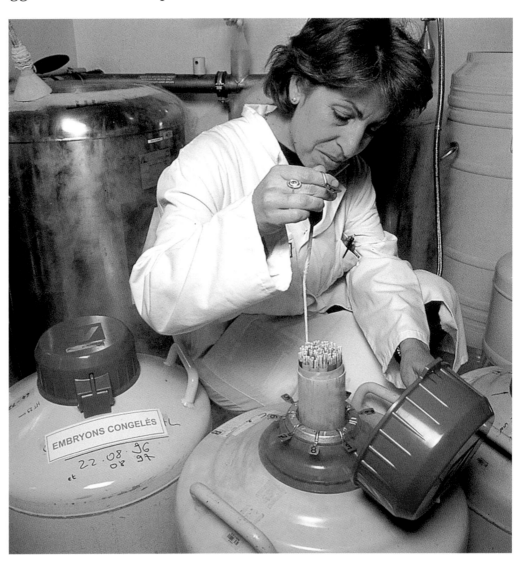

This technician is removing frozen embryos from storage prior to transfer to the recipient. The embryos have been frozen in liquid nitrogen at -196 °C (-321°F).

Preparing donors

Most women produce only a single egg each month during ovulation, which means that egg donors need to undergo stimulation of their ovaries to provide enough eggs to make donation worthwhile; a recipient who receives only a single egg would have a minimal chance of becoming pregnant.

STIMULATION
The ovaries are stimulated by giving the donor hormone-containing drugs. The drugs are given daily in the form of a nasal spray or injections. The drugs are given in two stages, and serve two separate roles:
■ Suppression of the normal menstrual cycle
■ Stimulation of the ovaries to hyperovulate (production of several eggs at once).

During the stimulation process, the ovaries will be monitored closely by ultrasound. Once an adequate number of eggs is seen to be maturing, a final set of drugs is given to complete the maturation process.

This final injection must be carefully timed so that it is given around 34 to 38 hours before collection of the eggs, when they are mature but have not left the ovary.

SIDE EFFECTS
Unfortunately, the drugs can have some unpleasant side-effects, including hot flushes, headaches, mood swings and depression, as well as tenderness around the ovaries. The symptoms usually pass once the second-stage drugs are given.

STORAGE
Unlike sperm, donated eggs cannot be frozen and successfully thawed for future treatment.

The donated eggs can be fertilized, however, and the resulting embryos frozen for transfer to the recipient at a future date.

SYNCHRONIZATION
Alternatively, the ovarian cycle of the donor and the recipient can be synchronized in the month leading up to treatment so that embryos can be transferred to the recipient.

Retrieval and incubation of eggs

Unlike sperm donation, the recovery of donor eggs is a complex procedure. Stimulatory drugs must be taken before the eggs can be harvested via the cervix under local anaesthetic. The eggs will then be fertilized and implanted into the recipient.

Eggs, unlike sperm, cannot easily be obtained from donors. The eggs must be recovered from the donor in the same way as that used to obtain eggs from women having *in vitro* fertilization (IVF).

RETRIEVAL OF EGGS

Egg retrieval involves aspiration (withdrawal by suction) of the egg from each follicle in the ovary. This is performed by first introducing a probe into the vagina. A fine needle is inserted along the probe and, under ultrasound, directed into the ovary to aspirate the eggs.

The eggs are then incubated with sperm from the recipient's partner (or from a sperm donor if her partner is infertile). Incubation lasts for several days.

A surgeon removes eggs from a woman's ovaries using a fine needle. Ultrasound helps to guide the needle via the vaginal wall into the ovary.

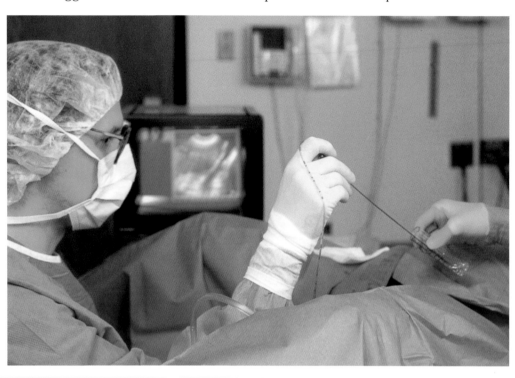

Embryo transfer

Each day the embryologist will check the eggs and observe those which have been successfully fertilized and are developing into embryos.

EMBRYO TRANSFER

Transfer of the embryos is usually carried out two days after the eggs have been harvested. Before transfer, the embryos will be closely examined under a microscope to ensure that they are healthy.

Embryo transfer is fairly straightforward and does not require any sedation. A fine catheter is passed through the opening of the cervix, and up to three embryos are placed in the uterine cavity. There is a one in five chance of a pregnancy occurring.

EMBRYOS FROZEN

Any embryos that are not used may be frozen so that they can be used in future treatment cycles should the first attempt fail. These embryos may also be used for donation to other couples, if so desired.

Embryos are usually frozen at the eight-cell stage (after three divisions). They are thawed when required and transferred to the recipient's uterus.

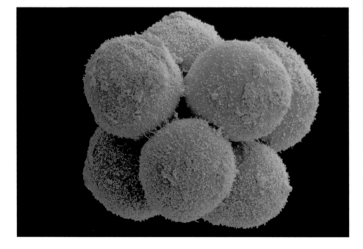

Preparing the recipient

The hormones progesterone and oestrogen are given to the recipient to prepare her uterine lining for the embryos. The recipient's blood hormone levels will be checked regularly and the uterine lining is monitored by ultrasound. It needs to be enriched with blood and at an optimum level of thickness for embryo implantation to occur.

Ideally, the ovulatory cycle of the recipient will be synchronized with that of the donor. The embryos can then be transferred without the need for freezing.

Recipients must be prepared for disappointment because it may take several treatment cycles before a successful pregnancy is achieved.

Prior to artificial insemination, the doctor examines the recipient. Her blood hormone levels and uterine lining will also be carefully monitored.

Embryo donation

Couples who are unable to produce healthy sperm or eggs, and thus cannot conceive naturally, may opt to use a donated embryo. This gives them an opportunity to experience pregnancy and childbirth.

In rare cases, a couple may find that they require both sperm and egg donation in order to start a family. This might occur when a man is found to produce no sperm (azoospermia) and his partner has ovarian failure or a premature menopause.

One option is to be the recipients of both sperm and egg donations; another option is to receive a donated embryo.

EMBRYOS FROM IVF
When undergoing *in vitro* fertilization (IVF), many couples find that they have too many embryos to be implanted safely at the time of their treatment.

To reduce the chances of multiple births, doctors usually place only two or three embryos in the uterus of women in a single treatment cycle.

In some centres, the couple have the option of freezing spare embryos, and these will be kept for them should the treatment cycle fail or should they wish later to have another baby.

However, some couples may decide not to use their frozen embryos and may opt to donate them to another couple.

Although a baby born from a donated embryo will not be genetically related to its parents, many couples still would prefer to undergo pregnancy and childbirth rather than adopt.

COUNSELLING
Recipient couples undergo rigorous counselling to make sure that they understand the processes involved and that they have thought through the issues that might confront them.

Sometimes, couples may need the donation of both sperm and eggs for the chance to have a baby. Embryo donation is an option for such couples.

A limited number of embryos will be used during IVF. Couples may choose to donate any remaining embryos to others wishing to undergo this form of treatment.

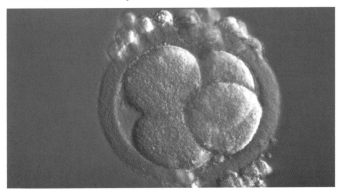

Storage of embryos

Embryos are stored routinely while couples are undergoing the IVF process. The embryos are frozen for up to five years, after which time couples are asked to indicate whether they wish them to be stored for a further period, or discarded.

MAXIMUM STORAGE
The regulatory body in the UK, the Human Fertilization and

Embryos are frozen for up to 10 years, during which time their condition remains unchanged. After this time, the embryos are donated or discarded.

Embryology Authority (HFEA), states that embryos may be stored for a maximum of 10 years. There is no evidence to suggest that freezing harms embryos during this period.

DONOR MATCHING
The physical characteristics of the donors (for example, height, build, eye and hair colour) are registered with the HFEA and used for matching with those of the recipient couple if possible.

The woman donating the embryos is usually aged 35 or under at the time the embryos were frozen.

Embryo transfer

Up to three embryos will be transferred into the recipient's uterus. For each embryo inserted, there is a 10 per cent chance that pregnancy will occur.

If the recipient is not undergoing a menstrual cycle (which is common in ovarian failure), she will be given hormone replacement therapy (HRT) to prepare her body for a pregnancy. This therapy is often started many months before treatment begins.

The quality of the recipient's endometrium (uterine lining) will be monitored closely by ultrasound scanning in order to determine the optimum time for embryo transfer.

TRANSFER
If a healthy endometrium is achieved, then two or three embryos will be inserted into the recipient's uterus. The embryos are transferred painlessly into the uterus via a fine catheter, which is passed through the cervix.

SUCCESS RATE
Like any other woman who is trying to become pregnant, the recipient must then wait to see if she misses her menstrual period and has a positive pregnancy test. Any resulting pregnancy is then allowed to continue in the normal way.

The chance of successful embryo implantation is about 10 per cent per embryo that is transferred.

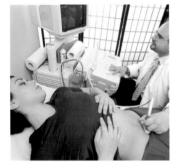

An ultrasound scan will reveal the quality of the recipient's uterine lining. This will help to determine the best time for insertion of the embryos.

A catheter is used to transfer the embryos into the recipient's uterus. Up to three embryos are transferred to maximize the chances of success.

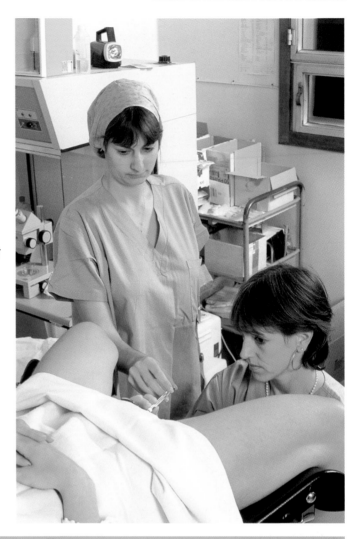

Donor counselling

Unlike egg and sperm donors, couples who donate their embryos will already have undertaken infertility treatment of their own. They will therefore already have received extensive counselling – both about their own treatment and about the possibility that any spare embryos could be donated to other couples at a later stage.

When a couple decide to donate their embryos, however, it may be several years after their treatment took place. They would therefore normally be invited to see a counsellor again to discuss their decision.

Personal decision
It is entirely a matter of personal choice as to whether those couples with embryos in storage decide to donate their embryos. Indeed, many embryos are donated for research purposes or are simply destroyed if unwanted.

Some countries have very strict rules surrounding embryo donation and the use of embryos in medical research; indeed, in a number of countries, both are strictly forbidden.

Medical research
Where the use of embryos for medical research is possible, it is tightly regulated and strict controls are placed upon the scientists regarding the use to which the embryos can be put.

Legal restrictions currently state that embryos cannot be stored for longer than 10 years.

Legal considerations
The counsellor will explain the legal situation with regard to the embryo donation and will ascertain the couple's feelings on the idea of genetic siblings of their own children growing up in other families.

Discussions will also inquire into how the couple's own children might feel about the existence of siblings when they grow older – if, indeed, the couple decide to tell them about their donation.

Embryo donors will already have received fertility counselling. When they wish to donate, however, they may be invited to undertake further counselling.

Endometriosis

Endometriosis is the abnormal growth of uterine tissue outside the uterus. The tissue passes through the same monthly cycle of swelling and bleeding, and can cause severe pain during a period.

Endometriosis is a condition that affects 5–10 per cent of women, in which cells that normally line the uterus become embedded outside the uterus, usually elsewhere within the pelvic area.

The endometrium is the lining of the uterus, which is shed during menstruation. Usually, any minor leakage of blood or cells from the endometrium into the pelvis via the uterine (Fallopian) tubes is quickly reabsorbed. However, in women with endometriosis, uterine lining tissue becomes attached to the pelvic wall, ovaries, Fallopian tubes, uterus, bladder or bowel.

Endometriosis is not restricted to these sites; it can also affect more distant structures such as the appendix, kidney, ureters and even the lungs.

MENSTRUAL EFFECTS
Because the tissue is the same as that which lines the uterus, during menstruation it secretes blood and forms a tiny bleb (a blister-like cyst) each month. Over time, the surface of the cyst becomes fibrosed and adheres to neighbouring structures in the pelvis.

Possible sites of endometriosis

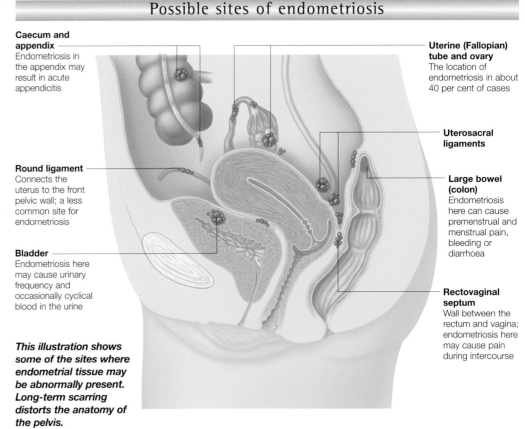

Caecum and appendix
Endometriosis in the appendix may result in acute appendicitis

Round ligament
Connects the uterus to the front pelvic wall; a less common site for endometriosis

Bladder
Endometriosis here may cause urinary frequency and occasionally cyclical blood in the urine

Uterine (Fallopian) tube and ovary
The location of endometriosis in about 40 per cent of cases

Uterosacral ligaments

Large bowel (colon)
Endometriosis here can cause premenstrual and menstrual pain, bleeding or diarrhoea

Rectovaginal septum
Wall between the rectum and vagina; endometriosis here may cause pain during intercourse

This illustration shows some of the sites where endometrial tissue may be abnormally present. Long-term scarring distorts the anatomy of the pelvis.

Symptoms of endometriosis

One of the most common symptoms of endometriosis is pain. This can occur during ovulation, menstruation or defecation, or during sexual intercourse. The pain may become progressively worse as the period continues and is quite different from 'period pains', which tend to be more severe at the beginning of the period.

However, not all women with endometriosis suffer from pain; even quite a large endometrioma (a swelling that fills with blood, also known as a 'chocolate cyst') on a patient's ovary can be completely painless unless it is attached to the peritoneum (the membrane lining the abdomen).

FERTILITY PROBLEMS
Many women with endometriosis are diagnosed only because they have trouble becoming pregnant. This may be the result of the formation of adhesions within

Abdominal pain is a common symptom of endometriosis. It is different in character from the more usual 'period pains'.

the pelvis, which restrict the ability of the uterine (Fallopian) tube to carry an egg from the ovary to the uterus. More rarely, the uterine tube itself may become blocked by the endometrial tissue.

Endometriosis may be diagnosed when a woman is having difficulty conceiving. Thirty to forty per cent of women with endometriosis will be infertile as a result.

Causes

The cause of endometriosis is unknown. One theory is that during menstruation some blood, instead of passing out of the body via the vagina, travels back up the uterine (Fallopian) tubes and settles in the abdomen. It is not known why this may occur in some women and not others, but it has been suggested that this may be due to the immune system not recognizing and removing endometrial tissue found outside of the uterus.

Hormones are known to influence the symptoms and spread of the condition, as endometrial tissue follows the action of uterine tissue during the menstrual cycle.

Treating endometriosis

Once a definitive diagnosis of endometriosis is made – often by using ultrasound and laparoscopy – the condition may be treated by drugs or surgery.

Endometriosis can be difficult to diagnose and has been mistaken for fibroids, back pain or irritable bowel syndrome. The doctor must bear in mind that fibroids may also cause pain and excessive menstrual bleeding. However, a woman who experiences pain during a period, which worsens as the period goes on, is likely to have endometriosis.

INVESTIGATIONS
The diagnosis can sometimes be made by the doctor carrying out a bimanual examination (externally and internally) of the pelvic organs. This is not reliable, however, as any tissue mass detected may not be due to endometriosis. Ultrasound can be very helpful in visualizing abnormal masses or cysts.

LAPAROSCOPY
Laparoscopy, however, is the definitive investigation for endometriosis, which is often seen as loops of bowel stuck together. In some cases, cysts are found on an ovary. Laparoscopy also allows biopsies to be taken from suspected sites to confirm the diagnosis histologically. The gynaecologist records the size and position of any endometrial tissue.

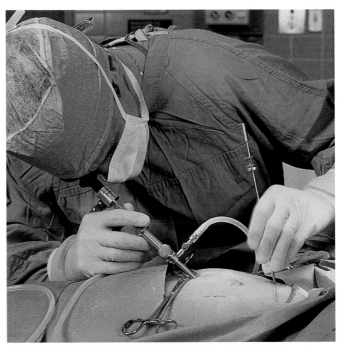

The technique of laparoscopy allows the surgeon to see inside the woman's abdomen and pelvis. Sites of endometriosis can thus be identified.

Medical treatment

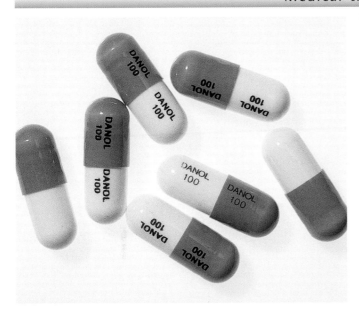

Treatment aims to remove or reduce the size of endometrial tissue, thereby relieving the symptomatic pain. A further aim is to restore fertility in those women who have been rendered unable to conceive.

HORMONE-BASED DRUGS
Drug treatments work to suppress the growth of endometrial tissue for an extended period of time (usually a minimum of six months) so that the abnormal tissue withers away. This can be achieved by suppressing oestrogen

Danazol (trade name Danol) is an anti-oestrogen drug widely used in the treatment of endometriosis. It is usually taken daily over a six-month period.

production, as the growth of endometrial tissue is sensitive to oestrogen.

The most effective hormone-based drug is danazol. Usually, a course of tablets is taken daily for 6–9 months. Danazol disrupts the menstrual cycle and can cause periods to cease altogether in some women.

Many drugs are synthetic analogues that inhibit the release of oestrogen by the ovaries, causing an artificial menopause. They can be given for up to six months at a time. Nafarelin and buserelin are given by a nasal spray morning and evening, whereas goserelin is given as a depot injection (allowing slow release of the drug) every 29 days for a maximum of six months.

Surgical options

When drug treatments have not proved successful, surgery may be undertaken. The aim of surgery is to relieve pain and to free the uterine (Fallopian) tubes and the ovaries from any adhesions that may prevent conception.

The operation is usually carried out laparoscopically and requires considerable skill. The surgeon uses the laparoscope to view the inside of the abdomen and destroys any endometrial tissue using either laser or diathermy techniques. The danger in using either diathermy or a laser, however, is that the bowel or

other unaffected tissue may be accidentally damaged.

Removing the ovaries will cure endometriosis completely, but this is not an option for women who want to have children. Removing the uterus but leaving the ovaries so that the woman does not have a permanent early menopause is not effective in curing endometriosis.

In severe endometriosis, a total hysterectomy may have to be performed. This involves the removal of the uterus and the ovaries.

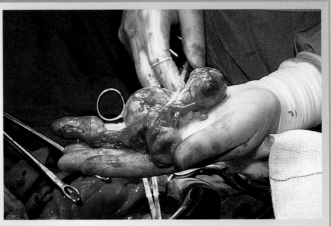

Failure to ovulate

Anovulation is the failure to make and release an egg each month. It is the commonest cause of female infertility, and can be treated using either hormone injections or laparoscopic surgery.

The vast majority of women with anovulation have an irregular menstrual cycle. This, by definition, is when the cycle length varies by more than five days from month to month. Regular cycles are usually a sign of healthy follicle development and egg release in response to the pituitary hormones: follicle stimulating hormone (FSH) and luteinizing hormone (LH).

SIGNS OF OVULATION

Some women know when they are ovulating as they experience pain (called mittelschmerz) and an increase in vaginal discharge at the time of ovulation. A temperature measurement taken first thing in the morning throughout the cycle is a simple way of checking for ovulation;

During normal ovulation, an egg is released from an ovary into the uterine (Fallopian) tube. Anovulation is the state when the ovaries fail to release an egg.

Anovulation is when a woman fails to release an egg (shown on this coloured electron micrograph) each month.

body temperature rises by about half a degree centigrade after ovulation has occurred.

Women who are trying to conceive, but have irregular cycles or no evidence of ovulation by temperature change or home testing with a kit, should see a doctor. Early diagnosis avoids many months of unnecessary misery and treatment is usually very simple.

The treatment of anovulation depends on the underlying cause. In the majority of cases, there is disruption to the normal hormonal signals that are sent from the hypothalamus or pituitary gland (FSH and LH) to the ovary. Ovulation detection kits are a much more accurate way of detecting ovulation and measure the rise in the hormone LH in the urine.

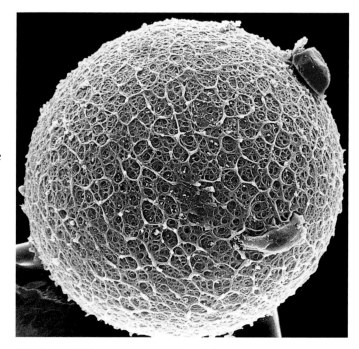

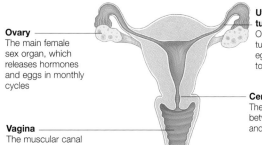

Ovary
The main female sex organ, which releases hormones and eggs in monthly cycles

Vagina
The muscular canal leading from the cervix to the exterior

Uterine (Fallopian) tube
One of the pair of tubes that carry the eggs from the ovary to the uterus

Cervix
The narrow opening between the vagina and the uterus

Polycystic ovary syndrome

The most common cause of anovulation is polycystic ovary syndrome. This is when the ovaries have small follicles, about 5–8mm ($^3/_{16}$ – $^5/_{16}$ in) in size, usually distributed around the edge of the ovary. The small follicles usually contain eggs that have stopped growing.

Polycystic ovaries can be identified on pelvic ultrasound in one in five women of reproductive age. Many women with polycystic ovaries have no symptoms, ovulate every month and are completely fertile. They

should be reassured that they do not have the syndrome and that having polycystic ovaries on an ultrasound scan is an incidental finding and not a health risk.

Some women, however, have irregular periods or no periods at all, and experience difficulty in conceiving. A further group may be aware of acne persisting long after puberty, increased body hair or hair thinning in a male pattern. Women who have both polycystic ovaries on ultrasound and symptoms are said to have polycystic ovary syndrome.

Prolactinoma

There are also some rarer conditions that affect the hypothalamus and pituitary gland and cause cycle disruption. Prolactinomas are small tumours of the pituitary gland that secrete excessive amounts of the hormone prolactin, a hormone that stimulates breast milk production. Although some women have no symptoms other than an irregular cycle, others notice visual disturbances or headaches.

Small tumours can be treated effectively with drugs that inhibit

the production of prolactin, such as bromocriptine or cabergoline. Usually these are sufficient to restore a regular cycle and fertility and will also shrink the tumour. Surgery to remove the tumour is usually necessary only if it is large (greater than 1cm/ ⅜in in diameter), and/or drug treatment has not been effective.

Small tumours in the pituitary gland, called prolactinomas, can sometimes cause breast milk to be produced as a result of increased prolactin levels.

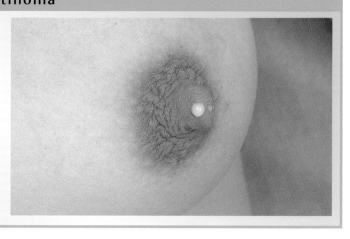

Causes of polycystic ovary syndrome

The precise cause of PCOS is still not clear, but current research points to an hereditary basis. Women who have polycystic ovaries are born with them, although the condition can only be clearly detected by ultrasound after puberty.

The tendency to develop symptoms of PCOS depends on a mixture of genetic and environmental factors. Although several genes are likely to be involved, the one that controls the production of male hormones by the ovary seems to be key to many of the symptoms that develop; levels of male hormone are typically higher in women with PCOS.

BODY WEIGHT

Genes involved in the regulation of insulin, the hormone involved in controlling blood sugar, also seem to be affected, particularly in those women with anovulation. Weight is important because both androgen and insulin levels tend to rise with body weight. Doctors can calculate whether body weight is excessive by an equation called the 'body mass index', or BMI. This is the weight in kilograms divided by height in metres squared.

A normal BMI is between 20 and 25 kg/m^2. Many women with PCOS and a BMI much above 27 kg/m^2 are anovulatory, and drug treatment alone is often ineffective in restoring fertility. Treatment therefore needs to be combined with a weight loss programme.

By contrast, excessive weight loss can result in periods stopping altogether because the FSH and LH signals from the pituitary are turned off. This condition is called hypogonadotropic hypogonadism. Although the condition can occur in women of normal BMI, low BMI (below 19 kg/m^2) is the commonest cause. However, psychological stress is also an important issue.

Excessive weight can be a contributory factor to PCOS. Treatment is often effective only when combined with dietary control to achieve weight loss.

Secondary symptoms of PCOS

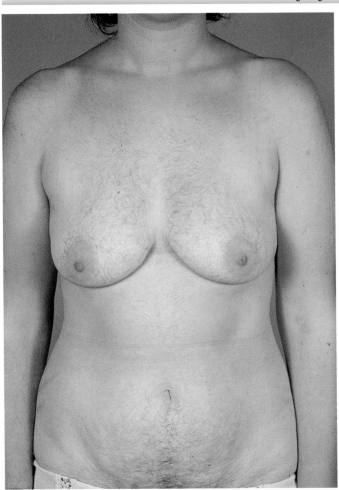

There is a wide spectrum in the severity of symptoms experienced by women with PCOS. Increased body weight often tips the balance between a woman experiencing no or very few symptoms and her developing amenorrhoea, oligomenorrhoea and menorrhagia (heavy, irregular periods) and/or hirsutism.

In terms of long-term health, women with PCOS are at increased risk of developing diabetes and heart disease in later life. Therefore, attention to diet, lifestyle and, in particular, regular exercise, is of paramount importance in these women.

There is no link between the small follicles of polycystic ovaries and ovarian cancer. However, women who have very few or no periods at all tend to develop an increased thickness in the endometrium (uterine lining) and, as a result, are at increased risk of developing cancer of the uterus.

Hirsutism in women is characterized by the presence of coarse hair on the face, chest, upper back or abdomen.

Some women with polycystic ovary syndrome may experience troublesome acne which persists long after puberty.

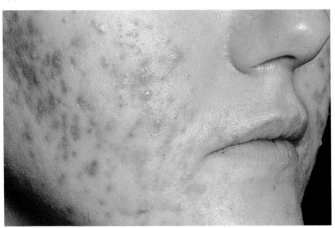

Treating anovulation

Polycystic ovary syndrome can be treated either by inducing ovulation, by administering hormones or by surgical intervention. The precise treatment depends on the symptoms experienced.

Ovulation induction is the term given to the drug treatment of anovulation. It is the first-line therapy for PCOS and hypothalamic hypogonadism. Once attention has been given to diet and lifestyle, women with PCOS should be given the anti-oestrogen drug clomiphene citrate. This is taken as a daily tablet for five days from the second day of menstruation.

ULTRASOUND SCANNING

Usually, the first month of treatment is monitored with a series of ultrasound scans throughout the cycle (called follicle tracking) to ensure that only one follicle (and egg) is developing. This reduces the risk of multiple pregnancy and ovarian hyperstimulation. The dose of the drug can then be adjusted. Thereafter the drug can be safely given at the correct dose for a total of six cycles.

Although 8 out of 10 women will ovulate on clomiphene, only 7 out of 10 will conceive after a six-month course of treatment. Side effects are minimal, although some women experience hot flushes, bloating, headaches and, occasionally, depression. The risk of twins is four times higher than in a

In the first month of treatment with clomiphene, ultrasound can be used to detect the presence of a multiple pregnancy.

Ovulation detection kits accurately detect ovulation by determining the rise of the hormone LH in the urine.

natural cycle (about 1 in 20 instead of 1 in 80).

Clomiphene is ineffective for women with hypogonadotropic hypogonadism. For them, and for those who fail to respond to clomiphene, injectable drugs are

the only option. These are called gonadotrophins and are either a mixture of FSH and LH, or FSH alone. They are given as daily or alternate day injections. Women who still do not menstruate may be given progesterone tablets for a few days to induce a period.

As with clomiphene, scanning is used to monitor the growth of the follicle and, once this has reached 18mm (¾in) in size, another hormone, called human chorionic gonadotrophin (hCG), is given in order to release the egg.

Side effects and risks of ovulation induction

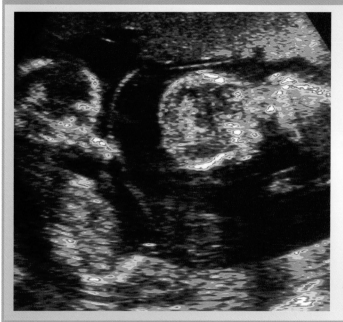

The risks of ovulation induction, particularly with injectable gonadotrophins, are multiple pregnancy and ovarian hyperstimulation. Tailoring the dose of drugs to the patient's response and the use of ultrasound monitoring are central to minimizing both. If more than three follicles develop to a size greater than 14mm (½ in), the cycle is abandoned and hCG is withheld. The patient is then advised to have protected intercourse or abstain.

Ovarian hyperstimulation syndrome is a rare condition that occurs when too many follicles

One of the main risks of ovulation induction is multiple pregnancy. This ultrasound scan shows a pair of twins developing in the uterus.

grow in response to drug stimulation. It is a very rare complication with clomiphene but can occur in women with PCOS who are given gonadotrophins.

Symptoms include abdominal distension and discomfort, nausea and, sometimes, difficulty breathing, and the ovaries become large and tender. The condition resolves itselfonce stimulation is stopped, although it may take longer if the patient has conceived because the hormone of pregnancy, hCG, tends to continue to stimulate the ovary. In extreme cases, admission to hospital may be necessary.

Recently, metformin – a drug traditionally used to treat diabetes, which works by lowering insulin levels – has been used to induce ovulation in women with PCOS.

Surgical treatment

As women with polycystic ovary syndrome are at high risk of developing ovarian hyperstimulation with injectable gonadotrophins, they are often advised to consider a surgical alternative. These operations are carried out using laparoscopic techniques.

Laparoscopic diathermy (when an electric current is used to burn tissue) can be used to excise ovarian cysts. This is usually carried out through an operating laparoscope. First, the patient is placed lying on the operating table with her legs supported and her knees bent. The head and upper part of the trunk is tilted head-down to enable the loops of intestines to come up out of the pelvis so that the surgeon has a clear view of the contents of the pelvis, and the risk of burning the bowel is minimized.

DIATHERMY
Carbon dioxide gas is used to distend the abdomen so that there is a space behind the abdominal wall into which the laparoscope is passed through a small cut in, or just below, the navel (umbilicus).

The surgeon then looks for the cysts on the ovary and passes a diathermy probe down into each cyst in turn. The diathermy current destroys the cyst.

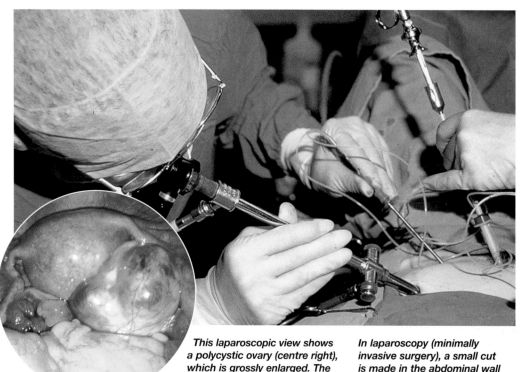

This laparoscopic view shows a polycystic ovary (centre right), which is grossly enlarged. The ovary is attached to the uterus (upper left) by a uterine tube.

In laparoscopy (minimally invasive surgery), a small cut is made in the abdominal wall through which the surgeon's instruments are passed.

Advantages and disadvantages of laparoscopic procedures

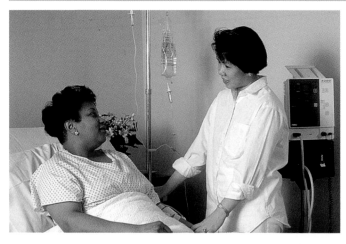

The main advantage of laparoscopic diathermy over older, open, surgery is the avoidance of a large incision in the abdominal wall. This generally means that the patient can go home the next day, and recovery is rapid.

The risks are that the bowel may inadvertently be burnt by the diathermic probe; this is very serious. Also, it is not only the cyst that is destroyed but some

Since only small incisions are made in laparoscopy, there are few after-effects and the patient can go home the following day.

surrounding ovarian tissue too. Thus the area from which ovulation can take place is diminished.

LASER TECHNIQUES
To overcome the risk factors, some surgeons now use lasers rather than diathermy; they control both these instruments using laparoscopic techniques. A laser fibre is inserted through the abdominal wall into each cyst through a small needle. Precise puncturing of the cyst with laser causes minimal damage to surrounding tissues in the ovary.

Wedge resections

The first operations to treat polycystic ovaries were performed in the early 1960s. These open procedures are called 'wedge resections'. The abdomen was opened through a small 'bikini cut' across the lower abdomen at the upper edge of the pubic hairline. The ovaries were delivered through the wound and a narrow wedge of tissue about 0.5cm (³⁄₁₆ in) wide and 3cm (1 ⅛in) long was cut out.

Non-absorbable sutures of sterile polyamide were placed close to the surface of the wedge in the ovary. However, adhesions of bowel to ovary still occurred. The operation was successful in about 50 per cent of patients.

This photograph shows two halves of an ovary after removal of a central wedge. The cysts (circled) can be seen protruding from the cut ends of the ovary.

Fibroids

Fibroids are common non-malignant growths within the tissue of the uterus. They may cause no symptoms or they may result in heavy menstrual bleeding and, in some cases, infertility.

Fibroids, or fibromyomata, are common non-malignant tumours of the muscular wall of the uterus. They can affect up to one in five women of childbearing age and are most often found in women over the age of 30. They are rarely found in the ovary, which is capable of producing almost any kind of tissue. Only very rarely do the fibroids become malignant, but they can grow to a large size.

DIAGNOSIS

It is not uncommon for fibroids to be discovered on routine pelvic examination, such as when screening for cervical cancer. A doctor may also make the diagnosis when examining a patient who experiences heavy or painful periods.

It may be difficult on physical examination to distinguish between large fibroids, ovarian swellings, an undiagnosed pregnancy and uterine malignancy. Ultrasound is therefore employed as the best method to determine the shape, size, position and consistency of any pelvic or lower abdominal mass. X-rays may be used in post-menopausal women and MR imaging is also occasionally used to clarify the diagnosis.

Common sites for fibroids

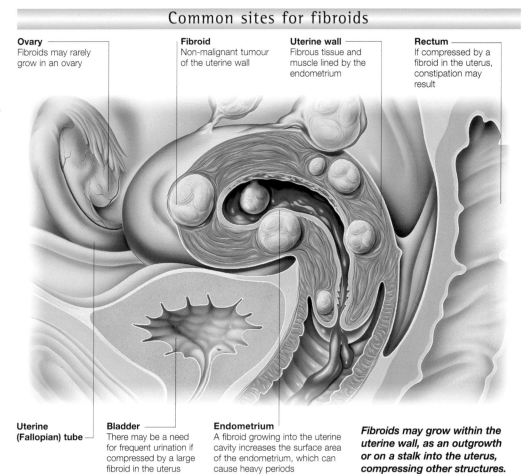

Ovary
Fibroids may rarely grow in an ovary

Fibroid
Non-malignant tumour of the uterine wall

Uterine wall
Fibrous tissue and muscle lined by the endometrium

Rectum
If compressed by a fibroid in the uterus, constipation may result

Uterine (Fallopian) tube

Bladder
There may be a need for frequent urination if compressed by a large fibroid in the uterus

Endometrium
A fibroid growing into the uterine cavity increases the surface area of the endometrium, which can cause heavy periods

Fibroids may grow within the uterine wall, as an outgrowth or on a stalk into the uterus, compressing other structures.

Clinical features of fibroids

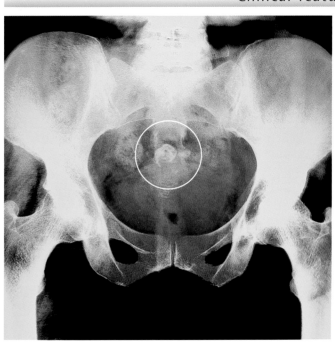

Small fibroids initially cause no symptoms, but those that grow into the uterine cavity increase the area of the endometrium (uterine lining), which is shed during menstruation. This results in heavy periods that may be longer in duration than normal. Heavy blood loss may lead to anaemia, which can be severe.

Infertility is probably the most common side effect of fibroids, which tend to occur more often in childless women.

Fibroids may outgrow their blood supply and become painful as they degenerate. In some cases, fibroids with an insufficient blood supply calcify. This can be a helpful change

because calcified fibroids stop growing and do not bleed.

If fibroids press on the upper part of the bladder, the patient will need to pass urine frequently; if the rectum is compressed, the patient will have difficulty in passing faeces and become constipated.

Fibroids are sometimes detected during routine cervical examination. A doctor will try to assess the size of the fibroids as this determines treatment.

Several forms of imaging can be used to visualize fibroids within the pelvis. Plain X-rays may aid diagnosis, but only if the fibroid has calcified, as shown here.

Types of fibroid

Fibroids always start their growth in the muscle wall of the uterus (intramural). If situated on the innermost part of the uterine wall, they may grow into its cavity (submucosal), where they are then covered with endometrium, the lining of the uterus. Occasionally, instead of growing diffusely, they may become pedunculated (on a stalk), with the main part jutting into the cavity of the uterus.

EXTENT OF GROWTH

If they grow outwards (which is common), they extend the outer surface of the uterus (subserosal), but often they just grow in bulk within the muscle wall of the uterus. When growing, they are surrounded by a capsule of condensed tissue.

Submucosal and cervical fibroids may be single, but many patients have multiple tumours. Growth is usually slow, tending to cease at menopause, after which fibroids may shrink. The worst effect of fibroids during reproductive life is heavy bleeding during periods and occasionally some bleeding between periods.

Intramural fibroids

Intramural fibroid
These common fibroids grow within the muscular uterine wall

Fibroids in the uterine wall
Fibroids that grow within the wall of the uterus are termed intramural fibroids. This is the most common type of fibroid.

Uterine cavity fibroids

Pedunculated fibroid
These grow into the uterus on a stalk

Pedunculated fibroid
May block the cervical canal

Fibroids in the uterine cavity
Pedunculated fibroids grow into the cavity of the uterus on a stalk. They increase the surface area of the endometrium.

Subserosal fibroids

Subserosal fibroid
The fibroids are located on the outer surface of the uterus, just below the outer lining; if large, these may press on other organs such as the bladder

Cervical fibroid
May be detected during a cervical examination

Submucosal fibroid
These grow under the endometrium (inner lining) and increase its surface area. This can cause heavy bleeding and discomfort

Fibroids outside of the uterus
Submucosal fibroids are found just under the endometrium. Subserosal fibroids grow on the outside of the uterus.

Treating fibroids

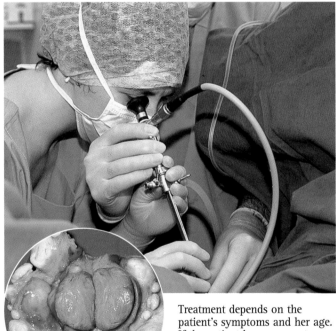

A large number of fibroids can be seen in this uterus, which has been dissected. In cases such as these, hysterectomy may be the most effective treatment.

Treatment depends on the patient's symptoms and her age. If the patient has no symptoms and an ultrasound shows only one or two small fibroids, there is no need for active treatment. However, an appointment should be given for a follow-up visit a few months later, when another ultrasound will be taken.

Anaemia is diagnosed by taking a full blood count (blood test) and treated by reducing the

Laparoscopy is used for visualizing fibroids on the outer surface of the uterus. The fibroids can sometimes be removed at the same time.

surface area of endometrial bleeding as well as by treating the iron loss with iron tablets or injections.

SURGICAL TREATMENT

Diathermy or laser may be used to destroy moderate-sized fibroids growing into the cavity of the uterus, via a hysteroscope. The tissue of the fibroid is devitalized, with the result that after a few months its volume has shrunk considerably.

A laparoscope is used to visualize fibroids on the outer abdominal surface of the uterus. It is also possible to remove fibroids, particularly those on a pedicle (stalk), in this way.

The older method of myomectomy (removal of fibroids) after opening the abdomen is still considered for the treatment of large fibroids by most gynaecologists.

Hysterectomy to remove the entire uterus is indicated for women who no longer wish to reproduce and who may be near the menopause.

HORMONE TREATMENT

Fibroids can be reduced in size using hormonal treatment, such as Zoladex – a hormone that affects the pituitary gland, thereby stopping the output of its stimulating hormone. This drug also thins the lining of the uterus. It is given by injection into the abdominal wall every 28 days for up to three months before surgery.

Women with fibroids should not receive hormone replacement therapy (HRT) after the menopause because the oestrogen in HRT will make the fibroids grow again.

This micrograph shows an intramural fibroid (dark mass) within the muscular uterine wall. It may grow to the size of an orange or even larger.

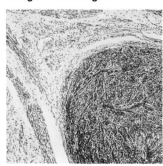

Hysteroscopy

The technique of hysteroscopy enables gynaecologists to look directly into the uterus and detect any abnormalities. Surgical procedures can also be carried out in this way.

Hysteroscopy is a procedure for viewing the interior of the uterus through an instrument similar to a telescope, called an endoscope, which is introduced through the cervix. Initially it was used only as a diagnostic tool, but it is now also widely used therapeutically. Although the concept is not new, the development of superior optical systems and of fibre-optic light sources, together with the increasing interest in minimally invasive surgery, provided a spur to progress.

Diagnostic hysteroscopy has replaced the procedure of dilatation and curettage (D and C) which is performed for similar reasons, but was just a blind scrape of the inner surface of the uterus. The direct visualization offered by hysteroscopy is much more precise.

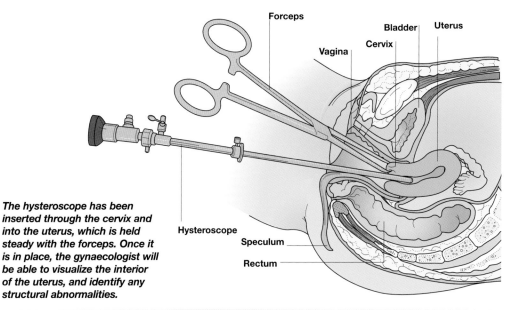

The hysteroscope has been inserted through the cervix and into the uterus, which is held steady with the forceps. Once it is in place, the gynaecologist will be able to visualize the interior of the uterus, and identify any structural abnormalities.

Types of hysteroscope

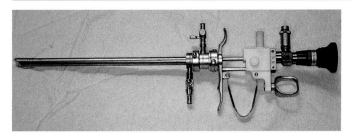

Surgical instruments can be passed through an operating hysteroscope.

■ Diagnostic hysteroscopes can be rigid or flexible. They consist of a telescope with fibre-optic bundles and a channel through which fluid can be irrigated. The fluid distends the cavity of the uterus and helps to wash away blood so that every aspect of the interior can be inspected. It can

Diagnostic hysteroscopes see inside the uterus. They are usually 3–4 mm (⅛ in) in diameter to allow easy passage.

be introduced with little, if any, dilatation of the cervix.

■ Operating hysteroscopes are about 8mm (³∕₁₆in) in diameter and incorporate a variety of surgical tools. The purpose of each of these is to cut away any abnormal structures inside the uterus, or to destroy the endometrium (inner lining of the uterus). In addition, a fibre carrying a laser beam can be fed down a special channel in the hysteroscope to enable surgical procedures. Fine biopsy forceps may also be passed so that tiny pieces of tissue which may be abnormal can be accurately removed for microscopic study.

Indications for diagnostic hysteroscopy

A hysteroscopy may be performed when abnormality of the uterine cavity is expected. The commonest reason will be abnormal uterine bleeding, such as heavy periods (menorrhagia), or irregular inter-menstrual bleeding. Abnormalities to be excluded are endometrial polyps or submucous fibroids. Although malignancy is uncommon before the menopause, this will also be looked for.

Postmenopausal bleeding is usually innocent, but may be malignantt. Hysteroscopy may allow a lesion to be identified by direct visual biopsy.

Hysteroscopy may be used when a congenital abnormality of the uterus is

suspected. This would apply to women with a history of recurrent miscarriage. In the fetus, the uterus develops in two halves, and these then fuse to create a single cavity. However, this process can be disturbed such that there is a division of the cavity. This may be partial, or there may be a complete double uterus.

Other, less common indications are for women whose periods have stopped prematurely, particularly after a miscarriage where adhesions have formed within the uterus. Another indication would be for a women with a 'lost' intrauterine contraceptive device that cannot be retrieved in the normal way.

The presence of a double uterus (shown here during a hysterectomy operation) may be detected by hysteroscopy.

Preparing for the examination

Before undergoing a hysteroscope examination, a woman will have the procedure and its aims fully explained to her by the gynaecologist.

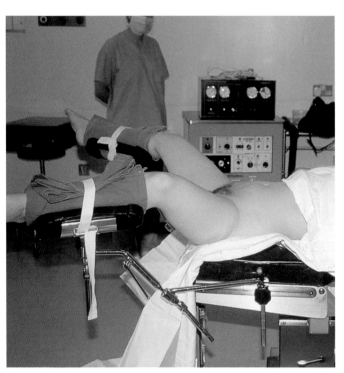

Hysteroscopy is often an outpatient procedure; on occasion, it may involve admission to a day surgical unit, and in the very elderly or medically unfit possibly admission as an in-patient.

EXAMINING THE PATIENT
The nature of the investigation will have been fully described so that the patient is not apprehensive. She will then be placed on a table with her legs elevated and supported on leg rests or in stirrups.

The position and size of the uterus will be assessed by bimanual pelvic examination, and any other pelvic abnormality will be excluded. Sometimes an ultrasound scan will have been performed, which may have prompted the hysteroscopy by suggesting some abnormality of the inner surface of the uterus. In women who have had children, when the entrance to the cervix is slightly open, it is often possible to pass a slim diagnostic hysteroscope without any form of anaesthetic.

Some women will require a local anaesthetic in the cervix; some will prefer to have a general anaesthetic. This will depend on the patient, the gynaecologist, what the expected pathology is and whether it is anticipated that it may be necessary to proceed to perform a more extensive procedure.

During hysteroscopy, the patient lies on her back with her buttocks hanging over the edge of the table. Her legs are supported on special rests.

Having the examination

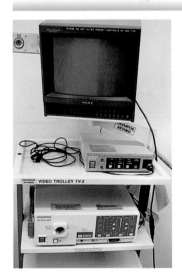

An instrument called a sound is first inserted to check the length of the uterine cavity, as the cervix may need a little dilatation in order to pass the hysteroscope. Once this is passed, irrigation fluid and a fibre-optic light source is attached.

Visualization may be directly through the instrument, but most surgeons use a video camera that attaches to the telescope and will view via a television monitor.

The trolley holds the monitor (top), where the view through the hysteroscope is displayed, and the light source for the hysteroscope and camera.

The cavity of the uterus will be systematically viewed. The openings to the Fallopian tubes will be identified, and the front and rear walls will be separated by the irrigating fluid so that they can be carefully inspected. The cervical canal is also viewed.

If an abnormality is seen, such as a polyp, a decision has to be made as to whether to proceed there and then or organize a subsequent admission. Curettings from the endometrial surface of the uterus will be sent for examination. This may be a biopsy of a particular area that looks abnormal, or just a representative sample if no specific abnormality can be seen.

This surgeon is using direct vision to inspect the uterus. There is often a video camera, which is linked to a monitor, attached to the hysteroscope.

Operative hysteroscopy

A diagnostic hysteroscopy may have been performed prior to the operative hysteroscopy, or the operator may decide to proceed at the time of the initial hysteroscopy.

The surgical procedures performed via a hysteroscope are, firstly, the removal of polyps (collections of endometrial cells with a stalk). These may produce irregular bleeding. Next, the resection of fibroids (benign tumours of the muscular wall of the uterus) if these impinge on the cavity. These may have caused heavy periods; even a small fibroid on the inner surface of the uterus can produce major menstrual problems. However, they are very amenable to local resection, which can significantly improve the situation.

The last of the common procedures is destruction of the whole endometrial layer

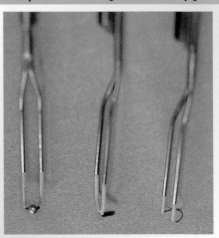

of the uterus – endometrial ablation. This procedure is a treatment for unacceptably heavy periods and may save the patient having to have the more major operation of hysterectomy.

Less common procedures to be performed with the use of a hysteroscope include the division of intra-uterine adhesions and the division of a congenital septum (dividing wall) within the uterus. There have also been attempts made to sterilize women by occluding (blocking) the uterine tubes via the hysteroscope.

A variety of surgical instruments can be attached to the end of the hysteroscope. Shown here are a roller ball (left), a probe (centre) and a diathermy loop (right).

Menopause

The menopause, the cessation of a woman's menstrual cycle,
occurs when the egg supply is exhausted naturally or artificially due
to surgery or disease. It is associated with a variety of symptoms.

The menopause is the permanent cessation of menstruation, signalling an end to a woman's reproductive ability. The average age for the menopause in the UK is 51, but it can range between the ages of 46 and 56. It may occur earlier, however, and when menopause occurs before 40, it is said to be premature.

HORMONAL INFLUENCES
The female menstrual cycle is controlled by the hypothalamus and the pituitary gland in the brain. The pituitary gland (under the control of the hypothalamus) releases two important hormones, follicle-stimulating hormone (FSH) and luteinizing hormone (LH), which stimulate the ovaries to produce oestrogen and progesterone and to ovulate.

A feedback mechanism exists by which high levels of oestrogen and progesterone in the circulation inhibit the production of FSH and LH by the pituitary gland.

CHANGES AT MENOPAUSE
At menopause, the pituitary gland continues producing FSH as well as some LH, but the ovaries no longer respond by producing oestrogen. The excess production of these hormones is thought to be the cause of many of the signs and symptoms of the menopause.

Hormone changes at the menopause

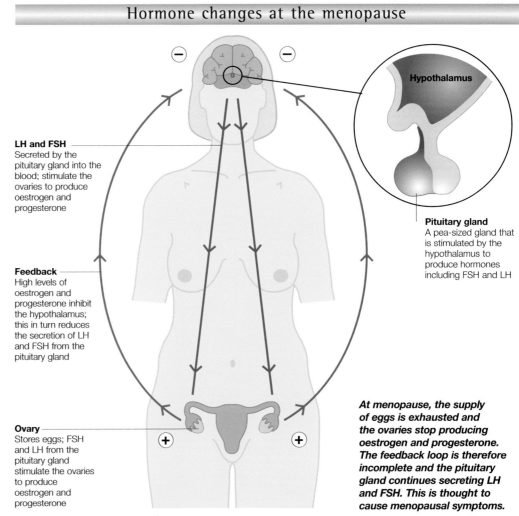

LH and FSH
Secreted by the pituitary gland into the blood; stimulate the ovaries to produce oestrogen and progesterone

Feedback
High levels of oestrogen and progesterone inhibit the hypothalamus; this in turn reduces the secretion of LH and FSH from the pituitary gland

Ovary
Stores eggs; FSH and LH from the pituitary gland stimulate the ovaries to produce oestrogen and progesterone

Hypothalamus

Pituitary gland
A pea-sized gland that is stimulated by the hypothalamus to produce hormones including FSH and LH

At menopause, the supply of eggs is exhausted and the ovaries stop producing oestrogen and progesterone. The feedback loop is therefore incomplete and the pituitary gland continues secreting LH and FSH. This is thought to cause menopausal symptoms.

Symptoms and signs of the menopause

The excess production of FSH and LH, together with the loss of oestrogen, probably causes most of the symptoms and signs of the menopause. These include:
- Irritability
- Lethargy
- Occasional intense hot flushes, night sweats
- Heart palpitations
- Depression
- Headache
- Insomnia
- Genital atrophy and vaginal dryness
- Osteoporosis

Unpleasant symptoms of the menopause are thought to be due to a hormonal imbalance. Irritability, lethargy and depression are common.

- Skin changes
- Cardiovascular disease
- Forgetfulness – this occurs in women (as well as men) from the age of 50, and is not necessarily due to the menopause
- Psychological symptoms – many women experience a loss of self-esteem at the time of the menopause
- Weight gain – this may be due to a more sedentary lifestyle at this age, rather than the menopause
- Increased libido – a lot of women experience increased libido. This increase in sex drive is even more likely as a result of hormone replacement therapy (HRT), given to replace oestrogen and progesterone.

Managing the menopause

Many women choose to have HRT to counteract the symptoms of the menopause. Dietary supplements and non-hormonal drugs may be used instead of HRT.

In the lead-up to the menopause, menstrual periods tend to become erratic. The menopause is understood to have occurred in a woman who has not menstruated for at least a year.

Hormone tests can confirm that the menopause has occurred. Blood may be analyzed to estimate the levels of FSH – which is raised at the menopause – and the level of oestrogen, production of which almost ceases at the menopause.

THE ROLE OF HRT

Not all women are given hormone replacement therapy. Whether to have it or not is a decision a woman has to make together with her partner and her doctor. Women who are encouraged to have HRT are those who have had a hysterectomy (especially if accompanied by removal of the ovaries), and those who have a family history of osteoporosis.

HRT is not recommended for some women, including those with fibroids or migraine, or a history of thrombosis or lumps in the breast.

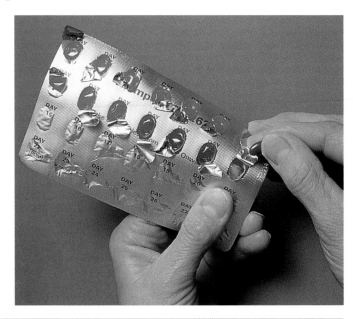

HRT is used to replace hormones that are deficient after the menopause. This can help to prevent osteoporosis.

Prevention and treatment of menopausal osteoporosis

Osteoporosis is amongst the most disturbing side effects of the low levels of oestrogen associated with the menopause. It is a condition in which the bones become weakened due to the loss of minerals, such as calcium. The total mass of bone is reduced and the bone tissue becomes porous and at risk of fractures, particularly in the wrist, hip and spine.

Osteoporosis tends to occur during and particularly after the menopause. Preventative measures include eating a healthy diet with sufficient calcium and vitamin D, reducing alcohol intake and undertaking regular weight-bearing exercise to prevent bone loss.

TREATMENT

Postmenopausal osteoporosis may be treated with a combination of biphosphonate drugs, either alone (Fosamax) or combined with calcium (Didronel PMO). Patients on these drugs will be closely monitored for side effects. Fosamax is particularly associated with severe oesophageal reactions and must be taken with a full glass of water before the first food of the day.

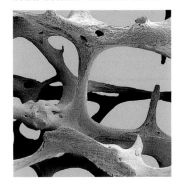

An electron micrograph of osteoporitic bone reveals the porous structure caused by loss of bone tissue.

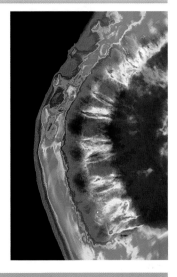

Osteoporosis can cause compression of the vertebrae. This results in curvature of the spine, as seen in this X-ray.

Healthy living during the menopause

While HRT is certainly very helpful for large numbers of women, it is not the only treatment, and it is not necessary when there are no symptoms. Regular medical check-ups are recommended, particularly for women around the menopause to check for cardiovascular disease and other complications of the menopause.

Exercise, such as walking, is essential for health and can help to build and maintain bone density in women of all ages.

Diet and supplements

Vitamins and minerals that are needed particularly at the menopause are normally obtained from a well-balanced diet. A menopausal woman's diet should contain sufficient fresh fruit and vegetables. Salt intake should decrease as blood pressure increases after the menopause. Meat should be eaten in moderation and fat kept to a minimum, as cholesterol levels increase after menopause. The fatty content of fish is an exception, because it includes healthy omega-3 fats that strengthen the immune system and helps fight heart disease.

Herbal supplements, particularly those containing phyto-oestrogens (plant-based substances similar to oestrogen) are found in soya, linseed oil and red clover sprouts, as well as rhubarb, yams, celery and parsley. These plants have some reported oestrogen-like effects which may serve to alleviate symptoms of the menopause.

Herbal medicine may be useful for some menopausal women. St John's wort, camomile and other herbs can relieve symptoms, but should be taken with caution.

Hormone replacement therapy

During the menopause, or following the removal of the ovaries, a woman's body becomes hormonally imbalanced. The risks associated with this can be reduced by hormone replacement therapy.

The menopause is defined as the date of a woman's last period, caused by the gradual failure of the ovaries to produce the female hormone oestrogen. On average, the menopause occurs at 51 years of age, but symptoms of the declining level of the hormone start some five years earlier and continue afterwards. This period around the menopause is known as the perimenopause.

As well as during the natural cycle of a woman's life, the menopause can be triggered by the surgical removal of the ovaries (oophorectomy), and a hysterectomy with conservation of the ovaries will often result in the menopause occurring two years earlier than would have occurred naturally.

BALANCING HORMONES
The lack of oestrogen results in unpleasant side effects, and the treatment – hormone replacement therapy (HRT) – is aimed at maintaining premenopausal hormone levels. Prescribing oestrogen with another hormone, progesterone, protects the menopausal woman against the risk of cancer of the endometrium (womb lining).

In the perimenopausal period, the progesterone is given for a two week period to stimulate menstruation every one to three

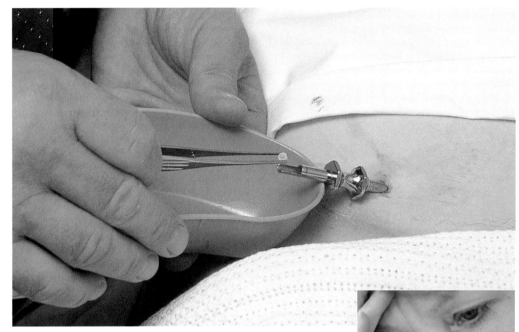

months. In the post-menopausal period, it can be given continuously with oestrogen to suppress the endometrium, resulting in the complete cessation of menstruation. Women who have had hysterectomies do not need to take progesterone.

The sooner HRT is started, the sooner its protective effects begin. Age is no disadvantage; indeed, the benefits of treatment increase with age. At first,

Pellets containing oestradiol, a female sex hormone, can be implanted into women to administer HRT. This is used in the treatment and prevention of postmenopausal symptoms, which include osteoporosis and vaginal dryness.

patients experiencing symptoms should be given a four-month HRT trial. However, patients who have had their ovaries removed should start HRT immediately.

The menopause results in an imbalance of hormones, often causing depression and fatigue. HRT can help to alleviate these periods of emotional distress.

Effects of the menopause

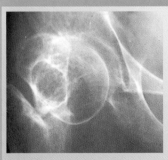

The menopausal depletion of calcium can lead to osteoporosis and fractures (as seen in this X-ray of a femur).

The symptoms of menopause vary enormously. Some women notice only that their periods stop, while others suffer from a variety of disabling physical symptoms that can cause acute distress. These include general heat intolerance, hot flushes of about 60 seconds' duration and occurring up to 30 times a day, night sweats and other sleep disturbances, and vaginal dryness.

Many women also suffer from psychological symptoms such as irritability, depression and lack of confidence.

The risk of several diseases increases quite dramatically after the menopause. While the cause is not known, there is evidence suggesting that this is due to the lack of oestrogen. These diseases include:
- Osteoporosis (loss of bone tissue) resulting in fractures and premature death
- Heart disease, the commonest cause of death in women
- Stroke
- Alzheimer's disease
- Cancer of the colon
- Cataracts.

A cataract is a lack of transparency in the lens of the eye. It is one of many possible side effects of the menopause.

Administering hormone replacement therapy

FORMS OF THERAPY
The type of hormone replacement therapy depends upon the patient's preference and previous medical history, as well as side effects and cost.
- Oral: Tablets are the cheapest option, allowing flexibility in dosage; however, only 30–70 per cent of the drug is metabolized after ingestion.
- Transdermal: Skin patches are usually applied twice-weekly.
- Subcutaneous: This involves the insertion of implants, requiring a minor operation, usually every six months.
- Vaginal: This form of therapy usually has a local effect only; available as cream, pessaries (a drug 'plug' fitted into the vagina) or tablets.

WHEN TO STOP
The decision of when to cease HRT is based on the patient's well-being, side effects and the relative risks and benefits of treatment. Generally, treatment is continued for about 10 years, but this is likely to be extended, as the benefits of HRT become more apparent with time.

WHEN NOT TO OFFER HRT
Some cancers grow under the influence of oestrogen; if these are advanced, they may be exacerbated by HRT. However, some breast cancer patients with severe menopausal symptoms benefit from HRT. Women who have severe liver disease, thrombophlebitis (inflamed superficial veins) or undiagnosed vaginal bleeding should not start HRT. It is also not recommended for women who are pregnant or breast-feeding.

The graph indicates oestrogen secretion throughout the life of an average woman. At menopause, the production of the hormone comes to a halt.

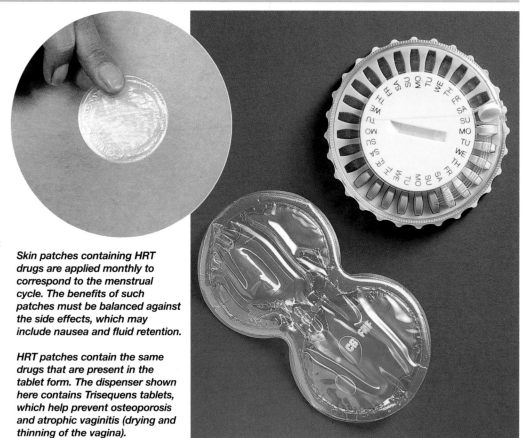

Skin patches containing HRT drugs are applied monthly to correspond to the menstrual cycle. The benefits of such patches must be balanced against the side effects, which may include nausea and fluid retention.

HRT patches contain the same drugs that are present in the tablet form. The dispenser shown here contains Trisequens tablets, which help prevent osteoporosis and atrophic vaginitis (drying and thinning of the vagina).

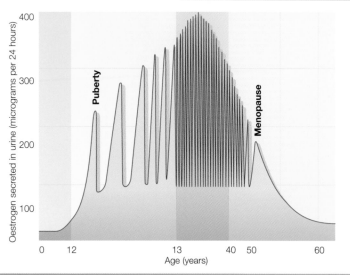

Graph: Oestrogen secreted in urine (micrograms per 24 hours) vs Age (years). Y-axis marked 100, 200, 300, 400. X-axis marked 0, 12, 13, 40, 50, 60. Labels: Puberty, Menopause.

THE FUTURE OF HRT
SERMs – Selective Oestrogen Receptor Modulators – are a new category of drug licensed for the prevention of osteoporosis. They block oestrogen receptors in the breast and thus slow the growth of breast cancers.

SERMs have beneficial effects on bone and blood cholesterol, preventing osteoporosis and, theoretically, heart disease. It is possible that they will have all the benefits of HRT without the risks. However, the use of SERMs has only just begun, and more research into their effectiveness is needed.

Risks and benefits of HRT

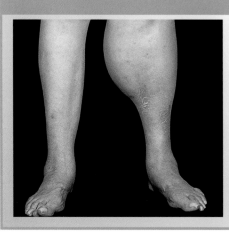

The swollen left calf of this patient is caused by a deep-vein thrombosis (a blood clot). The swelling is owing to sluggish blood flow and coagulation, and is often a side effect of HRT.

Risks of HRT
- **Breast cancer.** With HRT, there is a small increase in breast cancer incidence: women who have taken the drugs for five years increase their risk by 0.2 per cent; after 15 years, this rises to 1.2 per cent.
- **Deep-vein thrombosis** (clots in the deep veins of the legs). There is a lower incidence of DVT in menopausal women, but this is reversed with HRT.

Benefits of HRT
- **Osteoporosis.** By the age of 70, women will have lost 50 per cent of their bone tissue, largely owing to a deficiency of oestrogen. HRT slows down this process.
- **Ischaemic heart disease.** HRT reduces the of risk of heart disease by 40–50 per cent, and possibly reduces the risk in those already suffering with heart disease.
- **Alzheimer's disease.** Studies suggest that HRT gives a 20 per cent protective effect, and may also benefit sufferers.
- **Stroke.** Research suggests a reduction in risk of about 20 per cent.
- **Sexual sensitivity.** Sexual pleasure and arousal appear to be heightened with HRT.

Stress incontinence

Stress incontinence is a common condition in women, and often initially occurs after pregnancy. The weakened pelvic floor muscles can be strengthened by exercise or repaired by surgery.

Incontinence is the involuntary loss of control over the release of urine. It affects many more women than men, becoming increasingly common as women get older. Around five per cent of women under the age of 50 are affected, but this figure increases to over 25 per cent by the age of 80.

Fortunately, symptoms can often be resolved, but one of the main problems concerning incontinence is the sufferer's reluctance to ask for help.

TYPES OF INCONTINENCE
There are two main types of incontinence:
- Urge incontinence
- Stress incontinence.

Urge incontinence is also known as an unstable bladder. In this type of incontinence, the muscle of the bladder wall contracts involuntarily before the bladder is full. The urge to urinate is quickly followed by an uncontrollable complete emptying of the bladder.

In cases of stress incontinence, small amounts of urine leak as intra-abdominal pressure rises, such as when coughing, sneezing, laughing or exercising.

This is caused by the increased stress on the muscles that support the bladder – those of the pelvic floor.

Small rises in intra-abdominal pressure are caused by coughing or sneezing. This can result in an involuntary release of urine in those with stress incontinence.

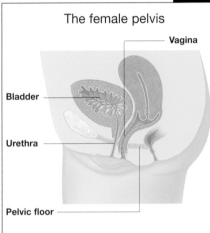

The female pelvis

- Vagina
- Bladder
- Urethra
- Pelvic floor

The muscles of the pelvic floor are weakened by childbirth. As these surround the urethra, their weakness leads to a loss of control over its action.

CYSTOCELE
In extreme cases, the bladder may bulge into the walls of the vagina, forming a protrusion called a cystocele. This adversely affects the ring of muscles holding urine within the bladder and urine leaks out.

Causes of stress incontinence

Pregnancy, with its resulting weakening of the pelvic floor, is the major cause of stress incontinence. The situation worsens during menopause.

The main cause of stress incontinence is a weakened pelvic floor. This can develop as a result of any of the following:
- Childbirth – stress incontinence is common during pregnancy and following childbirth. Up to 10 per cent of women leak urine in the postnatal period. The symptoms of stress incontinence initially caused by childbirth can worsen again in old age
- Hormonal disturbance, such as a lack of oestrogen after the menopause – this can cause thinning and weakening of the muscles of the pelvic floor.

Other causes
Other possible causes include:
- Infection – especially of the lining of the urethra. This requires antibiotic treatment
- Certain medications, such as lithium (used to treat manic depression), tricyclics (a type of antidepressant), and prazosin (a vasodilator)
- Certain conditions, such as parkinsonism, multiple sclerosis and diabetic neuropathy
- Local bladder causes, such as a bladder stone or pressure on the bladder from a myoma (benign muscle tumour)
- Constipation or any condition that increases abdominal pressure
- Obesity – a reduction in weight often resolves the problem.

Caffeine and alcohol may aggravate symptoms.

Diagnosis and treatment

Urine samples, vaginal examinations and urodynamic studies can build a comprehensive picture of the problem and dictate a suitable treatment.

A number of diagnostic tests can be carried out, either by a GP or in hospital.

GP TESTS
Some basic tests can be performed in a GP's surgery. The doctor or nurse can test a urine sample for signs of infection. An infection may precipitate stress incontinence, and treating the infection with antibiotics may resolve the incontinence.

A vaginal examination may be carried out to identify weakness in the pelvic floor muscle and to check for a cystocele or prolapsed uterus.

URODYNAMIC STUDIES
Urodynamic studies using contrast X-rays provide a wealth of information. The studies show the volume of urine the bladder can hold before leakage occurs and the stage at which the urge to pass water occurs. The rate and strength of flow during urination is also measured. X-rays are taken to enable visualization of the urinary tract.

Doctors are able to assess the severity of urinary incontinence through urodynamic studies. These assess all aspects of urine storage, release and flow.

Treatment for stress incontinence

A weakened pelvic floor is the most common cause of incontinence, so treatment usually focuses on strengthening the muscles using exercises.

First, the relevant muscles must be identified by the person performing the exercises. This is most easily done by trying to stop urinating midstream and noting which muscles are used.

PELVIC FLOOR EXERCISES
Pelvic floor exercises are performed as follows:
■ There are two phases – slow and fast. During the first set of exercises, the pelvic floor muscles are slowly tightened and then held for a count of five before being allowed to relax. This phase must be repeated at least five times

■ The second set is a repeat of this process, five times faster
■ The exercises should ideally be done at least 10 times a day, but strengthening the muscles may take several weeks
■ The exercises should become part of everyday life, and must be practised every day for the rest of the person's life to retain strength within the pelvic floor.

ALTERNATIVE TREATMENTS
The treatment chosen reflects the cause. For example:
■ Vaginal cones – this is another form of pelvic floor exercise.

Antenatal classes include lessons on performing pelvic floor exercises. These must be done both during and after pregnancy to avoid problems.

Here, weights are placed in the vagina, causing the muscles to react by contracting to hold the weight in place
■ Ring pessaries – these are plastic rings that are placed in the vagina to support the vaginal walls. They can be used to prevent a cystocele bulging

downwards and are suitable if a patient is not fit for surgery
■ Oestrogen creams – these can help postmenopausal women
■ General measures – drinking plenty of fluid (but avoiding caffeine and alcohol), losing weight, stopping smoking and increasing fibre in the diet.

Surgery

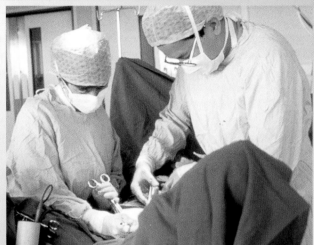

Surgery may involve a repair of the weakened pelvic floor muscles or the creation of a support for the bladder through colposuspension.

The literal meaning of colposuspension is 'suspension of the vagina'. It involves stitching the vagina to the structures above the pelvic bone. The aim is to elevate the neck of the bladder above the pelvic floor in order to prevent incontinence during times of increased abdominal pressure.

Surgical intervention in the form of a colposuspension is the last resort. The bladder is lifted above the pelvic floor to avoid response to pressure.

Success rates
Up to 50 per cent of symptoms can be controlled without resort to surgery.

Where surgery is thought necessary, around 75 per cent of cases are successfully treated and normal bladder control is restored.

Hysterectomy

The surgical removal of the uterus is one of the commonest gynaecological operations performed both before and after the menopause. The procedure may prove to be necessary for a number of medical reasons.

The medical indications (reasons for a course of action) for hysterectomy can generally be divided into those for women who are still menstruating and those for women past the menopause. In the former group, the commonest reason is menorrhagia (very heavy flow at menstruation), which may be accompanied by dysmenorrhea (painful periods).

However, there are alternatives to surgery. Drug treatment may resolve dysfunctional bleeding and endometriosis, which causes frequent and painful periods. Benign lumps in the uterus can often be removed with a specialized endoscope.

There are risks from any surgical procedure, but hysterectomy is a safe operation, and complications are rare, although damage to surrounding structures – the bowel or the urinary tract – can rarely occur. In pre-menopausal women, periods will cease after the operation and there will be an abrupt menopause if the ovaries are also removed. Hormone replacement therapy (HRT) may then be required.

CERVIX REMOVAL

The cervix may or may not be removed, depending on the reasons for the hysterectomy and the patient's wishes. In the past, the cervix was usually removed as a matter of course; arguments for this included the prevention of subsequent malignancy. Removal is often not surgically imperative, and the implications must be discussed before surgery.

Problems associated with the uterus

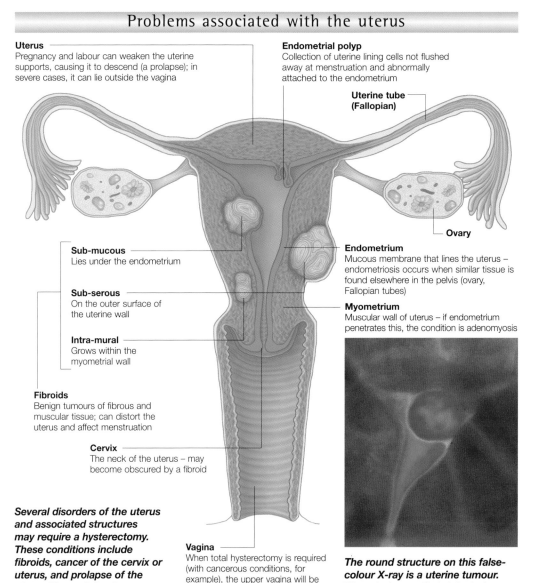

Uterus
Pregnancy and labour can weaken the uterine supports, causing it to descend (a prolapse); in severe cases, it can lie outside the vagina

Endometrial polyp
Collection of uterine lining cells not flushed away at menstruation and abnormally attached to the endometrium

Uterine tube (Fallopian)

Ovary

Sub-mucous
Lies under the endometrium

Sub-serous
On the outer surface of the uterine wall

Intra-mural
Grows within the myometrial wall

Fibroids
Benign tumours of fibrous and muscular tissue; can distort the uterus and affect menstruation

Cervix
The neck of the uterus – may become obscured by a fibroid

Endometrium
Mucous membrane that lines the uterus – endometriosis occurs when similar tissue is found elsewhere in the pelvis (ovary, Fallopian tubes)

Myometrium
Muscular wall of uterus – if endometrium penetrates this, the condition is adenomyosis

Vagina
When total hysterectomy is required (with cancerous conditions, for example), the upper vagina will be removed along with the cervix, uterus, Fallopian tubes and ovaries

Several disorders of the uterus and associated structures may require a hysterectomy. These conditions include fibroids, cancer of the cervix or uterus, and prolapse of the uterus (descent due to weakened tissues).

The round structure on this false-colour X-ray is a uterine tumour. The uterine cavity is injected with a contrast medium (blue).

Malignant disease of the uterus

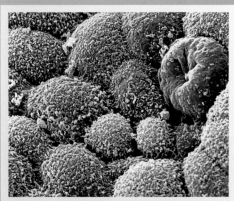

This false-colour micrograph shows cells of different shapes and sizes that typify the chaotic growth of a malignant ovarian tumour. They are covered in fine surface microvilli (projections).

Malignant (cancerous) disease of the uterus may occur within the cervix or within the body of the uterus, although this is uncommon in pre-menopausal women. Uterine disease is usually a malignancy of the endometrium (the mucous membrane lining the uterus). More rarely, however, there can be a sarcoma (malignant tumour) affecting the wall of the uterus itself.

Most malignant diseases of the uterus will initially manifest with irregular bleeding, although for the vast majority of pre-menopausal women this symptom has a benign origin. Malignancy, or suspected malignancy, of the ovaries will often require hysterectomy, but unfortunately such problems may be quite advanced before obvious symptoms occur.

In post-menopausal women, the reasons for hysterectomy are fibroids, prolapse of the uterus, or malignancy of the genito-urinary tract (this may also be marked enough to warrant hysterectomy in pre-menopausal women, but is less common).

Fibroids

Fibroids (also known as fibromyomata) are benign accumulations of muscle and fibrous tissue in the wall of the uterus. Some 30 per cent of women will have fibroids by the time they are 30 years old, but most of them will have no symptoms. Fibroids are most likely to cause menorrhagia when they are close to the inner surface of the uterus. Large fibroids on the outer surface of the uterus may cause few problems, while small ones close to the cavity may cause major menstrual disturbance.

Hysterectomy may be required when the degree of menorrhagia is unacceptable or if the fibroids are large enough to be felt on abdominal palpation. This is usually once they have exceeded the size of a 12-week pregnancy.

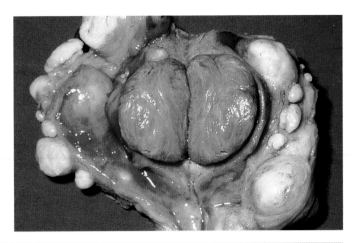

When fibroids are extremely large, removal will be necessary. Although they are benign (non-cancerous) tumours, they may result in pain and bleeding.

Menorrhagia

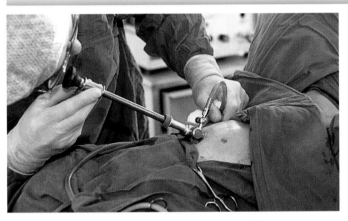

When menorrhagia (abnormally heavy menstrual bleeding) is not associated with any organic abnormality of the uterus, it is known as dysfunctional uterine bleeding, and is usually due to disturbed hormonal control. However, there may be some organic abnormality of the uterus to account for the menorrhagia which, for the

The gynaecologist may investigate the uterus with a laparoscope (left), hysteroscope or by ultrasound imaging.

majority of pre-menopausal women, will be due either to polyps or fibroids.

Polyps are collections of the cells that form the endometrium and are normally flushed out at menstruation. These cell bundles remain in the uterus, develop a stalk and attach to the inner uterine cavity. Occasionally, there is muscular tissue present, forming a fibroid polyp.

Polyps do not usually require hysterectomy and are removed by a hysteroscope, an endoscope passed through the cervix.

Types of hysterectomy

Abdominal hysterectomy
The operation is performed via an abdominal incision, which will usually be horizontal (along the 'bikini line') but may have to be vertical if a large mass or malignancy is expected. This route will be chosen if it is not suitable to remove the uterus vaginally. This may be because it is too large, there is no prolapse of the uterus or because complications are expected which can only be dealt with via an abdominal approach.

The operation may be a total hysterectomy – removal of the cervix and the body of the uterus – or subtotal, when the cervix is conserved. It may be necessary to remove one or both ovaries and their associated Fallopian tubes at the same time. This procedure is known as a salpingo-oophorectomy.

Vaginal hysterectomy
The uterus is removed via the vagina so that no abdominal incision is required. This will be the route of choice when there is prolapse of the uterus, especially if the uterus is not too large and no pathology involving the ovaries is suspected.

Laparoscopically assisted hysterectomy
Here, part or all of the operation will be performed via an endoscope inserted through the abdominal wall. It has the advantage of a shorter post-operative stay, but a specialist surgeon is required and the procedure has a greater potential for morbidity (subsequent illness). This may become a common approach as more experience is gained.

With the surrounding tissues and blood vessels cut and tied, surgeons proceed to excise the uterus, having gained access through the abdominal wall. The body of the uterus may then be lifted out, rather than removed through the vagina.

Endometriosis

The other common benign indication for hysterectomy in pre-menopausal women is endometriosis. This is the presence of tissue similar to normal endometrium in sites other than the lining of the uterus. The most common sites for this tissue are the ovaries or the space behind the uterus.

This tissue bleeds at each period and, because the blood is unable to escape, collections of blood build up. This causes irritation and can result in adhesion of the uterus to the bowel, ovary or other neighbouring structures in the abdominal cavity. A common feature of endometriosis is frequent, heavy and painful periods, with the pain starting before menstrual loss.

This coloured scanning electron micrograph shows endometriotic cells in an ovary. Removal of the ovary will alleviate symptoms.

Urogenital prolapse

A urogenital prolapse occurs when the female pelvic organs are displaced downwards from their normal position. Prolapse is caused by a weakening of the muscles and ligaments of the pelvic floor.

The word 'prolapse' is derived from the Latin term meaning 'to fall'. Urogenital prolapse describes the abnormal descent of the female pelvic organs when there is a weakness in the supporting structures (ligaments and muscles) of the pelvic floor.

ANATOMY OF THE PELVIC FLOOR
The muscles and ligaments of the pelvic floor form a cradle in the pelvis, supporting the uterus, bladder, urethra and rectum.

Anteriorly, there is a triangular sheet of dense fibrous tissue spanning the anterior half of the pelvis, which is pierced by the vagina and urethra. This sheet of tissue is known as the urogenital diaphragm. Posteriorly, there is the perineal body that lies between the vagina and the rectum and provides further support for the pelvic floor.

Prolapse is more common after the menopause, when reduced oestrogen levels result in a weakening of the pelvic floor ligaments. The condition is also more usually experienced by women who have had

children, as the muscles and ligaments are often weakened as a result of childbirth.

INCIDENCE
Today, increased life expectancy means that the majority of women spend a third of their lives in the postmenopausal state. One result of this is that

there is an increased incidence of urogenital prolapse.

Surgery for prolapse accounts for approximately one fifth of planned major gynaecological surgery, and this increases to almost two thirds of operations in the elderly.

Approximately one in 10 women will have surgery for

Although not usually life threatening, prolapse often leads to troublesome symptoms. The condition usually occurs only after the menopause.

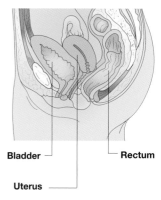

Bladder — — Rectum

Uterus —

▲ *The uterus lies in the pelvis, between the bladder and the rectum. In urogenital prolapse, the uterus or vagina is displaced downwards.*

prolapse during their lifetime and a third of these procedures are repeat operations for recurrent prolapse.

Classification of prolapse

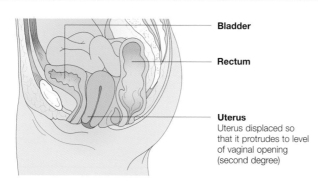

— Bladder

— Rectum

— Uterus
Uterus displaced so that it protrudes to level of vaginal opening (second degree)

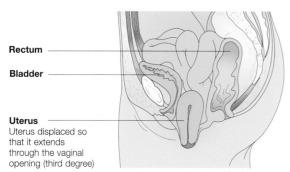

Rectum —

Bladder —

Uterus —
Uterus displaced so that it extends through the vaginal opening (third degree)

Urogenital prolapse is described according to the organ that is involved and the part of the vagina that is affected.

TYPES OF PROLAPSE
The four types of urogenital prolapse are:
■ Cystourethrocele – this describes the descent of the anterior vaginal wall and involves the bladder and urethra
■ Rectocele – this describes the descent of the posterior vaginal wall and is caused by the rectum pushing forward into the vagina
■ Uterine prolapse – this describes the descent of the uterus down the axis of the vagina
■ Vaginal vault prolapse – this term is used to describe the

Prolapse is graded according to the degree of the protrusion. A second-degree prolapse (top) is less severe than a third-degree prolapse (bottom).

descent of the upper vagina in women who have previously had their uterus and cervix removed at the time of hysterectomy.

GRADING OF PROLAPSE
The severity of prolapse depends on the size of the protrusion and the degree to which it protrudes into the vagina. The prolapse can be graded in the following way:
■ First degree – the lowest part of the prolapse descends halfway to the vaginal opening
■ Second degree – the lowest part of the prolapse extends to the level of the vaginal opening, but only through it on straining
■ Third degree – the lowest part of the prolapse extends through the vaginal opening and lies outside the vagina.

Procidentia describes a third-degree uterine prolapse in which the uterus lies entirely outside the body.

Causes and symptoms

The risk of prolapse is increased in certain situations.
Symptoms vary from a mild feeling of discomfort to
complete protrusion of the uterus through the vagina.

A number of factors increase the
risk of a prolapse occurring. Risk
factors are related to:
■ Age – the risk of prolapse
increases with age, affecting
over half of women over the age
of 50 years
■ Childbearing – prolapse is
more common after childbirth. It
is relatively unusual in women
who have not had children
■ Race – prolapse is generally
thought to be more common in
Caucasian women

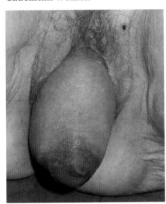

■ Hormonal factors – the
decrease in female hormones at
the time of the menopause is
thought to increase the risk
■ Smoking – smoking alone
does not increase the risk of
prolapse, although anything that
leads to a chronic cough will
increase the strain on the pelvic
floor muscles and thus increase
the risk of prolapse
■ Constipation – straining due
to constipation will increase the
pressure inside the abdomen and
so put the pelvic floor muscles
under more strain, increasing the
risk of prolapse
■ Exercise – heavy lifting as
well as sports such as
weightlifting and long-distance
running increase the risk
■ Surgery – gynaecological
surgery may increase the risk of
developing prolapse in later life.

*If a uterine prolapse is severe,
the most obvious symptom will
be a downward protrusion of the
uterus through the vagina. There
will be discomfort in the pelvis.*

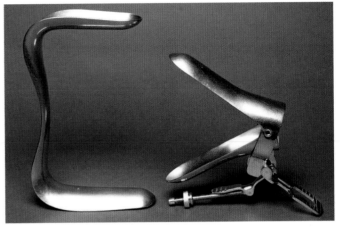

*Instruments called specula are
used to examine the vagina.
With the use of a light source,
they allow a clear view of
problems such as a prolapse.*

Over one third of women
develop symptoms following
hysterectomy, although far fewer
need further surgery.

SYMPTOMS
Most women with urogenital
prolapse complain of a feeling of
discomfort or heaviness within
the pelvis in addition to a
downward protrusion. Women
may also complain of pain on
intercourse, difficulty in
inserting tampons and chronic
lower back pain.
   A cystourethrocele may be
associated with bladder
symptoms of passing water
frequently and urinary urgency.
A rectocele may be linked to

difficulty in opening, or
incomplete emptying of,
the bowels.

EXAMINATION
Women are examined while
lying on the left side, using a
speculum, which allows the size
and position of the prolapse to
be identified. An internal
vaginal examination is also
performed to exclude a swelling
in the pelvis, which may be
causing the pain and discomfort.

Management of prolapse

There are a number of ways to
prevent prolapse prevented.

PREVENTIVE MEASURES
Methods of preventing prolapse
include the following:
■ Avoidance of constipation,
which has been implicated as
a major contributing factor to
urogenital prolapse for women
in Western society
■ Hormone replacement therapy
– this may also decrease the
incidence of prolapse, although
to date there is no evidence to
support this
■ Smaller family size and
improvements in obstetric care –
these have been implicated in
the prevention of prolapse

*Pelvic floor exercises, carried
out before and after childbirth,
can help to prevent a prolapse.
The exercises can also help to
manage a mild prolapse.*

■ Caesarean section delivery –
this may be important, although
studies have produced only
mixed results.

TREATING A PROLAPSE
In women who have developed a
prolapse, the condition may be
managed in a variety of ways.
These include:
■ Physiotherapy – pelvic floor
exercises may play a role in
treating women with
symptomatic prolapse, although

there are no objective evidence-
based studies to support this
■ Intravaginal pessaries –
pessaries offer a conservative
line of therapy for those women
who are not candidates for
surgery. Consequently, they may
be used in younger women who
have not yet completed their
family, in pregnancy and for
those women who may be unfit
for surgery. A pessary may also
offer symptomatic relief while
awaiting surgery.
   Ring pessaries are made of
silicone or polythene and are
available in a number of
different sizes. They are inserted
into the vagina and provide
support for the uterus and upper
vagina. Pessaries should be
changed every six months and
long-term use may be
complicated by vaginal
infections and ulceration
■ Surgery – surgical
intervention offers definitive
treatment of urogenital prolapse.
Operations are usually performed
vaginally under general
anaesthesia and require a
hospital stay of four to five
days.
   Prolapse surgery includes
pelvic floor reconstruction, with
or without vaginal hysterectomy,

depending on the degree and
type of prolapse present. After
the operation, a catheter is left
in the bladder and a pack in the
vagina for 24 hours.
   Women normally require four
to six weeks' convalescence and
should try to avoid any heavy
lifting, strenuous exercise and
constipation for the rest of their
lives in order to reduce the risk
of recurrent prolapse.

*Ring pessaries exist in a variety
of sizes. They are positioned
horizontally in the pelvis, where
they support the uterus and the
upper vagina.*

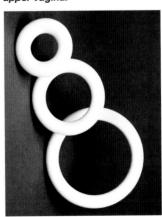

Contraception

There are a variety of methods of contraception available, all of which are intended to prevent pregnancy. Depending on the method used, the effect may be short-term or permanent.

Contraceptives either prevent fertilization of the woman's egg by the man's sperm, thus avoiding pregnancy, or prevent the implantation of the fertilized egg. Some contraceptives stop the sperm and egg from meeting, such as barrier methods (see overleaf), while others work by interfering with ovulation (egg release).

WHICH CONTRACEPTIVE?
The choice of contraceptive method depends on the couple, although some methods are unsuitable for medical reasons. Methods that are reversible can be divided into a number of categories.

■ **Chemical methods**
Spermicides are available in cream, gel, foam or pessary formulations, and all contain a chemical called nonoxynol-9, which works by killing sperm. Spermicides are not effective enough on their own and should be used with a barrier method.

■ **Barrier methods**
These include the diaphragm, cervical cap, male condom and female condom, and work by catching the male ejaculate. The male condom is also effective in helping to prevent sexually transmitted infections.

■ **Hormonal methods**
Hormonal contraception works in a variety of ways. The combined pill contains synthetic

A medical practitioner will be able to advise on the means of contraception most appropriate for each individual.

oestrogen and progestogen, which prevent ovulation. Progestogen-only pills work mainly by thickening the cervical mucus, making it impenetrable to sperm. Hormonal implants are inserted under the skin and release a progestogen. Injectables (intramuscular injections) also contain progestogens, and work by stopping ovulation.

Sterilization

Male and female sterilization both prevent sperm from reaching the egg. In men, it is called vasectomy and involves severing or blocking the vas deferens tubes which carry sperm from the testes, resulting in no sperm in the ejaculate.

Female sterilization involves the Fallopian tubes being cut, or clips being applied to block the Fallopian tube.

Sterilization is essentially irreversible, and is most popular in women and men over 30.

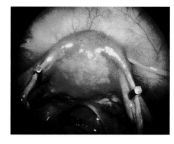

Female sterilization is achieved by fitting clips to the Fallopian tubes. This prevents fertilization, as sperm and egg cannot meet.

Effectiveness of different methods

Method	Contraceptive effectiveness (%)
Male sterilization	99.9
Combined oral contraceptives	99.9
Injectables	99.9
Contraceptive implants	99.8
Intra-uterine systems	99.8
Female sterilization	99.5-99.9
Progestogen-only pills	99
Intra-uterine devices	98-99.7
Fertility awareness* (rhythm method)	98
Male condom*	95
Female condom*	95
Diaphragm*	92-96
Cervical cap*	92-96
Persona*	94
Spermicides*	75
Withdrawal*	75

Contraceptive effectiveness is usually quoted as a percentage, and relates to the number of women who become pregnant when using this method for a year. The contraceptive effectiveness of the methods marked with a star (*) depends on how well the user follows the instructions for that method. Each is said to have a 'user failure' rate as well as a 'method failure' rate.

The perceived effectiveness of different contraceptives depends on how well the user follows the recommendations for each particular method.

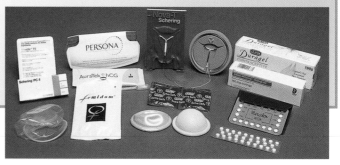

Physical methods

Couples can choose from a wide selection of contraceptive devices. A GP or family planning clinic can offer helpful advice if there is uncertainty.

Physical methods of contraception include barrier methods and intra-uterine devices, as well as fertility awareness and withdrawal.

BARRIER METHODS
Barrier methods prevent sperm from meeting the egg.
■ The male condom fits over the penis and collects the ejaculate. Male condoms are made of latex or polyurethane.
■ The female condom is made of polyurethane. It lines the vagina and collects the ejaculate.
■ Diaphragms and caps are made of latex and cover the cervix to block sperm from the reproductive tract. They are used together with a spermicide.

OTHER PHYSICAL METHODS
Intra-uterine devices (IUDs) are inserted into the uterus and remain effective for between

Sometimes two types of contraception need to be combined. The diaphragm, for example, is a reliable method of contraception when combined with a spermicide.

5 and 10 years, depending on the type used. All IUDs contain copper. The presence of the IUD in the uterus alters the uterine and tubal fluids, preventing fertilization.

Fertility awareness involves women being taught to recognize the different stages of their menstrual cycle. This enables them to identify fertile days and then either to abstain from penetrative sexual intercourse at this time or to use a barrier method.

Persona is a hand-held device that monitors the woman's cycle by measuring the hormones LH (luteinizing hormone) and estrone 3 glucronide in the urine. A red light shows on fertile days and a green light on other days.

If a couple opt for the withdrawal method, the man withdraws his penis from the woman's vagina before ejaculation. The withdrawal method is not an effective method of contraception since sperm is often released prior to ejaculation and many men do not withdraw early enough.

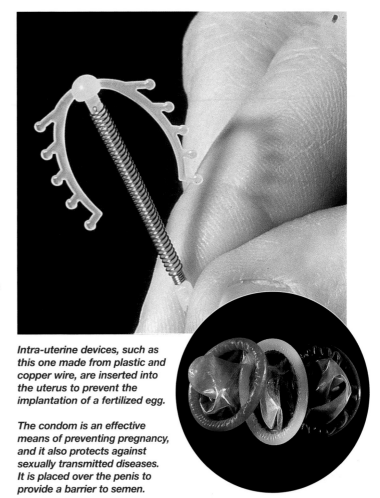

Intra-uterine devices, such as this one made from plastic and copper wire, are inserted into the uterus to prevent the implantation of a fertilized egg.

The condom is an effective means of preventing pregnancy, and it also protects against sexually transmitted diseases. It is placed over the penis to provide a barrier to semen.

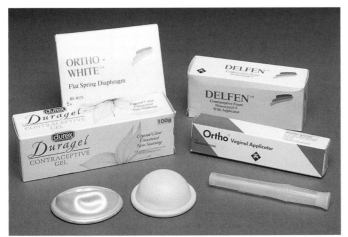

Popularity of methods

There are no comprehensive health service statistics published by the NHS on patterns of contraceptive use in the UK.

However, the annual General Household Survey provides information on contraception used by women aged between 16 and 49 and their partners.

The total exceeds 100 per cent because some couples use more than one method.

No method	27%
Contraceptive pill	25%
Condom	18%
Female sterilization	12%
Male sterilization	11%
IUD	4%
Withdrawal	3%
Diaphragm/cap	1%
Fertility awareness	1%
Spermicide	1%
Injectables	1%
Total	**104%**

Emergency or post-coital contraception

If a contraceptive method has failed, or no method has been used, then emergency contraception can be prescribed for use after intercourse has taken place.

Hormonal contraceptive, containing either synthetic oestrogen and progestogen or just progestogen, are given in two doses 12 hours apart.

The first dose must be given within 72 hours of unprotected sex. Alternatively, a woman can be fitted with an IUD within five days of unprotected sex or

within five days of the earliest date of ovulation.

DIFFERENT METHODS
A couple's contraceptive requirements may change over the years as their circumstances change. Contraceptive needs are not static – different methods are appropriate for people at different stages in their lives, and some methods are not advised in certain circumstances. A GP or family planning clinic will be able to give individuals further advice on this.

Where to get contraception

All methods of contraception have been free of charge since 1974, when the Family Planning Association clinics were transferred to the NHS.

In 1975, GPs began to provide free contraception (excluding condoms) in return for an item of service payment. Around 80 per cent of people obtain their contraception from GPs, and 20 per cent from family planning clinics.

Contraception is also provided by the following:
■ Brook Advisory Centres, which provide contraception and sexual health services to people under 21 years of age through clinics in 18 cities
■ Some genito-urinary medicine (GUM) clinics and sexual health clinics
■ Private clinics such as Marie Stopes Clinics and the British Pregnancy Advisory Service.

Natural family planning

Natural family planning offers an alternative to conventional contraceptive methods. It involves women being aware of when they are fertile so that they can assess the likelihood of becoming pregnant.

Natural family planning (NFP), or fertility awareness, is the term now used for what was traditionally known as the rhythm, or 'Billings', method.

This contraceptive method works by recognizing the naturally occurring signs of ovulation (release of an egg from the ovary), which enables the fertile and infertile phases of the menstrual cycle to be identified.

RENEWED INTEREST

The development of more sophisticated artificial methods of contraception (such as the contraceptive pill) have seen a move away from natural methods. However, trends change, and concerns over the long-term effects of some artificial methods of contraception have renewed interest in natural methods.

A knowledge of when a woman is fertile and when she is not means that she can decide whether or not to have sex, thereby either maximizing her chances of conception or minimizing them.

Natural family planning used to be considered an unreliable method of contraception. However, with care, it can be effective, allowing couples to choose when they have children.

Identifying fertile times

Ovulation, the crucial event in the menstrual cycle, is the result of a complex series of events influenced by pituitary and ovarian hormones. During the menstrual cycle, a mature egg is released 12–16 days before a woman's next period.

Once released, the egg is capable of being fertilized for up to a maximum of 24 hours. Since sperm can survive inside a woman's body for up to five

days, sex up to seven days before ovulation can result in conception. However, it is virtually impossible to get pregnant more than 24 hours after ovulation.

A woman may be able to identify her fertile time by recording body temperature daily throughout her cycle. This is done first thing in the morning.

This electron micrograph shows the release of a mature ovum (red) at ovulation. Knowing the time of ovulation is important for natural family planning.

FERTILITY INDICATORS

There are several indicators that can be used to identify a woman's fertile and infertile time. The three main ones are:
■ Cycle length – that is, the time between each menstrual period; if assessment of this is used alone, this is not a reliable indicator
■ Body temperature on waking – this changes after ovulation
■ Cervical secretions or mucus – the consistency of both of these changes with ovulation.

Using a combination of these indicators is recommended to maximize reliability.

PHYSICAL SIGNS

Some women may be aware of other physical signs to support these fertility indicators. These may include some or all of the following:

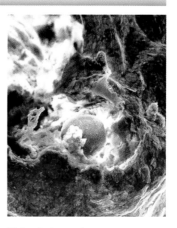

■ Ovulation pain
■ Changes in the position and softness of the cervix
■ Mid-cycle spotting or bleeding
■ Breast sensitivity
■ Bloating
■ Mood changes.

The more indicators that are used, the more effective NFP will be; noting several indicators may make this method up to 98 per cent effective as a means of contraception.

Advantages and disadvantages of NFP

Natural family planning can offer benefits over conventional contraceptive methods, but it may not be suitable for use by all couples.

ADVANTAGES
■ NFP increases women's awareness of fertility and how their body works
■ There are no physical side effects
■ Knowledge gained can help to plan or prevent a pregnancy
■ NFP is acceptable to all cultures and religions
■ Once the method is learnt, no further follow-up is required

■ Responsibility for contraception is shared with the partner, which can enhance the relationship.

DISADVANTAGES
■ It takes time to learn the method correctly
■ Daily observation and record-keeping is required
■ Commitment and motivation is required from both partners
■ High-reliability use requires periods of abstinence, so

Couples who wish to use NFP will need to learn what the technique involves from an experienced adviser.

spontaneity is lacking compared with some other methods
■ NFP can be difficult to learn with an irregular cycle, at times of stress or illness, after childbirth or miscarriage and during the menopause
■ Finding an NFP teacher may be difficult on the NHS and some teachers charge a fee

■ NFP is not suitable for those women who need to protect themselves against sexually transmitted infections.

Most NFP teachers advise abstinence from sex on fertile days if a woman does not want to conceive. No contraceptive method is foolproof, however.

Value of breast-feeding

Full breast-feeding (lactation) delays the return of ovulation after childbirth; amenorrhoea (absence of the menstrual period) is a marker that ovulation is not occurring. The contraceptive effect of breast-feeding is due to increased levels of the hormone prolactin, which inhibits ovulation.

The inhibition of ovarian activity is largely dependent on

Breast-feeding delays the return of ovulation after childbirth. It has a contraceptive effect in about 90 per cent of women, and lasts for several weeks.

the frequency of breast-feeding episodes day and night, and the time the baby spends suckling at the breast.

Exploiting lactational amenorrhoea is a valid and reliable method of contraception. It offers a woman up to 98 per cent protection against pregnancy when the following conditions exist:
■ A woman is exclusively breast-feeding her baby day and night at regular intervals
■ The baby is less than six months old
■ Menstruation has not returned after the birth.

Ongoing developments

New technologies have led to the development of several systems that monitor temperature, saliva and urine. The problems of daily observations and charting are gradually being resolved by these modern systems.

One example is Persona, which consists of a small, hand-held computer and urine test sticks. This system detects hormonal changes and ovulation, indicating with red and green lights when the fertile phase begins and ends.

Interestingly, this method is less effective than using natural

family planning. Currently, Persona is 94 per cent effective in preventing pregnancy if it is used according to instructions.

Research in this area continues in the attempt to find products that are effective at detecting a woman's fertile phase accurately, easily and cheaply.

The Persona contraceptive kit involves monitoring hormone levels in the urine. It is based on the principle that levels are highest around the time of ovulation.

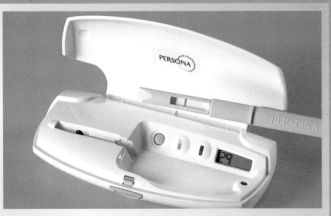

Intrauterine and barrier contraception

Two common forms of contraception are intrauterine methods (placing contraceptive devices inside the uterus) and barrier methods. These work by preventing the implantation of a fertilized egg in the uterus.

Intrauterine methods

The intrauterine device (IUD) and the intrauterine system (IUS) devices are small (3cm/1 ⅛in long), and are inserted into the uterus at a clinic or GP surgery.

Although both are fitted into the uterus they do differ in some respects. One of the main differences is that the IUS slowly releases small amounts of progestogen. This has the effect of thickening the cervical mucus, making sperm penetration difficult; it also makes the lining of the uterus unsuitable for implantation; in 85 per cent of women, it prevents ovulation.

In contrast, the IUD contains copper, which prevents fertilization and implantation.

ADVANTAGES
IUD and IUS both have several major advantages:
■ Its use does not interfere with intercourse
■ Long-acting, highly effective
■ Easily reversible – fertility returns as soon as the device is removed.

Apart from the initial check-up after insertion, only an annual follow-up check is required. For women who have heavy periods, the IUS can be advantageous, as it reduces menstrual bleeding over time and in some women stops their periods altogether. The IUD may also be suitable

Before starting to use intrauterine contraception, it is advisable to consult a GP. The doctor will be able to give advice on which methods may be most suitable.

for emergency contraception if fitted within five days of intercourse, or within five days of the earliest time that ovulation could have occurred.

DISADVANTAGES
Some period-type pain and a small amount of bleeding can occur on fitting an IUD or IUS. Side effects of using the IUS are often temporary but can include:
■ Irregular bleeding (for up to three months)
■ Acne
■ Headaches
■ Negative mood change
■ Breast tenderness.

The main side effect of using the IUD is heavier and longer periods, although this is less of a problem with the newer, smaller devices. Serious complications are very rare but can include:
■ Expulsion of the device
■ Infection due to the insertion and perforation of the uterus.

In the very rare event of a pregnancy occurring, the IUD or IUS is removed immediately if possible, to avoid later complications of a miscarriage.

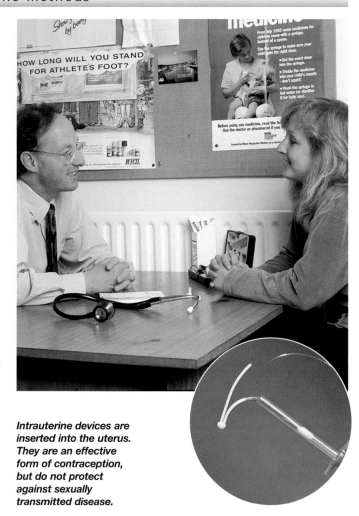

Intrauterine devices are inserted into the uterus. They are an effective form of contraception, but do not protect against sexually transmitted disease.

Using an IUD or IUS

Fitting of either device is done during or shortly after the menstrual period. The IUD is effective immediately, as is the IUS if fitted in the first seven days of the cycle. Both can be used immediately after a miscarriage or an abortion and 6–8 weeks after childbirth.

Removal of either device is usually done during a menstrual

Intrauterine devices are fitted by a doctor or nurse. Once inserted, and if no problems occur, the devices can prevent pregnancy for up to seven years.

period by the doctor or nurse pulling on the plastic threads which hang from the cervix.

CONTRA-INDICATIONS
Most women can use either of these methods with no problems. However, a history of an ectopic pregnancy, a sexually transmitted infection, unexplained vaginal bleeding, abnormalities of the cervix and uterus, a heart abnormality, active liver disease, a heart attack, stroke or an allergy to copper could exclude a woman from using these methods.

Barrier contraception

Barrier methods prevent pregnancy by stopping the sperm from reaching the egg. Each method differs slightly and couples may need to try a number of different methods before deciding which is most suitable for them.

MALE CONDOMS

Condoms are suitable for most people. It is important, however, that only condoms carrying the BSI Kitemark (BS EN 600) and the European CE mark are used. They should not have passed their 'use by' date and not been damaged by strong heat, sharp objects, light or damp.

Instructions on how to use condoms are supplied in the packet and need to be followed exactly, making sure a new condom is used each time and that there is no contact with the vagina or penis before the condom is used.

Male condoms are rolled carefully down over the erect penis. As soon as the man has ejaculated, and before the erection is lost, the penis needs to be withdrawn from the vagina and the condom held firmly in place to avoid spilling any semen.

FEMALE CONDOMS

Male condoms, however, may not be a suitable method for men who have difficulty in

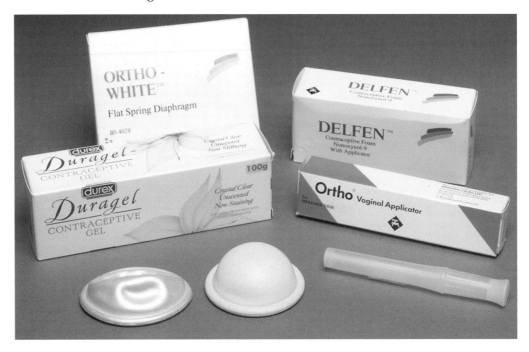

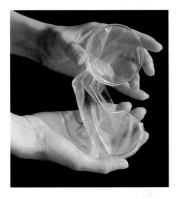

maintaining an erection during intercourse.

The female condom is inserted as far as possible inside the vagina using a small flexible ring which comes inside the condom, but which can be removed during sex. A fixed second ring at the open end of the condom stays outside the vagina when the condom is in place and is used to twist the condom as it is removed so that the semen stays inside.

The female condom has an open end and a closed end. As with the male condom, sperm cannot escape into the vagina, thus avoiding pregnancy.

Female condoms may not suit women who feel uncomfortable touching their genital area.

DIAPHRAGMS AND CAPS

There are three different types of vaginal diaphragm and three types of cervical cap. They are available in a variety of sizes and are currently all made of rubber, although new varieties of caps are made from silicone.

Cervical caps fit over the cervix, whereas diaphragms cover a larger area of the vagina as well as the cervix. A doctor or nurse will fit a woman with the correct size for her and teach her how to use the method. A check to see that

Diaphragms are inserted into the vagina, covering the opening to the uterus. Diaphragms are used in conjunction with spermicide cream or gels.

the size is still correct is only necessary every 6–12 months.

The diaphragm or cap is left in place for six hours after sex and is easily washed with warm water and a mild soap. Most women can use these methods, but it may be more difficult if the vaginal muscles cannot hold a diaphragm in place, the cervix is an awkward shape or is difficult to reach, or if a woman suffers from repeated urinary infections or is not comfortable touching her genital area.

Using barrier methods

Diaphragms are intended for use in conjunction with spermicide cream or foam. This provides further protection against fertilization.

What are the advantages of using barrier methods?
■ They need to be used only when having intercourse
■ There are no side effects
Condoms
■ Male condoms are easily available
■ They offer good protection against most sexually transmitted infections

■ A female condom can be put in any time before intercourse
Diaphragms and caps
■ Can be inserted any time before sex (but more spermicide must be used if more than 3 hours has elapsed)
■ May offer some protection against sexually transmitted infection and cervical cancer

What are the disadvantages of using barrier methods?
■ Very careful use is required with every episode of intercourse
■ Using them can interrupt intercourse

■ Rarely some people are allergic to latex or are sensitive to spermicide
Condoms
■ Female condoms are not widely available and are expensive
■ Male condoms can split or come off
Diaphragms and caps
■ It can take time to learn how to use them
■ Cystitis can be a problem
■ Some people find using spermicide messy
■ Need to be fitted by a doctor or nurse.

Hormonal contraception

Hormonal contraception is the most popular and effective method of pregnancy prevention for young women. One of the commonest forms is the combined oral contraceptive pill.

Hormonal contraception is used by over 50 per cent of women aged 18–24 in the UK. This mode of contraception falls into two main categories:
■ A combined method utilizing two hormones (the combined oral contraceptive pill)
■ Methods utilizing only one hormone (progestogen-only pill, injectables and implants).

Each has its own advantages and disadvantages, which women will weigh up when choosing their method.

COMBINED PILL

The combined pill, commonly referred to as 'the Pill', contains two synthetic hormones – oestrogen and progestogen – and works in three main ways.

The principal action is to affect the development of the ovum (egg) in the woman and to stop ovulation taking place. In addition, the sperm's ability to travel through the cervix, uterus and uterine (Fallopian) tubes is affected by making the cervical mucus less penetrable.

Finally, the combined pill alters the lining of the uterus to prevent it developing in a way that would allow a fertilized egg to implant. If used according to instructions, this method is over 99 per cent effective.

BENEFITS OF THE COMBINED PILL

Benefits include lighter and less painful periods and relief of premenstrual symptoms. The risk of cancer of the ovary and uterus is reduced and there is protection against some pelvic infections. The risk of ectopic pregnancy is also lowered and it may prevent the formation of ovarian cysts.

It is important that a woman's personal and family medical history are discussed prior to the Pill being prescribed to avoid any associated risks.

Hormonal contraception, such as taking the combined pill, is an extremely safe method of contraception. It can be used by most women.

Disadvantages and risks of the combined pill

Women may experience minor side effects when they start taking the Pill. These can often be the reason why women stop taking it; they include problems such as breakthrough bleeding (bleeding while taking the pill),

Some women will experience side effects, such as headaches, when taking the Pill. These side effects may be temporary and pass after a few months.

breast tenderness, nausea, weight gain and headaches. It is important to stress that many of these symptoms are often temporary, so trying the Pill for at least three months before changing is recommended.

POSSIBLE RISKS

There are some serious side effects, but these are very rare. A few women may develop a blood clot that can block a vein (venous thrombosis) or artery (causing a heart attack or stroke).

Combined pill users have an increased risk of breast cancer although this risk disappears

over a 10-year period of stopping the Pill. A link between using the combined pill and developing a rare liver cancer has also been shown.

A full medical history will be taken from the patient. Women over the age of 35 who smoke and women who have the following conditions (or who have previously had them) are advised not to use the Pill:
■ Thrombosis in a vein or artery, a heart abnormality or circulatory disease, including raised blood pressure
■ Very severe migraines
■ Breast cancer
■ Active disease of the liver or gall bladder
■ Diabetes with complications
■ Unexplained vaginal bleeding (such as bleeding between periods or after sex).

Women over the age of 35 who are smokers are advised not to use the combined pill. This is because smoking increases the risk of blood clot formation.

Different types of combined oral contraceptive pill

There are numerous types of combined oral contraceptive pill,
each with varying doses of hormones. Women may need to try several
different pills before they find one type that suits them.

There are over 20 different types of combined oral contraceptive pill. All but one of these contain the synthetic oestrogen ethinyloestradiol. These pills also contain one of five synthetic progestogens (norethisterone, levonorgestrel, desogestrel, gestodene and norgestimate) in varying doses. Every woman has her own hormonal balance, so if she experiences side effects a change to a different brand may solve the problem.

USING THE COMBINED PILL

The most commonly used type of combined pill is the monophasic 21-day pill. Each pill in the packet contains the same level of oestrogen and progestogen. The pills are taken at approximately the same time every day for 21 days and then stopped for seven days. During this break the woman usually experiences a withdrawal bleed – this is simply a response to stopping taking the hormones. Pill-taking is then resumed on the eighth day and the cycle is repeated.

Combined pills with varying hormone doses in each packet (phasic pills) are also commonly prescribed. Taking these in the right order (as indicated on the packet) is important.

Everyday (ED) combined pills are available for women who find it difficult to remember to restart pills after their pill-free break. These pill packets contain 21 active pills and seven inactive pills. As with the other pills, the woman experiences a withdrawal bleed. During the pill-free week, a woman's body begins to get ready to produce an egg. It is therefore extremely important that pills on either side of the pill-free break are not forgotten.

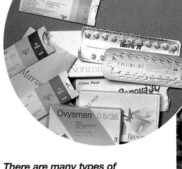

There are many types of combined contraceptive pills, each with a different combination of hormones. Most women will find a suitable pill.

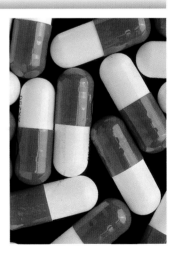

Reasons for the pill becoming less effective

It is important that a doctor asks about other drugs a woman may be using before prescribing the Pill. Certain drugs reduce the Pill's contraceptive effect.

There are certain circumstances when the contraceptive pill may become less effective:
- Pills taken more than 12 hours late
- Vomiting within three hours of taking the Pill
- Episodes of severe diarrhoea
- Taking the Pill at the same time as some other medication (including some antibiotics). The Pill should not be taken at the same time as St John's wort.

In each of these situations, extra precautions are needed for at least seven days and often for longer; in some cases, the Pill-free week will need to be omitted.

Some medications, such as antibiotics, may affect the natural bacterial flora of the bowel. This interferes with the effectiveness of the Pill.

Emergency contraception

Emergency contraception can be given up to five days after sex to prevent an unwanted pregnancy. Methods include the morning after pill, and the copper-bearing intra-uterine device.

Emergency contraception is a safe and effective way of preventing an unwanted pregnancy. It is defined as any contraceptive method that is used after sexual intercourse has taken placed.

MODERN METHODS
Post-coital contraception has been used for thousands of years, although methods employed in the past – such as the use of dung, wine and garlic pessaries in ancient Egypt – were messy and often failed.

Emergency contraception involves using oestrogen and progesterone as found in the contraceptive pill or the copper-bearing intra-uterine device.

Emergency contraception may be required in the following circumstances:

■ When sexual intercourse has occurred without contraception – for example, under the influence of alcohol or drugs
■ In cases of rape or mental handicap
■ Contraceptive failure: split or 'lost' condoms, accidents with caps, expulsion of an intra-uterine device (IUD) and missed contraceptive pills.

A woman may require emergency contraception if she has had unprotected sex or the contraception method failed. A GP will advise on the options.

The copper-bearing intra-uterine device is one form of emergency contraception. It can be used up to five days after unprotected sex and is very effective.

Types of emergency contraception

Hormonal methods of post-coital contraception either prevent or delay ovulation.

Later in the cycle they may also prevent implantation by disrupting the development of the lining of the uterus. In some cases, ovulation may simply be delayed, meaning that barrier methods of contraception should be used for the rest of the cycle as a precaution.

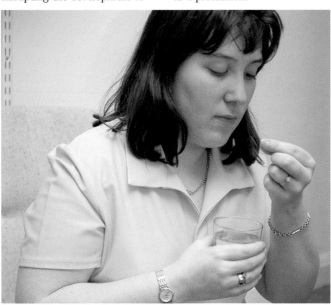

HORMONAL METHODS
Hormonal methods include:

■ Yuzpe or combined method – consists of two doses of two tablets, each containing levonorgestrel (a progesterone) and ethinyloestradiol (an oestrogen). The tablets are taken 12 hours apart, up to 72 hours after a single episode of unprotected sex. If the patient has a history of thrombosis or a focal migraine, then this method cannot be used. Side effects include nausea, and sometimes vomiting, but this is less likely if the pill is taken with food
■ Ho/Kwan or progesterone only method – involves taking two doses of levonorgestrel (progesterone) only, taken 12 hours apart. Until recently in the UK, this involved taking up to

Hormonal methods of post-coital contraception prevent or delay ovulation and implantation. They are taken in pill form and are very effective.

25 tablets of progesterone-only contraceptive pills. However, it is now marketed as a pack of two tablets under the name of Levonelle-2. These may cause nausea in some women. Clinical studies have demonstrated that this form of pill is more effective than the combined method as a form of emergency contraception.

THE COPPER-IUD
The copper intra-uterine device (IUD) contains copper ions, which are toxic to the egg and sperm and therefore reduce fertilization capacity. The copper also blocks implantation.

This method can be used up to five days from the earliest episode of unprotected sex. It can also be used if there has been unprotected sex on multiple occasions. It has a very low failure rate – less than 1 per cent per cycle. However, it does require a procedure to insert the coil, and it is not suitable for all women.

Using emergency contraception

Emergency contraception can be obtained from a GP or family planning clinic. In some countries, the emergency pill can be bought over the counter.

Before dispensing or prescribing emergency contraception, certain facts need to be ascertained.

CALCULATING THE TIME OF OVULATION
The GP or pharmacist will need to know the time of the last menstrual period and whether or not the woman's periods are regular or not.

From this information, the GP will be able to ascertain the most likely day of ovulation (usually about day 14 in a 28-day cycle). This will give an indication of the fertility of the woman at that particular time, so that the most appropriate action can be taken.

NORMAL CYCLE
After taking the morning after pill, most women will have their next period at about the right time. Some have a small bleed a couple of days after taking the emergency contraceptive pill, but this is not a period. If the next period is late or abnormal in any way, a pregnancy test should be carried out.

FAILURE
Unfortunately emergency contraception is not 100 per cent effective (and is less effective than regular contraception) and may fail. This is more likely if it is more than 72 hours after the unprotected sex, or if the second pill was not taken 12 hours after the first.

SIDE EFFECTS
Hormonal methods may cause vomiting, which can stop the pill being absorbed, but this is very rare since anti-emetic drugs are usually given to prevent vomiting.

As emergency contraception can disrupt the normal menstrual cycle, ovulation may be delayed. For this reason, contraception should be used after taking the emergency pill as a precaution.

If a woman requires emergency contraception, she will need to know when her last period was. This allows her degree of fertility to be calculated by the doctor.

Availability

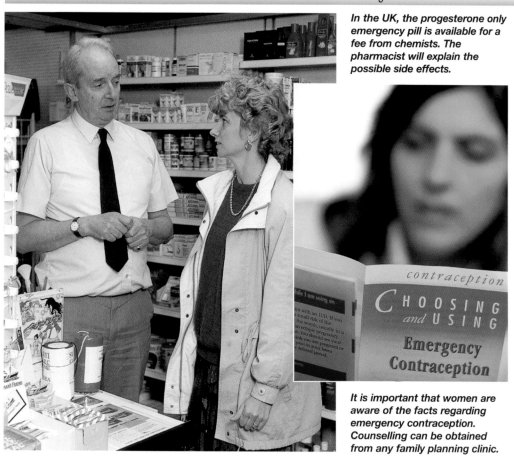

In the UK, the progesterone only emergency pill is available for a fee from chemists. The pharmacist will explain the possible side effects.

It is important that women are aware of the facts regarding emergency contraception. Counselling can be obtained from any family planning clinic.

For emergency contraception to be effective and prevent unwanted pregnancies, it is important that all women are aware of the options and how they can obtain them

Many women assume that it is too late for contraception after sex, even though emergency contraception can be effective for up to 72 hours following unprotected sexual intercourse.

PHARMACIES
In some countries, the progesterone-only emergency contraceptive pill is sold from pharmacies. In the UK, Levonelle-2 has been available from pharmacies, without a prescription, since 1 January 2001. The main advantage of such availability is that access to emergency contraception is improved, although the high cost of the drugs may deter some people. In addition, the local chemist is not always an ideal place to discuss the consequences of contraceptive failure or future needs. However, emergency contraception, counselling and advice are available from most family planning clinics.

Termination of pregnancy

The decision to abort a pregnancy is not always an easy one,
and every woman must be informed of all the options available.
Counselling, both before and after the procedure, is also provided.

Termination (abortion) is the medical term for the expulsion of the fetus from the uterus before it is able to survive independently. The term abortion is generally understood to mean ending a pregnancy by medical intervention, often at the woman's request but also because of medical complications.

Medically, the term 'abortion' is used to cover six categories of pregnancy loss:

■ Therapeutic abortion – a termination by medical intervention
■ Spontaneous abortion – a miscarriage
■ Missed abortion – a pregnancy that has ended but with the fetus and placenta remaining in the uterus
■ Incomplete abortion – the products of conception have not all been expelled from the uterus
■ Inevitable abortion – when the woman has vaginal bleeding and the fetus has died but has not yet been expelled
■ Stillbirth – the fetus is born dead after 24 weeks' gestation.

MEDICO-LEGAL ASPECTS

Legal termination of pregnancy, as defined by the 1967 Abortion Act, may be carried out, provided that two registered medical practitioners agree that:

■ The continuation of the pregnancy up to 24 weeks involves risk, greater than if the pregnancy were terminated, of injury to the physical or mental health of the pregnant woman or any of her existing children.
■ Termination (at any stage of pregnancy) to prevent serious, permanent injury to the physical or mental health of the pregnant woman, or there is risk to the life of the pregnant woman, greater than if the pregnancy were terminated.

Termination will also be considered if there is substantial risk that the baby, if born, would suffer from such physical or mental abnormalities as to be seriously handicapped (1967 Abortion Act, amended by the Human Fertilization and Embryology Act, 1990).

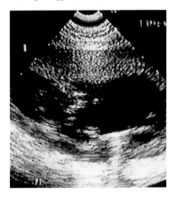

An ultrasound scan may be used prior to abortion procedures. This determines the stage of the pregnancy, which in turn determines the method for pregnancy termination.

For those who have lost a wanted pregnancy, the use of the terms 'spontaneous', 'missed' and 'inevitable' abortion can cause distress, and the term miscarriage is preferred.

Age of women having abortions

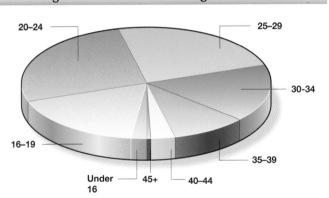

20–24
25–29
30–34
35–39
40–44
45+
Under 16
16–19

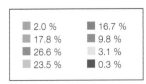

■ 2.0 %	■ 16.7 %
■ 17.8 %	■ 9.8 %
■ 26.6 %	■ 3.1 %
■ 23.5 %	■ 0.3 %

All abortions performed under the 1967 Abortion Act are notified to the Department of Health. This chart shows the age of women having abortions in England, Wales and Scotland in 1997.

Timing of abortions

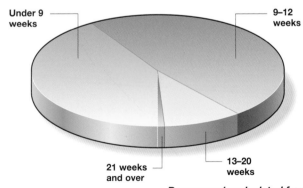

Under 9 weeks
9–12 weeks
13–20 weeks
21 weeks and over

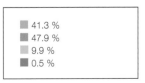

■ 41.3 %	
■ 47.9 %	
■ 9.9 %	
■ 0.5 %	

Pregnancy is calculated from the first day of the woman's last menstrual period. Each year, fewer than 100 abortions are carried out at 25 weeks and beyond, almost all because of fetal abnormality.

Role of counselling

The aim of counselling is to ensure that a woman considering an abortion makes the best decision for her circumstances by considering all the options.

As well as providing a women with the necessary facts about aborting a pregnancy, counselling can also take the form of assessment, to ensure that the woman has grounds for an abortion.

For women who are sure about their decision, the counsellor will supply information to ensure that the woman understands what to expect before, during and after the abortion. Future contraceptive use may also be discussed.

Around 20 per cent of women need or want counselling to help them make a decision. Women who are more likely to need counselling include those who:
■ Are very young and not yet living independently
■ Have mental health problems
■ Would want the pregnancy in other circumstances

Abortion can happen spontaneously. This human embryo is undergoing necrosis (tissue death), which can be due to genetic disorder or developmental problems.

■ Are ambivalent about the pregnancy, such as when abortion is against their religious or moral beliefs
■ Are considering abortion because of fetal abnormality.
Counselling may be provided by formally trained counsellors, nurses, doctors, social workers or trained lay counsellors. The following points are the main areas covered, although the structure of the counselling sessions will depend on the individual woman's situation:
■ Why is this pregnancy unwanted?
■ Was the pregnancy a result of a contraceptive failure, risk-taking or subconsciously wanting a pregnancy?
■ What family and emotional support does she have?
■ How did she feel immediately after finding out that she was pregnant?
■ How do those close to her feel about the pregnancy including the potential father (if informed)?
■ What are her views on abortion in general and for herself in particular?

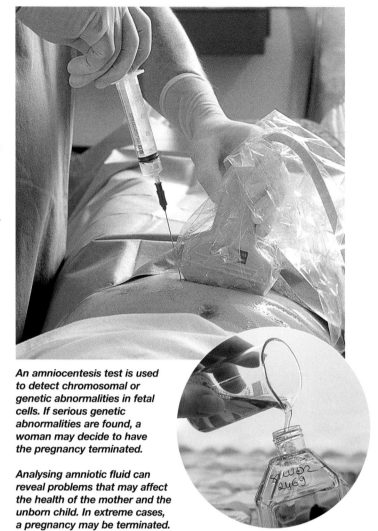

An amniocentesis test is used to detect chromosomal or genetic abnormalities in fetal cells. If serious genetic abnormalities are found, a woman may decide to have the pregnancy terminated.

Analysing amniotic fluid can reveal problems that may affect the health of the mother and the unborn child. In extreme cases, a pregnancy may be terminated.

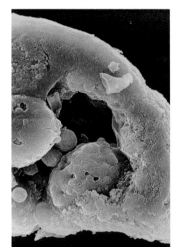

Psychological problems associated with abortion

A women may feel guilty about an abortion, both before and after the procedure. Counselling is always made available.

The most stressful and emotionally difficult time for the majority of women facing an abortion is when they are making the decision whether or not to undergo the procedure. It is therefore very important that women are made aware that they can see a counsellor after the abortion if they want or need to, as some can experience feelings of guilt and remorse.

The majority of women do not need post-abortion counselling, because once the abortion has been done, the 'problem' they were dealing with is resolved. For this reason, the most common emotional response after a termination is one of relief.

However, around 10–20 per cent of women experience short-lived negative feelings, such as guilt or sadness, after an abortion. A small minority of women will experience more severe psychological problems, and may seek professional counselling. In extreme cases, the woman may need further assistance in coming to terms with her strong emotions.

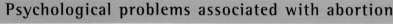

Types of abortion

MEDICAL ABORTION
In 1991, the use of the drug mifepristone was approved for use to terminate pregnancies under nine weeks (63 days) gestation. Mifepristone works by blocking the action of progesterone, a naturally occurring steroid hormone that is necessary to maintain a pregnancy. A drug called a prostaglandin (a hormone-like substance that cause smooth muscles to contract) is given 48 hours later and this causes the fetus and placenta to be expelled from the uterus.

Late medical abortion involves admission to hospital. Labour is induced using prostaglandins which are inserted into the uterus, via the cervix or into the amniotic fluid. Since 1995, mifepristone has been used for abortions between 13 and 20 weeks gestation and speeds up the procedure, which usually takes 8–12 hours.

SURGICAL ABORTION
Up to 13 weeks gestation, the cervix can be dilated with the use of drugs and the contents of the uterus removed by vacuum aspiration (suction). This operation can be done using a local anaesthetic, but a general anaesthetic is more common. The operation takes just 10 minutes and is usually performed as a day case.

Beyond 13 weeks, dilation and evacuation is an option. The cervix is dilated and the fetus can be removed using forceps. This is a procedure that is usually performed under general anaesthetic.

Pelvic pain in women

Pelvic pain describes pain or discomfort that arises from within the pelvis, which protects the genital tract, bladder and rectum. There are a number of possible causes, and treatment varies accordingly.

Non-serious causes of pelvic pain are usually short-lived. However, the pain can be very severe, such as occurs in dysmenorrhoea, a condition caused by spasms of the uterus during menstruation.

Some of the more common and serious causes of chronic or severe pelvic pain are pelvic inflammatory disease, ectopic pregnancy and endometriosis.

OTHER CAUSES OF PAIN
Pain in the anus and rectum can also cause pain in the pelvic area, normally around the lower back. Pelvic pain can be caused less commonly by a variety of other conditions, such as fibroids, appendicitis, bowel problems, bladder problems and cancer of the pelvic organs. If any pain is prolonged without remission, specialist help should be sought.

In investigating pelvic pain, it is essential that the doctor takes a detailed history from the patient and conducts a full examination.

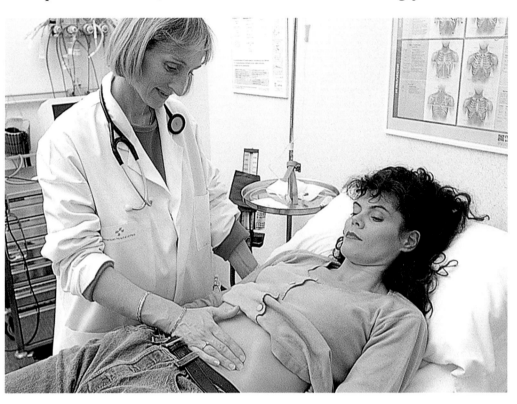

Pelvic inflammatory disease

Pelvic inflammatory disease (PID) describes inflammation of the uterus, uterine (Fallopian) tubes and ovaries, owing to infection. The most common cause is the sexually transmitted disease chlamydia, which is involved in 50–80 per cent of cases of PID. Other causes include gonorrhoea and anaerobic bacteria.

Although PID can arise spontaneously, it may also occur following surgical procedures in the pelvis or after insertion of an intrauterine contraceptive device (IUCD). This latter situation is most likely if a woman is already unknowingly infected with chlamydia.

SYMPTOMS
Pain usually comes on over several hours and is felt as a dull ache across the lower abdomen and above and around the pubic area; it can sometimes be quite severe and may also worsen during sexual intercourse.

Chlamydia trachomatis *bacteria are visible as the green/brown spheres in this micrograph of infected uterine tube cells.*

Spasms of pain do not occur unless there is sudden movement. The pain may improve if the woman lies or sits quietly. Other associated symptoms can include pain on urination and fevers. The pain can be so severe that the woman is unable to move and she may also feel sick or vomit, but this is unusual; mild cases can also occur.

DIAGNOSIS
There is no individual test that confirms whether a woman has PID, so diagnosis is based on the doctor's examination findings. Of particular importance is tenderness in the cervix and fornices (the 'gutter' around the neck of the cervix) on vaginal

An intrauterine contraceptive device (IUCD) is seen (circled) within the uterus on this composite picture. PID can occur after the fitting of an IUCD.

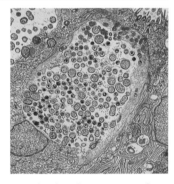

examination. Laparoscopy of the internal organs may sometimes be performed.

TREATMENT
Serious cases have to be treated as hospital in-patients with intravenous antibiotics. The majority are treated out of hospital with oral antibiotics. Most women with suspected PID should be tested for chlamydia and ideally be seen in a genito-urinary medicine clinic. Clinics may also offer a chlamydia test or antibiotics prior to termination of pregnancy or IUCD insertion.

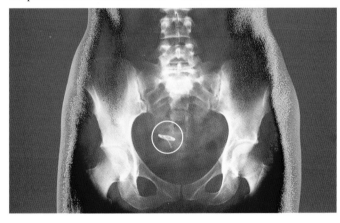

Ectopic pregnancy

An ectopic pregnancy is when the fetus develops outside the uterus, most often within the uterine (Fallopian) tube. This may be due to scarring of the uterine tubes, often as a result of previous chlamydia infection. Around two to four weeks after conception, the pregnancy bursts through the tube, causing pain and bleeding.

SYMPTOMS
The pain is usually on one side of the lower abdomen and often starts suddenly. Many women have difficulty walking because the pain is so severe. However, the symptoms may occasionally be quite mild, deceiving both doctor and patient, who may fail to recognize the nature of the problem.

If there has been significant internal bleeding, the patient will look pale and feel faint and may collapse if she tries to stand. The woman's period is usually late or abnormal and she will often be experiencing symptoms of early pregnancy. Sometimes, however, the ectopic pregnancy may cause problems before the period is due.

DIAGNOSIS
When the doctor performs a vaginal examination, there will be tenderness in the fornix (area of vagina next to the cervix) on the same side as the pain.

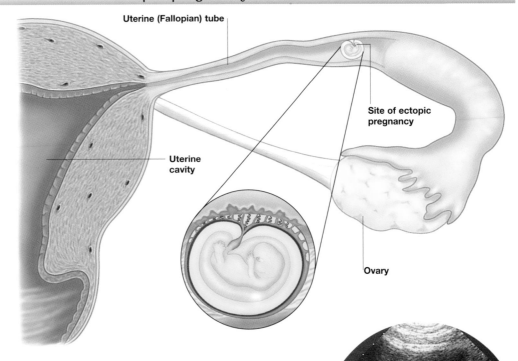

A swollen uterine tube is also often felt, which is confirmed on an ultrasound scan. A pregnancy test is usually positive.

TREATMENT
Ectopic pregnancy should be treated as an emergency, as it can be fatal. Most cases will require either open surgery or laparoscopy. Rarely, it can be treated by injections of the drug methotrexate.

The commonest site for an ectopic pregnancy is in the ovary or uterine tube. This causes abdominal pain and often internal bleeding if the tube ruptures.

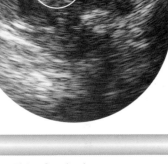

An ectopic pregnancy will usually be apparent on an ultrasound scan. In this case, an eight-week-old embryo is present in the right uterine (Fallopian) tube (circled).

Endometriosis

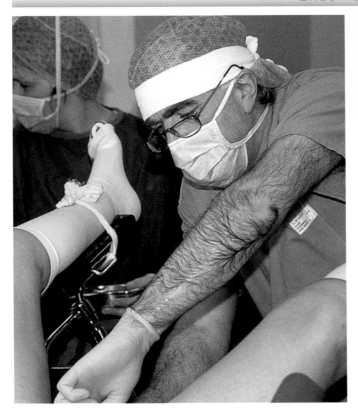

Endometriosis is a condition in which the endometrium, the tissue that lines the uterus, has spread to other parts of the body – most usually within the pelvis. The condition probably arises when some of the menstrual products spread back through the uterine (Fallopian) tubes rather than passing through the cervix and vagina as normal.

Endometriosis may also be caused by spread by the blood or even by tissue growing spontaneously on the outside of the uterus. It is estimated to affect 5–10 per cent of women, usually starting around the ages of 25–35.

SYMPTOMS
The endometrial tissue swells under the influence of female hormones in the same way as the lining of the uterus.

Investigations to determine the extent of endometriosis will be necessary before treatment can begin. Often, drug therapy is combined with laparoscopy.

This often leads to symptoms such as pelvic pain, which is usually worse on one side, mainly around the time of the period. Sex can be very painful due to discomfort felt deep inside. This disease can also lead to infertility.

DIAGNOSIS
It can be difficult to distinguish the symptoms of endometriosus from those of PID, although the pain of PID does not usually wax and wane and is not especially related to the period. A diagnosis is made by performing a laparoscopic examination of the pelvis.

TREATMENT AND PREVENTION
Treatment depends on the symptoms and severity of the condition, but may include hormonal treatment or surgery. Treatment often lasts for many months or even years. There is no way to prevent the condition, although it is less common in women who undergo pregnancy.

Vaginal pain and discomfort

Pain in the vagina is often a discomfort that can be described by the sufferer as burning or itchy. There are three main causes: infection, lack of hormones and spasm of the muscles around the vagina.

Infection is by far the most common cause of vaginal discomfort, and it is usually due to thrush (infection with the fungal organism *Candida*), but it can also be caused by the sexually transmitted infection trichomoniasis. Uncommonly, the cause is bacterial vaginosis or other infections.

Women with thrush usually describe it as an itchy condition and there may be an associated soreness of the vulva. There is frequently a vaginal discharge which is usually thick and white,

Vaginal infections caused by Candida albicans (shown here) can usually be successfully treated with antifungal drugs.

but in some cases may be more watery and green or yellow. These symptoms can sometimes be worse just before or after a menstrual period or after sexual intercourse.

Trichomoniasis often causes a more intense, burning discomfort. Most women will have a heavy, watery vaginal discharge which can be yellow, green or white. The discharge normally has a smell, which is similar to the fishy odour of bacterial vaginosis and may be frothy.

DIAGNOSING INFECTION
Diagnosis is easily established by examining a sample of the discharge under a microscope. The bacteria can also be grown in the laboratory from vaginal swabs. A genito-urinary medicine clinic can quickly perform tests; attendance is especially appropriate if there has been a recent change of sexual partner or the problem is not resolved after treatment by a GP.

When an infection is suspected, a doctor will take a sample from inside the vagina using a swab. The swab is then sent to a laboratory for testing.

Treating vaginal infections

At a laboratory, material from a swab is cultured so that the causative organism of the vaginal infection can be identified and then treated.

Thrush normally resolves after insertion of a vaginal pessary containing an antifungal antibiotic, but treatment also comes in the form of vaginal creams or tablets to swallow. Some women suffer from frequent attacks of thrush, which might be due to diabetes or other underlying illness. Antibiotics may also precipitate thrush.

For women with frequent thrush, there is often no known cause and they may need regular preventative treatment. Very tight clothing, especially

when made from artificial materials, may make the condition worse, as may over-use of soap on the genital area.

Trichomoniasis is treated with an antibiotic called metronidazole. As it is sexually transmitted, the male partner or partners will also need treating. It is important for a woman and her partner to abstain from sex until they have both completed treatment and the infection has been shown to have gone on repeat testing. It is also important that they have tests for other sexually transmitted infections.

Apart from these measures, there is little that can be done to prevent thrush, but trichomoniasis can be prevented by the use of condoms.

Vaginitis

Secretions in the vagina tend to be fairly acidic, due to the presence of lactic acid produced by bacteria which reside in the outer layer of the vagina. These bacteria are most prevalent between puberty and the menopause, and their acid secretions protect against infections. Girls who have yet to reach puberty and post-menopausal women are therefore particularly susceptible to infections. Typical causative organisms include *Candida, Shigella, Streptococcus* and *Staphylococcus.*

YOUNGER PATIENTS

Childhood vaginitis is the most common gynaecological problem in prepubescent girls. Besides the lack of oestrogen and a lack of acidic bacteria, there are a number of reasons for this, including poor hygiene. A foreign body may be a precipitating factor for the condition, for example.

Treatment will depend on the specific cause. If poor hygiene is a problem, advice should be given regarding cleaning and bathing habits. A number of creams are available to provide symptomatic relief. Bacterial infections may require the use of antibiotics to treat them.

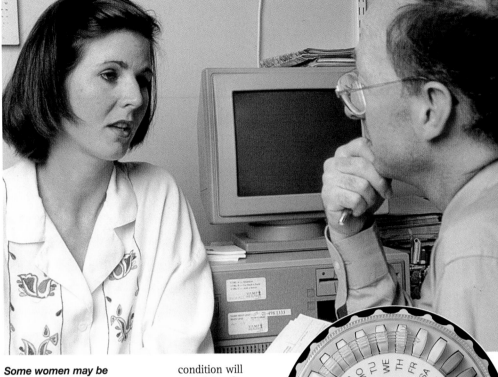

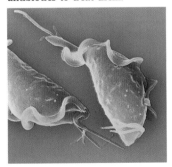

Some women may be embarrassed about approaching their doctor with problems such as vaginitis. However, most treatments are straightforward and successful.

OLDER PATIENTS

Atrophic vaginitis is a condition that normally occurs after the menopause. Lack of female hormones leads to mucosal thinning and infection of the vagina, exacerbated by the lack of acid-producing bacteria. A woman suffering from this

Vaginitis is a non-specific infection of the vagina with, for example, Trichomonas vaginalis. It is exacerbated by a lack of acid-producing bacteria.

condition will complain of soreness, vaginal discharge and uncomfortable sexual intercourse.

A diagnosis is usually confirmed by the typical appearance of the vagina on examination by a doctor – if necessary, a specimen may be taken for laboratory investigation. The condition usually responds to hormonal treatment such as hormone replacement therapy (HRT), which can be combined with oestrogen creams in the vagina and antibiotic creams.

Atrophic vaginitis usually occurs after a woman has passed the menopause. Hormone replacement therapy (HRT) can help to treat the condition.

Vaginismus

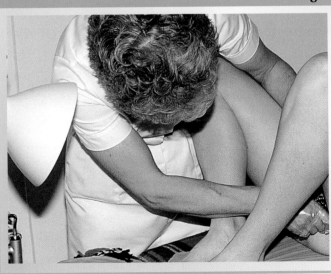

Spasm of the muscle around the lower vagina can cause pain, which is normally only experienced during sexual intercourse. The spasm may be triggered by fear of pain if the woman has recently suffered from a painful vaginal condition. Some cases may be due to psychological upset, leading to a fear of sexual intercourse.

The condition is diagnosed on the description of the pain and its

Vaginismus is often thought to be a psychological problem in which the vagina undergoes involuntary spasms. Such spasms may also occur during a physical examination.

incidence, especially if it occurs on attempted sexual penetration. The spasm may also occur when a doctor tries to examine the woman's vagina. Treatment of painful infections of the vagina or vulva may lead to resolution of the problem.

Women who do not have a continuing physical cause can be treated by a psychosexual specialist, who may use relaxation techniques. A woman suffering from vaginismus with a suspected psychosexual cause is often asked to use vaginal dilators – implements of increasing size that can be introduced into the vagina – to overcome the fear of penetration.

Dyspareunia: painful intercourse

For many women, sexual intercourse results in pain, either within the vagina or deep within the pelvic area. Whether physical or psychological in origin, the condition requires careful treatment.

Dyspareunia is the medical term used to describe the type of pain experienced by a woman during penetration. The pain can range from discomfort during certain sexual positions to severe pain that prevents any form of penetration.

Dyspareunia is classified into two types, according to where the pain is felt:
■ Superficial – pain is felt on the labia (lips), near the entrance to the vagina (introitus) or on the walls of the vagina
■ Deep – pain is felt within the pelvis, either within the innermost section of the vagina or around the cervix.

SUPERFICIAL DYSPAREUNIA
Dyspareunia may be caused by:
■ Arousal disorder – pain is due to hormone deficiency or failure of genital response (which may also include psychological factors)
■ Iatrogenic (medically induced) factors – pain is due to the

Women suffering from dyspareunia may begin to fear sexual intercourse and try to avoid close sexual relations. This leads to conflict in relationships.

aftermath of medical intervention, such as an episiotomy following childbirth, or vaginal surgery
■ Pathological factors – this is the most common cause of superficial dyspareunia, pain being caused by infection or dermatological problems
■ Psychological – this is a common cause of dyspareunia, and sometimes arises as a complication of a physiological disorder.

ANATOMICAL CAUSES
Rarely, dyspareunia may be due to anatomical causes, such as:
■ Congenital absence of the vagina – where the vagina has failed to develop
■ Hymenal remnants – when the hymen (the tissue covering the

vagina at birth) is broken by intercourse or physical activity, small remnants may remain. These then become caught between the vagina and penis

during coitus, which causes pain
■ Vaginal stenosis – narrowing or under-development of the vagina.

Deep dyspareunia

Deep dyspareunia involves pain experienced deep inside the vagina and pelvis during penetrative sexual intercourse. The causes may be either physical or psychological.

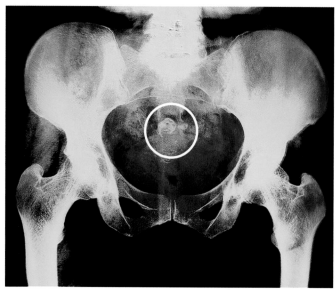

PHYSICAL CAUSES
The presence of any of the following conditions may result in deep dyspareunia:
■ Uterine fibroids – these are muscle bundles that sometimes

form within the wall of the uterus
■ Chlamydial cervicitis – this is a common sexually transmitted disease caused by bacterial infection, which often remains undiagnosed for some time
■ Endometriosis – this is caused by pieces of the lining of the uterus breaking away and becoming attached to organs in the pelvic cavity. The condition affects as many as one in five women of childbearing age
■ Pelvic inflammatory disease (PID) – this is an inflammation of the reproductive organs, which may develop as a result of sexually transmitted infections or infection following childbirth. It may cause severe pain, and requires antibiotic or (rarely) surgical treatment

Fibroids (an example shown) grow within the uterine wall. Pain in the pelvis during sexual intercourse may be the only presenting symptom.

■ Uterine retroversion – this refers to an unusual positioning of the uterus, in which it is tilted backwards instead of forwards within the pelvis, causing pain during intercourse
■ Infections of the bladder or bowel, causing pain by pressure.

UNKNOWN CAUSE
In almost two thirds of women with deep dyspareunia, there is no identifiable physical cause. There are thought to be three possible reasons for this:
■ Pain is due to an early disease process that cannot yet be detected
■ Pain is due to vascular changes or pelvic congestion syndrome (varicose veins within the pelvis, affecting the uterus, ovaries or vulva)
■ Pain is due to psychological causes.

All cases of deep dyspareunia need thorough examination to rule out the possibility of cancer within the reproductive organs.

Pathological causes

Infections of the genital and urinary tracts commonly cause pain during sexual intercourse. These include sexually transmitted diseases such as gonorrhoea, viral, bacterial and fungal diseases and infestations such as scabies.

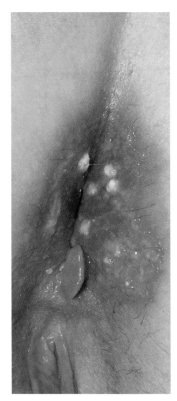

Pathological conditions are common causes of dyspareunia. Genital herpes is a recurrent virus causing painful blisters and ulcers around the vaginal area.

Superficial dyspareunia is perhaps most commonly caused by infection or dermatological (skin) abnormalities.

INFECTION
Any infection that affects the vulva or introitus can cause superficial dyspareunia. For example, trichomonas, a relatively common bacterial infection, often causes vulvovaginitis (inflammation in and around the vagina), resulting in pain on penetration.

The fluid-filled blisters that surround the vagina in genital herpes cause a burning sensation and intense pain with physical pressure or penetration.

Infections higher up the genital tract, such as chlamydial cervicitis, may also cause a discharge which can be an irritant to the vulval mucosa. One infection can also lead to another: chlamydial cervicitis, for example, may lead to pelvic inflammatory disease, adding to the pain of dyspareunia.

DERMATOLOGICAL CAUSES
Dermatitis, such as eczema or psoriasis, may affect the vulva and cause superficial dyspareunia. However, the most common dermatological problem is a sensitivity to certain ingredients within shampoos, shower gels and soap.

This problem is easy enough to solve, by avoiding use of any product within the bathwater and washing with aqueous cream.

Infections causing superficial dyspareunia

Bacterial	
Gonorrhoea	Discharge/no symptoms
Bacterial vaginosis	Offensive discharge
	Itching/soreness
Syphilis	Genital ulcers
Chlamydia	Discharge/no symptoms
Viral	
Herpes	Blisters and ulcers
Warts	Lumps, itching, no symptoms
Protozoa	
Trichomonas	Offensive discharge
	Soreness/itching
Fungal	
Candida (thrush)	Discharge
	Itching/soreness
Tinea	Red rash with scales
Infestations	
Lice/nits/scabies	Itching
	Soreness

Unfortunately, discomfort caused by dermatological conditions often presents as itching. This has led to many women seeking relief from such discomfort to be treated incorrectly for thrush (candida) infection. Any woman suffering recurrent problems of this nature in which fungal medication is not effective should seek advice from a local genitourinary medicine clinic.

Most dermatological problems are easily diagnosed and respond well to treatment.

Iatrogenic causes

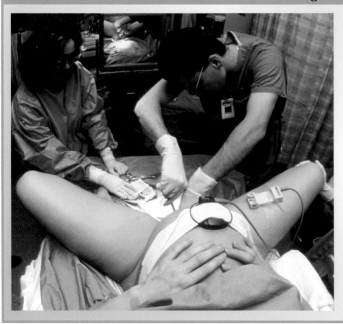

'Iatrogenic' refers to damage caused by medical intervention. An episiotomy scar (when the entrance to the vagina is cut to allow the birth of a baby and then subsequently sutured), is one of the most common iatrogenic causes of superficial dyspareunia.

It is estimated that 30–40 per cent of women who have episiotomies suffer some degree of dyspareunia afterwards. However, persistent pain in the area of the scar is rare, and almost all women will have no pain three to four months after delivery.

The pain results from the scar tissue that forms during the

An episiotomy scar may heal badly, forming a hard swelling (granuloma). Its proximity to the vagina makes it likely to cause pain during penetration.

healing process, which is inevitably less elastic than the surrounding skin. When required to stretch during penetration, this can cause considerable pain. Where necessary, this problem can be successfully treated by further surgery.

Vaginal surgery
In women who have previously had vaginal surgery (to treat prolapse of the vagina, for example) or a hysterectomy, penetration of the vagina may subsequently be painful.

Any deep pain experienced may be due to infection or vault haematoma (blood clots around the upper walls of the vagina). It may also occur due to an ovary adhering to the vault. Persistent deep dyspareunia may require surgical exploration.

Vaginal discharge

Most women will experience an increased or abnormal vaginal discharge at some time in their life. Although this can be distressing for the patient, the cause is usually simple to treat and not serious.

Women with abnormal discharge from the vagina should seek medical advice as soon as possible in order to rule out malignancy and to secure the correct treatment. In most cases, this is straightforward.

BACTERIAL VAGINOSIS
Probably the most common cause of abnormal vaginal discharge is bacterial vaginosis (BV). This arises when the normal vaginal bacteria (lactobacilli) are replaced by a mixture of other bacteria.

What triggers BV is not fully understood; however, it does not occur in women who have never had sexual intercourse, and seems to be more common in women who excessively wash inside the vagina (douching).

Women who feel that they may be at risk from a sexually transmitted disease (STD) should visit their GP as early as possible for treatment.

Symptoms of bacterial vaginosis

One of the typical symptoms of BV is an increased vaginal discharge, which can be clear or yellow. This is often described as smelling like fish, and may also contain small bubbles. The latter symptoms are due to a gas produced by the causative bacteria. Soreness does not usually occur in BV and would indicate a separate condition.

There is no real evidence for sexual transmission of BV, so treating male partners makes no difference to the frequency of relapses or severity of symptoms.

Bacterial vaginosis is an annoying condition, and can be distressing for women who suffer frequent attacks, but it rarely causes harm. Many women can be infected with BV without having any symptoms, in which case they often subsequently lose the infection without the need for treatment.

POTENTIAL PROBLEMS
BV can cause more serious problems in two circumstances:
■ There is a definite link in pregnancy between BV infection and some cases of premature labour or late miscarriage
■ There is also a possible link between BV and pelvic inflammatory disease arising after insertion of an intrauterine contraceptive device.

BV is diagnosed if a woman's discharge is less acidic than normal (has a high pH), and if it has a fishy smell that is accentuated by mixing with potassium hydroxide (the 'whiff

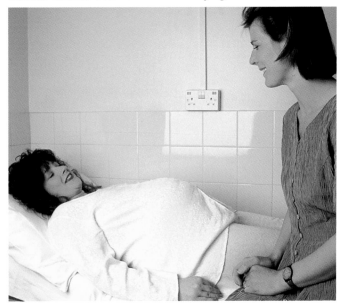

Some pregnant women are now screened for BV, and may benefit from antibiotic treatment if they have had similar problems in previous pregnancies.

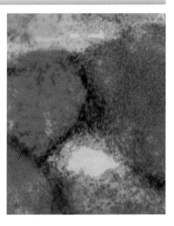

The characteristic appearance under the microscope of abnormal bacteria that coat the vaginal cells ('clue cells') leads to the accurate diagnosis of BV.

test'). The condition will disappear after treatment with an antibiotic called metronidazole, or a vaginal cream containing clindamycin. Ideally, douching should be discontinued by the patient, but there is no other effective treatment or way of preventing the relapses that some may suffer.

Thrush (candidiasis)

Several different types of yeast may cause thrush, all of which are commonly found in the environment. As with BV, there is no evidence of sexual transmission for this infection, and treatment of male partners does not help unless they also suffer with symptoms of thrush.

It is thought that the thrush bacteria are normally carried on the body and in the intestine, which acts as the 'reservoir' of infection from which spread to the vagina occurs.

SYMPTOMS
The discharge due to thrush is usually thick and white, cream or yellow, often being described as similar in texture to cottage cheese. Most women experience vaginal itch and there is often also discomfort and redness around the vulva.

Most cases of thrush arise spontaneously for no apparent reason, though they may be brought on by taking antibiotics.

Some diseases such as diabetes and HIV also trigger attacks. The problem is easily diagnosed by finding the thrush germ on testing a swab taken from the vagina. However, some doctors may make the diagnosis on the basis of typical symptoms plus an improvement of symptoms after using antifungal vaginal pessaries.

TREATMENT
Many women self-diagnose thrush and buy the appropriate treatment from a chemist. However, BV is more common than thrush, so a diagnosis made without tests is often wrong.

Antifungal tablets taken by mouth as one or two doses are an effective treatment for thrush. Other treatments include:
■ Live yoghurt – some women report an improvement and relief from itching if they instill live yoghurt into the vagina
■ Not washing the genital area with soap and avoiding bubble baths and genital toiletries
■ Wearing loose-fitting clothing made of natural materials (such as cotton); this may help reduce the severity of symptoms or the frequency of relapse.

A small proportion of women get frequent attacks, often at the same time as their period. These women may benefit from taking regular thrush treatment just prior to the time of an expected attack, every month for three to six months.

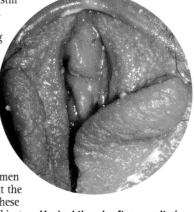

Vaginal thrush often results in discomfort and itching. The area around the vulva can become very red and sore, and a creamy discharge is also common.

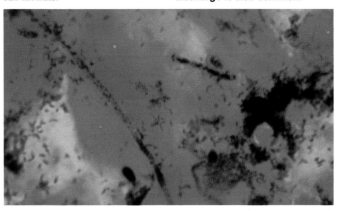

Antifungal vaginal pessaries are often used to treat thrush. The pessaries are inserted high into the vagina to combat the uncomfortable fungal infection.

Candidiasis is a common yeast infection of moist areas of the body. This shows a close-up of a vaginal candida infection, usually known as thrush.

Non-infective causes of discharge

Some women can have heavy 'normal' vaginal discharge that is clear in colour and does not smell or cause itching. This may persist for months or years and does not improve with antibiotics or thrush treatment. Why this happens is unknown, although it may start with the use of hormonal contraceptives such as the Pill. There is no effective treatment for this discharge, but most women are reassured when they find that there is no serious cause.

CERVICAL ECTROPION
In a small proportion of women, the cervix (neck of the womb) may be found to be covered by the soft tissue that normally only lines the inside of the

Starting on the contraceptive pill can sometimes trigger a heavy, but otherwise normal, clear discharge in some women. This should not be a cause for alarm.

cervix, a condition called cervical ectropion or ectopy. As the tissue is less resilient than the tougher tissue normally found on the outer cervix, it may produce mucus leading to discharge. This condition can be treated by destroying the soft tissue by freezing it under local anaesthetic (cryosurgery).

Cryosurgery is the use of extreme cold to destroy unwanted tissues. The technique may be used to treat cervical ectropion.

Sexually transmitted causes of discharge

Discharge that results from unprotected sex tends to have more serious consequences than non-sexually transmitted causes of discharge. It is important to seek early diagnosis and treatment.

TRICHOMONIASIS

Trichomoniasis (or TV) is caused by the bacterium *Trichomonas vaginalis* and is caught after unprotected sexual intercourse. Symptoms usually start one to four weeks after infection and normally include a heavy yellow, green or white discharge that is very similar in appearance to that seen in bacterial vaginosis (BV).

As in BV, the discharge frequently has a fishy odour and may contain bubbles. Unlike BV however, there is often vulval and vaginal soreness and occasionally pain felt deeper inside the pelvis. A significant proportion of women have mild symptoms and some have no symptoms at all.

TREATMENT

Diagnosis is made by examining the discharge microscopically.

The woman and her sexual partner(s) will need to be treated with a course of an antibiotic

named metronidazole, and must abstain from sexual intercourse until the infection has been shown to have gone.

Very rarely, the organism will not respond to metronidazole and other more specialized therapies will be needed.

Fortunately, although TV is unpleasant, it does not cause any permanent harm. The presence of one STD may mean that the woman is at risk of others and should have a thorough check-up at a genito-urinary medicine (GUM) clinic.

Condoms help prevent the spread of sexually transmitted diseases. Latex-free condoms will lessen the risk of allergies.

Testing for Trichomonas is usually performed at a department of genito-urinary medicine. The bacterium can also be grown in the laboratory from a swab.

Gonorrhoea and chlamydia

The majority of women suffering from gonorrhoea and chlamydia will not have symptoms. Those that do, usually complain of pelvic pain or bleeding after sexual intercourse.

A minority of women will get a clear or yellow discharge that occasionally contains blood. This is due to infection of the cervix, which will be seen to be red and inflamed on examination. Both infections are caught through unprotected sex and normally cause symptoms one to three weeks after infection.

In some cases, a doctor may mistakenly think that the cause

For diagnosis of gonorrhoea or chlamydia, swab tests are required. These need to be taken during a vaginal examination.

of the discharge is thrush and will only realize there is another problem when the women fails to get better after treatment. The tests can be efficiently taken at a GUM clinic, where treatment will also be given in the form of a regime of antibiotics. Of course, the woman's sexual partner(s) will also need to be treated, and abstention from sex must be undertaken until treatment has been successful.

ESSENTIAL DIAGNOSIS

It is particularly important to diagnose these two infections because, if they remain untreated, they may progress to cause inflammation of the uterine (Fallopian) tubes, pelvic inflammatory disease and possible infertility.

Vaginal discharge in children

While all of the causes of vaginal discharge mentioned above may also cause problems in children and post-menopausal women, other causes become more common in these age groups. At the extremes of life, the common factor is a lower production by the body of female sex hormones.

HORMONE LEVELS
Before the periods have commenced, the vaginal wall is thinner and less resilient than that of adults, due to lower levels of oestrogen and progestogens (female hormones) circulating in the blood.

One reason a child's vagina may become inflamed is as a reaction to a foreign body that the child has inserted into her vagina, which could be something as innocuous as a piece of fluff or a toy.

INFECTION
The vagina can also become infected in children as a result of poor hygiene, and occasionally threadworms may be the cause.

Detecting a vaginal discharge in a child can be distressing for the parents because of fears of accusation of sexual abuse, but doctors realize that in most cases this has not been the cause.

It is normally necessary for a doctor to take tests in order to ascertain the cause of the infection, and this may also require a very discreet examination of the vagina in case there is a foreign body still inside. This should be carried out gently with a minimum of fuss.

Successful treatment of the condition is usually quickly achieved with a combination of advice on hygiene and, perhaps, a course of antibiotics.

It is important for doctors to put the young patient and her parents at ease if a vaginal examination is deemed necessary. This will determine the cause of any discomfort, discharge or inflammation.

Vaginal discharge after the menopause

Many women remain sexually active well after the menopause and may still be at risk of the infections outlined above. However, another cause of discharge, atrophic vaginitis, becomes more common at this later stage of life.

CAUSES
This problem is thought to arise as a result of the thinning of the vaginal wall because the blood levels of the female hormones fall after the menopause. The vagina therefore becomes more susceptible to infection from germs that are found on the skin. There may also be fewer normal protective vaginal bacteria, known as lactobacilli, which normally afford resistance to outside bacteria.

TREATMENT
As a result, a woman may notice some discharge but also vaginal soreness and occasionally bleeding, especially after sex. The diagnosis is made by the doctor on seeing the typical changes of the vaginal wall at vaginal examination. A course of antibiotics as tablets or cream may then be prescribed. Hormone creams inserted into the vagina are also frequently used. In the long term, the vaginal wall will become more resilient if hormone replacement therapy (HRT) is undertaken.

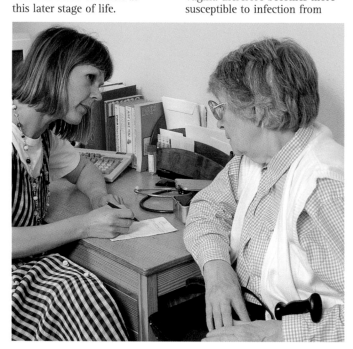

Sexually active older women are still susceptible to sexually transmitted diseases, but are also liable to other disorders, such as atrophic vaginitis.

Hormone replacement therapy (HRT) involves taking a combination of oestrogen and progestogen hormones to make good the deficiency of female sex hormones that occurs in women after the menopause.

Vulval itching

The vulva lies at a junction of mucous membranes and skin, making it rich in nerve endings and therefore prone to itching. Any persistent itching requires thorough examination.

Most women suffer from vulval itching or discomfort at some time in their lives. There are many causes and in almost all cases a complete cure is obtainable. Unfortunately, the diagnosis can be delayed for a variety of reasons, especially as individuals may suffer considerable discomfort before seeking medical attention or obtaining a definitive diagnosis. The most common cause of irritation of the vulva is contact with irritating chemicals:

■ Through inadequate rinsing of clothes washed in detergents and fabric softeners
■ Through use of perfumed soaps, gels and panty liners
■ Through inadequate rinsing of baths cleaned with strong detergent materials.

EXCLUDING CANCER

However, it is important to exclude infection and pre-cancerous lesions as the cause of persistent vulval itching or irritation. For this reason, a medical examination should always be carried out. Unfortunately the availability of over-the-counter medications for the treatment of candida (thrush) has resulted in many women opting to self-treat, and this may delay the diagnosis of conditions that are not candida.

The causes of vulval itching or discomfort are either infective or non-infective. If vulval itching or irritation persists after removal of possible skin irritants or treatment with an antifungal agent, specialized tests may be required to establish a definitive diagnosis of the cause. In some cases, this may even include a biopsy of the affected area.

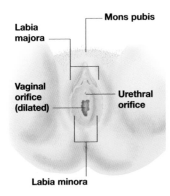

The external female genitalia are known as the vulva. The labia majora and minora, two pairs of fleshy folds, are commonly involved in vulval itching.

Labia majora — Mons pubis

Vaginal orifice (dilated) — Urethral orifice

Labia minora

Any case of vulval itching requires clinical examination. This ensures a correct diagnosis and treatment and can assuage fears of more serious disease.

Vulval infections

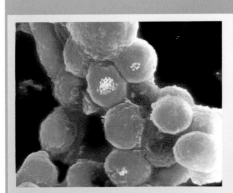

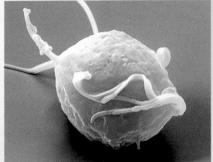

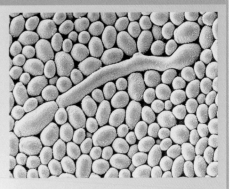

HERPES SIMPLEX VIRUS

The herpes simplex virus forms clusters of cells that bind to the wall of a host cell and inject their own DNA into it. This 'hijacks' the body's cell, turning it into a virus-producing entity.

The first exposure (primary infection) to the herpes simplex virus may result in a severely painful and ulcerated vulva and influenza-like symptoms. Later attacks (secondary herpes) are usually less severe and may just present as recurrent vulval irritation or itching. There is no long-term cure.

TRICHOMONAS VAGINALIS

Trichomonas vaginalis is a protozoan that causes a vaginal infection called trichomoniasis. The infection is transmitted sexually. Each organism (shown above) is a single-celled entity that is larger than a bacterium. The symptoms of trichomoniasis include vaginal and vulval soreness and irritation, and an offensive, frothy, yellow-greenish vaginal discharge. The infection can be identified through laboratory examination and culture from a swab test, and treated with antibiotics.

CANDIDA ALBICANS

Candida albicans is a yeastlike organism that is present in the vagina in a large proportion of women without causing any symptoms at all. However, in some individuals it can cause intense itching or soreness of the vagina and/or labia (skin folds around the vulva); this condition is commonly known as thrush.

In around 50 per cent of cases there is an accompanying thick, white, non-offensive discharge. Thrush is easily treated with antifungal agents such as clotrimazole, and symptoms should clear within 48 hours.

Non-infective conditions

Allergies or irritation of the vulval skin and mucosa are perhaps the commonest cause of vulval irritation. Products such as shampoos, soaps, hair gels and shower gels contain detergents that may be extremely irritating to the mucosal surfaces of the vulva. An allergic reaction may cause urticaria (an itchy rash caused by the release of histamine).

Sensitizing products may have been used for a long period of time before irritation begins. Treatment is simply to stop using all bath products and to wash and rinse hair separately from the rest of the body.

DERMATOSES
Any skin condition affecting the skin of the body may also affect the labia. Eczema, psoriasis and seborrhoeic dermatitis have all been known to affect the vulva. The diagnosis of these conditions can easily be missed by medical personnel because their appearance here may differ

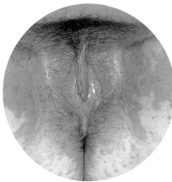

Psoriasis of the labia is a scaly, chronic skin condition which can spread over the labia and legs. It normally responds well to corticosteroid treatment.

Washing powders and fabric conditioners may cause skin reactions that result in vulval itching. Bath and hair products can also cause reactions.

quite markedly from other affected areas of the body.

Psoriasis of the labia is often accompanied by itching or discomfort around the anus or belly-button, but in many cases the vulva is the only area affected. Most of these conditions can be successfully treated with steroid cream.

LICHEN SCLEROSUS
This is an inflammatory skin condition of unknown cause which may also affect other areas of the body. Intense itching is the main clinical symptom, with accompanying tightening of the skin due to coalescing lesions. The area of skin affected is usually very pale. When the condition occurs around the vaginal entrance, intercourse may be painful. Lichen sclerosus is easily treated with steroid cream.

LICHEN PLANUS
Lichen planus is a fairly common disease that normally affects the wrists, ankles and mouth, and less commonly, the labia and vagina. It is an

inflammatory skin condition of unknown cause, characterized by very itchy, slightly raised, purplish lesions. It responds well to topical steroid treatment.

LICHEN SIMPLEX
This condition is the result of an 'itch-scratch' cycle. An initial event that causes itching (such as contact with a chemical irritant) results in the woman scratching. The more the area is scratched, the more irritated the skin becomes, releasing chemicals from the cells into the surrounding tissues. This, in turn, causes itching, and thus a cycle of 'itch-scratch' is established.

Once the diagnosis is made, the area is treated with a mild steroid and the individual is encouraged to cut her nails to

prevent further damage to the skin by scratching.

As scratching commonly occurs during sleep, wearing gloves may be necessary to prevent skin damage. The condition usually resolves quickly once the cycle is broken.

Menopause
The lack of oestrogen at the time of menopause or thereafter can result in quite marked shrinkage and thinning of the vulval mucosa due to a reduction of fat tissues.

This is often accompanied by a burning or itching sensation, which is easily relieved by the application of an oestrogen-containing cream.

Malignancy

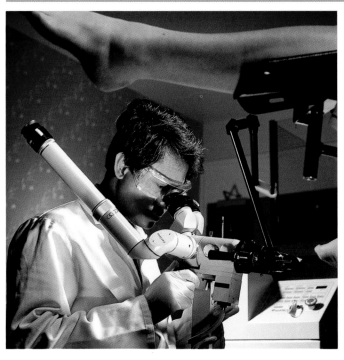

Cancer of the vulva makes up 3–4 per cent of gynaecological cancers. It most commonly affects elderly women, peaking between the ages of 60–80.

Although symptoms occur relatively early in the disease, diagnosis may not occur until it is fairly well advanced. This is partly due to a reluctance on the part of the woman to seek help for symptoms that may appear to be unimportant, or to the difficulty of early recognition of the disease or its precursor.

Recently, medical attention has begun to focus on vulval intra-epithelial neoplasias, which occur in much younger women and can have implications for gynaecological cancer.

Vulval intra-epithelial neoplasia (the presence of pre-cancerous cells) can be treated with laser. The gynaecologist directs the laser beam using a colposcope.

VULVAL INTRA-EPITHELIAL NEOPLASIA (VIN)
Vulval intra-epithelial neoplasia is a very slow, progressive condition that, in some cases, indicates the possible development of cancer. It may be preceded by a condition causing intra-epithelial lesions; one per cent of women with lichen sclerosus will develop malignant lesions.

Itching is the most common symptom of VIN at clinical presentation.

DIAGNOSIS
The widespread involvement of the vulval skin makes diagnosis of VIN difficult, requiring an experienced specialist. If diagnosed early enough, the condition can be treated with laser therapy before cancer develops. If the lesion is extensive, surgery with skin grafting may be necessary.

Urinary tract infections

Symptoms

The urinary tract is normally sterile, and does not house any infectious organisms. Bacterial urinary infections are, however, common, particularly in women.

Urinary tract infections are particularly common in women. A GP uses a urine dipstick that changes colour if an infection is present.

DRAINAGE SYSTEM
A urinary tract infection may involve all or part of the urinary drainage system, which includes:
■ The kidneys
■ The ureters – a pair of tubes, 25–30cm (8–10in) long, which connects the two renal pelves to the bladder. The junction between the ureters and bladder (vesicoureteric junction) acts as a one-way valve, allowing urine to enter the bladder, but shutting the ureters off when the bladder contracts
■ The bladder – a sac-shaped muscular organ. Urination occurs when the bladder contracts
■ The urethra – drains the bladder. It is 3.5–4 cm (1 $\frac{3}{8}$–1$\frac{1}{2}$ in) long in women and 20cm (8in) long in men. In women, the opening to the urethra is fairly close to the anal area.

CLINICAL FEATURES
Symptoms of infection in the lower part of the urinary tract involving the bladder and urethra include:
■ Pain when passing urine (dysuria), often described as 'passing razor blades'
■ The urge to pass urine very frequently, only small amounts being passed each time
■ Pain and tenderness in the lower abdomen
■ Blood in the urine (haematuria)
■ Offensive-smelling urine
■ Fever.

PYELONEPHRITIS
Acute infection of the urinary tract involving the kidney and its pelvis is known as pyelonephritis. Typically, this more severe infection is

accompanied by :
■ High fevers
■ Attacks of shivering (rigors) due to the high temperature
■ Pain in the lower back
■ Nausea and vomiting.

ROUTINE CHECK
In some people, however, symptoms of infection in the urinary tract are mild or non-existent and the infection is detected only by a routine urine examination.

Causes

Bacteria entering the urinary tract via the urethra cause most urinary infections. Infection via the blood or lymph circulations is less common. Once in the bladder, the infection often travels up to the kidney. Any abnormality that impedes the flow of urine increases the risk of infection.

Escherichia coli, which normally inhabits the bowel, causes about 80 per cent of urinary tract infections in the community and about 50 per cent in hospital patients. A variety of other bacteria cause the remainder.

The presence of more than 1,000,000 of the same species of bacteria per millilitre of urine indicates the presence of a urinary tract infection.

PREDISPOSING FACTORS
Certain groups are at increased risk of urinary tract infections:
■ Females – women have short urethras. Infection often occurs during sexual intercourse
■ Older men with enlarged prostate glands – incomplete bladder emptying can occur
■ Children with anatomical defects – a congenital abnormality of the implantation of the ureters into the bladder wall often causes recurrent upper urinary tract infections by allowing the urine to pass back into the upper urinary tract during urination (vesicoureteric reflux). The reflux improves or resolves with growth
■ Pregnant women – the ureters and renal pelves dilate, disturbing the flow of urine
■ Patients with diabetes and immunosuppressed patients
■ People with a tumour in the urinary tract, abdomen or pelvis

Urinary tract infections are often caused by the rod-shaped bacterium, E.coli. Here, it is shown magnified on the cells of the bladder (blue area).

may develop a urinary tract infection. Stones in the urinary tract also increase the risk of infections
■ Patients with long-term urinary catheters (drainage tubes) left in place to drain the bladder.

Incidence
At least eight per cent of girls and two per cent of boys have a urinary tract infection in childhood. Boys have more infections before the age of three months, as they have more congenital malformations of the urinary tract than girls.

Adult women, particularly if sexually active, are at higher risk than men. At least 50 per cent of women have at least one urinary tract infection at some time. After the age of 60, urinary infection in men increases as the incidence of prostate enlargement increases. Up to six per cent of pregnant women have bacteria in their urine. If untreated, 20 per cent of these women will go on to develop pyelonephritis (kidney infection).

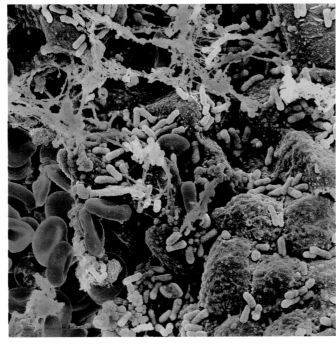

Diagnosis

A definite diagnosis of urinary tract infection can be made only by culturing a sample of urine for bacteria, as some patients with symptoms of a bladder or urethral infection (cystitis or urethritis) have no evidence of infection in their urine.

Urine culture should be done when a urinary tract infection is suspected, but it is not always necessary if a sexually active woman has mild cystitis.

SPECIMENS

A urine specimen is collected in a sterile bottle, using a clean technique so bacteria from the skin do not contaminate the specimen, and sent to the laboratory or refrigerated.

Examination of the urine provides information about the likelihood of infection by detecting white blood cells and the products of inflammation.

Other investigations that may be undertaken include:
■ Ultrasound scanning
■ Intravenous urogram or pyelogram (IVU or IVP) – X-rays of the urinary tract are taken after an intravenous injection of a contrast medium that is concentrated and excreted by the kidneys
■ Cystourethroscopy – an illuminated endoscopic instrument is passed through the urethra into the bladder
■ Micturating cystourethrogram – first, a contrast medium is introduced; then an X-ray is taken while the patient urinates, to record the bladder emptying.

Infections are often diagnosed by sending a urine sample to a laboratory. Drops of urine are spread on an agar plate to encourage bacterial growth.

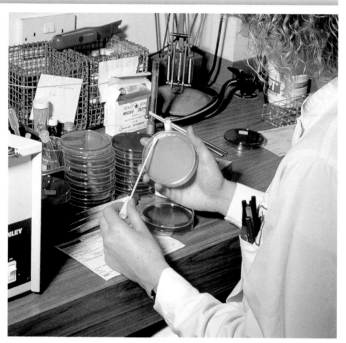

Treatment

In general, treatment aims to eliminate bacteria from the urine and correct abnormalities of the urinary tract. Treatment includes:

■ Antibiotics – a short course of an antibacterial drug, such as trimethoprim or amoxicillin, is often sufficient for cystitis (bladder infection). Acute pyelonephritis (kidney infection) requires a longer course of antibiotics and may need hospital admission
■ Fluid therapy – increasing fluid intake flushes the urinary tract and reduces the pain
■ Analgesics.

Pregnant women with urine infections should always be prescribed antibiotics. These drugs do not harm the developing fetus.

RISK GROUPS

Management of specific patient groups includes the following:
■ Pregnant women with infected urine should be treated with antibiotics, even if they have no symptoms
■ Elderly women often have bacteria in their urine but, unless they develop symptoms, are best left untreated
■ Sexually active women with recurrent infections are helped by long-term, low-dose antibacterial treatment taken last thing at night or after intercourse. In older women, hormone replacement therapy (HRT) may help
■ Children should be treated with antibiotics until the urine is sterile. The use of long-term antibiotics may be needed to prevent recurrences.

Prognosis

Urinary infections are usually mild and easily treated. Some groups, however, such as young children, pregnant women and people with diabetes, are at high risk of a serious illness that may affect kidney function.

The prognosis is much improved if each episode of infection is treated with antibiotics. In some cases, the long-term preventive use of antibiotics is also necessary. Surgery involving re-implantation of the ureters into the bladder may be considered in severe cases.

Prevention

The following measures can be taken to prevent infection of the urinary tract:
■ Empty the bladder completely when urine is passed
■ Drink plenty of fluids regularly throughout the day to flush out the urinary tract. Water is ideal, and try to avoid very sweet drinks
■ Wipe only from front to back after going to the lavatory. This will prevent *Escherichia coli* bacterium (which lives in the bowel) from entering the urinary tract – this bacteria is the main cause of urinary tract infection
■ Use a vaginal lubricant during intercourse

■ Always empty the bladder immediately after intercourse
■ Avoid the use of deodorants or scented soaps around the genital area
■ Wear loose-fitting underwear made out of cotton instead of man-made fibres
■ If a diaphragm is used as a contraceptive device, it is important to check the fit with a doctor. If this method is causing infections, it may be worth considering a different form of contraception
■ Antibiotics may occasionally be used as a long-term preventive measure if the infection keeps recurring.

Drinking plenty of water will help to prevent the recurrence of bladder infections. Keeping fluid intake high is particularly important during pregnancy.

Breast cancer

Breast cancer is the most common female cancer in the UK, affecting about 1 in 14 women at some stage in their lives. However, there are a variety of treatments and over two-thirds of patients are cured.

Breast cancer is the most common female cancer by far, with more than 30,000 new diagnoses every year in the UK. It is also the leading cause of cancer deaths in British women.

However, unlike many other types of cancer, such as lung or pancreatic cancer, which kill the vast majority of the patients who develop them, breast cancer is cured in around two-thirds of cases.

AT-RISK WOMEN

Despite concern among many young women about developing breast cancer, predominantly it is a disease of older women who have passed the menopause.

The risk of developing breast cancer before the age of 35 is only about 1 in 2500. It rises to 1 in 50 by the age of 50, and is 1 in 10 for women who reach the age of 80.

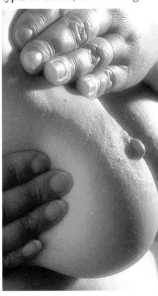

◀ *Regular self-examination can help to detect breast cancer early. The earlier a malignant abnormality is detected, the more effective the treatment.*

▶ *Mammography is an X-ray technique that reveals the presence of breast abnormalities. Many countries have breast screening programmes for at-risk women.*

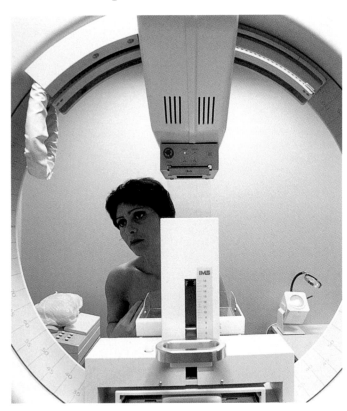

Risk factors for breast cancer

The development of breast cancer is a chance event for the majority of patients. There are, however, a number of clearly documented risk factors for its development. These include:
■ Increasing age
■ Family or personal history of breast cancer
■ Previous non-cancerous breast lumps
■ Excessive exposure to the female sex hormone oestrogen – this means that women who start their periods early, go through the menopause late, or who take hormone replacement therapy (HRT) after the menopause have a slightly increased risk of developing breast cancer
■ Diet and alcohol intake – these have also been implicated.

CANCER GENES

Women from families with several members who develop breast cancer, particularly young first-degree relatives (mothers, sisters or daughters), have an extremely high risk of developing the disease themselves. This is related to carrying an inherited breast cancer gene.

Two breast cancer genes have been identified, and these are known as BRCA1 and BRCA2. The chance of breast cancer developing during the lifetime of a patient carrying either BRCA1 or BRCA2 is 87 per cent.

The BRCA1 gene has been linked to the development of breast cancer. The gene is the red band (circled) on this fluorescent micrograph of chromosome 17.

Thus it is important to identify affected families and offer genetic counselling and, if appropriate, testing.

If a breast cancer gene is found in a patient with breast cancer, their offspring have a 50 per cent chance of inheriting that gene. Those family members inheriting the gene have a high risk of developing cancer.

OTHER FACTORS

Although the breast cancer genes are a very important cause of breast cancer, it should also be remembered that less than 10 per cent of all cases of breast cancer occur in individuals from families in which a specific breast cancer gene can be found.

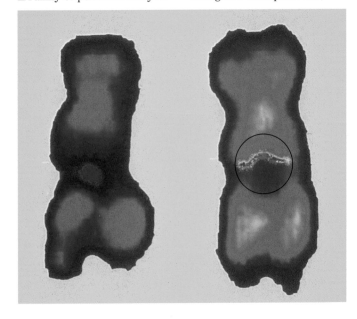

Risk of breast cancer by age	
AGE	RISK
30	1 in 2525
40	1 in 217
50	1 in 50
60	1 in 24
70	1 in 14

Breast cancer prevention

There are several strategies that may be employed to reduce the chance of developing breast cancer. Their use is generally confined to women in high-risk groups, particularly those individuals who have been shown to have inherited one of the breast cancer genes.

TAMOXIFEN

The anti-oestrogen drug tamoxifen has been used in breast cancer prevention trials. A recent US trial in women at a moderately increased risk of breast cancer showed that those who took tamoxifen for five years were less likely to develop breast cancer than those who did not. However, there was an increased risk of endometrial cancer (cancer of the inner lining of the uterus) and thromboembolic disease (blood

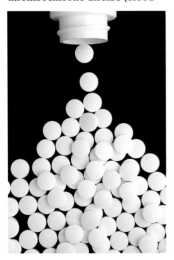

Tamoxifen is an anti-oestrogen drug that may prevent breast cancer in some women. However, the results of clinical trials have not been conclusive.

Removal of breast tissue is an effective method of preventing recurrence of breast cancer. The reduction of risk is linked to the amount of tissue removed.

clots in the leg veins or lung) in women taking tamoxifen. Women who took tamoxifen have not been shown to be less likely to die of breast cancer than those who did not.

Preliminary results from an ongoing UK study in women with a family history of breast cancer have shown no advantage from the use of tamoxifen. This collection of conflicting trial results makes it hard to formulate clear treatment guidelines.

Women contemplating tamoxifen chemoprevention for breast cancer should discuss this with an appropriate specialist and should, ideally, be treated in a relevant clinical trial.

PREVENTIVE SURGERY

■ Mastectomy

The most effective preventive strategy, supported by the best evidence, is bilateral mastectomy (or second mastectomy for patients who have already been treated for a first breast cancer). The removal of normal breasts cannot be undertaken lightly and it is vital that women

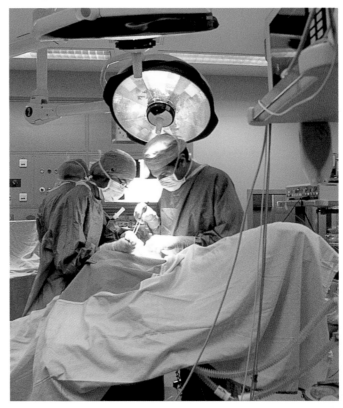

considering this procedure receive adequate pre-surgical counselling.

The reduction of cancer risk is directly related to the amount of glandular breast tissue removed. Thus subcutaneous mastectomy, which leaves the nipple intact, is not generally recommended, as it leaves about 10 per cent of this tissue behind. A traditional mastectomy leaves about one per cent of the glandular tissue.

■ Oophorectomy

For BRCA gene carriers ,there is also an increased risk of ovarian cancer and consideration should also be given to prophylactic oophorectomy (preventive removal of the ovaries).

Oophorectomy reduces the risk of breast cancer by reducing the main source of oestrogen production and has been shown to reduce the risk of breast cancer in BRCA gene carriers.

Detecting and diagnosing breast cancer

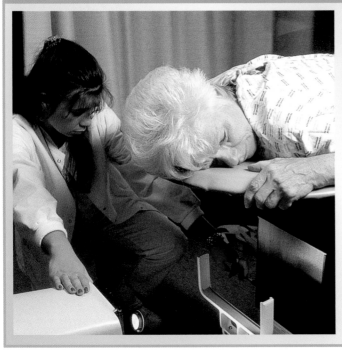

Patients can be alerted to the suspicion of breast cancer in one of two ways:

■ An abnormality can be detected on a screening mammogram, usually in the NHS Breast Screening Programme

■ A breast abnormality is noticed by the patient herself.

The commonest symptoms and signs of breast cancer are the presence of a lump, a change in shape of the breast, abnormalities in the skin of the breast, changes in the nipple or nipple discharge.

The diagnosis of breast abnormalities is usually made by a 'triple assessment', which includes clinical examination, mammogram and a needle

A breast biopsy may be taken under X-ray guidance. The biopsy needle takes a small tissue sample from the breast to be analyzed for cancer cells.

biopsy. However, mammography may not be useful in some women – particularly before the menopause when normal breast tissue is more dense – and common alternatives are ultrasound or magnetic resonance imaging.

After these investigations, the majority of women, particularly those who notice a breast lump, are found not to have cancer. For those with a positive diagnosis, the emphasis moves on to treatment.

Patients need a multidisciplinary approach to treatment, with input from surgeons, oncologists (cancer specialists), physiotherapists and other allied healthcare professionals. Specialist breast care nurses have an important role in counselling and helping patients to select appropriate treatment options.

Breast ultrasound

Ultrasound images may be used to examine breast abnormalities in women. Advances in technology have enabled the development of high-frequency ultrasound machines, making diagnosis easier.

Ultrasound examination is used as a routine part of assessing an abnormality found at breast screening or at a visit to the breast clinic. In women under the age of 35, it is the first-line examination for investigation of a breast problem, and may indeed be the only examination that is required. Ultrasound of the breast is an important adjunct to mammography and clinical examination in the further assessment of both palpable and impalpable breast abnormalities.

EXAMINATION OF THE BREAST
The breast is a relatively low contrast object and changes are subtle. For this reason, high-quality scanners are required when examining the breast. It is possible to scan most breasts with ease by positioning the patient correctly so that the breast is spread over the chest wall. This reduces the depth of breast tissue to be scanned. The breast is then approximately 3cm (1³/₁₆in) in thickness, and within the operating zone of high-frequency ultrasound probes.

LIMITATIONS
The use of ultrasound in breast imaging has several limitations:
■ It cannot reliably distinguish between benign and malignant solid lumps
■ It is difficult to visualize the sub-areolar region
■ It can miss small lesions at limits of probe resolution
■ The absence of surrounding tissue contrast makes some lesions invisible
■ It is not suitable as a screening procedure, as it is not very sensitive.

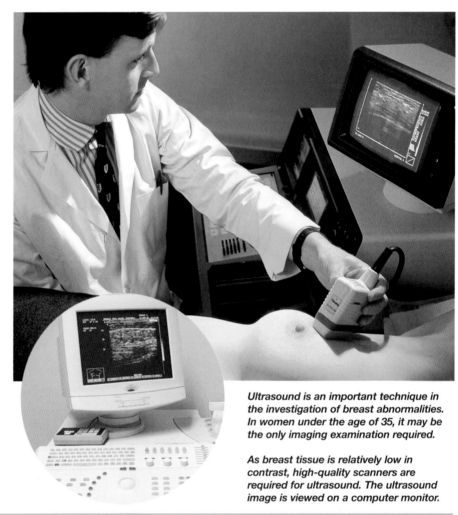

Ultrasound is an important technique in the investigation of breast abnormalities. In women under the age of 35, it may be the only imaging examination required.

As breast tissue is relatively low in contrast, high-quality scanners are required for ultrasound. The ultrasound image is viewed on a computer monitor.

Anatomy of the breast on ultrasound

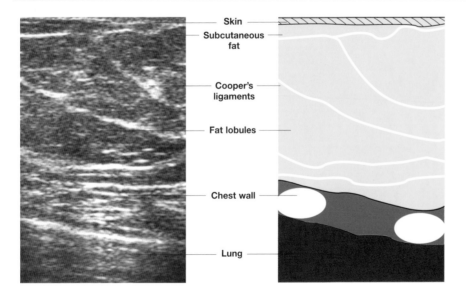

Skin
Subcutaneous fat
Cooper's ligaments
Fat lobules
Chest wall
Lung

Layers of tissue making up the breast can be seen by high-frequency ultrasound.
■ Skin: highly reflective double band along the surface of the breast
■ Fat: seen in lobules or as subcutaneous fat, which normally measures about 3mm (¹/₈in) in depth and is dark in contrast to the skin and underlying glandular tissue
■ Cooper's ligaments: seen as curvilinear structures attaching the fibroglandular tissue to the skin and pectoral fascia
■ Parenchyma (fibroglandular tissue): the reflective tissue seen within the fatty tissue of the breast, which varies, depending on the level of female hormones in the body at the time
■ Ducts: these show as long, low-echo lines, about 2–3mm (¹/₁₆–¹/₈in) thick.

A high-frequency ultrasound image of the breast shows the various layers of tissue. Ultrasound may help to determine if a mass is a benign cyst or a carcinoma.

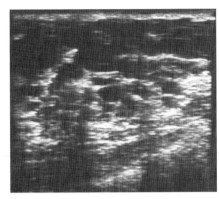

Ducts in the breast tissue can become distended and contain more secretions. On an ultrasound image, the ducts appear as black, sausage-like structures.

Benign breast change

Breast tissue becomes more responsive to oestrogens, and reacts by increasing in glandular density, and the ducts become distended. Cyclical increases in benign breast change are considered to be part of what is known as premenstrual syndrome.

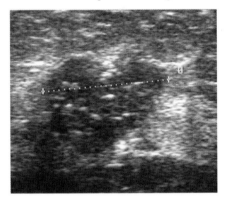

If the cancer contains microcalcification, this can be seen within the mass as fine reflections or speckles. It reflects the calcified in-situ component of the disease.

Breast cancer

The presence of microcalcification may be the only sign of breast cancer even in the absence of a visible mass. A mammogram will reveal the first signs of calcification; ultrasound will then be used to determine whether it is benign or malignant.

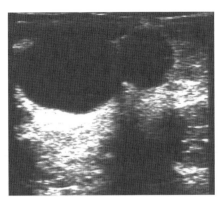

Breast cysts appear as round, well-defined lesions with a bright posterior wall. A diagnosis can be made using ultrasound if a cyst has all of these features.

Simple cyst

Simple cysts (single or multiple) are hormone-related and caused by a blocked duct, with subsequent dilatation of the breast lobule. Most small cysts change in size and shape over a menstrual cycle. Larger cysts may be tender and require drainage.

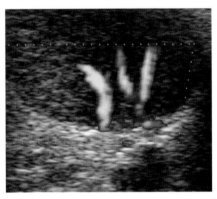

Using Doppler scanning can help the operator to avoid blood vessels during a biopsy. The blood vessels can be seen as red/orange signals from within the mass.

Doppler scanning

Doppler scanning is a good way of visualizing blood vessels in or around a mass lesion. It is helpful to determine whether the vessels are within the mass or around the periphery. Large vascular channels should be avoided when performing a biopsy.

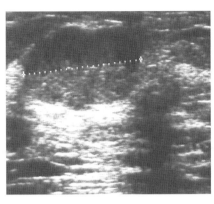

A fibroadenoma, seen here, is typically oval, less than 3cm (1 ¹⁄₈in) in size and wider than it is tall. It has smooth borders and is generally circumscribed.

Fibroadenoma

Fibroadenomas are the most common benign breast tumours found in young women. They have a uniformly low- or medium-level echogenicity, show enhancement behind the mass, have minimal shadowing and may be lobulated.

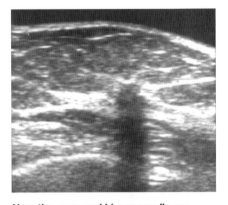

Here the mass and biopsy needle can clearly be seen. Using ultrasound to guide the needle, the operator can be sure the mass has been biopsied.

Guided breast biopsy

To investigate a lump further, a sample will need to be taken for analysis. Performing a biopsy of a breast lump is simple if using ultrasound. Even superficial masses, and those close to major structures can be successfully biopsied by this technique.

High-frequency scanning

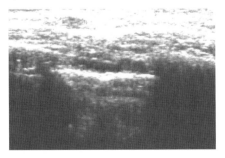

This low-frequency image shows an intra-mammary lymph node as a vague low-echo ovoid mass. Using low-frequency probes, it is difficult to visualize small objects with any certainty.

Latest developments in ultrasound technology include high-frequency scanning and power Doppler ultrasound. Machines are now available, dedicated for breast imaging, with small hand-held probes with frequencies in the region of 7.5 to 20 MHz.

Use of high-frequency ultrasound allows for detection of smaller lesions, with greater accuracy. By using a probe operating at 10 or 13 MHz, these smaller lesions can be seen with ease. It is possible to see the outlines of abnormalities more clearly, allowing diagnosis to be made more easily and with increased confidence. These two images show an intra-mammary lymph node imaged using both low and high frequencies.

This high-frequency scan shows a doughnut-looking low-echo mass with a reflective centre (the fat in the hilum of the lymph node). Such scans can avoid the need for biopsy.

Mammography

Mammography is a specialized low-dose X-ray examination used to image the breasts, and is used for screening for breast cancer, and in women with other breast disorders.

The breast is a low-contrast structure and ordinary X-rays machines are unable to cope with this. For this reason, dedicated mammography X-ray sets have been developed, which use both low power and specialized film and screen combinations to obtain a high-contrast image.

ANATOMY
The breast is composed of a mixture of fat, ducts and glandular tissue. Fat is relatively dark on X-ray, whereas glandular tissue is white (dense) and ducts may show up as tubular structures or nodular densities.

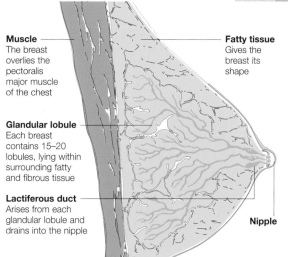

Muscle
The breast overlies the pectoralis major muscle of the chest

Glandular lobule
Each breast contains 15–20 lobules, lying within surrounding fatty and fibrous tissue

Lactiferous duct
Arises from each glandular lobule and drains into the nipple

Fatty tissue
Gives the breast its shape

Nipple

The breast is shaped by fatty tissue, with fibrous suspensory ligaments providing support.

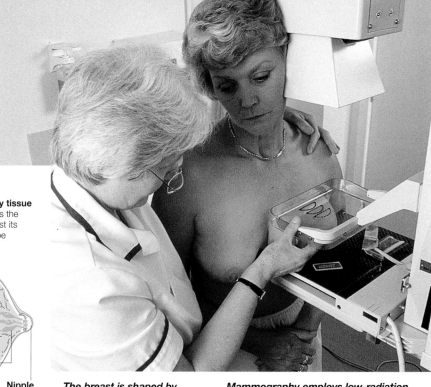

Mammography employs low-radiation X-rays to allow the visualization of breast tissue. In this way, the presence of any abnormalities can be detected.

Changes in the breasts

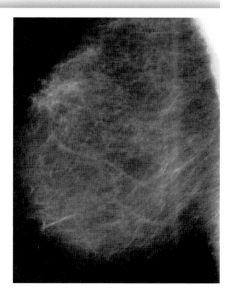

As women age, breast tissue becomes less dense, with glandular tissue being replaced by fat. These changes are reversed by hormone replacement therapy (HRT), and the breast once again becomes very dense.

To see an abnormality on a mammogram, a difference must exist between the absorption of X-rays by the tumour and that by the surrounding breast tissue ('tissue contrast'). If the densities are the same, the tumour will be invisible.

RECENT ADVANCES
As with most imaging methods, digital mammography is gradually being introduced. This is currently used for spot imaging of calcifications or distortions, stereotactic biopsy and localization biopsies. Some centres will use full-field computed radiography for symptomatic patients, until digital technology allows direct image capture by the mammography machine. Digital technology speeds up the examination, allows the image to be manipulated and enables calcifications to be seen more easily.

In younger (pre-menopausal) women, the glandular tissue of the breast is dense, and appears white on a mammogram. This is a medio-lateral oblique view.

In contrast, breast tissue in older women who have passed the menopause loses density as fatty tissue replaces glandular tissue. As a result, the image is darker.

Breast screening

Breast cancer is currently the commonest cancer affecting women in the UK, with one in 12 women suffering from the disease in their lifetime. The incidence of breast cancer increases with age, being most common in women above the age of 50.

The UK has a National Health Service Breast Screening Programme (NHS BSP) in which women are offered single-view mammographic screening on a three-yearly basis between the ages of 50 and 64 years.

PERFORMING A MAMMOGRAM
Mammography is the first-line investigation for a symptomatic woman who is 35 or older. In younger women, ultrasound is performed first, and mammography if there is a solid lump, or as a baseline for women with a family history of breast cancer.

TWO-VIEW MAMMOGRAPHY
Two views are taken of each breast. The breasts are gently squeezed between two plates and the exposure made. The compression evens out the breast tissue, produces a high quality image and reduces the radiation dose to the woman. The medio-lateral oblique (MLO) mammogram demonstrates the greater part of the breast tissue in one picture and is used routinely for screening. The top to bottom (CC) view demonstrates the medial aspect of the breast, not shown so well on the MLO view. Some cancers are only visible on the CC view.

Regular breast screening is available to all women in the UK over the age of 50. This has proved vital in reducing the number of deaths from breast cancer.

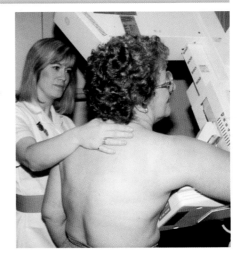

Breast abnormalities

A cyst (circled) is a fluid-filled swelling that is usually benign. They commonly occur in the breast, and mammography is used to distinguish them from malignant growths.

Cyst

When a duct becomes blocked with secretions due to hormone imbalance, the terminal lobule swells with fluid. If this pressure is not relieved, the swelling ends up as a cyst. On a mammogram, the appearance is similar to a fibroadenoma, but without the typical calcification. It is diagnosed with ultrasound scanning.

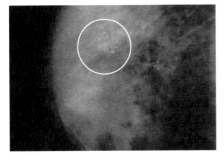

Micro-calcifications can be seen as specks of white (circled) on a mammogram. In this case, the cells of the lactiferous duct have become malignant.

Ductal carcinoma in situ

When malignant ductal cells have grown along, and are limited to, the ducts (not invading the glandular tissue), this is called ductal carcinoma in situ (DCIS). When the fast-growing cells die, they calcify and produce fine micro-calcifications along the ducts.

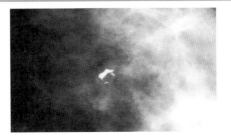

Fibroadenoma is the most common type of breast lump in young women. Mammography cannot reliably diagnose them as benign, so they are usually removed.

Fibroadenoma

A fibroadenoma is a benign tumour of fibrous tissue. On a mammogram, it is seen as a well-defined, circumscribed mass lesion. It may contain characteristic 'popcorn' type micro-calcification. A large benign-looking mass could be a special type of tumour known as a phyllodes (leaflike) tumour.

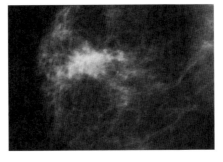

This mammogram shows multiple areas of calcification typical of an invasive ductal carcinoma. Calcifications in the breast tissue is a strong indicator of cancer.

Invasive ductal carcinoma

This is the commonest form of breast cancer that arises as a genetic mutation. It starts at a lobule and spreads around the ducts, invading the surrounding glandular tissue. It typically presents as a spiculate (starlike) mass, although frequently mimics benign lesions.

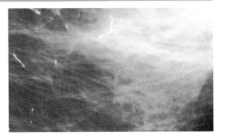

This mammogram shows fibrous strands of calcified tissue in the breast. The calcifications appear white on X-ray against the darker, healthy breast tissue.

Peri-ductal mastitis

In this benign condition, leakage of fluid from the ducts into the surrounding tissue may cause inflammation (mastitis), causing shooting pains and producing redness of the overlying skin. If chronic, typical ductal calcifications can be seen, with smooth, dense margins. Unlike DCIS (see next image), each calcification is quite large.

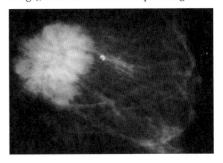

A large advanced cancer is revealed on this mammogram as a grey mass. With the advent of breast screening, breast cancers are usually detected at an earlier stage.

Advanced cancer

Rarely, a cancer can reach an advanced form with lymph glands enlarging as it spreads via the lymphatics draining the affected part of the breast. In the outer half of the breast, the lymphatics drain into the axillary nodes, and in the medial half, the internal thoracic (mammary) nodes.

Treating breast cancer

Advances in treating breast cancer have reduced death rates by 30 per cent in the last decade. Treatment may involve a combination of surgery, radiotherapy, hormone therapy or chemotherapy.

For the majority of patients, the first treatment used against breast cancer is surgery to remove the primary tumour in the breast.

SURGERY

For patients with large tumours, mastectomy (removal of the whole of the breast) is the appropriate operation. Surgical breast reconstruction may be considered afterwards.

For patients with small tumours, a lumpectomy, in which only part of the breast is removed, may be possible and may lead to a more satisfactory post-surgical appearance.

At the time of surgery, it is usual to remove some or all of the lymph nodes (glands) from the axilla (under the arm).

Following surgery, the tumour is examined under the microscope and a pathology report is issued. This describes the exact size of the primary tumour, histological grade, number of involved axillary lymph nodes and the oestrogen receptor status.

It is also usual to look for signs of spread of tumour to other parts of the body with a chest X-ray, blood tests and, for some patients thought to be at particular risk of distant spread of tumour, a bone scan and liver ultrasound. Advice on further treatment can be given once this information has been collected.

RADIOTHERAPY

Post-surgical radiotherapy to the breast is regarded as mandatory for patients who have a lumpectomy, and radiotherapy may be used as an alternative treatment to surgery for the axilla. There is evidence that, after any breast surgery, radiotherapy to the scar, underlying chest tissue and the axilla reduces the local recurrence rate. This, in turn, leads to a reduction in deaths from breast cancer.

Surgery is usually the initial treatment for breast cancer. Depending on the size of the tumour, all of the breast, or only a part of it, may be removed.

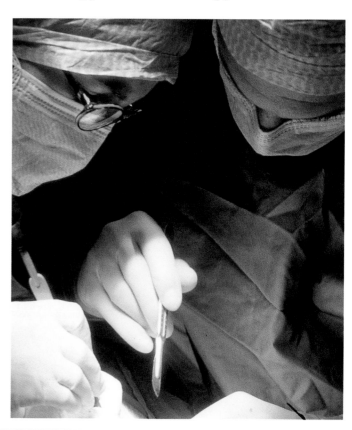

Systemic treatment

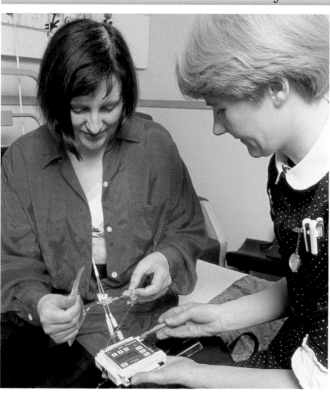

Chemotherapy and endocrine, or hormone, therapy are delivered into the veins or orally as post-surgical therapy. They are used to eliminate micrometastases, tiny fragments of cancer that have broken off before surgery and are elsewhere in the body, posing potential problems of recurrence in the future.

HORMONE THERAPY

Turnover of normal breast tissue is controlled by cyclical changes in oestrogen levels. Sixty per cent of breast cancers can be shown to have the oestrogen receptors needed for this controlling effect and can be treated with tamoxifen, which blocks the effects of oestrogen on receptor-positive breast cancer cells. This reduces the risk of spread or recurrence of the cancer.

Breast-cancer patients may be fitted with a portable drug pump. This is worn 24 hours a day, for four months, to deliver drugs that combat cancer cells.

Current evidence suggests that women with oestrogen receptor-positive tumours benefit from taking tamoxifen tablets for five years following the diagnosis of breast cancer.

CHEMOTHERAPY REGIMENS

It has been shown that almost all women with breast cancer under the age of 70 benefit from adjuvant (added) chemotherapy. The women who benefit most are those with the greatest risk of developing future recurrence.

There are a large number of chemotherapy regimens that have been shown to reduce the recurrence rate for breast cancer. CMF – a combination of the drugs cyclophosphamide, methotrexate and 5-fluorouracil – was one of the first regimens to be effective, and it is still in widespread use worldwide.

The addition of newer drugs – for example, doxorubicin and paclitaxel – is helping to improve the results of chemotherapy treatment.

Managing advanced breast cancer

For patients with metastatic breast cancer – cancer that spreads to other parts of the body – a cure may not be possible. However, treatments can offer relief of symptoms, and current research into new therapies aims to improve the chances of survival.

Unfortunately, despite significant advances in the treatment of breast cancer over the last few decades, breast cancer cannot be cured in every patient.

Patients with metastatic cancer (secondary deposits) at the time of diagnosis, or who develop metastases after their initial treatment, have an uncertain outlook. The most common sites of metastatic disease are bone, liver, lung, skin and subcutaneous tissues, as well as the brain.

TREATMENT OBJECTIVES
Treatment of these patients is directed at prolonging life and relieving symptoms (known as palliative treatment) and, while a minority of patients may live for several years with advanced breast cancer, it is unrealistic to talk of a cure.

The use of surgery and radiotherapy in metastatic disease is less important than chemotherapy and hormone treatments, which are able to get to all sites of secondary spread anywhere in the body. One exception to this is radiotherapy to bone metastases, which is a very effective treatment.

Bisphosphonates are a class of drug that reduce the rate at which cancer damages bones,

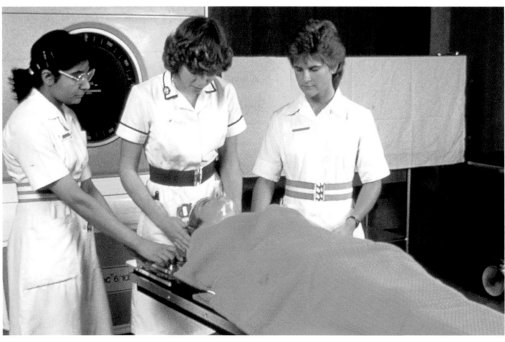

and reduce bone-related cancer complications, including pain and the risk of fractures.

The choice of treatment depends on the anatomical distribution of disease, previous therapies, pathological characteristics of the tumour and the degree to which the patient has been weakened by the cancer or other diseases.

QUALITY OF LIFE
Treatments should be planned carefully for each individual breast-cancer patient, with a high priority given to improving their quality of life.

It is an advantage to involve specialist palliative care doctors and nurses in the treatment of patients with metastatic disease to maximize the chances of

Radiotherapy may be used in cases of advanced breast cancer when the cancer has spread to bone. However, radiation therapy is not without side effects.

effective symptom relief. Pain control and other supportive treatments are vital at this stage of breast cancer.

New drugs and clinical trials

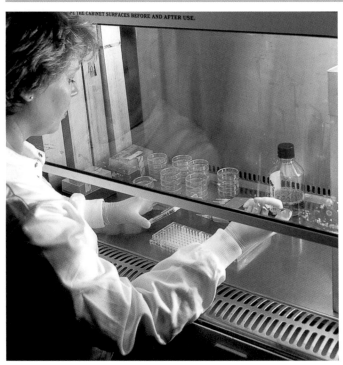

Scientists and doctors are constantly searching for new anticancer therapies and so patients with breast cancer are often offered experimental treatments. The commonest trials involve testing a current treatment alongside a newer and, hopefully, better treatment in a randomized study.

Other trials test the newest treatment without comparing it to one that has already been in widespread use, looking for evidence of drug activity and with a careful eye on toxicity.

◀ *Research is ongoing to test the effect of anticancer drugs on cancer cells. This research helps to determine why some patients do not respond to treatment.*

▶ *Gene research has shown that chromosome 17 is the site of the breast cancer gene. Here, DNA fragments making up chromosome 17 can be seen.*

CLINICAL TRIALS
Clinical trials define the best treatments and provide the evidence needed to push for funding of expensive new technologies. There is also evidence that clinical trials lead to better survival rates for those who take part in them.

The current trend is to move away from conventional chemotherapy treatments towards less toxic drugs tailored to individual patients' needs.

Cervical cancer

Symptoms

Cancer of the cervix (also known as cervical cancer) is one of the most common female cancers worldwide. However, it is usually slow-growing and, if detected early enough, it can be effectively treated. In developed countries, advanced cervical cancer has become a decreasing problem as a result of widespread cervical screening but, in many developing countries, screening is not generally available and cervical cancer remains the most common cause of cancer death.

CELL ABNORMALITIES
The cervix (the neck of the womb) is the lower third of the uterus. It projects into the vagina and surrounds the cervical canal, which links the vagina to the inside of the womb. Cells on the outer surface of the cervix sometimes develop abnormalities but often return to normal without treatment.

Occasionally, however, the abnormalities persist and after several years these cells may become cancerous. Abnormalities that are recognized as pre-cancerous can usually be simply treated, using a laser, freezing or diathermy and requiring only an out-patient appointment.

CLINICAL SYMPTOMS
Pre-cancerous changes in the cervix and early cervical cancer cause no symptoms, so cervical screening is vital to detect early disease. At a later stage, cervical cancer may cause abnormal vaginal bleeding between periods and a vaginal discharge, and discomfort may occur after intercourse. Women who have reached their menopause and who no longer have periods may develop new bleeding.

Pain is a late symptom of cervical cancer and a sign that the cancer has spread widely in the pelvis. Persistent mild fever, weight loss, anaemia and urinary and bowel problems may also occur in advanced disease.

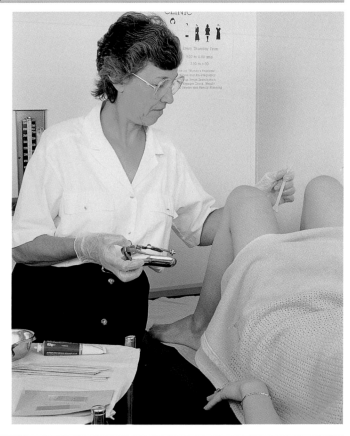

Cervical screening involves a smear of cells being taken from the cervix. This is then analyzed in a laboratory for cell changes.

Diagnosis

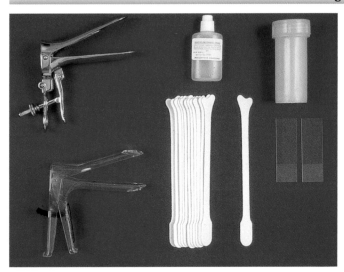

CERVICAL SMEAR TEST
In its very early stages, cervical cancer is diagnosed by the examination of cells taken from the surface of the cervix (a cervical smear). During a smear test, the doctor inserts an instrument called a speculum into the vagina in order to hold the vaginal walls apart and obtain a clear view of the cervix. A wooden spatula and/or a small brush is then used to take a sample of cells from the cervix. These samples are spread on a microscope slide and sent to a laboratory.

If the laboratory finds persistently abnormal cells or pre-cancerous (dyskaryotic) or cancerous cells, the woman will be asked to attend hospital for a colposcopy, an out-patient procedure involving the use of a magnifying instrument to view the cervix. Small

The equipment used for a smear test consists of a speculum, spatulas, a fixative and slides and containers for preserving samples for testing.

biopsies of cervical tissue may be taken and sent for laboratory examination.

CONFIRMING THE DIAGNOSIS
More advanced cancer of the cervix is not diagnosed reliably by a smear test, but the diagnosis may be suspected when the cervix is viewed through a speculum. Colposcopy and biopsy may therefore be needed to confirm the diagnosis and determine the extent of the disease.

Further tests may be conducted, including: blood tests, X-rays, an ultrasound examination and CT (computed tomography) or MR (magnetic resonance) imaging scans. In some cases, a pelvic examination under anaesthetic (EUA) may also be required.

A photograph may be taken of the cervix (cervicography). This enables the image to be examined by a specialist.

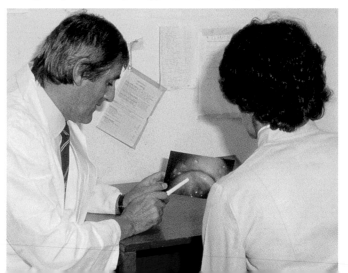

Causes and prognosis

Risk factors for cervical cancer include having sexual intercourse, having sexual intercourse at an early age and having several sexual partners. These all expose the cervix to the risk of infection with the human papilloma (wart) virus (HPV). HPV infection does not always lead to cervical cancer, but infection with a type 16 strain of HPV is an important risk factor. Some women appear to have an increased genetic susceptibility to cervical cancer. Smoking and conditions that affect the immune system also increase the risk.

The outlook for women with cervical cancer depends on the stage of their disease. Cervical cancer can often be very successfully treated in its early stages, before it has spread to the lymph system. If the cancer has spread, however, the outlook is less favourable.

Only about 65 per cent of women treated for advanced cervical cancer will survive for five years.

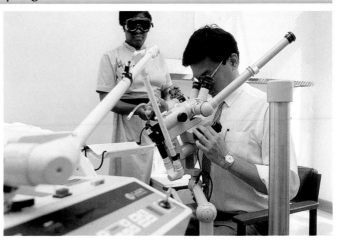

A gynaecologist uses a laser to treat cervical cancer. This can be effective in the very early stages of the disease.

Stages of cancer of the cervix

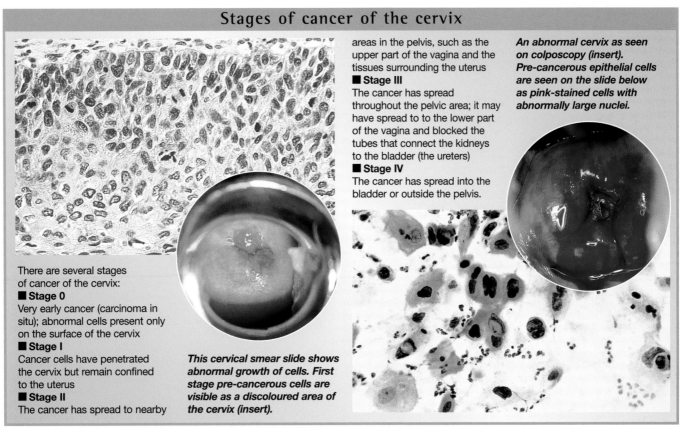

There are several stages of cancer of the cervix:
■ **Stage 0**
Very early cancer (carcinoma in situ); abnormal cells present only on the surface of the cervix
■ **Stage I**
Cancer cells have penetrated the cervix but remain confined to the uterus
■ **Stage II**
The cancer has spread to nearby

This cervical smear slide shows abnormal growth of cells. First stage pre-cancerous cells are visible as a discoloured area of the cervix (insert).

areas in the pelvis, such as the upper part of the vagina and the tissues surrounding the uterus
■ **Stage III**
The cancer has spread throughout the pelvic area; it may have spread to to the lower part of the vagina and blocked the tubes that connect the kidneys to the bladder (the ureters)
■ **Stage IV**
The cancer has spread into the bladder or outside the pelvis.

An abnormal cervix as seen on colposcopy (insert). Pre-cancerous epithelial cells are seen on the slide below as pink-stained cells with abnormally large nuclei.

Incidence

Cancer of the cervix is rare below the age of 25, but the incidence rises until the age of about 54, when it peaks and then levels off. The disease kills about 7500 women in the European Union each year, and is responsible for two per cent of all cancer deaths.

The effectiveness of cervical screening in reducing the incidence of cervical cancer has been shown in several countries. In the UK, it is estimated that screening for cervical cancer has reduced deaths due to the disease by over 60 per cent in women under the age of 55. In Sweden, where cancer of the cervix was once the third most common cancer in women in their early 60s, it has now fallen to 14th place.

A nurse places a specimen of cells, taken during a smear test on a slide. Screening for abnormal cells has reduced the incidence of cervical cancer.

Treatment

The treatment of cervical cancer will vary according to the stage at which the disease is diagnosed. Surgical removal of the womb (hysterectomy) and radiotherapy may be necessary if the cancer has progressed beyond its very earliest stage.

Recent research suggests that the effectiveness of radiotherapy may be increased if the patient is also treated with the effective anti-cancer drug, cisplatin. Antibiotics may also be needed to improve the patient's general condition, and treating underlying or associated problems, such as anaemia, may help to improve response to treatment.

Cervical smear tests

One of the greatest advances in the prevention of cervical cancer was the establishment of a regular screening programme. Cervical smear tests allow the detection of abnormal or precancerous cells in the cervix.

Working in the United States in the 1940s, Dr G. N. Papanicolaou developed a method of staining cells taken from the vagina and cervix so that the maturity of the cells could be examined histologically (under a microscope). It was noticed that immature-looking cells were associated with the subsequent development of cervical cancer. From this pioneering work, the modern cervical smear test (or 'Pap' test, as it is known in the United Sates) was developed.

NATIONAL SCREENING PROGRAMME

The examination of stained cells from the cervix has been carried out in Britain since the 1960s, but an organized national screening programme was not established until 1988. At that time, less than 50 per cent of eligible women had been tested, and the number of cases of cervical cancer was increasing, particularly in young women.

Before 1988, population screening in places such as British Columbia and Iceland had been linked to a reduction in new cases of cervical cancers. With this knowledge, the

The collection of cervical cells during a smear test is a painless procedure. The nurse or doctor taking the smear keeps the woman relaxed and comfortable.

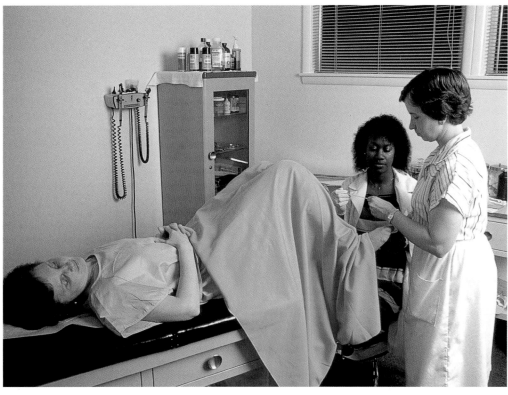

National Health Service began inviting women for testing at regular intervals of 3–5 years after their 20th birthday. The reason for this timescale is that it takes an average of seven years for normal cervical tissue to progress to an invasive cancer, and this is only likely to develop in women over 20.

Screening stops at 64 in England and Wales, and 60 in Scotland.

The percentage of population screened closely mirrors the numbers of lives saved, and GPs are now given an incentive payment if more than 80 per cent of the eligible women on their list of patients have been screened in the previous five

The regular smear test has been instrumental in reducing the number of deaths from cervical cancer. Most women are tested every three to five years.

years. Since 1988, the number of deaths from cervical cancer in England and Wales has fallen by 50 per cent.

Equipment

The equipment used for performing cervical smears is of a standard design and differs little wherever the test is performed. It consists of:
■ A bivalve Cusco's speculum made of stainless steel or plastic to hold open the vagina during the examination. The speculum is coated in lubricating jelly and inserted in the closed position. It may then be opened to allow examination of the cervix.
■ A disposable wooden spatula is used to harvest the cells from the surface of the cervix and the cervical opening into the uterus.
■ Glass slides, onto which the cellular material from the cervix is spread from the spatula. They are then sprayed with a fixative.

The speculum is shown in the closed position. To the right are wooden spatulas and a tube of lubricating jelly. The two bottles contain fixative.

INVITATIONS FOR SCREENING

The NHS has a register of almost the entire population of the UK, listed by sex and date of birth. This register is used by district health authorities to produce lists each month of women in each GP practice area who are due to have a smear test. Individual GPs check this list against their own records in order to update addresses and other details, and to discount those women who have had a total hysterectomy (and thus no longer have a cervix) or are past the testing age limit.

A letter is sent out to every eligible woman at her home address, informing her that she is due for a smear test, along with a leaflet explaining the procedure. The invitation letter may include an appointment date and time, or give a telephone number for the woman to ring in order to make an appointment.

Most smear tests are carried out in GP surgeries, but women may opt to have the test at their family planning clinic, or other health centre. Having the test performed by a female nurse or doctor should always be possible if the woman so requests.

HAVING THE TEST

At the clinic, basic identification details are recorded, and the nurse or doctor performing the test asks the date of the woman's last period and whether she has had any treatment to the cervix or previous abnormal tests.

Cervical cancer is associated with sexual intercourse, so although all women over 20 are invited, only those who are sexually active need to be tested. Women who have never had

The sample of cervical cells is spread evenly onto a glass slide. The slide is covered in a fixative spray for preservation, and sent to the laboratory for analysis.

Speculum insertion into the vagina

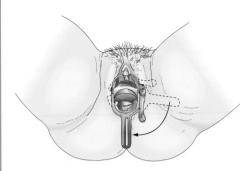

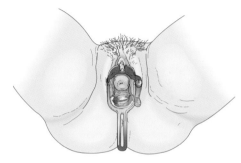

Pubic bone
Bladder
Uterus
Cervix
Anus

STEP ONE
The closed speculum is held under a stream of warm water, and coated in lubricating jelly. It is then introduced gently into the vaginal opening and rotated 90°.

STEP TWO
The speculum is in place when it has been inserted along the length of the vagina and its blades are aligned along the anterior and posterior (front and back) walls.

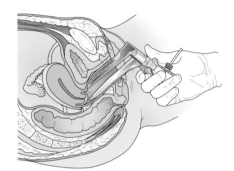

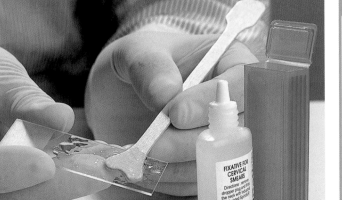

STEP THREE
Using the mechanism in the handle, the speculum is hinged open. Any necessary adjustments are made and the blades are locked in place. This allows access to and visualization of the upper vagina and cervix.

STEP FOUR
The person taking the smear directs a suitable source of illumination through the speculum and on to the cervix. The surface can be examined and the sample is taken with the spatula. Once this is done, the speculum is withdrawn.

intercourse are at little or no risk of cervical cancer and may not need to be screened.

Once the woman's details have been recorded on the request form for the laboratory, the smear will be taken. The woman is asked to remove clothing below the waist, although a loose-fitting skirt may be left on.

She then lies down on an examination couch so that the speculum can be introduced into her vagina to expose the cervix, which is situated at the top of the vagina. The person taking the smear directs a bright light on to the cervix so that a good view is obtained.

A scrape of cells is taken from around and just inside the os (opening of the cervix into the uterus) with a standard sampling device, the bifid (divided-end) wooden spatula. Only cells from this area of the cervix are appropriate, because this is the

site where malignant disease will develop.

Once the cell sample has been taken, it is spread thinly and evenly from the spatula onto three prepared glass microscope slides, which are labelled with the woman's details. The cells are preserved by coating the slide in a fixative solution.

The slides are then dispatched to the histopathological laboratory for cytological (cellular) microscopic analysis.

Notification of results

After the test, the woman is told when she can expect to receive the results and how this will be notified to her. She is informed that the smear may need to be repeated if the laboratory is unable to assess the first sample. She will be assured that the purpose of the smear test is to detect cell changes that may lead to cancer in the future, not a test for cancer, and that she should not be overly concerned if the result is abnormal.

Once the health authority has been informed by the laboratory that the smear test has been processed and the results sent to the woman's GP, it sends a letter to the woman.

To ensure that all eligible women are tested, a health authority that does not receive a test result for a woman within a set time will send her another invitation letter as a reminder that a test is due and her attendance is required.

Treating cervical cancer

Once cervical cancer has been diagnosed, treatment depends on the
stage of the cancer and the extent to which it has spread.
The treatment options available include surgery and radiotherapy.

The treatment of cervical cancer
depends on the extent of the
disease as defined by the FIGO
staging system.

TREATMENT OF CIN
If CIN is confirmed, it is usually
treated by local excision or
destructive treatment (laser,
cryosurgery, electrocoagulation).
If CIN 3 is untreated, it may
progress to invasive cancer.
Effective treatment of high-
grade CIN significantly reduces
the risk of progression to
invasive cancer. However, the
risk remains higher than for the
general population and careful
follow-up is indicated for at
least five years after treatment.

MICROINVASIVE DISEASE
Patients with microinvasive
disease may be managed with
a cone biopsy (removal of the
central portion of the cervix).
If excision of the lesion is
complete on microscopic
examination of the tissue, no
further treatment is needed.

*There is abnormal bleeding and
ulceration around the os
(opening) of this cervix. Such
a lesion would be further
investigated by colposcopy
before treatment.*

SYMPTOMS OF INVASIVE CANCER
Common symptoms of invasive
cervical cancer include:
■ Bleeding – this may occur
after sex (post-coital), in-
between periods (intermenstrual)
or after the menopause (post-
menopausal)
■ Offensive vaginal discharge.
  Pain normally does not occur
until the advanced stages of
the disease.

*Laser surgery via a colposcope
may be used to treat cervical
intraepithelial neoplasia (CIN).
The areas of abnormality are
visualized first with staining.*

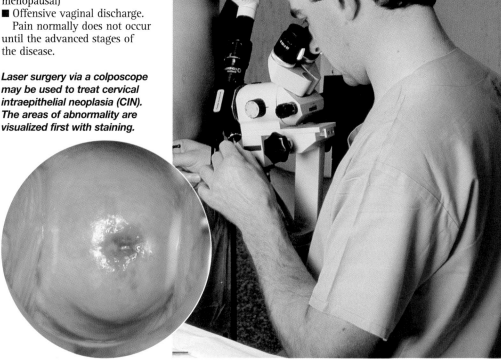

Surgery for invasive cervical cancer

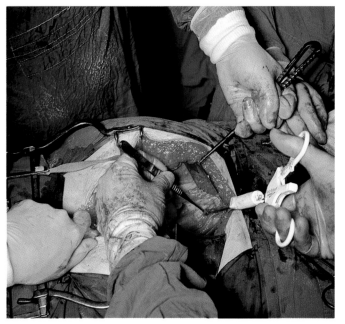

Patients with stage Ib to IIa
disease may be offered either
surgery or radiotherapy.
These have identical cure rates.

HYSTERECTOMY
Surgery is the treatment of
choice for young, fit women
since it offers the following
advantages:
■ Avoidance of vaginal scarring
and shortening by radiotherapy
■ Retention of ovarian function
– the disease does not spread
to the ovaries and so they are
not removed
■ Avoidance of the small risk
of a late, radiation-induced
second malignancy.

*Total hysterectomy will usually
be offered to women who have
cervical cancer that has not
spread beyond the cervix and
upper vagina.*

Surgery for cervical cancer
involves a radical hysterectomy
and pelvic node dissection.
Cervical cancer tends to spread
into the tissues around the
uterus and vagina. It may also
spread through the blood into
nodes such as those that lie
alongside the major arteries to
the pelvis.

AIMS OF SURGERY
Surgery for malignant cancer
aims to remove the cancer and
a margin of normal tissue. Thus
a radical hysterectomy involves
removal of the cervix, uterus,
parametrial tissues (adjacent to
uterus) and a cuff of vagina.
The pelvic lymph nodes are also
removed. The para-aortic nodes
may be biopsied. Patients with
lymph node metastasis or
tumour at surgical margins will
require adjuvant radiotherapy.

Fertility-preserving surgery

Young patients who have not given birth, who have small-volume disease up to stage Ib and who wish to retain their fertility, may be offered a radical trachelectomy.

This is a relatively new technique, in which the cervix is excised with a zone of paracervical (around the cervix) tissue and a cuff of vagina. The remaining part of the vagina is connected to the body of the uterus and a stitch is inserted into the lower end of the uterus to maintain competence during pregnancy. Pelvic lymph node dissection may be carried out laparoscopically. If pregnancy occurred, the woman would be monitored carefully for threatened miscarriage and delivery is by Caesarean section.

It must be explained to patients that this is a relatively new technique and that the standard treatment remains radical hysterectomy.

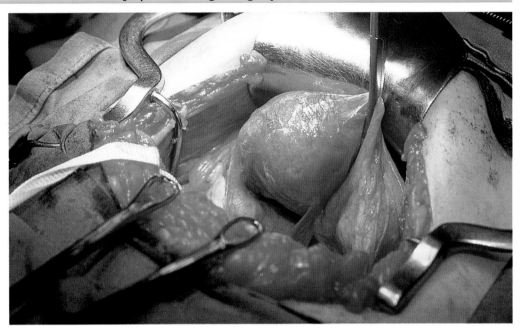

In a hysterectomy, the uterus is removed, making the patient infertile. New techniques that preserve fertility may be offered to young women who have not had children.

Radiotherapy

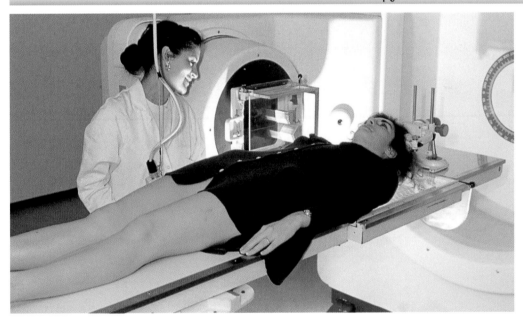

Radiotherapy almost always destroys ovarian function in pre-menopausal women. These women should thus be offered hormone replacement therapy.

The aim of radiotherapy is to treat the tumour and the areas at risk of cancer spread. Radical radiotherapy may be offered to women with stage I or IIa disease who are unfit for surgery and to women with more advanced disease.

SIDE EFFECTS
Radiotherapy has side effects, which include:
■ Loose, more frequent stools
■ Frequency and urgency of urination
■ Dryness and shortening of the vagina – this may lead to dyspareunia (painful intercourse).

COMBINATION THERAPY
Recent studies have shown that the combination of radiotherapy and chemotherapy (the use of drugs to treat cancer) with cisplatin, a platinum-based drug, achieves results superior to those of radiotherapy alone.

Prognosis

The prognosis for cervical cancer patients depends mainly on the stage that the cancer has reached by the time of treatment. If the cancer has spread to the lymph nodes, the five-year survival rate will be reduced by half for each FIGO stage.

Involvement of para-aortic lymph nodes is a marker for widespread dissemination, and very few patients are alive five years after diagnosis.

Lymphovascular space involvement (tumour in blood or lymphatic vessels) is of prognostic significance in that it is an indicator of probable lymphatic involvement.

The histological differentiation of the tumour – that is, how similar in appearance the tumour is to the native tissue – is also significant. Poorly differentiated tumours carry a worse prognosis than well differentiated tumours.

STAGE	DEGREE OF LOCAL INVASION	FIVE-YEAR SURVIVAL
I	Confined to Cervix	90 per cent
II	Invasion of upper part of cervix or adjacent tissues	75 per cent
III	Spread to pelvic side wall, lower vagina or ureters	30 per cent
IV	Invasion of rectum, bladder wall and/or beyond pelvis	10 per cent

Ovarian cancer

Ovarian cancer is the fifth most common cancer affecting women. The disease can remain undetected in a large number of women until the latter stages of the disease.

Malignant ovarian tumours account for 5000 deaths in women every year in the UK and 6000 new cases are diagnosed each year.

OVARIAN TUMOURS
Ovarian tumours are classified according to the cell type from which they originate. Tumours may be solid or cystic, benign (non-cancerous) or malignant (cancerous). Many ovarian tumours produce active hormones.

WHO IS AT RISK?
Ovarian cancer is more common in those women who:
■ Are over the age of 50, especially those who are nulliparous (have never had a child) or have had pregnancies after the age of 30. Ovarian cancer affects 1 in 2500 women over the age of 55, and 1 in 3800 over 25
■ Have previously developed cancer of the uterus, breast, colon or rectum
■ Have a long fertile period (start menstruating early and undergo a late menopause)
■ Undergo IVF treatment, involving superovulation therapy (hyperstimulation of the ovaries), although this is controversial
■ Belong to blood group A
■ Have genetic abnormalities. In 50 per cent of ovarian cancers, a mutation (spontaneous fault) in the p53 tumour suppressor gene can be identified. This gene would normally act to prevent ovarian cancer from developing.

FAMILY HISTORY
About three per cent of ovarian cancers have been found to be due to problems in the inherited gene BRCA1, which is also implicated in breast cancer. Where there is a strong family history of ovarian or breast cancer, it may be possible to test for the faulty BRCA1 gene in an affected living relative. Other family members may then be similarly tested. It must be emphasized that, even with the faulty gene, it does not follow that ovarian cancer will develop.

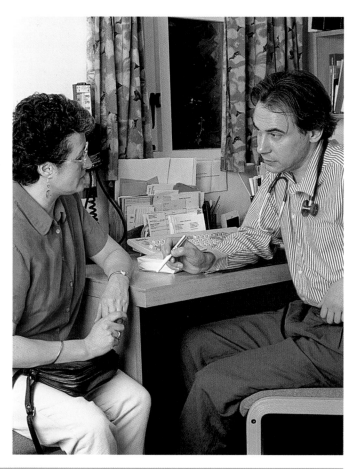

Ovarian cancer involves the growth of a malignant tumour in one or both ovaries. The cancer occurs more frequently in post-menopausal women.

Clinical features

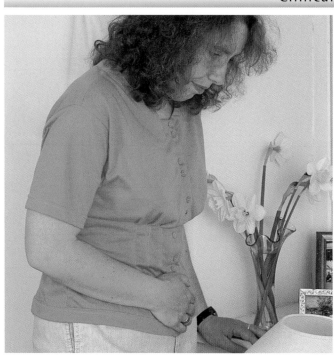

Symptoms of ovarian cancer include swelling and discomfort in the lower abdomen. Pain is very rare, however, and the cancer often goes undetected.

Ovarian cancer may remain undetected in a large number of women until a late stage of the disease. This is because there are often either no symptoms or only a few symptoms, which may be easily overlooked.

If the cancer is left untreated, it may spread to other organs in the body – for example, the lungs or the liver.

SYMPTOMS
In cases when symptoms of ovarian cancer do occur, these may include:
■ Discomfort in the lower abdomen
■ Nausea
■ Swelling of the abdomen caused by the tumour or ascites (fluid accumulating in the peritoneal cavity)
■ Frequent need to pass urine, due to external pressure on the bladder
■ Erratic menstruation, sudden appearance of excess body hair and a deepening voice – these symptoms are caused by the hormonal secretion of some tumours
■ Swollen ankles, caused by pressure on the pelvic veins leading to venous congestion
■ Malaise
■ Loss of appetite
■ Weight loss
■ Dyspareunia (deep pain as a result of intercourse)
■ Increasing constipation, due to pressure on the bowel.

Women suffering from any of the above symptoms should seek prompt advice from their doctor. It is important to point out, however, that most will not have ovarian cancer.

Diagnosing ovarian cancer

Ovarian cancer can be difficult to diagnose because the position of the ovaries allows them to enlarge without pressing on other organs. Blood tests, imaging techniques and laparoscopy can all be used to confirm diagnosis

After examination by the doctor, a number of different techniques may be utilized to diagnose ovarian cancer. These tests help to stage the tumour, which assists in determining treatment.

BLOOD TESTS
If ovarian cancer is suspected, the doctor may arrange for a CA125 blood test. If high levels of CA125 are detected, a pelvic ultrasound scan may be performed. Other blood tests (full blood count, kidney and liver function tests) can indicate whether the cancer has spread.

In addition to these tests, a fuller assessment by a consultant in hospital is usually needed. A vaginal (and possibly rectal) examination is performed.

IMAGING
A CT or MRI scan can give further valuable information about tumour size and spread. If there is any fluid causing swelling of the abdomen, the doctor can remove some using a syringe. The fluid can then be examined under a microscope.

LAPAROSCOPY
A laparoscopy may be necessary. This is a surgical procedure in which a viewing instrument is inserted through the abdominal wall. This allows the ovaries to be examined and a biopsy can be taken for examination.

Sometimes, it is not possible to make a diagnosis unless a laparotomy (an exploratory operation) is performed. This involves making a surgical incision in the abdominal wall to allow direct inspection of the abdominal contents.

HISTOLOGY
A tissue diagnosis is dependent upon microscopic examination of a sample of the tumour. Histology may be carried out on fluid aspirated from a cyst, a biopsy sample or the whole tumour following surgery.

TUMOUR TYPES
Ovarian cancers may originate in the ovary (primary tumour) or elsewhere in the body (metastatic tumours). There are several types of primary tumour, including epithelial (such as adenocarcinoma), germ cell (such as teratoma) or sex cord stromal (such as granulosa cell) tumours.

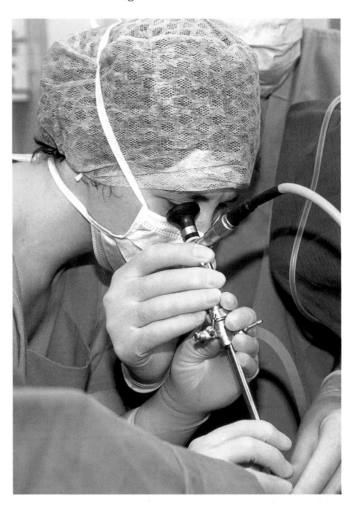

Diagnosis of ovarian cancer can be made using laparoscopy. A viewing instrument is inserted through the abdominal wall to examine the ovaries.

Screening

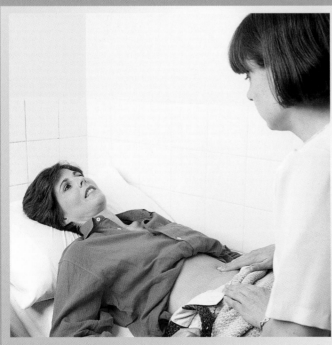

Physical examinations are one way of screening for ovarian cancer. This method is only suitable for the detection of large tumours, however.

Screening can detect early cases of ovarian cancer, although it is useful only if it detects the cancer early enough to make treatment more effective. Ovarian cancer that is confined to the ovary (Stage 1) can usually be successfully treated.

The decision as to whether or not an individual woman should be screened depends on her family history of the disease. As such, it should be reached only after careful discussion with her doctor and/or a genetic counsellor.

Methods
There are three methods used to screen for ovarian cancer:

■ Regular internal examination – this can identify large tumours but even experienced doctors are not able to detect early, small tumours. This method is therefore not effective for early diagnosis
■ CA125 blood test – CA125 is a protein released into the circulation in high levels in most women with ovarian cancer. In addition to screening, the test is valuable in monitoring the response to treatment and in detecting recurrence
■ Ultrasound scanning – in ovarian cancer, the ovaries increase in size and their structure looks abnormal, although some benign conditions may also look suspicious on an ultrasound scan.

Scans can be performed by placing a probe on the abdomen, but better pictures can often be obtained by inserting the probe into the vagina.

Treating ovarian cancer

The treatment of ovarian cancer is dependent on the type, stage and grade of the tumour, and the patient's level of health. Treatment options include surgery, chemotherapy and radiotherapy.

The type of treatment offered to a woman with ovarian cancer depends on the stage the tumour has reached. Other factors affecting treatment include the type and grade of tumour and the patient's general health.

The type of tumour is determined after examination under the microscope. The grade of the tumour is referred to as low, intermediate or high, depending on how aggressively the tumour grows and spreads (low-grade tumours have a better outlook than high-grade tumours). Secondary tumours, usually from a primary cancer in the stomach or breast, may spread to the ovaries.

One type of ovarian cancer is an adenocarcinoma, shown here under the microscope. The cancerous cells are seen growing in irregular shapes.

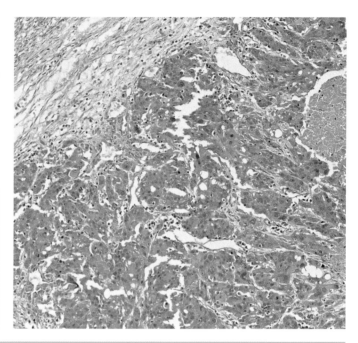

Stage	Features
1	Confined to the ovary
2	Spread to the pelvis
3	Spread to the abdominal cavity
4	Distant spread, such as to liver/lungs

Surgery

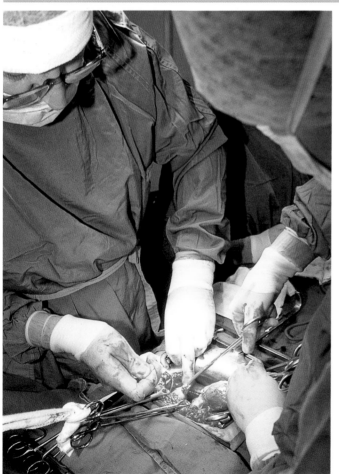

All patients who have operable disease will be offered surgery, which aims to remove as much of the tumour as possible. A total abdominal hysterectomy is performed; the uterus is removed through an abdominal incision along with the uterine (fallopian) tubes and both ovaries.

OMENTECTOMY
An omentectomy (removal of the sheet of tissue covering the abdominal organs) is also performed. All other abdominal contents and the lymph glands are inspected, and biopsies are taken of suspicious areas.

Surgery, involving a hysterectomy, is the mainstay of treatment for ovarian cancer. The uterus is removed through an incision in the abdomen.

In patients with stage 1 disease, a normal CT scan following surgery and normal CA125 levels, no further treatment is needed. However, they will be closely monitored with regular CT or ultrasound scans and CA125 tests.

ADVANCED CASES
In those patients who have more advanced cancers, adjuvant (additional or supplementary) therapy, such as chemotherapy and radiotherapy, is given. Following such treatment, these patients are closely monitored.

A cancerous ovary (left, black) can be seen in these female reproductive organs, excised during a hysterectomy. The normal ovary is shown right.

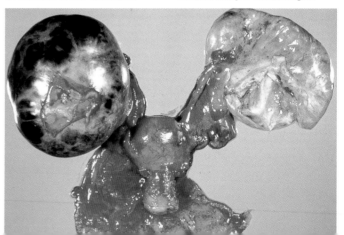

Chemotherapy

For patients with stage 2 and 3 disease, courses of intravenous drugs that kill residual cancer cells (chemotherapy) are offered following surgery. Until recently, this treatment consisted of one of the platinum drugs – either cisplatin or carboplatin.

Recently, a new drug called paclitaxel has been introduced. This drug, in combination with one of the platinum drugs, has been found to prolong survival by up to one year.

The combination is associated with a greater occurrence of side effects, but the quality of life is equivalent to that when the platinum drugs are used alone. The combination of the two drugs is given for a minimum of six cycles at monthly intervals.

With modern chemotherapy, overall five-year survival figures can be up to 50 per cent for more advanced cases. However, the side effects of the drugs can be unpleasant and are potentially dangerous.

ADVANCED CASES
For stage 4 disease, the prognosis is poor, which means that treatment is often not indicated. However, if the patient's general condition is good, a course of chemotherapy may be tried.

Most cases of ovarian cancer are treated with chemotherapy. Multiple anti-cancer drugs are administered to patients via intravenous cannulae.

Recurrence

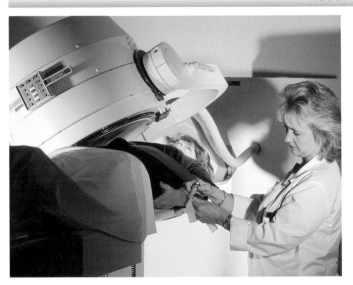

If ovarian cancer recurs after treatment, or has spread widely at the time of diagnosis, the prospect of cure is remote. Treatment is then directed at ensuring a good quality of life.

When initial surgery has been carried out, it is unusual to perform a second operation. If the patient has not been offered combination chemotherapy, this may now be considered. Other chemotherapy drugs, such as topotecan or etoposide, are sometimes prescribed.

Radiotherapy may be useful in easing the symptoms of advanced cancer. However, radiotherapy is not a cure for ovarian cancer.

PALLIATIVE CARE
Radiotherapy is not usually used as a curative treatment, but it can be helpful in reducing the size of large pelvic tumours or in controlling bleeding from a tumour that has invaded the vagina. Where there is pain from bony spread, radiotherapy can give valuable pain relief.

Fluid that accumulates in the abdominal cavity (ascites) can make the patient feel very uncomfortable but can be drained off when required. Doctors and nurses with special expertise in palliative care can help maximize both pain and symptom control. Their role becomes increasingly important in advanced disease.

Developments in treatment

A number of new treatments are currently being investigated, and it is hoped that these will both increase the chance of cure and prolong survival.

Maintenance chemotherapy
Clinical trials are in progress to investigate the concept of maintenance chemotherapy. It is thought that low doses of the drugs, administered for a prolonged period after the initial six cycles, could be more successful than conventional chemotherapy in increasing survival rates.

Intraperitoneal therapy (injecting a solution of a chemotherapy drug into the peritoneal cavity) is another method of giving chemotherapy. It is hoped that this will be as effective as intravenous therapy, but with fewer side effects.

A drug (marimastat) belonging to the group known as matrix metalloprotease inhibitors has been found to significantly slow down the rate of rise of CA125 in advanced cases. It is not yet known whether this drug treatment increases survival rates.

Other therapies
Monoclonal antibody (antibody produced artificially from a cell clone) therapy has been investigated as a treatment. Trials are due to start on the drug theragyn, which, in earlier studies, significantly increased five-year survival compared to best standard therapy.

Intraperitoneal chemotherapy is a relatively new treatment. It involves instilling the drugs directly into the patient's peritoneal cavity.

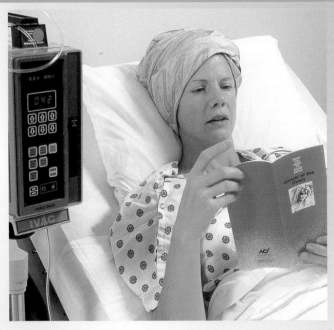

Endometrial cancer

Cancers of the uterus usually affect post-menopausal women.
The most common cancers are those of the endometrium
(uterine lining), and tend to occur in women over the age of 50.

The uterus, or womb, is made up of two main elements:
■ The myometrium (muscular wall)
■ The endometrium (lining).
Cancer can occur in either of these areas, although endometrial cancer is far more common than cancer of the myometrium (uterine sarcoma).

PREVALENCE
Endometrial cancer is relatively common in the developed world. It has a high incidence in Caucasian populations of western Europe and North America; it is the most common gynaecological cancer in North America, although in England and Wales it occurs less frequently than ovarian and cervical cancer. It is uncommon in Asian women.

AGE AT DIAGNOSIS
Endometrial cancer is a disease of post-menopausal women, with over 90 per cent of women aged 50 years and over at diagnosis. Less than five per cent of women diagnosed with this cancer are under 40 years old.

Location of the endometrium

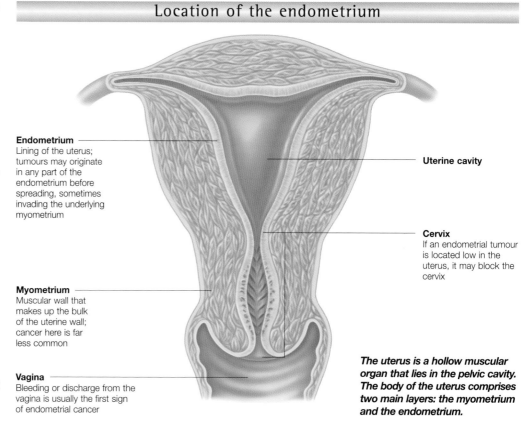

Endometrium
Lining of the uterus; tumours may originate in any part of the endometrium before spreading, sometimes invading the underlying myometrium

Uterine cavity

Cervix
If an endometrial tumour is located low in the uterus, it may block the cervix

Myometrium
Muscular wall that makes up the bulk of the uterine wall; cancer here is far less common

Vagina
Bleeding or discharge from the vagina is usually the first sign of endometrial cancer

The uterus is a hollow muscular organ that lies in the pelvic cavity. The body of the uterus comprises two main layers: the myometrium and the endometrium.

Risk factors for endometrial cancer

Various factors are associated with endometrial cancer, such as:
■ **Anovulatory cycles**
An anovulatory cycle is a menstrual cycle in which an ovum (egg) fails to be released and so progesterone is not produced. The endometrium is therefore exposed to oestrogen alone for the whole of the cycle.

If this occurs frequently, the endometrium becomes hyperplastic (thickened), increasing the risk of endometrial cancer.

Anovulatory cycles are common at the time of the menarche (start of menstruation) and before the menopause. Early menarche or delayed menopause

may increase the number of anovulatory cycles experienced and thus increase the risk of developing endometrial cancer.

■ **Oestrogen**
In hormone replacement therapy, a patient is rarely treated with oestrogen without progestogen therapy also being administered, because of the known risk of endometrial cancer. If a woman has had a hysterectomy, progestogens are unnecessary.

■ **Tamoxifen therapy**
The drug tamoxifen, widely used to treat breast cancer, has weak oestrogen-like effects on the female genital tract.

Patients receiving tamoxifen need careful monitoring and any abnormal vaginal bleeding should be investigated promptly,

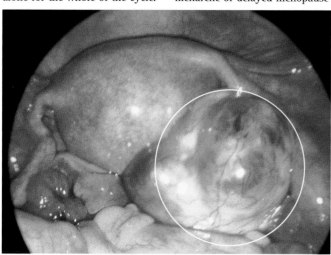

A grossly enlarged ovary (circled) is visible here. This is due to polycystic ovarian syndrome, which carries an increased risk of endometrial cancer.

as they are at increased risk of developing endometrial cancer.

■ **Polycystic ovarian syndrome**
This syndrome is associated with prolonged periods of anovulation. Without appropriate management, the syndrome will lead to an increased risk of developing endometrial cancer.

■ **Obesity**
Peripheral body fat contains an enzyme, aromatase, that converts androgens (male sex hormones), produced by the adrenal glands, to oestrogen.

The greater the body weight, the greater the peripheral conversion of androgens to oestrogen. Thus, endometrial cancer is more common in obese post-menopausal women.

■ **Other risk factors**
The risk of endometrial cancer is also increased in women of low parity (who have had few or no children) and those with high blood pressure or diabetes.

Symptoms and signs of endometrial cancer

The most common symptom of endometrial cancer that patients see their doctor with is abnormal vaginal bleeding. This may occur:

■ Between periods (intermenstrual bleeding)
■ After the menopause (post-menopausal bleeding)
■ After sex (post-coital bleeding).

As most women with endometrial cancer are over 50 years old, post-menopausal bleeding is the symptom most frequently experienced.

Women may also have a yellow vaginal discharge that may be due to pyometra (an infection that causes the uterine cavity to fill with pus).

ADVANCED DISEASE
Rarely, there may be symptoms of advanced or metastatic disease, such as shortness of breath secondary to lung metastasis (spread). Occasionally, symptomatic anaemia – due to prolonged bleeding – may be the first indication of disease.

Endometrial cancer generally affects post-menopausal women. Women who experience unusual vaginal bleeding should report it to their doctor.

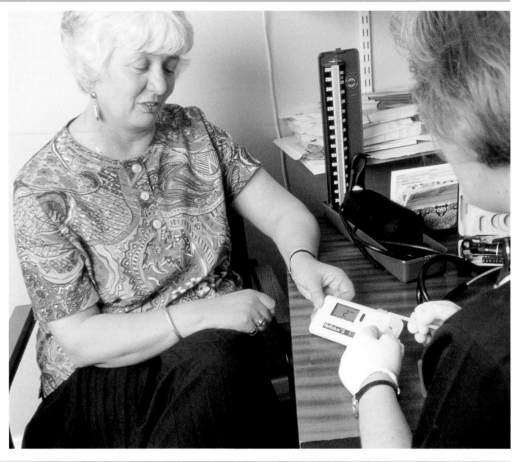

Investigations

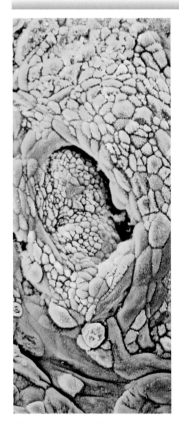

This micrograph shows an adenocarcinoma of the endometrium. The cancer cells appear large and brown, and are invading the uterus surface.

Although there are several causes of post-menopausal bleeding, all women with this symptom must be investigated to exclude endometrial cancer.

Atrophic vaginitis (thinning of the vaginal tissues that occurs with age and oestrogen withdrawal), endometrial polyps or alterations in hormone replacement therapy (HRT) regimens may cause bleeding, but there is a 10–20 per cent risk of endometrial cancer, particularly with increasing age.

TESTS
In addition to a careful clinical examination, the most important tests are:

■ Transvaginal scan of the pelvis. The purpose of the scan is to measure the thickness of the endometrium. The risk of endometrial cancer is almost negligible if the endometrial thickness is less than 5mm (about ³/₁₆ in).

■ Biopsy of the endometrium. An endometrial biopsy can be obtained in the out-patient clinic with a number of devices designed to sample or aspirate (draw out by suction) cells from the endometrium.

If this procedure is poorly tolerated or fails to yield sufficient material for diagnosis, a hysteroscopy (examination of the interior of the uterus) should be carried out. A small endoscope is used to inspect the endometrium for any obvious areas of abnormality, which are then sampled.

PREPARING FOR SURGERY
Once a diagnosis of endometrial cancer is established, investigations are tailored towards ensuring that the woman is fit for surgery.

A full blood count is performed to exclude anaemia, and electrocardiogram examinations and chest X-ray often indicated. Magnetic resonance (MR) scanning may be used to determine the depth of myometrial invasion, but there is no good evidence that this contributes to the subsequent management of the cancer.

A hysteroscopy examination allows a gynaecologist to investigate the inside of the uterus. A fibre-optic endoscope is inserted through the cervix.

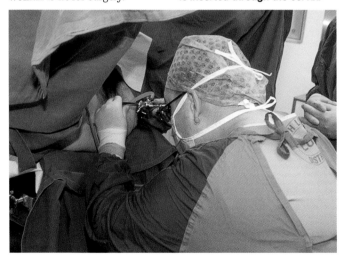

Managing endometrial cancer

Surgery is the mainstay of treatment for endometrial cancer; radiotherapy also plays an important role as primary radical treatment, as an adjunct to surgery and for relief of symptoms.

The majority of endometrial cancers are adenocarcinomas – cancers that arise from the glandular elements of the endometrium. The commonest uterine adenocarcinomas, accounting for 90 per cent of tumours, are endometrioid – that is, they closely resemble the native endometrium.

DIFFERENTIATED TUMOURS
Sometimes the cells within the cancer can change their microscopic appearance from glandular epithelium to squamous (skinlike) epithelium, a phenomenon known as squamous differentiation.

Such differentiated tumours (adenoacanthomas) are found in 20–25 per cent of endometrioid tumours and carry a similar prognosis to pure endometrioid tumours. More rarely, the squamous element may be malignant (adenosquamous carcinoma).

In endometrial cancer, the patient's prognosis will depend on the type of tumour. This can be gauged by microscopic examination of cancerous cells.

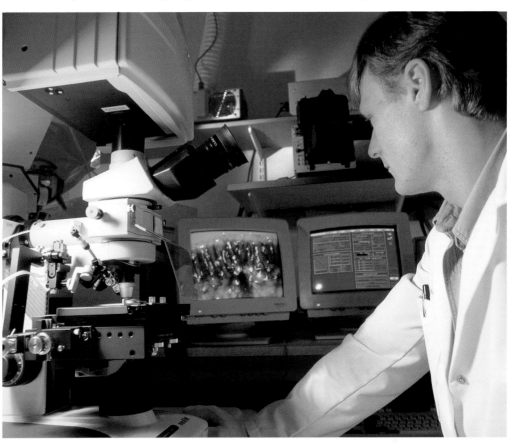

Grades and stages of cancer

The differentiation of the tumour (the extent to which it resembles the native epithelium) has a bearing on the prognosis for the patient.

Three grades of endometrial cancer differentiation are recognized. Grade 1, or well differentiated tumours, are almost identical to the normal endometrium and carry a good prognosis. Grade 3 or poorly differentiated tumours, however, have a poor outlook. Moderately differentiated tumours come between these two extremes.

METASTASIS
Endometrial cancer can spread to other parts of the genital tract and to distant sites via the blood or lymphatic system. The degree of spread (stage of the disease) is classified by the International Federation of Gynaecology and Obstetrics (FIGO).

The degree of differentiation and stage of the cancer affect treatment options. A full hysterectomy will need to be carried out in many cases.

Staging endometrial cancer

The degree of spread of the disease has been classified by FIGO as follows:
STAGE I
Endometrial cancer is confined to the body of the uterus
■ **Stage IA:** tumour limited to endometrium
■ **Stage IB:** invasion to less than one half of the myometrium
■ **Stage IC:** invasion to more than one half of the myometrium
STAGE II
Endometrial cancer involves the uterus and the cervix, but has not extended outside the uterus
■ **Stage IIA:** endocervical glandular involvement only
■ **Stage IIB:** cervical stromal (connective tissue) invasion

STAGE III
Endometrial cancer extends outside the uterus but is confined to the true pelvis
■ **Stage IIIA:** tumour invades serosa (smooth membrane) and/or adjoining parts and/or peritoneum
■ **Stage IIIB:** vaginal metastases
■ **Stage IIIC:** metastases to pelvic and/or para-aortic lymph nodes
STAGE IV
Endometrial cancer involves the bladder or bowel mucosa or has metastasized to distant sites
■ **Stage IVA:** tumour invasion of bladder and/or bowel mucosa
■ **Stage IVB:** distant metastases, including intra-abdominal and/or inguinal (groin) lymph nodes

Treating endometrial cancer

Treatment options for endometrial cancer depend on the differentiation of the tumour and the degree to which the disease has spread outside the uterine lining.

The treatment of endometrial cancer will depend upon the grade of endometrial cancer differentiation.

SURGERY

Surgery involves the removal of the uterus, including the cervix (total hysterectomy), and both uterine tubes and ovaries (bilateral salpingo-oophorectomy).

Samples from the surrounding pelvic lymph nodes are generally taken for examination under a microscope to see if the disease has spread to other areas.

CHEMOTHERAPY

If cancerous cells are found in the lymph nodes, the patient will undergo chemotherapy. The female hormone progesterone will also be given, which slows down the growth of the cancerous cells.

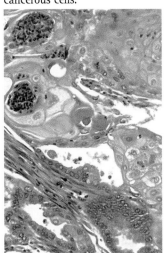

Light micrograph of endometrial cells showing the effects of radiotherapy on endometrial cancer. Cellular changes can be seen in the top left of the image.

RADIOTHERAPY

Women may be offered radiotherapy for three main reasons:
■ Primary radical radiotherapy with curative intent
■ As an adjunct to surgery
■ For palliation (relief) of symptoms.

■ **Primary radical radiotherapy**
Patients with early endometrial cancer who are unfit for surgery may be offered radical radiotherapy. Treatment by primary radiotherapy is associated with a poorer outlook and more side effects than surgical treatment, and every attempt should be made, where possible, to offer surgery.

Radiotherapy is usually given as a combination of external beam and intra-cavitary treatment. Women with large tumours may be given external beam therapy to reduce tumour bulk prior to insertion of intra-cavitary sources of radiation.

Complications of radiotherapy may occur due to radiation damage to adjacent tissues and organs. Thus, irradiation of the gut may manifest itself in diarrhoea and the passage of blood through the rectum – characteristics of radiation enteritis. Radiation cystitis, irritation of the bladder, may give rise to symptoms of

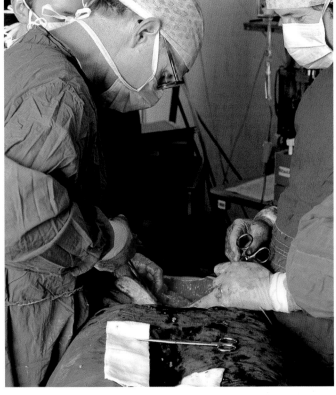

discomfort on passing urine or haematuria (blood in the urine). Symptoms often improve three to six months after the course of radiotherapy is completed.

■ **Adjuvant radiotherapy**
The commonest site for the local recurrence of endometrial cancer is in the vaginal vault (the upper end). To minimize the risk of vault recurrence, those at risk may be offered vault (intra-cavitary) radiotherapy. All patients are at risk except those whose tumours show absent or minimal myometrial spread or those with Grade 1 or 2 histology.

Surgery is the commonest treatment option for endometrial cancer. Patients may also need post-operative chemo- and radiotherapy.

External beam radiotherapy may also be given if there is risk of spread to the pelvic lymph nodes.

■ **Palliative radiotherapy**
The occasional patient who presents with late and incurable endometrial cancer may be offered radiotherapy to improve symptoms. Bleeding, in particular, responds well to radiotherapy.

Outlook for patients

Endometrial cancer has a good prognosis. This is because the majority of patients present with Stage I disease, associated with a five-year survival in more than 90 per cent of cases.

FIGO quotes a 72 per cent five-year survival rate. However, this is not disease-specific and reflects death from other causes in an elderly population with other medical problems.

In patients with positive pelvic nodes, 60 per cent survive for

There is a good prognosis for patients with endometrial cancer. This is because most patients are diagnosed when the disease is at an early stage.

five years or more. In those with advanced disease (which affects less than 10 per cent of women with endometrial cancer), approximately 10 per cent survive for five years or more.

Myometrial cancer

On rare occasions, cancer can occur in the muscular wall of the uterus (myometrium), causing uterine sarcomas. These sarcomas are highly malignant tumours, occurring in two per 100,000 women – and accounting for four per cent of all uterine cancers.

There are several types of uterine sarcoma, but the most common are leiomyosarcomas, accounting for 30–40 per cent of all uterine sarcomas.

Leiomyosarcoma
The majority of smooth muscle tumours in the uterus are benign fibroids, or leiomyomas. The

probability of malignant change in a fibroid is in the order of one in 1000 and only 5–10 per cent of leiomyosarcomas arise in an existing fibroid.

As with endometrial cancer, these tumours are treated surgically, but as spread tends to occur through the blood to distant sites, lymph node sampling is not routinely indicated. Adjuvant radiotherapy may be offered but there is no evidence that this improves survival.

The outlook for patients with these tumours is extremely poor, even for Stage I disease, which is associated with a two-year survival rate of only 45 per cent.

Chemotherapy and radiotherapy

The treatment of cancer largely depends on the type of the cancer in question. Chemotherapy and radiotherapy can be effective when used on their own or in conjunction with other treatments.

Chemotherapy is the treatment of malignant disease (cancer) with groups of anticancer drugs. Radiotherapy uses ionizing radiation to destroy cancerous cells. A combination of the two types of treatment is sometimes used to treat cancer and this is termed chemoradiation.

The techniques and types of equipment that are used for radiotherapy and the drugs prescribed in chemotherapy are constantly being improved as a result of new technology and clinical trials.

COMBINING TREATMENTS

For some types of cancer – for example, the leukaemias – chemotherapy and radiotherapy are the only treatments possible. For many solid tumours, such as breast cancer, patients are given as adjuvant treatment after surgery to prevent a recurrence of the tumour.

Radiotherapy and chemotherapy may be given radically with the aim of long-term control or cure of a tumour. Equally, one or both types of treatment may be offered palliatively to control a tumour for which surgery may not be feasible or to relieve symptoms without expecting any

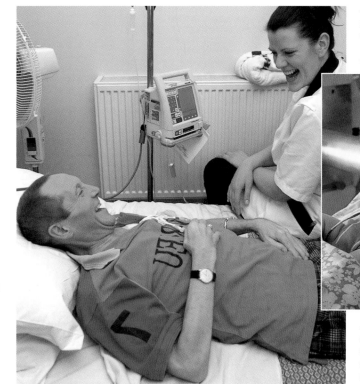

◀ *Improved chemotherapy drugs are more effective at destroying malignant cells. There are fewer side effects and treatment is less unpleasant.*

▲ *Using sophisticated equipment, radiotherapy can be accurately directed at a tumour. Children are usually sedated during the procedure.*

improvement in the survival of the patient. For example, radiotherapy may be used to treat severe pain in a patient with a secondary tumour (metastasis) of the bone.

NO TREATMENT

In people with cancer, there are many different instances when neither chemotherapy nor radiotherapy treatment would be the correct course of action for

the disease. For example, in the case of an inoperable lung cancer that is not causing any distressing symptoms, treatment with its potential side effects would be inappropriate.

The role of the medical oncologist

An oncologist is a doctor who specializes in the medical treatment of cancer. The oncologist will take many factors into account when making decisions about which treatments will most benefit a patient.

Patient assessment

The general health of the patient is carefully assessed and the presence of any other medical problems noted. A frail and

Treatment for cancer is discussed between the patient and the oncologist. The health and wishes of the patient often affect medical decisions.

elderly patient may not tolerate chemotherapy or radiotherapy as well as a younger, fitter patient, and this may affect any decision that an oncologist makes.

Risks and benefits

The stage, type and grade of tumour are all important considerations when planning cancer treatment. The attitude and wishes of the patient and their relatives also have a bearing on the chosen treatment.

Treatment is always a balance of the risks against benefits and the oncologist will point these out to the patient, who is then able to make an informed decision.

Side effects and adverse reactions

Chemotherapy does not usually cause serious long-term health problems. Sometimes, however, it can cause permanent damage to the heart, lungs, nerves, kidneys or reproductive system.

EFFECTS
The side effects of chemotherapy may include:
- Fatigue
- Nausea and vomiting
- Hair loss
- Anaemia (causes fatigue and shortness of breath)
- Problems with the central nervous system, such as confusion and depression
- Infections due to low white cell count
- Blood clotting problems (bruising and bleeding)
- Soreness in the mouth, gums and throat

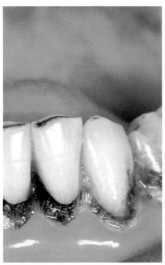

Radiotherapy to the head and neck may lead to dental decay. Side effects vary from person to person and in many cases there is no long-term damage.

- Diarrhoea and constipation.

There are now very effective anti-sickness drugs, which can prevent, or lessen, nausea and vomiting. Drugs are also available that stimulate the production of white blood cells by the bone marrow, and this lowers the risk of serious infection. These drugs, known as colony stimulating factors, also increase the platelet count, which can lessen the risk of bleeding. A hormone called erythropoietin can be given to people with a low red cell count or they may be given a blood transfusion. Many of the other symptoms can also be treated.

RADIOTHERAPY
Radiotherapy may cause both short- and long-term side effects:
- Short-term effects – the skin overlying the treated area can become inflamed and may peel. Treatment to the bowel may lead to diarrhoea and abdominal spasms. If the bladder is irritated by radiation, cystitis-like symptoms can develop. Radiotherapy to the head may lead to dental decay, a sore, dry mouth, poor appetite and weight loss. If the larynx (voice box) is treated, the voice may become hoarse. Hair loss can occur during treatment aimed at the

scalp and, sadly, with radical treatments it is often permanent. Radiotherapy to the chest can irritate the gullet, causing swallowing problems
- Long-term effects – after radical treatment doses, there are some uncommon complications that may present months, and even years, after treatment. The skin can be damaged and scarred. Portions of treated bowel may narrow, perforate or bleed and the irradiated bladder can scar, causing cystitis-type

Radiotherapy is frequently used to treat brain tumours. When directed at the scalp, the radiation can cause hair loss, which is often irreversible.

symptoms, with episodes of haematuria (blood in the urine). A patient who has had radical chest radiotherapy may be left with a permanent dry cough and breathing difficulties. There is a slight risk of inducing a second malignancy, but this is very rare.

Success rate

The success rate of chemo- and radiotherapy depends on the degree of susceptibility of the cancer.
- Leukaemias and lymphomas are very sensitive to chemotherapy. In acute lymphoblastic leukaemia – one of the commonest childhood leukaemias – over 60 per cent survive 10 years in their first remission (when the blood count and bone marrow are normal). in Wilms' tumour (a childhood kidney cancer), the cure rate approaches 90 per cent for stage 2 disease, where the tumour has been excised but extends beyond the kidney capsule. Wilms' tumour is a good example of the combined use of chemo- and radiotherapy
- Tumours of the breast, bowel and ovary are of moderate sensitivity to chemotherapy. In ovarian cancer, chemotherapy

has increased the five-year survival rate for even advanced disease to up to 50 per cent
- Cancer of the cervix is very resistant to chemotherapy. The drugs that have been tried have toxic side effects and this outweighs the benefits. In fact, radiotherapy is a much more successful option
- Localized Hodgkin's disease is usually cured with radiotherapy
- Thyroid cancers – radio-iodine is very successful in treating these type of cancers after surgery has been undertaken.

When cure is not feasible, palliative radiotherapy can prolong life and offer useful symptom relief.

Many cancers in children, such as leukaemias, respond well to radio- and chemotherapy. A course of treatment often results in long-term remission.

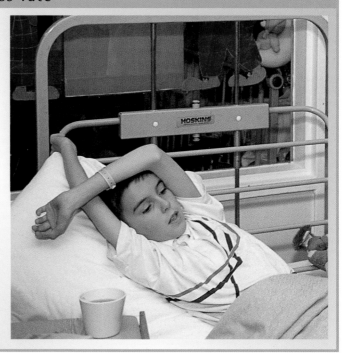

Acne

Acne, medically known as acne vulgaris, is a common condition.
It varies in severity from a few spots to large areas of infected and
inflamed pustules. Most cases readily respond to treatment.

Acne vulgaris, or common acne, is one of the most prevalent skin conditions. While classically affecting teenagers, one in 20 women still has acne at the age of 40. It can occur in children less than one year old, and in people in their 50s and 60s.

Acne is found on the face, which tends to be worst affected, and also the back and chest.

Acne vulgaris is a chronic skin disorder in which there is an overproduction of sebum. Sebum secretion increases with the onset of puberty.

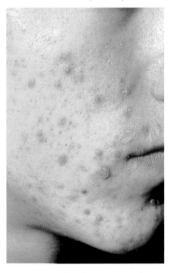

Acne is principally a disorder of the pilosebaceous glands. These glands originate in the deeper levels of the skin and produce an oily substance called sebum, which is emptied through the pores at the head of the glands, onto the skin surface.

HOW ACNE FORMS
Sebum production is controlled in part by androgen sex hormones. Androgen production increases at puberty, accounting for the increasing skin oiliness from which so many teenagers suffer.

As the sebaceous gland produces more sebum, the surface pore often becomes blocked. The sebum, unable to escape onto the skin surface, builds up and creates a blackhead. This then provides an ideal medium for the growth of certain skin bacteria, particularly *Propionibacterium acnes*. Infection with *P. acnes* is principally responsible for the inflamed pustules and cysts seen in the more severe forms of acne.

Hair follicles contain sebaceous glands, which release lubricating sebum. When too much sebum is produced, it cannot escape and becomes infected.

Section through a skin follicle

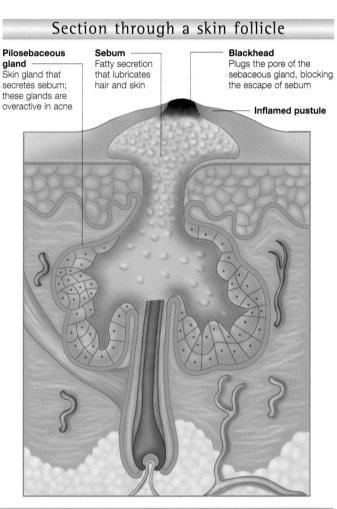

Pilosebaceous gland
Skin gland that secretes sebum; these glands are overactive in acne

Sebum
Fatty secretion that lubricates hair and skin

Blackhead
Plugs the pore of the sebaceous gland, blocking the escape of sebum

Inflamed pustule

Classifying acne

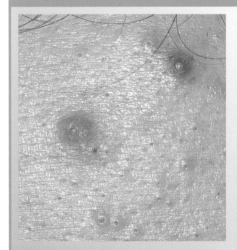

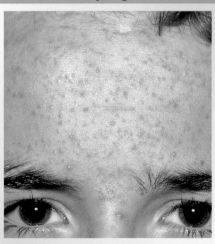

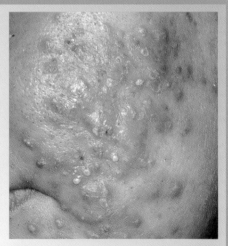

1 Mild acne. Acne is so widespread in adolescence that it could be deemed universal. The condition is associated with increased oiliness of the skin.

2 Moderate acne. The early lesions of acne are known as comedones, or blackheads. These then develop into inflamed papules and pustules.

3 Severe acne. This is a more persistent form, and large areas of the face – as well as other parts of the body, such as the back and chest – may be affected.

Treating acne

Depending on the severity of each case, the treatment of acne will usually involve topical applications and sometimes antibiotics. The aim is to prevent scarring.

Acne can have a severe effect on a sufferer's self-esteem, social life and even job prospects. Furthermore, the physical scars produced by acne can be life-long. It is important, therefore, that the condition is treated seriously and not just dismissed as a teenage disorder, something to 'grow out of' in time.

TREATMENT OPTIONS
There are many types of treatment for acne; their suitability depends largely on the site and severity of the acne.

Treatments can be topical – that is, lotions or creams applied directly to the affected skin. Systemic treatments usually involve antibiotic tablets that are taken orally.

However, there is no evidence that other remedies such as dietary manipulation help to reduce acne.

Acne can have a serious effect on a sufferer's self-confidence. However, most cases can be managed with over-the-counter preparations.

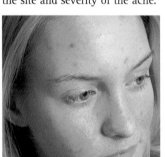

Mild acne is usually treated with topical applications, such as those containing 5–10 per cent benzoyl peroxide.

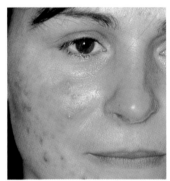

When acne is more severe or widespread, help from a GP may be appropriate. Prescription-only medication may then be given.

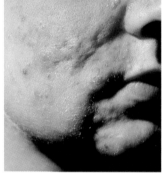

Topical acne treatments are not without possible side effects; some patients may suffer from mild skin inflammation.

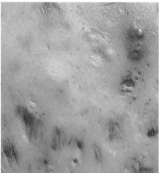

Even severe acne can be successfully treated in most cases. However, scarring may have already occurred.

Topical and systemic treatments

■ Topical treatments
Benzoyl peroxide lotion, cream and gel are available on prescription or over-the-counter, in various strengths. They act directly against *P. acnes*, help to

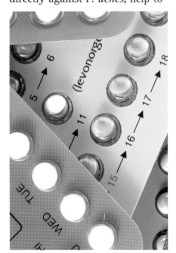

Hormonal therapy may be suitable for female acne sufferers who do not respond to other treatment. This also has a contraceptive effect.

unblock the pores and have a mild anti-inflammatory effect. Azelaic acid is a treatment that has a similar mode of action to benzoyl peroxide. Nicotinamide gel also has anti-inflammatory properties.

Retinoids that are derived from vitamin A act directly on the sebaceous gland. Retinoids cause dryness of the skin and must not be used in women who are, or may become, pregnant. Adapalene is another new agent, available as a gel. Topical antibiotics include tetracycline and erythromycin.

■ Systemic treatments
Antibiotic tablets commonly given for acne include tetracyclines (oxytetracycline or minocycline), erythromycin and trimethoprim.

Oxytetracycline cannot be taken by children or in pregnancy, and must be taken on an empty stomach. Erythromycin is often associated with gastric upsets. Although minocycline is the antibiotic

most likely to be effective against *P. acnes*, it is expensive and has several possible side effects, including dizziness and increased skin pigmentation.

Cyproterone acetate is a steroidal anti-androgen. It reduces the amount of circulating androgen in the body, and thus reduces the amount of sebum produced. It is combined with ethinyloestradiol in a preparation called Dianette. As well as being an efficient acne treatment, Dianette is an effective contraceptive. This makes it a suitable acne treatment for women who also need contraception; it cannot,

of course, be used for men.

Isotretinoin is a highly effective treatment for severe acne, which acts directly on the pilosebaceous glands, causing a reduction in sebum production and a reduction in pore blockage. It must be taken for several months and has several unpleasant side effects. These include joint pains, liver disturbance, and headaches.

Topical antibiotics act against P. acnes. The greatest problem is that of antibiotic resistance, which can render antibiotic treatment ineffective.

Common skin infections

The skin's surface is covered with harmless organisms, but infective organisms can sometimes invade. Most skin infections, however, are not serious and respond well to antibiotics at an early stage.

The skin has several mechanisms for preventing infection:
- A tough outer layer – the stratum corneum
- The constant shedding of surface cells
- Immunoglobulins in sweat
- An acidic pH
- Normal skin flora.

Skin infections occur with trauma, such as a break in the skin; excessive hydration of the skin; inflammation in the skin; or pre-existing skin disease – eczema, for example. Infection can result from an overgrowth of the natural flora or from contact with contaminated objects or people.

The commonest infective organisms are staphylococcal and streptococcal bacteria.

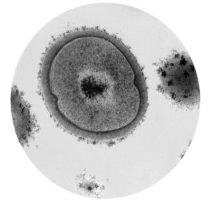

Staphylococcus aureus is often present on healthy skin and mucous membranes. It may become pathogenic (disease-causing) and is responsible for several types of skin infections.

Impetigo

Impetigo is caused by streptococcal or staphylococcal bacteria. The bullous variety is usually caused by staphylococci and the crusted variety by beta haemolytic streptococci. Impetigo is highly contagious, and is usually a childhood infection. It often occurs in epidemics, and as a result has a number of synonyms, such as 'school pox'. Infection usually begins on the face, hands or legs. Often a skin abrasion or insect bite triggers the infection. Other family/school members soon become infected.

TYPICAL SIGNS
Lesions start as raised red papules, which blister and then form pus. After rupturing, they release a golden coloured exudate, which is the typical appearance of the infection. The lesions may itch but are usually painless, and they clear of their own accord without scarring. However, a rare complication of a streptococcal infection is a post-streptococcal glomerulonephritis.

Younger children are more likely to develop the bullous form of the disease; rarely, certain strains of staphylococcal infection produce a toxin causing the superficial skin to peel off. This is called scalded skin syndrome, which carries a five per cent chance of death. Mild localized infections are treated with topical antibiotics; more widespread infections are treated with oral antibiotics.

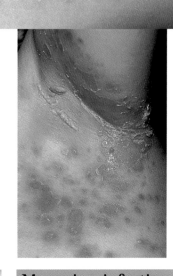

Impetigo has reached the crusted stage of the infection, with the typical lesions on the face. It usually affects the nose and mouth areas.

The armpit of a two-year-old with impetigo is seen here in close-up. The infection is most common in babies and children, and usually heals in 7–10 days.

Ecthyma

Ecthyma is an infection very similar to impetigo but affecting the deeper layers of the skin (the dermis). It is commoner in tropical areas and is associated with poor sanitation and nutrition. The legs and buttocks are usually affected, with deep, crusted lesions on ulcerated skin. Due to the deep nature of the infection, the lesions are slower to heal and often scar.

Ecthyma is an ulcerative form of impetigo, in which the infection spreads below the top layers of skin. The inflammation on this woman's lower leg is extensive.

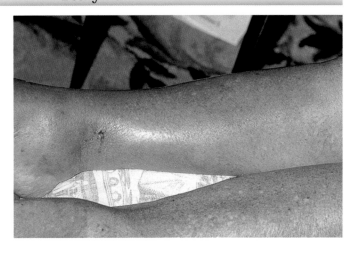

Managing infection

Most skin infections respond well to antibiotics. Other measures reduce the risk of contamination. Patients should:
- Avoid touching infected areas of the skin
- Wash the lesions with mild soap and water
- Gently remove the crust prior to applying antibiotic cream/ointment
- Wear gloves while applying cream/ointment to all affected areas
- Use their own flannel and towel, which should be washed daily.

Types of infections

Infections of the skin can occur at any age, and symptoms range from rashes to swelling and inflammation. The most serious skin infections may be accompanied by symptoms such as fever or organ failure; in these cases, urgent treatment is required.

Folliculitis

Folliculitis is a staphylococcal infection of the hair follicles. If the infection produces pus, the lesions are known as furuncles (boils), commonly occurring on the face or legs in adolescent boys. Sometimes, multiple adjacent hair follicles are infected and produce pus. A carbuncle (group of boils) that occurs on the neck may be associated with diabetes.

Oral antibiotics and occasionally surgical drainage of large furuncles are required to remedy an infection.

This scalp has the distinctive crusted lesions of folliculitis. The follicles become infected, especially if they have been blocked by keratin, a form of protein.

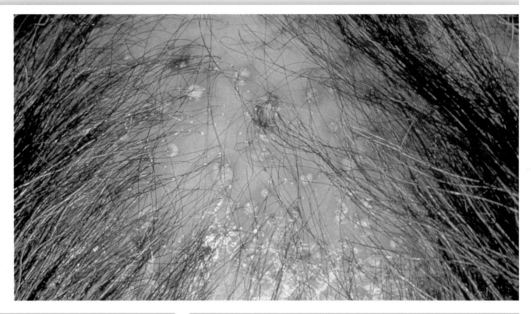

Cellulitis

Cellulitis is an infection below the skin in the subcutaneous tissue, caused by staphylococcal or streptococcal bacteria. The

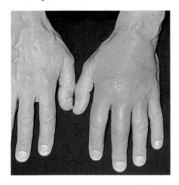

condition often follows local trauma (such as a wound) that allows infection to enter.

The edge of the infection is poorly defined and there are few systemic symptoms, although the patient may develop a fever. Treatment should be aimed at reducing the peripheral oedema (swelling due to fluid retention) and giving oral antibiotics.

Cellulitis occurs when bacteria infect the connective tissue underlying the skin. As a result, this patient's left hand has become swollen, red and tender.

Necrotizing fasciitis

Necrotizing fasciitis is an inflammation of the superficial fascia (the connective tissue membrane underneath the skin), and is a rare complication of

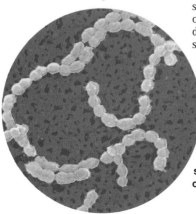

untreated cellulitis. Streptococci and other pathogens, including anaerobes, invade and destroy the tissues. The patient experiences shock and sometimes organ failure. The overlying skin has a rash and is discoloured dusky grey, and the sufferer is seriously ill. Even aggressive surgical debridement (removal of infected tissue) and systemic antibiotics may not prevent death in those most vulnerable.

Healthy humans carry Streptococcus pyogenes in their throat or nose, but certain strains of Streptococcus can cause very serious infections.

Erysipelas

Erysipelas is a streptococcal infection usually affecting the cheeks, and is common in the elderly. The infective organism is usually introduced through a crack in the skin, which becomes red and swollen, with the edge of the infected area well demarcated. The patient feels ill and has a fever.

Left untreated, erysipelas can be fatal, but it responds readily to penicillin. Recurrent infections affecting the same area can

occur. Low-dose prophylactic (preventative) penicillin may be required.

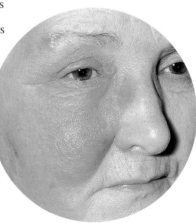

This woman's right cheek is swollen and inflamed due to erysipelas, which is caused by Streptococcus pyogenes. The rash often affects the face.

Recurrent infections

Some people are prone to recurrent staphylococcal infections. They may have diabetes; a low level of resistance due to other illness; be taking medication which suppresses their ability to fight infections; or simply be chronic carriers of the bacteria on the surface of the skin.

Many bacteria are resistant to penicillin-derived antibiotics. However, cloxacillin and flucloxacillin are still effective against staphylococci.

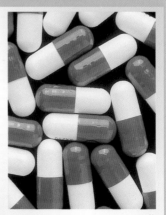

Hair disorders

Hair can be affected by a variety of disorders which, although often distressing, do not pose a threat to health. These disorders fall into two distinct groups – excessive hair growth and hair loss.

Healthy hair growth is dependent on balanced physiological conditions within the body. If these are upset – for example, by hormonal changes or stress – the phases of hair growth can become disrupted. The resultant hair disorders can be classified into two distinct groups: excessive growth and alopecia (hair loss).

CAUSES

Some hair disorders develop as a result of an underlying health problem. There are a number of clinical conditions that may affect hair growth, or even have an adverse effect on the condition of the hair itself. Other hair disorders are caused by localized skin diseases or by certain drug treatments.

Although not serious in themselves, hair disorders can be unsightly and very distressing for those affected.

DANDRUFF

Dandruff is not a hair condition, but it inevitably affects the appearance of the hair. Excess dead skin is shed from the scalp and is deposited as white flakes in the hair. The condition can be extremely embarrassing but is easily treated by regular use of medicated shampoos.

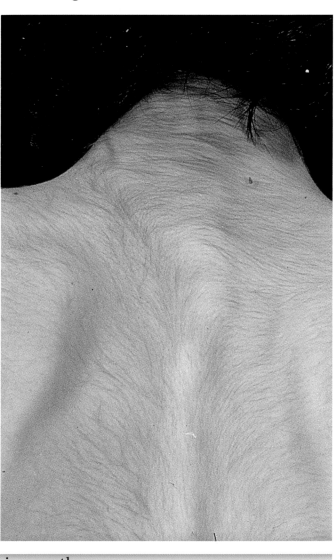

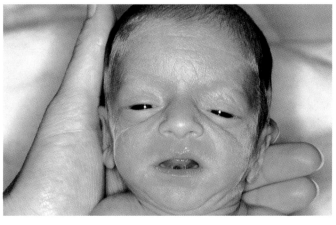

Premature babies are covered in downy hair called lanugo. This hair eventually disappears, but the same type of hair can develop in adults due to disease.

People with anorexia nervosa sometimes develop fine hair growth, much like lanugo, on the body. This is thought to be due to hormone disruption.

Excessive hair growth

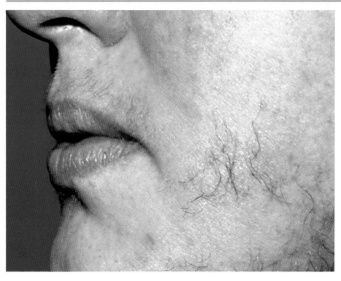

The development of excess terminal hair in women is known as hirsutism. This excess hair growth can be a sign of polycystic ovaries.

There are two main types of excessive hair growth: hirsutism and hypertrichosis.

HIRSUTISM

In hirsutism, a woman grows excess hair in a pattern that is normally specific to males – for example, on the face and lower abdomen. Hirsutism is usually due to abnormal hormone levels – for example, an excessive production of androgen (male) hormones. Excess hair growth can also be a symptom of the hormonal condition, polycystic ovarian syndrome (multiple benign ovarian cysts).

If hormone levels are normal, the only treatment for hirsutism is cosmetic, such as bleaching, electrolysis or laser treatment.

HYPERTRICHOSIS

Hypertrichosis, which can affect both men and women, describes excessive hair growth in a more random pattern.

Hypertrichosis is often localized, for example in the area of a mole, or over the lower spine in association with spina bifida. Other causes include malnutrition, porphyria cutanea tarda (a rare metabolic disorder) and some drug treatments.

Alopecia (hair loss)

Alopecia (hair loss) can occur in any area of the body, although the loss of hair from the scalp is more noticeable than that from other areas. There are a number of different types of alopecia. These include:

■ Telogen effluvium
Telogen effluvium is the excess shedding of hair (which can be marked), which often occurs about four months after major illness or childbirth. At times of prolonged physical stress on the body, hairs enter the telogen (final stage of hair growth) phase, but their shedding is delayed. Recovery leads to an increase of new hair growth, pushing out the old hairs. This condition can be alarming, but regrowth is usually complete.

■ Diffuse alopecia
Diffuse alopecia, which does not spontaneously resolve, is associated with a variety of systemic illnesses.

Malnutrition can be a major cause in the developing world, with kwashiorkor (protein deficiency) causing hair to become thin and red.

Iron and zinc deficiency can also lead to hair loss.

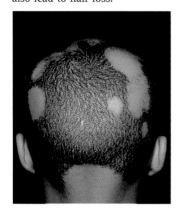

Hormonal disturbances associated with the thyroid, adrenal or pituitary glands are sometimes implicated.

Drug treatment, especially with certain hormones, anticoagulants or epilepsy medication, can cause alopecia. Chemotherapy can cause a temporary total alopecia.

■ Alopecia areata
Alopecia areata is an autoimmune disorder and is another relatively common cause of hair loss.

A discrete bald patch appears on the scalp, although the underlying scalp is healthy. There is usually no obvious cause, although stress is sometimes implicated.

Hair regrowth usually starts after a period of two to six months. Recovery is normally complete, although it may take up to two years, and the hairs may grow back white.

Treatment is often not necessary, but strong steroids, either creams or local injections, may help some people. Occasionally, the alopecia spreads to involve the entire scalp (alopecia totalis) and even body and facial hair may be lost (alopecia universalis). Regrowth is less likely in this case.

■ Traction alopecia
Traction alopecia refers to hair loss that is caused by continued pulling on the hair root. This condition may be caused by certain hairstyles that pull on the scalp.

In alopecia areata, bald patches develop on the scalp. People usually recover from the disorder, although steroid treatment may be required.

■ Scarring
Hair can be permanently lost due to scarring of the scalp – for example after burns, in which the skin tissue is destroyed.

■ Skin disease
Hair loss can be caused by skin diseases, such as lichen planus (in which the nails can be lost too), or by discoid lupus erythematosus (a chronic inflammatory disease).

Increased hair loss can also be the result of a scalp infection, such as ringworm.

Malnutrition is a common cause of alopecia in the developing world. Low levels of vital nutrients affect hair growth and cause hair to fall out.

■ Other causes
Trauma is a relatively common cause of hair loss.

Less commonly, a person will deliberately and consistently pull out hair (trichotillomania). Odd-shaped bald patches appear, with hairs broken off unevenly down their shafts. Psychological counselling is often necessary.

Baldness

Normal male pattern baldness, associated with androgen hormones, may first occur in some men in their teens; others show little sign even into old age. However, most men have some male pattern baldness by the time they are in their thirties. The individual hairs first become thinner and paler until, finally, the roots become inactive. Hair is lost first from the temples, then the forehead, then the crown.

Medication
Certain drug treatments will help hair regrowth. Minoxidil, for example, will help some hair to regrow in about 30 per cent of

men, but the effect is only temporary; when treatment stops, the new hair will fall out again. Hair loss due to male pattern baldness can be dealt with on a more permanent basis by having a hair transplant.

Age-related hair loss in women tends to be far more diffuse and less noticeable. However, male pattern hair loss in a woman should raise suspicion of abnormal hormone levels.

The majority of men have a degree of male pattern baldness by the time they are in their third decade. Some drugs will aid hair regrowth.

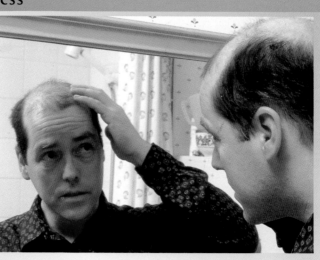

Psoriasis

Symptoms

Psoriasis is a common, chronic, non-contagious skin disease, which results in scaly, itchy patches (plaques) forming on the skin. The areas of the body that are particularly affected are the elbows, knees and scalp.

COMMON PSORIASIS
The more common types of psoriasis include:

■ Plaque psoriasis
This is the commonest form of psoriasis, also known as psoriasis vulgaris. The plaques are raised, red and scaly and there is a sharp demarcation line between the plaques and normal skin. They are often found on the extensor surfaces where straightening occurs at the knees and elbows. If the lesions are gently scraped, the surface becomes whiter and more scaly.

■ Guttate psoriasis
This form of psoriasis is often seen in children and young adults. A sudden outbreak of small, red, scaly papules may appear on the trunk and back. Two-thirds of these patients have had a recent bacterial throat infection.

■ Seborrhoeic psoriasis
Red, scaly lesions affect the scalp, shoulders, armpits, groin, face and skin behind the ears.

■ Nail psoriasis
Over 50 per cent of patients show abnormal nail changes, characteristically pitting ridges, and a separation of the nail plate from the nail base.

RARE PSORIASIS
The rarer forms of psoriasis include:

■ Pustular psoriasis
This form of psoriasis is often severe. Small blisters filled with non-infective pus develop on the hands or feet.

■ Inverse psoriasis
This mostly affects elderly people. Large, red areas appear in folds of the skin, affecting the groin and the skin under breasts and armpits.

■ Erythrodermic psoriasis
The whole body is affected, the entire skin surface being red and scaly. It can be triggered by drugs or withdrawal of steroids.

Psoriasis is characterized by red patches, or plaques, covered with a scaly, flaky surface. Skin on any part of the body may become red and inflamed.

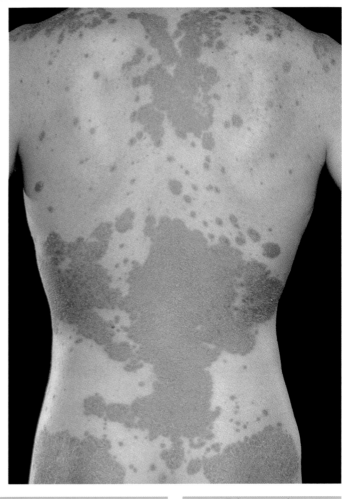

Causes

Psoriasis is caused by new skin cells being produced faster than dead skin cells are lost, resulting in excess thickened skin.

CAUSAL FACTORS
Various factors are responsible:
■ Genetic predisposition – about two thirds of cases are inherited

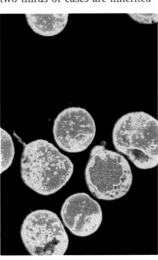

■ Autoimmune disorder – psoriasis may due to an abnormal immune reaction. Following exposure to a virus or bacterium, a sub-group of white blood cells (T cells), which normally protect the body from infection, become activated against skin proteins. This leads to inflammation and excess skin cell multiplication.

AGGRAVATING FACTORS
Symptoms may be triggered by:
■ Trauma – including lacerations, insect bites, burns
■ Medications – including drugs

These blood cells, known as T cells (orange), normally help the body fight infection. In psoriasis, T cells mistakenly attack skin protein, causing inflammation.

In someone who has psoriasis, skin injuries, such as cuts or burns, can trigger a flare-up in that area. Knees and elbows are prone to such injuries.

used for the treatment of hypertension, antimalarials, and antidepressants
■ Viral and bacterial infections
■ Excess alcohol
■ Obesity
■ Stress
■ Cold climate
■ Sunburn or lack of sunlight.

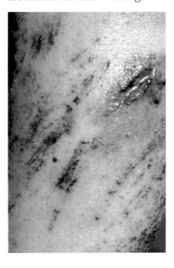

Diagnosis

Psoriasis is diagnosed by clinical examination of the skin. Diagnosis may be difficult, as psoriasis can sometimes resemble other skin conditions.

The characteristic rash is dry and red with silvery scales. Scraping the surface of lesions produces white discoloration and more scaling.

DIAGNOSTIC TESTS
A skin biopsy (sample) may be taken for histological examination under a microscope. A blood test to look for the HLA antigen (protein) may be positive in psoriasis.

Incidence

Psoriasis affects about two per cent of the population. It occurs equally in men and women and usually develops between 15 and 35 years of age. The condition can affect any part of the body.

Treatment

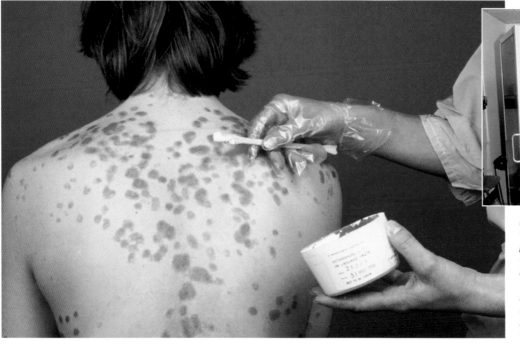

Phototherapy is an effective treatment for some forms of psoriasis. The patient receives UV light directly to the skin inside a special light box.

Plaque psoriasis is often treated using topical applications. Dithranol paste is messy and time-consuming to apply but often has excellent results.

All treatments for psoriasis aim to control symptoms rather than cure the disease. Treatment is determined by the type of psoriasis, its extent or severity, and the patient's medical history, age and sex.

TOPICAL TREATMENTS
Topical treatments, applied directly to the affected skin, can sometimes effectively clear psoriasis:
■ Corticosteroids – topical steroids are one of the most common therapies prescribed for mild or moderate psoriasis. There is a risk with potent steroids of skin thinning and the disease recurring, so long-term use should be avoided. Steroids should not be applied to the face
■ Topical vitamin D_3 analogue – calcipotriene ointment is used to treat mild to moderate psoriasis and is easy to apply
■ Coal tar – this can be messy but is very effective, especially when applied in increasing concentrations in plaque psoriasis
■ Dithranol – applied as paste or cream in varying strengths
■ Bath solutions – help to descale the skin especially when followed by moisturizing medication
■ Coconut oils – can be rubbed into the scalp at night in association with a tar shampoo.

PHOTOTHERAPY
Exposure to ultraviolet light may be recommended when psoriasis is resistant to other therapies. The options include:
■ UVB – ultraviolet light is administered using a light box. At least three treatments a week for several months are required
■ PUVA – for people with severe or extensive psoriasis, this combines taking psoralen, a light-sensitive drug, with exposure to ultraviolet light, using cabinets containing fluorescent tubes.

DRUG THERAPY
Severe psoriasis may require:
■ Oral retinoid drugs – which increase the rate at which the outer layers of skin are shed
■ Antibiotics – when an infection has triggered psoriasis
■ Cyclosporin – which is an immunosuppressant drug.

COUNSELLING
Embarrassment, frustration, fear and reduced self-esteem are common feelings among patients and may need to be addressed through counselling.
Doctors should explain the nature of the skin condition and what can be done to alleviate symptoms. It must be emphasized that psoriasis is not an infectious condition.

Prognosis

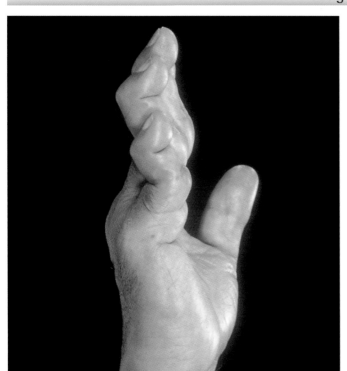

In some patients with psoriasis, psoriatic arthritis may develop. This often affects the fingers, causing inflammation of joints.

The course of chronic plaque psoriasis is variable. The condition may persist for several years with no apparent change, it may undergo spontaneous remission, or it may spread and become more extensive.
In the majority of patients with guttate psoriasis, the condition resolves without specific treatment.

Some patients may develop a polyarthritis associated with their psoriasis (psoriatic arthropathy).

PSORIATIC ARTHRITIS
Psoriatic arthritis is an inflammatory joint condition that is associated with psoriasis but is considered to be a separate condition.
It affects between seven and 42 per cent of people with psoriasis, and of these some 80 per cent have psoriatic nail changes.

Prevention

In view of the known effect of infection, stress and certain drugs, it should be possible to minimize exacerbations by trying as far as is practicable to avoid these. Sore throats that are not obviously associated with colds may require treatment with a course of penicillin.

Sunburn

An individual's susceptibility to sunburn depends on their skin type, but absorption of UV energy damages skin regardless of its type. Avoiding exposure or using dermatological sunscreens is the best way to avoid burning.

WHAT IS SUNLIGHT?

Sunlight contains ultraviolet (UV) radiation types A and B. When the skin is exposed to sunlight, it reflects some UV radiation and absorbs and re-emits the remainder. When UV radiation enters the skin, it collides with skin cells. Chemical reactions occur, leading to sunburn, premature skin ageing and sometimes skin cancer.

The wavelength of UVB is 280 to 315 nanometres (nm); the UVA wavelength is 315 to 400. UV radiation below 300nm is largely absorbed in the upper skin layer, the epidermis. UV radiation above 300nm passes mainly to the lower skin layer, the dermis. Some of this energy is then reflected back out from the dermis.

Sunlight is the main source of UV radiation, and outdoor workers and frequent sunbathers are particularly at risk. Sunbeds used for artificial tanning also expose the skin to UV radiation in high concentrations. Burning can occur when using a sunbed, and it is particularly dangerous when using some drugs with photosensitive side-effects.

TANNING

Melanin is a natural pigment produced in cells called melanocytes. When melanocyte cells are damaged, by excessive light exposure, the production of melanin increases. Also, when new melanocytes are formed by cell division, they increase in size, producing even more melanin. The melanin then transfers from the melanocytes to adjacent cells in the epidermis called keratinocytes.

The resulting increase in pigment accumulation causes tanning, which appears over a period of hours to days and lasts for weeks or even a few months.

Thickening of the skin cells also occurs. This too develops over hours to days, especially following UVB exposure, and can last for a period of one to two months.

Ultraviolet radiation in sunlight can destroy cells in the outer layer of skin, causing burning and blistering. (Dead cells are shed later as the skin peels.) It can also damage the capillaries beneath the surface of the skin.

Sun damage can occur from a very early age. Children tend to spend a great deal of time in the sun. Wearing sunscreen and a hat can help to prevent any permanent damage to their skin.

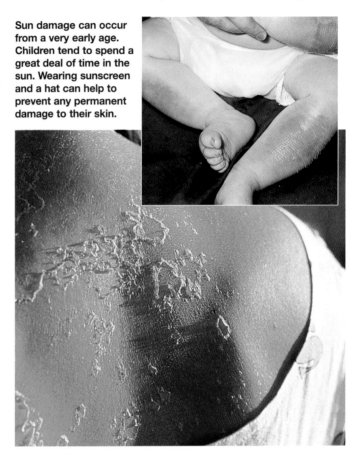

Effects of sunlight on the skin

Stratum corneum
On exposure to the sun, the epidermis, and especially the stratum corneum, thicken two- to four-fold due to greater cell division. This has a protective function against further UV damage

Stratum spinosum

Stratum basale
This layer contains the only keratinocyte cells (in normal skin) that undergo cell division. The daughter cells then move up through the epidermis

Dermis
Mainly composed of collagen, through which runs a fine network of elastic fibres. When the dermis is damaged, skin loses its elasticity

Langerhans cell
These cells of the immune system are involved in fighting infection and inflammation. Damage and destruction of some of these cells occurs after sun exposure. In the longer term, the immune system helps to fight off tumour formation, and loss of these cells may contribute to the risk of future skin cancers

Melanocytes
These cells contain the skin's natural pigment, melanin. With sun exposure, melanin production is increased. New melanocytes are formed by cell division and existing melanocytes increase in size

Melanin granules

Merkel cell
Function thought to be related to cutaneous sensation. The Merkel cell tumour is a rare but aggressive tumour than can arise from sun damage

Sensory nerve ending

Absorbed UV energy causes widespread epidermal and dermal cell damage. This damage encourages the release of chemicals, which results in a build up of inflammatory cells of the immune system in the skin. Blood vessels respond by dilating and allowing more fluid to escape into the skin. This results in redness, pain, warmth and swelling, which develops over hours or days. After UVB exposure, the inflammation is immediate and lasts for two to three days. The deep red effects of UVB persists for days after the effects of UVA exposure.

This diagram shows the layers of the epidermis of the skin. Light of different wavelengths is absorbed by different layers of the skin. UVB, which causes most burning, is absorbed by the upper layers. UVA, once thought to be benign, is now known to burn, penetrating deep into the skin and causing further damage.

AVOIDING SUNBURN

UV intensity is greater in summer, especially between 11am and 3pm on cloudless days, and also at high altitudes and low latitudes. Other factors include reflection of sunlight from snow, sand and water. It is especially important to minimize exposure when there is higher UV intensity.

Clothing of close weave is excellent at reducing the amount of UV light that reaches the skin. To assess the weave, hold it up to the light and look at the gaps between fibres – smaller gaps are preferable. A broad brimmed hat is excellent for face and scalp protection.

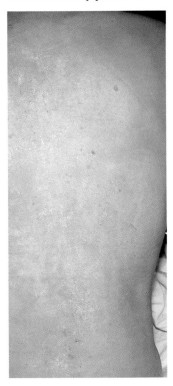

Light from a sun bed can result in burns if the skin is exposed for too long. This can produce photosensitive reactions as extreme as blistering of the skin and damage to the eyes.

Applying sunscreen also helps reduce the effects of UV light. Sunscreens either absorb or reflect UV light, or perform a combination of the two effects. Products that absorb UV energy are cosmetically more acceptable – they rub into the skin less noticeably. They work well in absorbing UVB light. However, these products are less effective against UVA, and some people become allergic to some of the active ingredients. Reflectant preparations, such as those containing titanium dioxide or zinc oxide, are particularly efficient against UVA as well as UVB, and are less likely to cause skin allergy. They are less cosmetically appealing, as they are more obvious on the skin, producing a whitening effect.

Recently, smaller 'micronized' reflectant particles, such as dibenzoylmethanes, have been introduced and these offer protective reflection with greater cosmetic acceptability.

SUNBURN TREATMENT

If burning occurs despite these precautions, symptom relief is advised. Drink plenty of fluids, and apply soothing bland moisturizer. Creams with ingredients from the aloe vera plant are considered soothing.

If the sunburn is more active, a topical steroid cream, such as one per cent hydrocortisone, is helpful. In severe cases, seek the advice of your doctor.

Sun Protection Factors (SPFs)

Different skin types have varying susceptibility to burning. There are five major categories:
- **Type 1** Always burns, never tans (e.g. fair skin, freckles, red hair)
- **Type 2** Usually burns, sometimes tans
- **Type 3** Sometimes burns, mostly tans
- **Type 4** Never burns, always tans (e.g. Asian skins)
- **Type 5** A lot of natural pigmentation (e.g. black skins)

The measure of a sunscreen's effectiveness is given by a sun protection factor (SPF). This represents the increased time that can be spent in the sun before burning occurs (an SPF of 2 means that twice as long can be spent in the sun). Applying a sunblock, however, can give a false sense of security, tempting people to be out in the sun for longer and risking more exposure to UV. There is no substitute for minimizing exposure by sitting in the shade, and wearing clothes and a hat.

Sunburn is mostly induced by UVB, and SPFs refer especially to protection against UVB. High SPF (15–25) products also provide substantial UVA protection.

For skin types 1 to 3, higher SPFs of 15–25 are suitable.

Lower levels of protection of 10–15 are generally satisfactory for darker skins and moderate exposures. If a sunblock is to be effective, however, it must be applied evenly to all exposed areas. After swimming, the sunscreen should be re-applied to ensure that adequate cover is maintained.

The reddening of the skin on this person's arm and back is the result of six hours' exposure to strong sunlight. This case is relatively mild – extreme sunburn can result in blistering. In the long term, the skin damage can result in wrinkles and loss of elasticity.

Long-term effects of sun exposure

Skin cells at the top have been destroyed by UV light and are sloughing off. Further damage is shown by the irregular shapes of dead cell debris below and to the wave-like basal cell layer.

With long-term sun exposure, the structure and function of the skin deteriorates due to the cumulative cell damage and chronic inflammation. Both epidermis and dermis are affected mainly by UVB, but the dermis is also affected a great deal by UVA. Wrinkling, laxity, dryness, yellowing, mottled pigment deposits and the formation of tiny dilated blood vessels visible on the skin's surface are all features.

SKIN CANCER AND MELANOMA

- Non-melanoma skin cancers occur on sun-exposed sites, especially the face and neck, and are caused by UVB and, to a lesser extent, UVA.

There are two types: basal cell carcinoma and squamous cell carcinoma.
- Malignant melanoma occurs on sun-exposed sites, more commonly on the back in men and on the calves in women, and is caused by UVB and UVA.

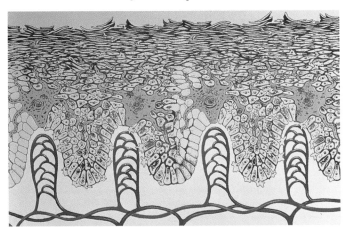

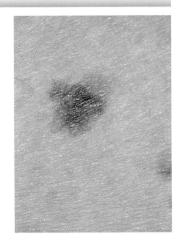

A malignant melanoma caused by sun damage on the surface of the skin. Melanomas are cancerous tumours of the skin's melanin-producing cells, which are responsible for pigmentation.

Anorexia nervosa

Anorexia nervosa is an psychogenic eating disorder, meaning that it originates in the brain. It is characterized by the patient's refusal to acknowledge their condition, but its effects are apparent over the whole body.

Anorexia nervosa is the name given to the condition affecting people who are usually, but not exclusively, young and female, do not eat enough and become very thin. Males who develop anorexia nervosa make up between 5 and 10 per cent of patients referred to specialist clinics; the proportion of boys to girls may be higher in a younger age group.

PROGNOSIS
Affected adults and older teenagers lose weight. Younger children, who should still be gaining weight to match their increase in height, cease to get taller and fail to gain weight as expected. As time progresses, the illness takes an ever firmer grip. The drive for thinness becomes even more determined and the consequent avoidance of high-calorie (usually high-fat) foods

In long-term anorexia nervosa sufferers (five years or more), X-rays may reveal osteoporotic fractures. Bones become brittle and are liable to fracture easily as a result of both a lack of calcium in the diet and low hormone levels.

becomes even more obsessive and total.

People who suffer from established anorexia nervosa will sacrifice anything to remain in control of their food intake, in order to avoid, as they see it, 'getting fat'. However low their actual weight, any weight gain will make them feel fat, even as little as 200g (14oz).

The illness can take a prolonged and severe course, resulting in marked and chronic emaciation. As well as the harmful physical effects,

This woman is suffering from advanced anorexia nervosa, and displays the characteristic signs of extreme emaciation. If the condition persists, a high-calorie intravenous solution will be necessary to avoid death.

including low bone density and osteoporotic fractures, anorexia nervosa has profound psychological effects. Personal and emotional relationships deteriorate, leading to social isolation and poor employment and study prospects.

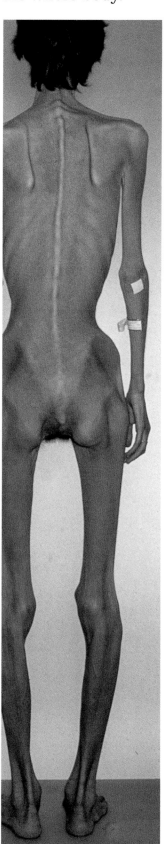

Biological effects of starvation

Anorexia nervosa is a psychoneurotic condition, whereby a person has a psychogenic (mental, rather than physical) aversion to food. The desire to avoid eating overrides any appetite or hunger pains, and gradual starvation leads to

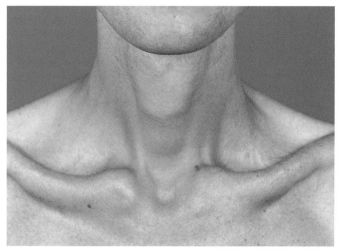

emaciation. In advanced cases, this has serious consequences for the person's physical condition, including the following:
- Parotid (salivary gland) enlargement
- Amenorrhea (cessation or lack of menstruation)

- Low pulse and blood pressure
- Erosion of tooth enamel
- Impaired endocrine function
- Metabolic and biochemical abnormalities
- Subnormal body temperature
- Oedema of the lower body

In spite of the obvious physical degradation, those suffering from anorexia are frequently in denial about their condition, and doctors have to repeatedly explain and draw attention to the condition. In some cases, the patient may 'play along' with the doctor and lie about food intake, or surreptitiously vomit any food that is eaten. Death from inanition (exhaustion caused by lack of nutrients) may occur in extreme cases.

Anorexia is characterized by emaciation, with bones prominent. Up to 25 per cent of total body weight may be lost.

Causes of anorexia nervosa

It is thought by some experts that there may be an inherited aspect to anorexia nervosa. This would imply that relatives who have eating disorders themselves, or who suffer from an obsessive-compulsive disorder or are chronic worriers, seem to be able to pass on, in their genes, their tendency to react to stress by developing an eating disorder.

What remains unclear is whether transmission of the disorder from generation to generation is solely by the handing on of genetic material from parent to child, or by example and teaching also.

Each family unit develops and passes on its own household traditions, and this is especially true about the culture, values, attitudes and beliefs that surround ordinary meals and feast-day celebrations. The traditions surrounding food may well determine who eats what, and under what specific circumstances. This influence is likely to affect us without our even realizing it.

We absorb such teaching and example even before we can talk, as research is beginning to demonstrate. For instance, detailed observations of mothers feeding their first-born child at the age of one show previously unsuspected variations in the mother—child interaction around feeding and associated habits.

Personality aspects, as well as physical characteristics, are passed on from parents to children in their DNA. It is thought that a predisposition to anorexia may be inherited.

From infancy, customs and assumptions concerning food are instilled in the child, often subconsciously. The exact role of family influence in the development of anorexia is unknown, but it may be a factor.

Mental health and anorexia nervosa

Anorexia nervosa is reported by the Department of Health as having the highest mortality of any single psychiatric diagnosis (14 per cent).

However, in spite of the obvious and visible damage that is done to the bodies and minds of sufferers, the illness is often dismissed as foolish. The behaviour is seen as that of vain young girls who have 'caught' anorexia nervosa because they want to look like the latest waif-like fashion model or pop singer.

This view trivializes the internal emotional conflict and distress of the sufferer. Usually, she lacks somebody to confide in, and seeks alternative ways of coping. About 50 per cent of patients also exhibit a depressed mood. Family attitudes, values and beliefs and the sufferer's own genetic inheritance all combine to create a neurotic perfectionism and a mode of thought that can see issues only in terms of extremes.

Low self-esteem, or a fixed and poor estimate of one's own

It is oversimplistic to assume that images from fashion and the media force people to become anorexic. However, there is undoubted pressure to conform to a physical 'norm'.

self-worth, are universal features of all eating disorders, and this applies especially in the case of anorexia nervosa.

As with other eating disorders, a characteristic of anorexia is a distorted self-image. This produces an inability to accept that a very low weight is undesirable.

Identifying and treating anorexia nervosa

Identifying anorexia nervosa may be straightforward for a doctor, but convincing the sufferer of their condition can be extremely difficult. Counselling, drug treatment and, occasionally, force-feeding may be required.

DIAGNOSTIC CRITERIA

There is no diagnostic laboratory test to identify anorexia nervosa. However, initial weight loss, not associated with any other medical illness, followed by the subsequent maintenance of a body weight that remains significantly below normal for an individual of the same height, age and sex as the sufferer, is one diagnostic feature of the condition. The peak onset is in the mid–late teens.

HORMONAL DISTURBANCE

Another criterion is a profound hormonal disturbance, which takes different forms in males and females. Young women who have reached puberty and started to have regular periods find that their menstrual flow lessens and their periods become irregular. In many cases, menstruation ceases completely (known as amenorrhea).

The equivalent hormonal disturbance in males reduces the frequency of ejaculations, and eventually limits the ability to have erections. Unfortunately, the accepted definitions of

A common side effect of anorexia is scurvy, caused by a deficiency of vitamin C (ascorbic acid, found in fruit and vegetables). Scurvy often results in bleeding gums and haemorrhaging under the skin.

anorexia do not list such hormonal effects that may be apparent in males.

Three consecutive months without a menstrual period is taken to be one of the three main diagnostic features of anorexia nervosa in females. The other two are the low weight and the central overriding preoccupation with dietary restriction and an absolute avoidance of weight gain. Taken together, these features have been described by one expert as together constituting a 'phobic avoidance of normal weight'.

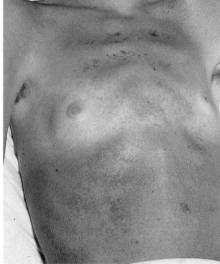

Brain chemistry
A psychogenic (in the mind) aversion to food may affect the chemical balance of the brain, thus affecting mood and mental balance

Breasts
May retain shape, despite overall physical atrophy (muscle wastage) and emaciation

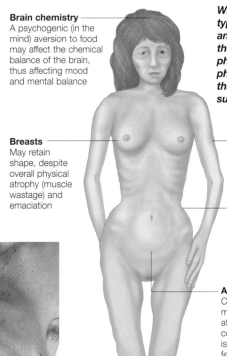

Whilst there is no single, typical picture of an anorexic's appearance, there are a number of physical and physiological changes that are common to many sufferers of the disorder.

Low pulse and blood pressure
(hypotension)

Fine, downy body hair
Lanugo hair may be present on the patient's body, especially on the back

Amenorrhea
Cessation of menstruation for at least three consecutive months is a diagnostic feature of anorexia; total failure of sexual function is rare

Oedema
Swelling of the lower limbs due to fluid accumulation in the tissues may occur in advanced cases

---

Anorexia nervosa and brain function

Living with a very low body weight has profound effects on the way the brain works. This is particularly applicable to thought processes and the way in which the brain processes information.

Recent research suggests that differences may be visible on brain scans of teenage girls with anorexia, compared with girls who do not have it. What is not yet clear is whether the lesions that can be seen develop as a result of the illness or were there before the girls developed their illness. What happens after

recovery has not yet been established. It is known that people can inherit genetically determined constitutional traits or personality characteristics. This may predispose a person to develop anorexia nervosa if the environmental factors are unfavourable.

Evidence of damage to the hypothalamic region of the brain, which controls hunger, thirst and sexual function, may be revealed by brain scanning. Whether this is a cause or an effect of the disease is not clear.

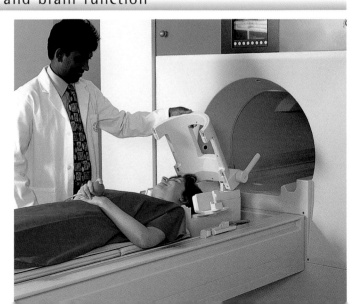

Recovery

Recovery can be a long and difficult process. The patient first needs to regain body weight, before embarking on a course of long-term psychotherapy.

Weight gain by itself does not constitute a recovery. However, without restoring weight to at least the lower end of the normal range, recovery cannot take place, as constrained mental functioning means the sufferer cannot grasp new ideas or process new information.

Researchers have different views about how attitudes typical of anorexia sufferers are created and maintained. All agree that restoration of near-normal weight by feeding and counselling or psychotherapy are essential to achieve an increase in self-esteem and establish habits of more flexible thinking. A reward system is sometimes used to encourage weight gain.

Someone who has recovered from anorexia is able to eat enough regular, nutritious meals to maintain a near-normal weight. This enables them to live a normal life in all areas, including sustaining fruitful personal relationships. Weight gain will also restore any damage to fertility.

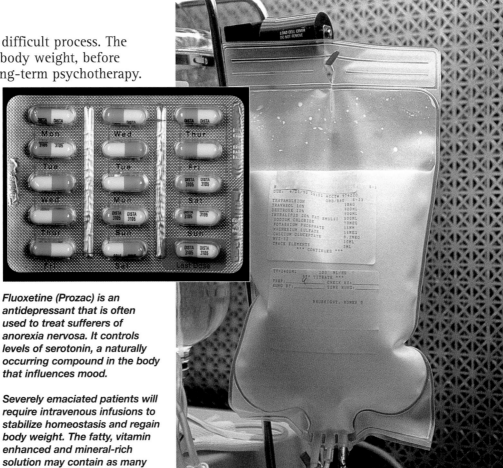

Fluoxetine (Prozac) is an antidepressant that is often used to treat sufferers of anorexia nervosa. It controls levels of serotonin, a naturally occurring compound in the body that influences mood.

Severely emaciated patients will require intravenous infusions to stabilize homeostasis and regain body weight. The fatty, vitamin enhanced and mineral-rich solution may contain as many as 3000 calories.

Long-term recovery and support

People with anorexia nervosa require evaluation and treatment focused on biological, psychological and social features of this complex, chronic health condition. Assessment and ongoing management should be

After the patient has regained weight, counselling can begin. These intensive therapy sessions may last for months or even years, and are designed to help the sufferer overcome the negative self-image they have of their body.

interdisciplinary, and is best accomplished by a team consisting of medical, nursing, nutritional and mental health professionals. Treatment should be provided by healthcare providers with expertise in managing patients with eating disorders, and knowledge about normal adolescent physical and psychological development.

Hospitalization is necessary in the presence of malnutrition, clinical evidence of medical or psychiatric decompensation or failure of out-patient treatment.

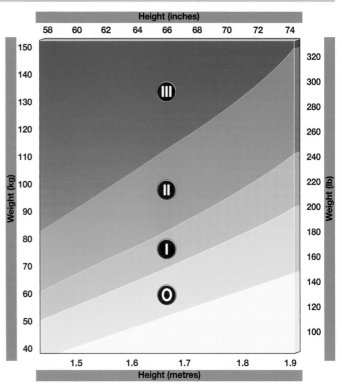

Doctors determine the body mass index (BMI) from an individual's weight and height. The formula is: BMI = (weight in kg)/(height in m)^2. On the above chart, III, II and I denote grades of obesity and 0 indicates the boundaries of desirable weight. A BMI reading of less than 17.5 indicates possible anorexia.

Body dysmorphic disorder

Body dysmorphic disorder is a mental illness in which sufferers are obsessed with their appearance. The condition causes distress and often disrupts an individual's personal and professional life.

Body dysmorphic disorder (BDD) is a preoccupation with an imagined defect in a person's appearance. If a slight physical anomaly is present, the preoccupation is excessive.

Many people are concerned to a greater or lesser degree with some aspect of their appearance. To be diagnosed with BDD, however, the preoccupation must cause significant distress or impairment in a person's social or occupational functioning.

COMMON CONCERNS

Complaints about shape, or symmetry of facial features are the most common, although any part of the body may be the focus of concerns.

Sufferers often have multiple preoccupations, which can be specific or very vague, such as feeling that they are ugly.

People with body dysmorphic disorder are excessively concerned with how they look. They may scrutinize themselves in a mirror, looking for defects.

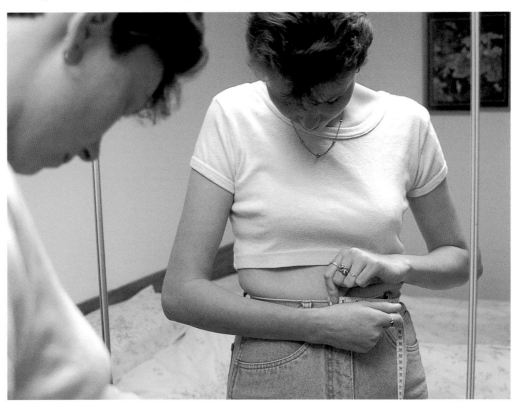

What are the symptoms?

BDD is difficult to control, and sufferers spend several hours a day thinking about their appearance. They often avoid a range of social and public situations to prevent feeling

uncomfortable. Alternatively, they may enter such situations but remain very anxious and self-conscious.

Sufferers may try to hide their perceived defect by using heavy make-up, changing their posture, or wearing particular clothes. They often feel compelled to repeat certain time-consuming rituals such as:

■ Checking their appearance either directly or in a reflective surface (for example a mirror, CD or shop window)
■ Excessive grooming
■ Picking at their skin to make it smooth
■ Comparing themselves against models in magazines or television
■ Dieting and excessive exercise or weight-lifting.

Such behaviours usually intensify the preoccupation and exacerbate patients' depression and self-disgust.

BDD sufferers may become obsessed with exercise in an attempt to 'improve' their body. They may try weight-lifting to change body shape dramatically.

DEGREE OF IMPAIRMENT

Some sufferers acknowledge that they may exaggerate problems. Others are so convinced about their defect that they are regarded as having a delusion.

Although sufferers often realize that others think their appearance is normal, and have been told so many times, they usually distort these comments to fit in with their views (for example, 'They only say I'm normal to be nice to me'). Alternatively, they may remember one critical comment about their appearance and dismiss a hundred other complimentary comments.

SEVERITY

Although BDD concerns may sound trivial, a high percentage of sufferers will require hospitalization, become house-bound, undertake unnecessary cosmetic surgery or even attempt suicide.

Causes of BDD

Although the condition was first defined over a century ago, there has so far been very limited medical research into body dysmorphic disorder.

In general terms, there are two different levels of explanation: psychological and biological, both of which may be accurate.

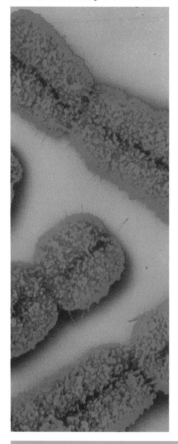

PSYCHOLOGICAL CAUSES
A psychological explanation emphasizes that an individual may judge themselves almost exclusively by their appearance, and therefore excessively focus their attention on themselves. Consequently, they may develop a heightened perception of their appearance and become increasingly obsessed about every slight imperfection.

Eventually there is a discrepancy between what they believe they should ideally look like and how they see themselves. Avoiding social situations or using certain behaviours prevents them testing out some of their fears, which in turn maintains their excessive self-focused attention.

BIOLOGICAL CAUSES
A biological explanation emphasizes that an individual has a genetic predisposition to a mental disorder, which may increase their likelihood of developing BDD. Certain stresses or life events, especially during adolescence, may precipitate the onset of the condition.

Once the disorder has developed, there may be a chemical imbalance of serotonin or other chemicals in the brain.

This micrograph shows human chromosomes, which carry our genetic information. A predisposition to conditions such as BDD may be genetic.

Who is affected?

The incidence of BDD is unknown; studies that have been done have either been too small or unreliable. The best estimate is that one per cent of the population might be affected. BDD may be more common in women than in men in the community, although clinic samples tend to have an equal proportion of men and women.

SEEKING HELP
BDD usually begins in adolescence – a time when people are generally most sensitive about their appearance.

However, due to shame and embarrassment, many sufferers wait for years before seeking help. When they do seek help through mental health professionals, they often have other symptoms such as depression or social phobia and do not reveal their real concerns because they fear that others will think them vain.

The physical changes that occur in puberty can be difficult for many people to deal with. BDD is most likely to arise during the teenage years.

Behaviour therapy and medication

Although BDD can be difficult to treat, certain therapies have led to successful outcomes. To date, however, there have been no controlled trials to compare different types of treatment and determine the most effective.

However, there have been a number of case reports and

small-scale trials that have demonstrated the effectiveness of two types of treatment, namely cognitive behaviour therapy (CBT) and anti-obsessional medication.

Cognitive behaviour therapy
CBT is based on a structured programme of self-help so that the individual learns to alter the way that they think about their appearance.

An individual's attitude to their appearance is crucial. This is demonstrated by people who have a physical defect, such as a port-wine stain on the face, and yet are well-adjusted because they believe that their appearance is just one aspect of themselves.

BDD sufferers have to confront their fears without avoidance (a process called 'exposure') and to stop all 'safety behaviours', such as excessive camouflage. This means repeatedly learning to tolerate the resulting discomfort.

Facing up to the fear becomes easier and the anxiety gradually subsides. Sufferers begin by confronting simple situations and

Cognitive behaviour therapy aims to change how patients perceive their appearance. They are encouraged to face their fears to reduce anxiety.

then gradually work up to more difficult ones.

Medication
Anti-obsessional medications such as fluoxetine (Prozac) are thought to be effective. They are called selective serotonin re-uptake inhibitors (SSRIs) and may be used alone or in combination with psychological treatment.

BDD has been linked to another condition, obsessive-compulsive disorder (OCD). SSRIs, which have been effective in the treatment of OCD, appear to reduce the obsessive thoughts, the emotional distress related to the thoughts and also the compulsive behaviour.

Although side effects are possible, the drugs are not addictive and may be stopped without experiencing withdrawal symptoms. Medication is especially helpful when a person is depressed, as it may help in improving their motivation.

Bulimia nervosa

Bulimia nervosa is an eating disorder. It is characterized by the affected person bingeing on food and then using various means to prevent themselves gaining weight.

In bulimia nervosa, the affected individual eats large amounts of food over a short period of time and then goes to great lengths to avoid weight gain.

Bulimia nervosa affects both women and men and can occur on its own, or as part of another eating disorder such as anorexia nervosa. Unlike people with anorexia, however, people with bulimia may be of normal weight, or even overweight.

COGNITIVE PROCESSES
People with bulimia have an intense fear of becoming fat and this fear grows to dominate their lives. They feel, to an extreme degree, that their weight reflects their worth as a person and thus determines their self-esteem.

Fears and beliefs about the importance of weight make it almost impossible for bulimic individuals to return to a normal eating pattern. Over-estimation of bodily size and a refusal to accept that they are not fat are adhered to rigidly, despite reassurance from family, friends and therapists.

BEHAVIOURAL PATTERNS
During a binge, the person feels that they are unable to stop eating and that their eating is out of control. However, once the binge is over, these thoughts are replaced by disgust at their

People with bulimia become obsessed with their weight. Affected individuals refuse to accept that they are not over-weight despite reassurances.

Bulimia is more common in women than men and usually develops between the ages of 18 and 30. This disorder is linked with low self-esteem.

behaviour and at the amount of food that has been eaten.

The person then takes steps to prevent weight gain. They may induce vomiting immediately, take laxatives, or follow a

vigorous exercise regime.

A diagnosis of bulimia nervosa is usually made if this pattern is repeated at least twice a week for three months or longer.

PREVALENCE
Some studies suggest that one per cent of women and 0.1 per cent of men have symptoms that are severe enough to interfere significantly with their lives.

Physiological complications

Bulimia is associated with binge eating followed by vomiting. This causes physical problems, such as dehydration, which should be explained to patients.

Most people with bulimia nervosa regularly induce vomiting. This can have several immediate consequences; if vomit is accidentally inhaled, damage to the lungs may occur, and forced vomiting can tear or even rupture the walls of the stomach. Frequent vomiting exposes the teeth to stomach acid, which accelerates decay.

Individuals may also lose fluid and potassium through frequent vomiting, and as a result can become dangerously dehydrated. Low potassium levels may lead

to heart arrhythmias and kidney impairment.

LONG-TERM EFFECTS
In the long term, it seems that the metabolic changes induced by alternately gorging and starving the body are associated with the development of Type 2 diabetes and polycystic ovary syndrome. The link in both cases appears to be the development of insulin resistance.

People with bulimia nervosa tend to binge on foods that have a high sugar and high fat content. Rapid rises in blood sugar and consequent insulin secretion followed by fasting may affect the body's ability to metabolize carbohydrates satisfactorily in the longer term.

Genetics and personality

Bulimia seems to be caused by a combination of factors – genetic, personality and environmental.

GENETICS
Eating disorders tend to run in families, and studies on identical twins suggest that genetics may be a major factor. However, it is more likely that certain genes predispose to personality traits that are a factor in bulimia, rather than directly predisposing to the disorder itself. There is also a high incidence of depression and substance addiction among close relatives of bulimics.

PERSONALITY
Individuals with bulimia tend to have certain personality traits – typically, perfectionism, obsessiveness and impulsiveness, coupled with low self-esteem, mood instability

Studies in twins have shown that genetic factors may greatly increase the likelihood of developing an eating disorder.

People affected by bulimia tend to have certain personality traits. These may include obsessive behaviour, low self-esteem and anxiety attacks.

and anxiety. They may also have a borderline personality disorder.

Bulimic individuals often have difficulty maturing and dealing satisfactorily with puberty, parental relationships, marriage and sexuality. They also tend to score low on tests of social co-operation. These personality traits are almost always set against a background of a poorly functioning family. The family may be goal-orientated and high-achieving, but may be affected by destructive interpersonal relationships.

ORGANIC CAUSES
Although there are few studies in this area, it is suspected that in some people, a malfunction of the serotonin-mediated satiety signaling system makes it difficult to stop eating. PET scans of people with bulimia have shown abnormalities of the hypothalamus in the brain, but these disappear if normal eating patterns are re-established.

Environmental factors

It is fashionable to blame the promotion of ever-skinnier models and film stars for the escalating incidence of eating disorders. However, there is little evidence that the media has influenced the behaviour of those people with severe eating disorders, although personal remarks from their peer group may contribute to the condition.

Eating disorders are more prevalent among dancers and athletes, suggesting that the demand for individuals to maintain a low level of body fat in order to optimize performance is a causative factor.

Images of thin models have been blamed for the rise in eating disorders. However, negative personal experiences have a greater influence.

Treatment and prognosis

There is little specific treatment for bulimia, but antidepressants may help in treating any associated depression. Potassium supplements are given to compensate for losses caused by repeated purging. In some cases, high doses of fluoxetine (prozac) halves the frequency of bingeing and also lowers the frequency of the subsequent weight-reducing activities.

Cognitive-behavioural therapy
Cognitive-behavioural therapy (CBT) may help to address the individual's low self-esteem and their preoccupation with their body, weight and food. CBT also addresses eating habits, dieting

People with bulimia may be referred to a therapist who specializes in eating disorders. The aim of treatment is to establish regular eating habits.

and ritualistic exercise. Patients are asked to monitor their feelings and behaviour. CBT provides cognitive methods to challenge rigid thought patterns. It also suggests techniques to improve self-esteem and to identify and appropriately express feelings.

A combination of CBT and drug treatment is the most effective treatment for bulimia.

Prognosis
Sadly, treatment does not often lead to cure. One study showed that 40 per cent of patients remained bulimic after 18 months; another showed that 50 per cent still had an eating disorder after 5 years.

Bulimia tends to be a lifelong condition, although it may vary in intensity. There is a small risk of sudden death, but generally the damage to physical and mental health occurs over the long term.

Depression

Depression is a mental state that involves mood disorder, leaving the sufferer feeling 'low'. There are a variety of symptoms, both physical and mental, which can be mild or severe.

An episode of depression may occur singly or recurrently (with intervening periods of normal mood). In both cases, the condition is referred to as unipolar depression, because there is only one direction of mood change.

Some people, however, develop depression in the context of a manic-depressive illness, called bipolar affective disorder. In this case, there are manic ('high') episodes as well as low mood swings.

Although the vast majority of features of unipolar depression would apply equally to bipolar depression, it is thought that there may be some subtle differences between the two.

CLASSIFYING DEPRESSION

As well as the distinction that is currently made by psychiatrists between unipolar and bipolar disorders, classification is based on its severity, recurrence and the presence or absence of psychotic symptoms.

Only rarely, however, does a depressive illness become so severe that the individual loses touch with reality and becomes psychotic (whereby delusions or hallucinations are experienced).

Depression is primarily a disorder of the mood. This is in contrast to mania, in which there is elation and elevation of mood.

Some people are reluctant to visit their GP to discuss feelings of depression, but this is often the first step towards receiving treatment.

Who is affected?

At any given time, approximately 10–15 per cent of people in this country will be suffering from moderately severe depression and 2–3 per cent from severe depression.

Every year, about 10 per cent of the population develop a depressive illness, although many more cases may remain undetected. Typically, onset is in the late 20s and, overall, women are twice as likely as men to get depressed. Inner-city housing, low social class, unemployment, poor education and being single are other important associations that have been recognized.

New mothers are also at risk of becoming depressed – in the six weeks following childbirth, 10–15 per cent become depressed enough to warrant some kind of help.

Among the many factors that can increase vulnerability to depression are a lack of social support and a difficulty in forming close relationships.

What causes depression?

Attempts have been made to distinguish between depressive episodes, which are understandable in terms of traumatic life events (reactive or neurotic depression), and those which occur spontaneously, depending on factors within the individual (endogenous depression). Although it is tempting to classify further on this basis, the initial observation that 'reactive' depression is less severe, and forms a separate entity, need not necessarily be true. In every case, there must be a mixture of causes that are both internal and external.

Genetic factors appear to be important (more so in bipolar depression), as are hormonal changes, such as increased cortisol levels and abnormal control of thyroid hormones.

Adverse events, especially those associated with losses such as bereavement and physical illness, can trigger depressive episodes. It seems that underlying vulnerability to such events can be increased by circumstances – for example, abuse or parental separation in childhood, unemployment, low social class and poor self-esteem.

CHANGES IN THE BRAIN

There is known to be a change in the function of several neurotransmitters and their receptors in the brain during periods of depression. Most research has concentrated on serotonin and noradrenaline, the hypothesis being that depression is associated with decreased activity of both of these chemicals. It is now accepted that this represents a huge oversimplification and that many other neurotransmitters are likely to be implicated.

Symptoms of depression

The key features of depression are a persistent lowering of mood and loss of enjoyment, interest and motivation. There are also important changes in biological function, thinking and behaviour.

■ **Biological symptoms**
These are most prominent in severe depression and include: sleep disturbance, typically with early morning wakening; decreased appetite; weight loss; reduced sex-drive; fatigue; aches and pains; psychomotor disturbance – slowing of movements, thought and speech or, in rare cases, agitation.

The mood is often worse in the morning and lifts as the day goes on. In very severe, life-threatening cases, an individual will refuse to eat or even drink.

■ **Mental symptoms**
Thought content is extremely negative, with ideas of guilt, worthlessness and hopelessness. People can find it hard to imagine any sort of future, and ideas of self-harm or suicide may be common. Concentration and memory can be severely impaired; in some cases in the elderly, the degree of impairment

Frontal lobe
The part of the brain concerned with controlling voluntary movement and other functions; it is also the centre for conscious emotion

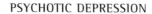

Area of abnormal activity
It is thought that in depressed people, part of the cortex of the frontal lobe is overactive, leading to an abnormal fixation on emotional state

Research has attempted to identify the specific areas in the brain that are affected when an individual is depressed. This cross-section through the brain shows one such area.

can be such that it is difficult to distinguish between depression and dementia.

Other symptoms that occur as part of a depressive illness include anxiety and phobias, obsessions, irritability, agitation and restlessness.

■ **Behavioural symptoms**
The ability to function from day to day, both socially and at work, is decreased – at least to some extent. People may avoid leaving home and isolate or neglect themselves, and facial expressions and body language of the severely depressed may be easily recognizable.

MILD DEPRESSION
Anxiety and obsessive symptoms in particular appear to occur more frequently in mild episodes; indeed, rather than differing merely in terms of severity, mild depression may represent a separate syndrome. Other important differences of mild depression include a tendency to initial insomnia (difficulty falling

A common feature of mild and severe depression is insomnia. A chronic lack of sleep can serve to exacerbate symptoms of fatigue.

asleep with subsequent oversleeping in the morning), an increase in appetite and the presence of few biological symptoms. The pattern of variability throughout the day can vary, with a worsening of mood in the evening.

PSYCHOTIC DEPRESSION
It is important to identify psychotic symptoms, as they represent a very severe illness, in which the individual has begun to lose touch with reality. Symptoms are usually in keeping with the patient's mood: delusions often concern illness, death, punishment, guilt or persecution; hallucinations (which occur less frequently and are usually auditory) are unpleasant and distressing – for example, a voice that accuses, urges suicide or confirms the patient's low self-esteem.

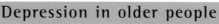

Depression in older people

Although the prevalence of depression is almost identical in elderly and middle-aged people, the diagnosis of the condition can often be missed in the older group. This is probably because the features of low mood can be less obvious; elderly people may not complain of feeling depressed or suicidal at all, perhaps going to see their doctor with physical problems or simply sleep disturbance, a degree of which is normal in old age.

It is always important for the doctor to bear the condition in mind, however, because of the relatively poor prognosis in this

group. Elderly depressed patients (especially men) are at a high risk of suicide and, for this reason alone, early detection and treatment is of paramount importance. It is also very important in preventing relapse and depressive episodes of long duration, which are more likely in people of this age group than in younger people.

It is easy to overlook depression in older people, but the problem is significant. It is often difficult to diagnose, as it can be hard to distinguish between depression and dementia.

Managing depression

Before taking steps to manage depression, it is important to recognize the type of depressive illness that the patient is suffering from. The most appropriate treatment can then be administered.

The diagnosis of depression would, at face value, appear relatively straightforward but in practice can be rather difficult.

IDENTIFYING DEPRESSION

It is important to distinguish between depression and the normal sadness that would be expected in response to bad news or a significant loss, such as a bereavement or the development of a major physical illness. To justify the diagnosis, there must exist some degree of other characteristic symptoms in addition to low mood; the severity and duration of change is also vitally important.

Depression should also be distinguished from adjustment reactions (representing abnormal psychological responses to such life changes as redundancy, divorce or moving house), which often result in a mixture of anxiety and depression. Neither of these will be sufficiently severe to justify a clear-cut diagnosis of anxiety or depression alone, however, and the biological symptoms of the latter will be absent.

PERSONALITY DISORDER

Borderline personality disorder (one of many recognized personality disorders which represent lifelong maladaptive patterns of behaviour, attitude and experience that cause distress to the individual or society) has, as one of its core features, an instability of emotion; people with borderline personalities typically complain of chronic lack of enjoyment and frequently have a low mood and suicidal ideas.

It is very difficult to distinguish between someone who has a low mood in the context of an abnormal personality alone, and someone with a borderline personality disorder who has developed a superimposed depressive illness.

In fact, even attempting to make such distinction merely serves to grossly oversimplify an extremely complex situation; in practice, if someone who meets the criteria for a borderline personality disorder appears to be markedly depressed they would usually be offered antidepressant medication.

DISTINGUISHING OTHER PROBLEMS

Other important conditions that may be hard to differentiate clinically from depression include generalized anxiety disorder, obsessive-compulsive disorder, chronic schizophrenia (a prominent symptom of which is flattening and blunting of emotions and mood), hormonal disorders (such as Cushing's syndrome and underactivity of the thyroid gland), cancer, malnutrition and post-viral fatigue syndrome.

General stress or worry can often leave one feeling low. However, this mood state does not necessarily equate to a depressive illness.

The symptoms of depression need to be distinguished from those that may arise as a result of thyroid dysfunction (the cause of this person's swollen neck).

Evaluating the patient

Initially, the most important step in the management of depression is to make an assessment of severity and risk to the patient in terms of self-neglect and suicidal behaviour.

All cases of psychotic illness and those patients thought to represent a high suicide risk should be admitted to a psychiatric hospital. The vast majority of cases, however, are managed by a general practitioner. Referral as an outpatient to a

Most patients with depression are seen and treated by their GP. However, if their illness becomes more severe, specialist attention may be necessary.

consultant psychiatrist is warranted if there is concern about the severity of the illness, a failure of response to commonly used treatments or recurrent episodes of depression.

It is very important for the doctor to take a history of any abnormal upswings of mood as well as the depressive episodes. Any predisposing factors will also be noted, as will triggers or precipitating events and maintaining factors (which keep the illness going). This helps in the identification of possible targets for change during treatment to prevent deterioration, relapse or recurrent episodes of depression.

Treatment for depression

Most people who suffer from depression will be managed by their GP, using antidepressant drugs. In some cases, however, specialist psychiatric care, involving psychotherapy or behavioural therapy, may be required.

Medication

Antidepressant medication is used to treat episodes of all severities. Overall, the response rate to such treatment is good (60–70 per cent) and continuing antidepressants for six months following recovery from a first episode can significantly reduce the risk of relapse.

The classes of drugs most commonly used are the tricyclic antidepressants (TCAs) and the selective serotonin reuptake inhibitors (SSRIs, of which Prozac is an example). Such drugs are thought to exert their influences through effects on neurotransmitters and their receptors, although the exact mode of action remains unclear.

TCAs and SSRIs have different side effects, but neither is without the potential to cause unpleasant or even intolerable symptoms. It is important that patients are warned that although the unpleasant symptoms may appear rapidly, the antidepressant effect will take longer to emerge (2–6 weeks); for this reason, some degree of perseverance is necessary.

COMBINATION THERAPY
Antidepressants can be used alone or in combination, either with other antidepressants or other types of drug. One example is the use of lithium to augment the effects of antidepressants; this approach can be used to treat depression which fails to respond to antidepressants alone.

Patients who suffer from recurrent episodes (especially if they have a strong family history of depression or early

Selective serotonin reuptake inhibitors are widely used in the treatment of depression. One of the best known SSRIs is fluoxetine (trade name: Prozac).

age of onset) benefit from long-term preventative treatment to reduce the risk of recurrence.

Lithium can also be used as a long-term treatment to prevent the recurrence of depression in patients with unipolar depression, and of both depression and mania in those with bipolar affective disorder.

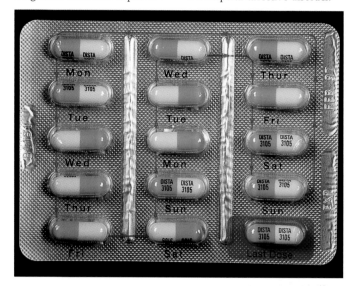

Other therapies

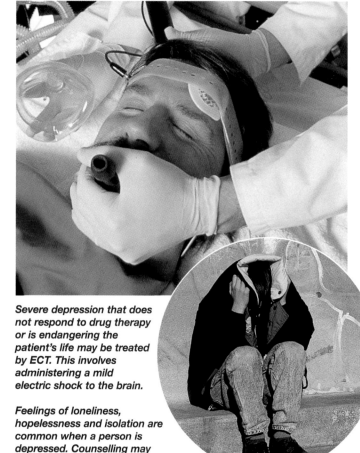

Severe depression that does not respond to drug therapy or is endangering the patient's life may be treated by ECT. This involves administering a mild electric shock to the brain.

Feelings of loneliness, hopelessness and isolation are common when a person is depressed. Counselling may help to overcome these feelings.

Psychotherapeutic techniques can be of great value. The most widely studied is cognitive behavioural therapy (CBT – originally devised to treat depression but since found to have wider applications). In the short term, CBT is just as effective as medication in treating depressive episodes and it may even be more effective at preventing relapses in the future; in practice, medication and CBT are often used in combination.

In some cases, counselling alone may be deemed sufficient for milder forms of depression without the need for psychotherapy or medication.

TREATING SEVERE DEPRESSION
Electroconvulsive therapy (ECT) is reserved for the most severe cases, especially when rapid treatment is required (for example, if there is refusal to eat or drink) and for situations in which drugs fail to work or cannot be tolerated. In cases of psychotic depression, antipsychotic medication may be added, in doses similar to those used for the treatment of other psychotic illnesses such as schizophrenia.

Prognosis

Although a single episode of depression usually lasts between three and eight months, 20 per cent last for more than two years. The severity of the first episode is related to the risk of developing further depressions – a risk of 50 per cent in moderately severe cases, rising to 80 per cent in the more severe.

Psychiatric illness in general (but especially depression) is strongly associated with suicidal behaviour. Among those with severe depression, there is a 15 per cent chance that patients may attempt to kill themselves.

The risk of suicide is not necessarily related to the depth of depression. It is important that all patients receive appropriate attention.

Munchausen's syndrome

Munchausen's syndrome is a psychological disorder that leads people to seek medical treatment for a non-existent illness. The condition frequently proves difficult to diagnose and treat.

Munchausen's syndrome is a psychological condition in which an individual endeavours to obtain medical treatment for an illness that is non-existent. The condition is named after Baron von Munchausen, a fictional character renowned for telling extraordinary stories.

HOSPITAL ADMISSIONS

If medical staff are unfamiliar with Munchausen's syndrome, and have not encountered the condition before, they may be misled by the often convincing medical history and symptoms. People with Munchausen's syndrome frequently undergo numerous investigations and procedures – there are cases of individuals with more than 200 hospital admissions.

Every patient with persistent symptoms will be thoroughly examined. In people with Munchausen's, however, tests are continually negative.

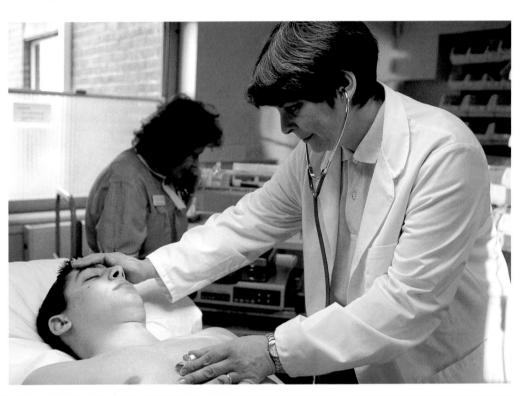

Diagnosis

Munchausen's syndrome is defined by the intentional production of symptoms or illnesses in order to assume the 'sick' role. People with Munchausen's syndrome contrast with those in whom fictitious symptoms may provide financial gain – for example, enable them to claim sick pay. Moreover, although patients may receive drugs as treatment, they are not drug addicts and the procurement of drugs does not appear to motivate them.

DIFFERENTIAL DIAGNOSIS

Doctors may suspect that a difficult patient with unusual or persistent symptoms has Munchausen's syndrome, especially as there are certain symptoms classically associated with the condition. However, other conditions, including real and rare diseases, should always be considered. Munchausen's syndrome can develop from a real illness. For example, a diabetic patient with the disorder may, in order to gain attention, induce episodes of hypoglycaemia (low blood sugar levels) by injecting too much insulin. Such behaviour makes the diabetes extremely difficult to manage.

PSYCHIATRIC DISORDERS

Munchausen's syndrome should be distinguished from other psychiatric disorders, such as somatization. Like those with Munchausen's syndrome, people with somatization have nothing physically wrong with them, but they differ in that they consciously believe that their symptoms are real.

Specific symptoms, such as breathlessness, will always be investigated. 'Real' disorders must be ruled out before a diagnosis is made.

Investigations

Normal tests are usually carried out to investigate any symptoms that a person may present with. In the absence of any positive results, however, suspicions may be raised.

In these cases, medical staff may, if they feel it is appropriate, refer a person for psychiatric assessment. During interviews, the psychiatrist may be able to extract enough information to make a diagnosis.

Some affected people may inject themselves with adrenaline to cause a rise in blood pressure. In this way, they are able to gain medical attention and treatment.

Behaviour

Almost every branch of medicine has experience of individuals who present with Munchausen's syndrome.

SYMPTOMS

Most frequently, those affected by the disorder complain of abdominal, neurological or psychiatric symptoms. They tend to display certain typical patterns of behaviour, and these include:
■ Self-admission to hospital Accident and Emergency departments, often relating stories about dramatic events or serious, and frequently fatal, accidents
■ A high level of medical knowledge
■ A belligerent attitude towards medical staff, especially if challenged about behaviour
■ A willingness to undergo any number of investigations or operations. For example, an individual may prefer to have a leg amputated, rather than allow self-inflicted injuries to heal and the leg be saved.

Numerous scars indicate that many operations have taken place. This physical evidence may cause doctors to suspect Munchausen's syndrome.

SUSPICIONS

Although Munchausen's patients may be knowledgeable about the medical condition they imitate, there are often certain clues that may alert medical staff.

For example, some individuals have multiple scars as evidence of their previous hospital admissions. Others may complain of a weak leg, for example, but when the 'good' leg is examined, the examining physician may detect that the other leg moves involuntarily.

Some people may imitate unconsciousness, putting up with very painful forms of stimulation without moving or complaining. Yet, if their hand is raised above their head and allowed to fall, it almost never falls onto their face.

It has also been known for people to complain of epileptic

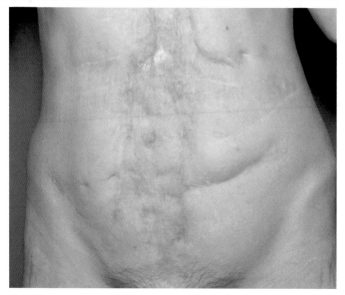

fits, but they have never bitten their tongues and are never witnessed to be incontinent.

PSYCHIATRIC

It is not uncommon for those people affected by Munchausen's syndrome to imitate psychiatric symptoms. For example, they may claim to have had hallucinations and delusions. As a result, medical personnel may mistakenly treat these individuals by prescribing varying amounts of psychotropic (mood-affecting) medication.

Management

People with Munchausen's syndrome seem unable to control their behaviour and have little awareness of their own motivation.

Referral to a psychiatrist is often helpful in treating people with Munchausen's. However, many people with the syndrome refuse to see a specialist.

CONFRONTATION

Management of the disorder generally involves confronting an individual about their condition. At this stage, most individuals discharge themselves from hospital. Very few will accept a psychiatric referral and, if asked about their condition, they are usually non-committal and unclear. They often leave one hospital to arrive at another with a similar illness.

Rarely, it may be possible to develop a constructive relationship with the patient, in which their symptoms and underlying fears about illness are discussed. However, people affected by Munchausen's syndrome are often severely disturbed and highly manipulative, and they make little real progress.

Although hospitals frequently exchange information about individuals seeking drugs as well as those feigning illness, issues of patient confidentiality need to be considered.

Munchausen's by proxy

Munchausen's by proxy is a state whereby the patient deliberately harms others (frequently children) to attract medical attention. Most commonly, a mother inflicts harm on her child.

The 'illnesses' may be bizarre in nature, and will never be directly witnessed by healthcare staff. The symptoms rarely follow an accepted medical pattern and typically disappear when the child is admitted to hospital.

Safety of child

These cases must be carefully managed as the safety of the child is paramount, and it is usually very difficult to make an individual accept their behaviour.

In extreme cases, especially where the illness continues in hospital, covert surveillance can be used to monitor the child. Ultimately, this is the only method of providing definite evidence of such abuse. Accusations made without direct evidence can be extremely damaging and, if unfounded, cause inestimable distress to all concerned.

Injuries inflicted on a child, often by its mother, may be signs of Munchausen's by proxy. In these cases, the child will need to be monitored.

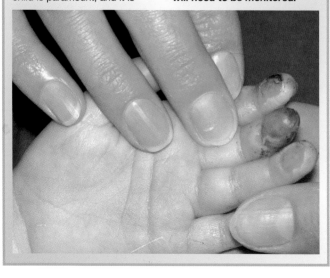

Obsessive-compulsive disorder

Obsessive-compulsive disorder (OCD) is a rare condition, comprising obsessional thoughts, ideas and actions. Patients may be treated by a combination of psychotherapy and medication.

Characteristically, OCD involves a subjective sense of compulsion overriding internal resistance; in other words, the sufferer feels overwhelmingly compelled to perform a particular action, or series of actions, despite struggling against it and knowing that it is an unreasonable series of actions.

The majority of patients have both obsessions and compulsions. Obsessions are characterized by intrusive, distressing ideas or thoughts that do not go away, such as the belief that the front door has not been shut. Compulsions are actions that result from obsessive thoughts, such as repeatedly checking that the front door is shut. The condition was first described at the beginning of the nineteenth century, and was initially termed a 'monomania' – meaning that once the sufferer had got a fixed idea into his head, he could not get rid of it.

People suffering from OCD exhibit a range of symptoms. The desire to obsessively arrange and rearrange household items is common.

What causes OCD?

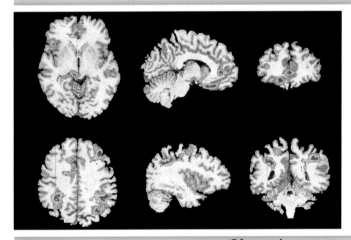

Imaging techniques, such as PET scanning (left), can show which brain regions are active during OCD behaviour.

There are various theories about the causes of OCD, but none of them provides a full, satisfactory explanation for the condition. Current theories include:

■ Genetic
Between 5 and 7 per cent of OCD patients have parents with the disorder, suggesting an inherited tendency for the condition. Upbringing, however, seems of little relevance.

■ Brain disorder
Advanced imaging techniques to view the brain, such as positron emission tomography (PET), suggest disturbance in brain structures, whilst anomalies of serotonin metabolism indicate a definite brain malfunction.

■ Psychoanalytical
Attempts have been made to describe OCD as caused by subconscious aggressive or sexual impulses that trigger internal conflict.

■ Learning theory
This suggests the symptoms are ploys to reduce anxiety.

Obsessive-compulsive symptoms

OBSESSIONS

Obsessions are mental fixations that the patient is unable to 'turn off':

■ Obsessional thoughts are recognized by the patient as inappropriate. They may be sexual, obscene, blasphemous, frightening or nonsensical

■ Obsessional fears (also termed phobias) include those of doing something dangerous to oneself or someone else. Common fears are of contamination or unspecified disaster: they may lead to compulsive acts

■ Ruminations comprise the endless reviewing of the simplest actions or brooding over abstract subjects

■ Obsessional doubts are about tasks one may have omitted to do, such as turning off an oven, or actions that may have harmed other people, such as driving past a cyclist too fast.

COMPULSIONS

Compulsions include repetitive acts, fixed 'rituals' and obsessional slowness:

■ Compulsive acts are those which develop into rituals, such as repeatedly checking that the front door is locked

■ Fear of contamination leads to washing oneself or other objects or elaborate avoidance of places where there may be dirt

■ Fear of bad luck leads to using the 'magic' of numbers to ward off disaster: doing actions a certain number of times, or performing everyday activities, such as getting dressed, in a rigid and inflexible order.

Other symptoms vary depending on the patient, but can include:

■ Depersonalization, a strange feeling of unreality whereby a patient feels unreal, or feels that the outside world is unreal

■ Anxiety, often driving the compulsive acts. These acts are intended to reduce anxiety, but sometimes make it worse. A patient who is performing a ritual feels mounting anxiety until they have completed it

■ Depression, common in OCD, is sometimes the primary illness.

Obsessive cleanliness is a typical feature of OCD. Some patients may feel compelled to wash hundreds of times a day.

Managing OCD

One person in 100 suffers from OCD at any time, but patients can be successfully
treated using several methods. Drug therapies, using antidepressant drugs, can be useful
and counselling and cognitive behavioural therapy are also very effective.

Psychotherapy

A number of psychotherapeutic approaches are used to treat patients with OCD. In more severe cases, medication will also be used.

The patient may find that the initial assessment with the therapist, involving the unburdening of distressing symptoms, is in itself a relief. The therapist should explain that the symptoms are exaggerations of thoughts and impulses that everyone has sometimes, and do not indicate incipient madness.

Self-help programmes, with encouragement, if possible, from a friend, partner or group can also help. Distractions and physical exercise may be useful. The most effective psychological treatment is cognitive

Cognitive behavioural therapy is often very successful in helping patients with OCD. It is necessary for the therapist to be skilled and experienced.

behavioural therapy, which can reason the patient out of their faulty reactions. Other techniques include:
- Systematic desensitization: a gradual approach. For example, exposure for an hour daily to a situation likely to provoke symptoms, such as doing housework, but without going through the usual rituals
- Response prevention: usually it is sufficient for the therapist to say 'don't'
- Modelling: providing an example for the patient to follow.

Treatment with drugs

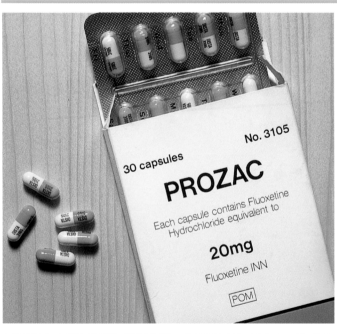

One of the best-known SSRIs is fluoxetine, which is often prescribed for patients with OCD. It is also known by the proprietary name of Prozac.

Recent experience has shown that selective serotonin re-uptake inhibitors (SSRIs), such as sertraline, citalopram and paroxetine, and the tricyclic antidepressant clomipramine can help to improve the symptoms of OCD. Mirtazapine, a serotonergic enhancer that is used in depressive illness, may also be prescribed.

There are possible side effects with all of these drugs, although the more modern SSRIs tend to be safer. Alcohol and benzodiazepines are banned, because of the risk of the patient becoming dependent on them.

Drug treatment will be considered in many OCD cases, especially if there is a danger that a certain compulsion may lead sufferers to harm themselves or others.

Who is affected?

A little over one in a 100 people will have OCD at any one time, and up to three per cent of the population are at risk of developing it at some time between the ages of six and 70. It is equally prevalent in both sexes.

The condition usually begins in adolescence or early adulthood, with the peak age of onset around the age of 20. Only 15 per cent of sufferers first have symptoms over the age of 35. Many patients, however, do not seek medical advice about their condition until they reach middle age.

The onset of the condition is usually gradual – although in some cases it can be acute – and the condition tends to run a chronic course, with the severity of the symptoms changing over time. Prognosis is a fluctuating course of symptoms with a 60–80 per cent likelihood of recovery within a year.

Case study

Mrs J had always been meticulous over her appearance, but this had developed into a decontamination ritual: every time she entered her house, she felt compelled to remove all her clothes in the hallway, take a bath and put on clean garments. She was able to conceal her compulsion from everyone except her husband, whom she drew into it. She would not allow him past the door unless he also changed his clothes. Her feelings were so strong that she could not withstand them.

Her GP thought she was psychotic and prescribed the drug amisulpiride, but she became depressed and her compulsive behaviour was unabated. The GP reviewed the diagnosis and prescribed SSRI antidepressants.

After four months, Mrs J's symptoms were greatly improved, but her husband had moved out.

Acupuncture

Acupuncture is a form of Chinese medicine that is increasingly being used by conventional doctors. This complementary therapy uses needles in the skin to treat a wide range of conditions.

Acupuncture is a system of medicine in which very thin needles are inserted in the skin in order to treat disease.

HOW DOES ACUPUNCTURE WORK?

In traditional Chinese medicine, acupuncture is believed to work by harmonizing the flow of energy (Qi) through invisible channels in the body, known as meridians.

However, there is now scientific understanding of how acupuncture works: it stimulates the release of various chemicals (neurotransmitters) in the body, including endorphins (the body's natural painkillers), serotonin and noradrenaline; and it also stimulates the release of certain hormones. The way the nervous system operates is essential to how acupuncture works.

Acupuncture literally means 'needle piercing'. The therapy involves inserting thin needles into selected parts of the body to relieve symptoms.

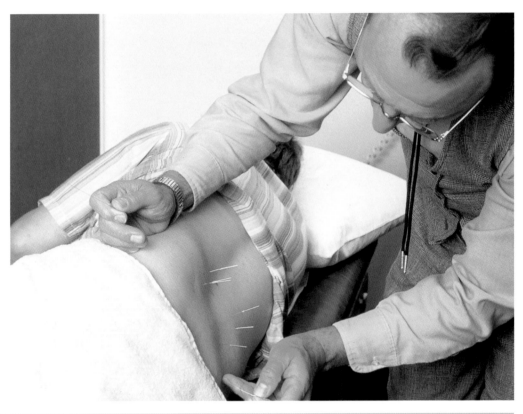

Benefits of acupuncture

There is now good scientific evidence for acupuncture's effectiveness in treating certain conditions. These include:
■ Musculoskeletal problems – such as osteoarthritis, and sports injuries such as tennis elbow

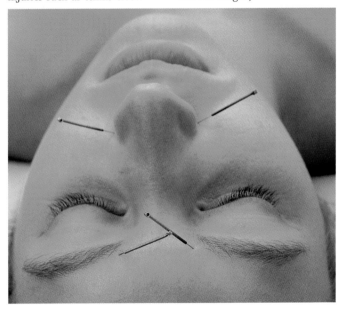

■ Pain – such as back pain, migraine, period pain, angina and trigeminal neuralgia (a sensory nerve disorder of the face causing sudden stabbing pain in the cheek, lips, gums, chin or tongue)

Needles are used to stimulate specific areas. For example, inserting needles into the face is thought to be beneficial to other parts of the body.

■ Nausea – relieving nausea associated with surgery, pregnancy and chemotherapy
■ Bowel problems – such as irritable bowel syndrome and colitis
■ Urinary problems – research has suggested that acupuncture can help in bedwetting
■ Allergies – including asthma, hay fever and urticaria (an allergic skin condition causing itchy, raised, pink patches)
■ Stress and addictions – acupuncture can help people overcome smoking, eating disorders and drug addictions, as well as stress relating to work or personal matters
■ Stroke – acupuncture may aid in recovery after a stroke; a large controlled trial is currently under way in the UK
■ Breech presentation (when the fetus is positioned incorrectly for

delivery) – correction of this requires turning the baby in the uterus; acupuncture aims to achieve this using moxibustion (burning of herbal agents near to the skin)
■ Fertility problems – many practitioners have claimed success using acupuncture in the treatment of couples who have problems trying to conceive.

Acupuncture may be used for treatment of addictions such as smoking. This form of treatment can help smokers overcome their habit permanently.

History of acupuncture

Acupuncture is an ancient system of medicine believed to have originated in China. The first definitive text on acupuncture was the *Huangdi Neijing*, or *The Yellow Emperor's Classic of Internal Medicine*, which was compiled between 500 and 300 BC. Acupuncture was probably brought to Europe in the seventeenth century by Dutch traders. Recent interest in acupuncture only really began in the West in the 1960s.

Western scientific acupuncture has adapted some traditional practices. There is now scientific evidence for the pain relief afforded by acupuncture.

According to traditional Chinese beliefs, illness is due to an energy imbalance. This imbalance is corrected by inserting needles in the skin.

TRADITIONAL CHINESE ACUPUNCTURE

Most acupuncture initially practised in the West was based on traditional Chinese medicine (TCM). This is founded on the ancient principles of yin and yang, energy flow, the five 'elements' (wood, fire, earth, metal and water) and the Zang-Fu system, which is based on the main 'organs' of the body and their functions.

Each of the main organs is related to a corresponding meridian, or a channel. Energy, or Qi, is believed to flow through the meridians, covering the whole body. According to TCM, disease occurs when the flow of Qi through the body is impaired.

Needles are inserted along the meridians in order to clear blockages in the flow of Qi and to restore the body's natural balance. There is little scientific evidence to support TCM theory, but it is based on many years of clinical experience.

WESTERN SCIENTIFIC ACUPUNCTURE

Some practitioners in the West have developed methods based on scientific understanding of the nervous system of the body. These are now grouped together under the term Western scientific

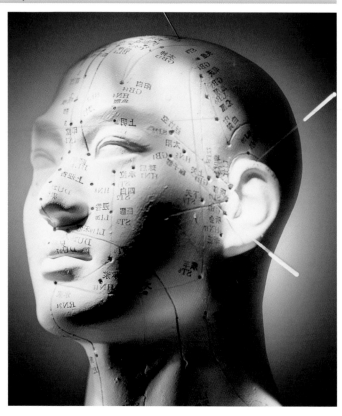

acupuncture, and include:
- Trigger point acupuncture – inserting needles into tender points on the body
- Periosteal acupuncture – needling the surface of bone
- Single point acupuncture – for example, on a specific point on the forearm to treat nausea
- Segmental acupuncture – based on the distribution of the nerves to the organs, muscles and skin.

EAST MEETS WEST

Not all of the 'Western scientific' methods of practising acupuncture are different from traditional methods. For example, Chinese acupuncturists have always used tender trigger points. Many TCM practitioners would also approve of single point therapy. There is no reason that these different theories and methods cannot exist side by side.

Acupuncture and pregnancy

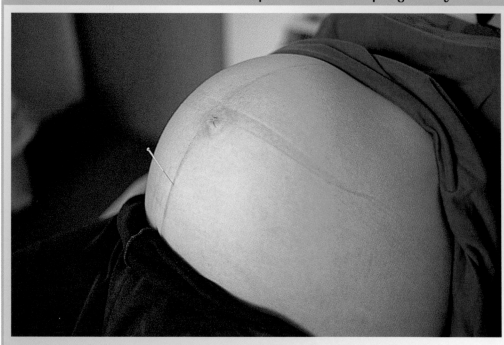

Some midwives have found that acupuncture has a particular place in pregnancy and childbirth. Acupuncture is offered at three NHS maternity units in the UK. It is most commonly used to treat the following conditions associated with pregnancy:
- Nausea
- Backache
- Sciatica
- Carpal tunnel syndrome
- Headaches
- Constipation
- Piles.

Occasionally, acupuncture can be used to induce delivery or for pain relief during labour, either during a normal delivery or a Caesarean section.

In some cases, acupuncture reduces the need for drugs used in pregnancy and birth. Such drugs may cross the placenta and affect the fetus.

Visiting an acupuncturist

Acupuncturists, like all holistic therapists, assess their patients as a whole person and not just in terms of specific disorders. This approach is reflected in the treatment, which may vary in method.

The first visit may be longer than subsequent sessions and its content will depend on the medical condition. In all cases, patients will be asked about their specific problem. The practitioner will need to know if a patient is taking any medication, especially as some can affect the acupuncture treatment. The acupuncturist will also need to find out if the patient suffers from any other illness.

EXAMINATION
Patients will undergo a physical examination, but a traditional Chinese acupuncturist will pay special attention to the condition of the tongue and the pulses at the wrist, where experienced acupuncturists believe they can assess the condition of each of the body's 12 main meridians and accompanying organs.

INSERTING NEEDLES
A number of needles – typically between four and 10, but possibly only one – are inserted into the skin from 5mm (¼ in) up to several centimetres in depth. They are traditionally left in for 10 to 30 minutes, but some practitioners needle for only a few seconds.

Needles are commonly inserted at or near to the area of the body which is affected, but are often inserted in acupuncture points some way away such as on the hands, feet or ears.

STIMULATING NEEDLES
Acupuncture needles are very thin and do not hurt in the same way as an injection. Needles may be stimulated by manual twirling or a small electrical current (electro-acupuncture).

Though the treatment may be completely painless, some acupuncturists will attempt to produce a sensation called 'de Qi'. This is a heaviness, soreness or feeling of warmth around the needle and is believed to be a sign that an acupuncture point has been correctly needled.

During and for a short while after treatment, people often experience a heaviness in the limbs or a pleasant feeling of relaxation. For this reason, patients are advised not to drive a vehicle immediately after receiving treatment.

Needles are inserted into acupoints on the body. The depth and length of time of insertion can vary depending upon the points that are used.

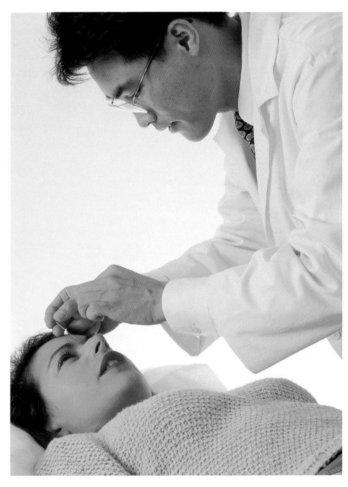

How often is treatment needed?

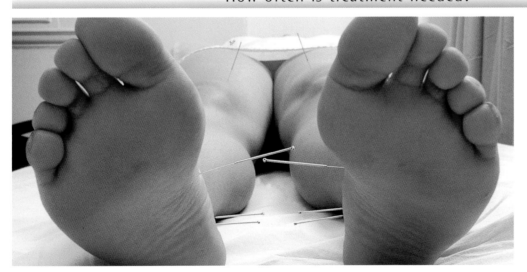

For new problems, such as a muscle strain, patients may need only one treatment. However, it is more common to have a course of treatment, typically weekly for 4-6 weeks. Conditions that patients have had for a long time, perhaps for many years, are likely to require more treatments.

However, if there is no improvement at all after six weeks, it is unlikely that acupuncture will help.

The length of treatment depends on the type of illness and the individual being treated. However, there is usually an improvement after six weeks.

Other methods of acupuncture

There are a number of different techniques that acupuncturists may use, including:

■ Ear acupuncture – tiny needles are inserted in the ear, and these are often stimulated electrically. The whole body is thought to be represented in the ear, with the head at the bottom in the lobe of the ear and the feet at the top.

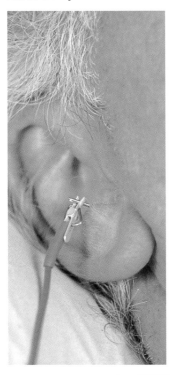

■ Electro-acupuncture – this involves attaching electrodes to the needles in order to cause an electrical stimulation. This can often be felt as a tingling or twitching but is not usually uncomfortable.

■ Acupressure – this refers to pressing acupuncture points with the thumb or finger. This can be an effective from of self-treatment, though the effect is generally less powerful than having needles inserted.

■ Moxibustion – this is used by some traditional acupuncturists. This involves the burning of the herb *Artemisia* (mugwort), either wrapped around the handle of a needle or as a cigar-shaped stick held over an acupoint.

■ Laser acupuncture – this is an experimental form of treatment being used by only a few practitioners. A laser beam is used to stimulate acupuncture points without piercing the skin. There is current uncertainty over the effectiveness of this form of acupuncture treatment.

Electro-acupuncture is a modern adaptation of traditional methods. A small electric current is used to stimulate a needle inserted in the skin.

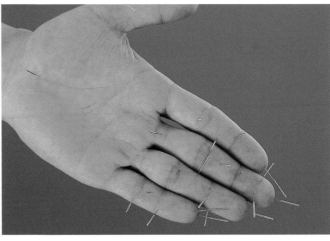

▲ *The traditional method of rotating a needle manually can be used on different parts of the body. Needles are inserted to stimulate the energy flow.*

▼ *Moxibustion involves burning a dried herb (mugwort) near to the skin. It is used to warm a needle inserted in the skin, stimulating the acupoint.*

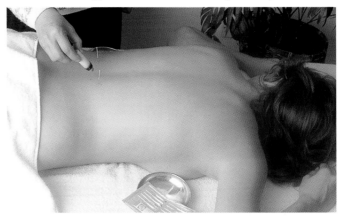

Are there any risks?

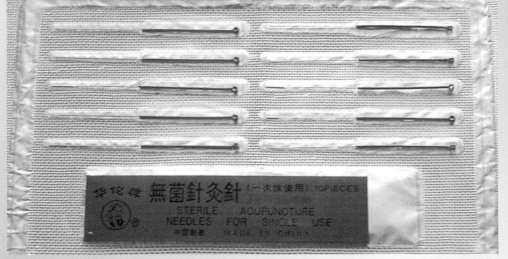

Acupuncture practitioners should use sterile disposable needles. This is to minimize the risk of infection.

What qualifications should an acupuncture practitioner have?
People wishing to receive acupuncture therapy should seek treatment from either a medical doctor or a well qualified lay acupuncturist. All members of The British Medical Acupuncture Society are doctors who are competent to practise acupuncture safely.

Where to find out more
The British Medical Acupuncture Society (BMAS) was founded in 1980 as an association of medical practitioners interested in acupuncture. There are now 1700 members who use acupuncture in NHS general practice, and in hospital or private practice. The BMAS recommends the practice of acupuncture by trained health care professionals.

Before embarking upon acupuncture, it is imperative that patients have a diagnosis made by a doctor to ensure that acupuncture is the most appropriate treatment.

Not all conditions are suitable for treatment with acupuncture. For example, there is no evidence that acupuncture can treat cancer, though it could be used effectively for pain relief.

Acupuncture is safe when used by a qualified practitioner. However, occasional side effects include an increase in pain (usually only temporary), bruising, dizziness and, very rarely skin infections, or even more rarely a punctured lung (though this should not occur if treated by a properly trained acupuncturist).

To minimize the risk of infection acupuncture should only be given using sterile disposable needles. Special precautions need to be taken in pregnancy.

Alexander technique

The Alexander technique is not strictly a therapy; rather, it teaches people how to regain natural posture and use their bodies efficiently. It can alleviate joint pain, breathing problems and nervous tension.

The Alexander technique is the practical study of certain aspects of the relationship between a person's mind and body. The technique looks, in particular, at the mechanisms given by nature for the body to support itself against gravity.

Under normal conditions, a two-way flow of information and feedback maintains appropriate muscle tone. This information flow can, however, become disturbed as a result of injury, illness, post-operative stress or inappropriate lifestyle. Most commonly, however, the flow is affected by the various mental, physical and emotional bad habits associated with modern life.

HISTORY
The technique was developed by an Australian, Frederick Alexander, who was born in 1869. He discovered that it is possible to learn, firstly, how to recognize the various ways in which we interfere with our natural support system, and then to learn how to prevent this interference from recurring.

This primarily involves taking responsibility for oneself and one's actions, in terms of how we do things, rather than what we do. The Alexander technique uses the tools of observation, awareness and attention.

HUMAN MOVEMENT
As a young man, Alexander pursued a career in the theatre. Severe and recurrent vocal and respiratory problems almost forced him to give up his chosen profession, but an absolute determination to find the cause of his difficulty led him to the discovery of certain fundamental truths about human reactivity, co-ordination and movement.

Having overcome his own problems, he became known for his exceptional vocal technique. It was not long before he began to teach what he had learned to others – initially, singers and actors.

GENERAL BENEFITS
As Alexander's reputation grew, many doctors sent patients with respiratory problems to him. It soon became apparent that his method was of benefit to people in many other ways than just the treatment of vocal and/or respiratory problems.

Alexander believed that he had discovered a key to resolving many hitherto unexplained complaints from which people suffer.

The Alexander technique teaches people how to utilize their bodies more efficiently. It is taught by verbal instructions and manual guidance.

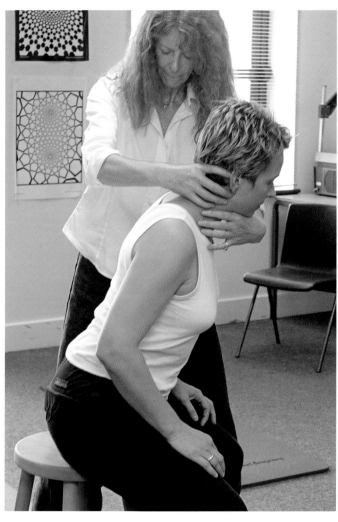

How does it work?

The Alexander technique is a method for regaining the natural co-ordination of the body, primarily by learning how to eliminate the physical and mental patterns (habits) which interfere with what nature has given us.

HOLISTIC APPROACH
The technique is based on the principle that mind, body and emotions form part of a potentially harmonious whole. Rather than trying to address specific problems, such as

The Alexander technique can address bad postural habits developed over time. Even dancers, known for their good posture, can benefit from it.

backache or a stiff neck, it focuses on the source of such problems, which are very often the result of a general disharmony in our functioning. It has been found in many cases that, by restoring the natural co-ordination between the parts of the body, specific complaints often disappear.

NATURAL POISE
The technique seeks to help people rediscover the natural grace and agility with which they moved as children. This natural poise is soon lost, with many people leading sedentary lifestyles bent over desks and computers; problems usually described as 'postural' can therefore easily develop.

Principles of the Alexander technique

The Alexander technique is based on the following principles:

■ Recognition of force of habit
The ways in which people make ordinary movements can feel so familiar to them that they usually do not recognize that they may have formed some very harmful habits – these are then incorporated into activities in which they engage, at work or leisure.

Once pupils recognize that what seems normal and 'right' – even though it may be causing them pain – is just the familiarity of habit, there is the possibility of making changes.

■ Faulty sensory awareness
Once bad habits have become established, people can no longer rely on the feedback from the body in terms of co-ordination and muscle tension. The Alexander technique greatly improves sensory awareness – once people are aware of tensions, they can let them go.

■ Inhibition
Alexander defined inhibition as the power to withhold consent to do something. People usually react very quickly to all stimuli. If these automatic reactions and movements are based on habits and faulty sensory awareness, the same problems constantly recur.

With sufficient mental alertness, it is possible to receive a stimulus and to choose not to react to it. If a response is made,

it can be done in a way that does not involve all the harmful habits. This process can be executed very quickly – at the speed of thought.

■ Direction
Muscle tone is maintained by a flow of 'information' from the brain. It is possible to learn how to direct this flow of information more consciously, not so much by the superimposing of something on the body, as by

affirming and co-operating with what is already there underlying the bad habits.

■ Means to an end
Most people are familiar with the saying, 'more haste, less speed'. In the majority of activities, people are hurrying to achieve results. The effect of this is that not enough attention is given to how activities are being carried out. Habits, faulty sensory awareness, inhibition

There are five principles behind Alexander technique. These are aimed at helping pupils to improve their co-ordination and posture, for work and leisure.

and direction are all about how activities are performed. By paying attention to the process and not just the result, it is possible to remain calm and co-ordinated – and the job is performed just as well, if not better.

Going to a teacher

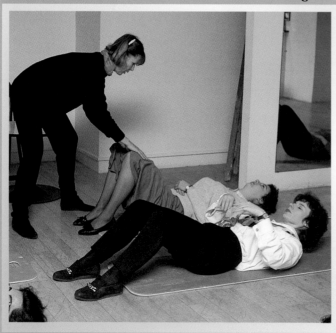

Teachers of the Alexander technique learn a unique way of using their hands to give pupils a direct experience of the principles of human functioning. Teachers train for a minimum of three years to acquire the necessary understanding of the principles in operation and the skilful use of heir hands.

One-to-one sessions
The technique is taught in a series of one-to-one sessions. Usually about 25–30 sessions over a period of around six months are required, with the sessions occurring more frequently in the early stages and

Lessons, taught over a period of months, usually last 30–45 minutes. After a series of private one-to-one sessions, group classes may be helpful.

then with less frequency as the principles and practice are assimilated by the patient.

An experienced teacher can bring about a change in a pupil in a matter of minutes; however, to sustain the process of change, practice by the pupil will be necessary between sessions.

At the beginning, especially, much of the work is 'hands-on', until the pupil becomes familiar with the technique. Change occurs most effectively when the pupil discovers something uniquely applicable to him/herself.

Group classes
When a pupil has had a series of lessons, group classes with other people who share a similar level of understanding can be a useful, interactive way of further exploring the ideas on which the technique is based.

Using the Alexander technique

The technique is taught in a series of lessons, over a period of months. By means of special techniques and regular practice, pupils gradually learn how to address and rectify their postural problems.

Every teacher has their own individual way of working, but usually the pupil can expect to be asked what their reason is for wanting Alexander lessons; they may have a specific illness or medical condition that the teacher should know about.

ASSESSMENT
The pupil will remain fully clothed throughout the lesson (tight-fitting clothes are not suitable, and women should wear trousers).

The teacher may ask the pupil to make a simple movement – to walk across the room or sit down, for instance – while watching how the pupil uses their body.

Then, using his or her hands, the teacher will bring about a subtle change in the relationship between the head, neck and back. This is usually experienced by the pupil as a feeling of lightness, release of tension or expansion.

RELEASING TENSION
The pupil may be asked to lie down, and the teacher will show them how to lie in a way that already allows for some release of bodily tension.

The teacher will then, by using the hands in a very gentle way, help the pupil to let go of tension in the neck; this is of vital importance in bringing about a release of contraction in the deep layer of muscles running between the vertebrae. The back then tends to spread out, the ribcage begins to loosen and breathing becomes easier.

EMOTIONAL HARMONY
To an outside observer, it may seem as though little is happening during the lesson.

A trained eye, however, may see in the pupil some greater freedom of movement, an increase in height or improved posture, but the significant changes are those experienced internally: the sense of calm and well-being, the feeling of integration and the decrease in tension.

Each teacher of the Alexander technique has his or her own system. However, the principle of re-educating pupils about posture is shared by all.

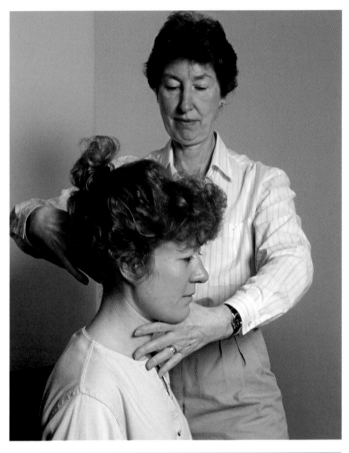

Typical techniques

1 *In an early session, the teacher may ask the pupil to lie down. The teacher shows the pupil how to lie so that some tension is released.*

2 *The teacher may use their hands gently to help the pupil relax the neck muscles. This will help to release the muscles between the vertebrae.*

3 *The teacher guides the pupil in simple activities, such as sitting and bending. This enables the pupil to cultivate the necessary awareness in activity.*

As the pupil begins to experience improvements in performing simple activities, such as sitting or bending, more complex activities can be explored. These might include playing a musical instrument, using a keyboard or singing.

APPLYING THE TECHNIQUE
Between lessons, pupils begin to apply what has been learned. This is done by:
■ Spending 10 or 15 minutes a day lying down in the way in which they have been shown, to allow the muscles of the back and neck to release tension
■ Bringing more attention and awareness to daily activities
■ Beginning to notice how certain patterns of stimulus and response tend to recur.

Benefits of the Alexander technique

The most immediately noticeable benefits of the Alexander technique are physical in nature.

PHYSICAL WELL-BEING

For many people, having lessons gives them for the first time the experience of 'letting go' and a sense of well-being in the body. They may now start to view their body as a sensitive and integral part of the self.

Typical complaints which have been helped by the Alexander technique include:
■ Stiff neck and shoulders
■ Repetitive strain injury (RSI)
■ Prolapsed, herniated or worn intervertebral discs
■ Lower back pain
■ Hip problems
■ Angina
■ Respiratory problems.

EMOTIONAL HEALTH

Not only can the Alexander technique be of great benefit in alleviating physical complaints, but it can bring about improvements in mental and emotional health. Stress-related conditions, anxiety and nervous tension, panic attacks and general fatigue are all believed to be helped by the technique.

Pupils receiving both physical and emotional benefits from the technique will cease to think of the mind, body and emotions as separate entities. Rather, they will become aware of the integration of mind and body and may find it possible to return to a more balanced state.

The possibility of consciously using one's potential to 'give or withhold consent' can have far-reaching implications. Even at a very basic level, people trying to put this idea into practice report a sense of having greater control over their lives.

APPLICATIONS

The Alexander technique has, for many years, been taught in major colleges of music and drama in Europe and the USA. It is increasingly being used in the commercial sector, and thousands of men and women in all spheres of life the world over have benefited from learning and using it.

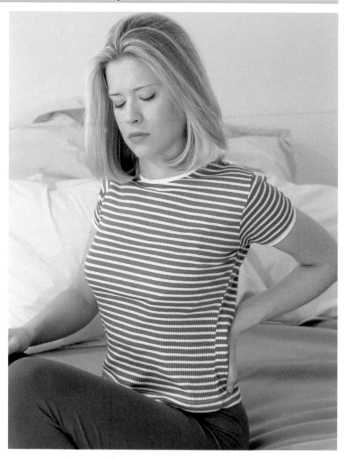

Back pain is one of a number of complaints that can be alleviated by Alexander technique. Improvements can become evident after just a few sessions.

RSI and Alexander technique

Good posture at work can help to prevent RSI. Desks and chairs should be correctly positioned and the lower back should always be supported.

Office workers tend to hunch over their computers. Over time, this bad posture, and repetitive actions, can lead to soft tissue injury and backache.

Repetitive strain injury (RSI) is a term used to describe a number of different types of soft tissue injury, including backache and carpel tunnel syndrome. The condition is usually caused by bad ergonomics, poor posture and repetitive actions.

While the symptoms will respond to treatment, the injury will recur if the underlying cause is not treated. The key to dealing with RSI lies in tackling the original cause of the repetitive injury.

Repetitive strain injuries are often caused just as much by poor posture as by overuse. The Alexander technique is extremely effective at addressing postural problems, by aiming to correct bad habits that may have been practised over many years.

Preventing RSI at work
The workplace is a common factor in RSI, since many people tend to carry out the same tasks every day, sitting in the same position for long periods of time, or possibly carrying heavy loads. Many office workers tend to slouch in front of a computer.

To prevent RSI, it is important that the work space is well-planned. This includes:

■ Positioning the desk and chair at appropriate heights, so that both feet can rest flat on the floor
■ Ensuring that the chair faces the computer, so that no awkward twisting motions are involved when using the computer
■ Adjusting the chair so that it supports the lower back.

It is also a good idea to take regular breaks and to change position to avoid over-straining the same muscles and joints.

Reflexology

Reflexology is a complementary technique used to treat a wide range of disorders. It involves manipulation of the 'reflex' areas of the feet or hands to influence and stimulate corresponding areas of the body.

Reflexology is a holistic treatment that involves gentle pressure massage of the feet. It is based on the principle that each part of the body is mapped onto a corresponding part of the foot as a reflex point or area, and that pressure applied to these sites stimulates the body's natural balancing and healing processes.

THE HISTORY OF REFLEXOLOGY

Reflexology has been in use for thousands of years; its origins date back to ancient times, when it was first practised by

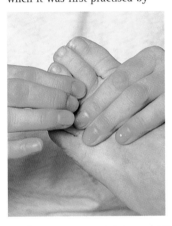

the early Indian, Chinese and Egyptian peoples. However, the technique in its current form was initiated and developed by an American ear, nose and throat surgeon, Dr William Fitzgerald, in 1913.

Dr Fitzgerald discovered that pressure on specific parts of the body could have an anaesthetizing effect on a related area. He developed this theory into what is known as zone therapy. In zone therapy, the body is divided into 10 equal zones, ending in the fingers and the toes. Pressure on one part of a zone can affect everything else within that zone, thus linking reflex areas on the hands and feet to all other areas and organs of the body within that zone.

Reflexology has many applications – some women, for example, find that it can help with the aches and pains associated with pregnancy.

Reflexology relies on the use of manipulation and massage of the feet and sometimes hands. It is also believed to stimulate the immune system.

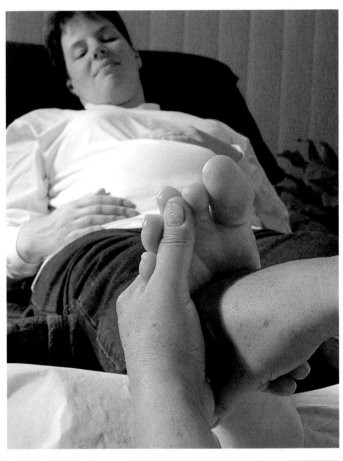

Visiting a reflexologist

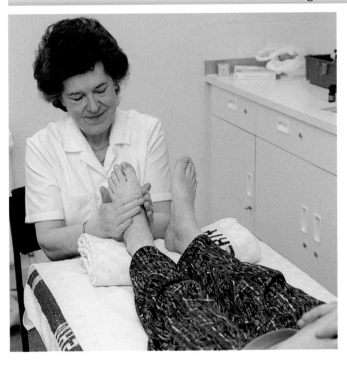

The first visit to a reflexologist begins with the therapist taking a detailed medical history to determine the general state of health of a patient, and to help the reflexologist decide which reflexes may need extra attention. Reflexology is not advisable in patients with any condition that may be worsened due to treatment, such as blood clots or lymphatic cancer.

A reflexologist should be consulted only after any serious medical conditions have been recognized by a physician.

THE CONSULTATION

After the medical history has been taken, the patient removes their shoes and socks and lies or sits on a couch while the

A session of reflexology should be relaxing and unhurried, with the therapist taking their time in treating the patient.

reflexologist carries out the treatment.

On the whole, reflexology should be an enjoyable experience. Some sites may be tender or painful: this discomfort usually indicates congestion or an energy imbalance and should only be momentary, easing as the reflex point is worked.

Reflexology encourages the body to increase elimination of toxins and some people may experience a 'healing crisis'. This may involve a slight headache and perhaps a temporary worsening of symptoms while the body is in this transitory state.

The number of treatments required varies according to the patient's needs and their responsiveness to treatment. It is not unusual for an improvement to be noticed after the first treatment; however, it may take much longer to see any change in more serious conditions.

Cross reflexes

Reflexology is based on the theory that the body is divided into reflex zones which allow one area of the body to be influenced by another using 'cross reflexes'.

The reflex zones extend throughout the whole body. The arms and legs are made up of the same zones, and a relationship exists between the right arm and right leg and the left arm and left leg and the joints in these limbs. These 'zone related' areas are commonly known as 'cross reflexes'.

The cross reflexes are hand to foot, knee to elbow, hip to shoulder and ankle to wrist. Cross reflexes can be used to affect bodily areas where, for various reasons, direct treatment cannot be applied. Treatment of these areas is known as 'referral'. For example, the referral zone of the elbow would be the knee.

HOW DOES IT WORK?

One theory is based around the concept that reflexology works primarily by improving the flow of blood and lymph around the body. This flow can be impaired by crystalline deposits of uric acid, which are found in the reflexes of the feet.

A reflexologist can break up and disperse these deposits by working over the reflexes. Often it is possible to feel these crystals, though sometimes their presence is made apparent only by watching the patient's response, as working over these crystals produces sensations ranging from slight tenderness to extreme sharp pain.

Map of the reflex areas of the soles of the feet

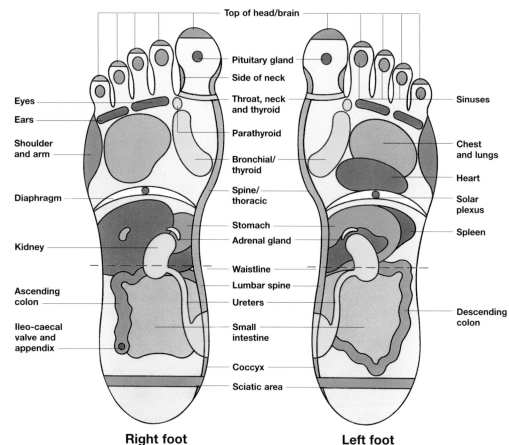

Top of head/brain — Pituitary gland — Side of neck — Throat, neck and thyroid — Parathyroid — Bronchial/thyroid — Spine/thoracic — Stomach — Adrenal gland — Waistline — Lumbar spine — Ureters — Small intestine — Coccyx — Sciatic area

Eyes — Ears — Shoulder and arm — Diaphragm — Kidney — Ascending colon — Ileo-caecal valve and appendix

Sinuses — Chest and lungs — Heart — Solar plexus — Spleen — Descending colon

Right foot

The organs of the body are mapped in corresponding reflex areas of the foot. Some areas are the same for both feet.

Left foot

Reflex areas may differ between practitioners; this diagram is based on a chart designed by Doreen Bayley.

Treating different zones

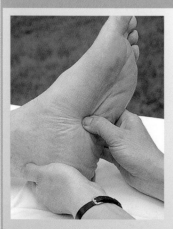

Small intestine
The small intestine reflex area is found on both feet. The thumb is used in a 'caterpillar' movement across the lower sole, working from the centre towards the inside of the foot.

Reproductive organs
The reproductive organ reflex sites are around the ankles on both feet. This shows the uterus or prostate point (same area in men and women) on the inside of the foot below the ankle.

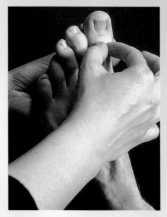

Neck
The neck area on each foot is massaged from the front of the big toe to the nail bed followed by the back of the big toe. This can be painful, especially when working towards the second toe.

Thyroid gland
The reflex area for this is found on both feet. A 'caterpillar' movement is used around the bottom of the first metatarsal bone toward the big toe. This area is then massaged in rows.

Applications of reflexology

Reflexology is used to treat many problems, from breathing difficulties to pain relief. The therapy is also increasingly being used to complement conventional medical treatments.

Reflexology is an effective form of therapy and it has many different applications. The therapy has been shown to bring relief to a wide range of acute and chronic conditions, including musculoskeletal pain, circulatory problems, digestive complaints, hormonal imbalances, sinus and breathing difficulties and migraine.

PAIN RELIEF

Studies have also shown reflexology to be effective in the alleviation of conditions where conventional medicine sometimes fails to bring relief from the symptoms, such as chronic fatigue syndrome and multiple sclerosis.

Reflexology is now being increasingly used in hospitals and in palliative care for the terminally ill. It has been shown to accelerate recovery times both from illness and surgery and is highly effective in relieving pain and distress and can reduce the need for pain relieving drugs, such as morphine. Reflexology may also reduce the need for medication in various other conditions.

Studies show a reduction in both heart rate and blood pressure following reflexology treatment, so it is important for anyone taking drugs for the purpose of controlling these physiological measures to inform their reflexologist.

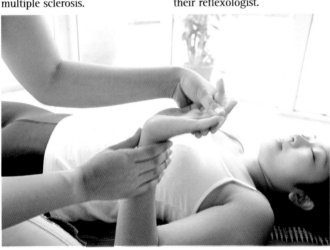

For people who are terminally ill, such as this AIDS patient, reflexology may be used to bring about the temporary relief of painful symptoms.

Musculoskeletal pain may be relieved by reflexology. This kind of therapy is increasingly available in hospitals throughout the UK.

Using reflexology for stress relief

Reflexology is in common use purely for stress relief and relaxation. Many people live and work in a stressful environment and find it difficult to relax. This takes its toll on the immune system, resulting in lack of sleep and illness.

Many large companies are now making reflexology treatment available to their staff

Many patients use reflexology as an aid for stress relief and relaxation. Regular sessions can also be useful in helping to regulate sleep patterns.

and have found it to reduce levels of sickness and absenteeism, increase productivity and develop staff enthusiasm and morale.

CONTROLLING SLEEP PATTERNS

Another useful application of reflexology is its effectiveness in treating jetlag. As sleep patterns are regulated by the endocrine system, the reflexologist can pay special attention to these reflexes, thus helping to bring the body clock back into balance.

Reflexology and drug and alcohol abuse

Reflexology has been found to be especially useful in treating people with drug- or alcohol-abuse problems. People who have problems of this nature will suffer from chemical and glandular imbalances, and will aslo be causing themselves serious physical damage. Reflexology helps immensely with rectifying these imbalances as well as speeding up the detoxification process.

EMOTIONAL EFFECTS

Reflexology is also useful in the treatment of drug and alcohol addiction because it works on an emotional level, which is the level at which most drug- and alcohol-related problems start. Reflexology has the ability to both release and calm negative emotions, and it is not uncommon for someone to become tearful after a treatment or to feel very calm, in stark contrast to the feelings of anger and rage that may of been felt at the start of the treatment.

A common problem for people with drug or alcohol addiction is that they find they cannot sleep or relax without the aid of drugs or alcohol; reflexology also helps greatly within this setting.

People who are addicted to alcohol often find they cannot sleep or relax without a drink. Reflexology can help to break this cycle of dependence.

Addiction to drugs such as cocaine can lead to chemical imbalances in the body. Reflexology has been shownto be of some help to people with this type of problem.

Reflexology and children

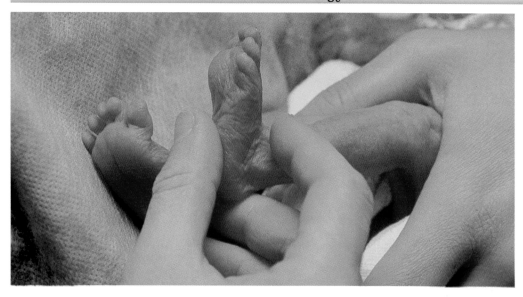

Babies and children can be treated effectively with reflexology once any serious medical condition has been excluded; however, children's feet are far more responsive than adults' and should be treated accordingly. The pressure used should be much lighter than that used on adults. For young babies, it is sufficient to use one finger very gently.

It is also important to take care when treating children approaching puberty, as the endocrine system is in a state of heightened activity.

Newborn babies can benefit from reflexology, but gentle pressure is necessary because their feet are very sensitive.

Hand reflexology

Reflexology may be applied to the hands instead of the feet. The hands have exactly the same reflexes as the feet, but as the hands are so much more mobile these reflexes are not so clearly defined. Due to the fact we use our hands all the time and they are constantly exposed to the elements, they are not as sensitive; tender areas may not be picked up as easily.

It is important for a reflexologist to be familiar with the reflexes in the hands so they can be worked on when for some reason the feet cannot be treated. In cases of injury to or amputation of a foot, great relief can still be given through the hands.

Another area where hand reflexology is useful is for self-help. It is much easier and more comfortable to treat yourself on the hands than on the feet. A practitioner may show a patient where certain reflexes are located to help with pain relief.

Reflexology can be applied to the hands as well as the feet. This may be useful in cases where self-help pain relief may be needed between sessions.

Aromatherapy

Aromatherapy uses essential oils to improve health and wellbeing. Oils are applied to the skin, or burned to allow calming or invigorating aromas to be released into the atmosphere.

Aromatherapy is the systematic use of essential oils in holistic treatments to improve physical and emotional wellbeing. These natural plant oils are the aromatic, volatile substances extracted from botanical sources by steam distillation or expression. These sources include flowers, plants, herbs, leaves, woods, fruits and gums.

The resulting highly concentrated essential oil then contains all the aroma and therapeutic properties of the source from which it was derived and can be used to promote positive health and prevent disease.

ORIGINS

Many ancient cultures understood and valued the healing properties of essential oils and their powerful influence on the emotions.

Ancient Ayurvedic Indian literature and Chinese medical scripts described healing with essential oils. Ancient Egyptians used balsams, perfumed oils, scented barks and resins, spices and aromatic vinegars as well as juniper, myrrh and cinnamon in mummification. For the Egyptians, plants played a crucial part in life, death and resurrection.

HEALING PROPERTIES

During World War I, essential oils were used in a variety of civilian and military hospitals. In the 1920s, a French chemist, Dr Rene-Maurice Gattefosse,

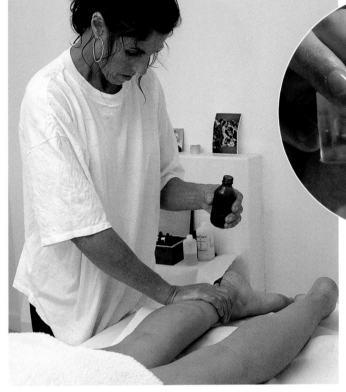

Essential oils are very concentrated and only a few drops are needed for each treatment. For massage, the oils are diluted in a base oil.

Massage is an ideal way to administer aromatherapy, as the oils are directly absorbed by the skin. Numerous problems are treated using essential oils.

researched the healing potential of essential oils following successful treatment with lavender oil of serious burns to his hands caused by a laboratory explosion. He discovered that many essential oils were more effective antiseptics than any synthetic products and coined the term 'aromatherapie'.

The French army surgeon Dr Jean Valnet furthered this research by successfully using oils in surgery during World War II. His protegé, Madame Arcier, subsequently introduced aromatherapy clinics to Britain in the 1950s through beauty therapy. Beauty therapists were taught to use blended essential oils in massage treatments.

WIDER USE

Since that time, aromatherapy has developed far beyond beauty therapy. Aromatherapy as a complementary therapy began to gain wider acceptance in the UK during the 1970s, since when there has been a renewed interest in this form of healing. This increase in use is mainly due to the search for gentler and more natural substitutes for chemically produced medicines. Today, aromatherapy is one of the most popular complementary therapies and is an important part of healthcare.

What problems can aromatherapy help?

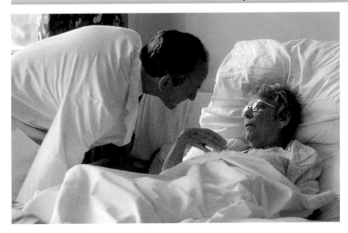

Aromatherapy is commonly used in the hospital setting. It has been found to be particularly helpful in relieving pain and promoting sleep in the very ill.

In common with all forms of holistic medicine, aromatherapy works on the whole body to improve general wellbeing.

Aromatherapy is particularly effective for alleviating:
■ Stress and anxiety-related conditions
■ Rheumatic pains and arthritis
■ Menstrual problems
■ Menopausal complaints
■ Skin problems
■ Digestive disorders
■ Insomnia
■ Depression.

Aromatherapy may also be used to improve the overall quality of life of elderly and terminally ill people and those with learning disabilities. It has also been shown to play a role in maternity units.

Treatment with essential oils is effective for health maintenance and therefore helps to encourage preventative healthcare and personal responsibility for health.

How aromatherapy works

Essential oils possess distinctive and unique healing properties. For example, the UK's most popular essential oil, lavender, is antiseptic, analgesic, antibiotic, decongestant, relaxant, anti-inflammatory and sedative. It therefore has a wide range of uses, from skin problems to sleep disorders and depression.

METHODS OF APPLICATION

Essential oils are applied in a variety of ways, which include:
- Massage – this is the most common form of treatment and is very effective. The combined effects of touch and the fragrance of the oils promote physical and emotional health
- Baths – any oil can be added to bath water. Footbaths can also be scented with oils
- Inhalations – these can be direct inhalations or steam inhalations
- Compresses – a piece of cotton is soaked in water containing a few drops of oil, and the compress is then applied to the skin. Compresses help to relieve skin problems, bruising, and muscle pain
- Application of pre-blended creams and lotions.

PSYCHOLOGICAL BENEFITS

The full psychological benefits of the aroma are obtained when oils are inhaled. The aroma sends an immediate signal to the limbic system of the brain – the centre of memory and emotions – where it can exert a powerful effect on the mind, mood and emotions to bring about a general feeling of wellbeing.

ABSORPTION

Essential oils are made up of tiny molecules that are easily absorbed by the membranes of the lungs and through the skin pores, hair follicles and the skin surfaces. The oils are broken down by the skin and their constituents spread to other areas of the body, causing gentle physiological changes.

Oil can be burned in an oil burner; this technique fills the room with the aroma. Lavender oil is particularly useful for relaxation.

Oils

There are many essential oils, each with its own particular healing property. There are several widely used oils, which include the following:

- Eucalyptus (*Eucalyptus globulus*) – antiseptic, decongestant – used to treat chest infections and colds

- Lavender (*Lavendula vera officinalis*) – antiseptic, soothing – used to treat skin problems, indigestion, headaches, burns

- Rosemary (*Rosmarinus officinalis*) – refreshing, stimulating – used to treat colds, aches and pains, poor circulation

Essential oils can be purchased from specialist shops. Each oil has individual properties and is used to treat particular problems.

- Lemon (*Citrus limonem*) – stimulating, refreshing – used to treat depression, acne, warts

- Geranium (*Pelargonium graveolens*) – relaxing, refreshing – used to treat premenstrual tension, menopausal complaints, anxiety

- Peppermint (*Mentha piperita*) – digestive, refreshing – used to treat bad breath, indigestion, toothache

Consultation and treatment

A skilled aromatherapist has specific expertise in how to optimize an individual's health and wellbeing. Prior to treatment, the aromatherapist will therefore carry out a full consultation, taking into account medical history, any current medical problems, general level of health and lifestyle.

MASSAGE

The aromatherapist then asks the individual to undress and lie down on a massage table. The therapist selects and blends appropriate essential oils in a carrier oil that is suitable for that person. If the individual has a preference for certain oils, these are generally used, because this

During a consultation, the nature of the problem is ascertained. The therapist then selects appropriate essential oils that suit the individual.

has been shown to enhance their treatment. The therapist usually applies oils in combination with traditional massage techniques, and will also prescribe home treatment.

BENEFITS

The carrier oils themselves have specific beneficial effects on bodily health and form a vital part of the treatment. The combination of the therapeutic properties of essential oils with massage and touch produces a powerful, health-giving treatment.

A full body massage generally lasts around 30–45 minutes. After the massage, the individual relaxes for a few minutes and is advised not to bathe or shower for several hours to ensure that the oils are properly absorbed and the scent of the oil lingers. Oils may be given to the recipient to use at home.

Chinese herbal medicine

Chinese herbal medicine has been used for thousands of years to treat a number of physical, mental and emotional conditions. Herbal infusions are the mainstay of treatment.

Chinese herbal medicine uses a variety of different herbal preparations, tailored to individual needs, to treat and prevent illness, whether it is physical or emotional.

TRADITIONAL CHINESE MEDICINE

Chinese herbal medicine is one of the treatment methods of Traditional Chinese Medicine (TCM). For several thousand years, TCM has been the dominant system of healing throughout eastern Asia.

TCM interprets how the body works using a model that is completely independent of the western bio-medical model. As a result, the practitioners of traditional Chinese medicine can often interpret a pattern of symptoms that do not fit easily into a bio-medical disease category.

In Chinese herbal medicine, herbs are prescribed to treat the underlying causes of illness. These herbs are dispensed in Chinese pharmacies.

Key aspects of Traditional Chinese Medicine

There are several key aspects of TCM, including:

■ **Yin and Yang**
The balance of Yin and Yang is a fundamental concept. All the body's functions and substances have two interdependent aspects: Yin – the cooling, relaxing, dark and quiet side; and Yang – the energetic, warm, bright side.

For the body to be in harmony, Yin and Yang must be in balance. A person who rushes around all day without resting at night, who is always hot and has no way of cooling, or whose life is full of sadness with no joy, will have a body that is not in harmony and will soon become ill.

■ **Qi (energy), blood and body fluids**
Qi, our life force or vital energy, is the second key aspect of TCM. Qi is derived from food and air

Yin and Yang are the two opposing forces in Chinese philosophy. Yin is the inward-looking force while Yang is more dynamic.

and adds to the Qi with which everyone is born.

Blood and other body fluids, such as tears or saliva, are seen as other aspects of Qi, which allow energy to flow around the body and maintain good health.

Qi must flow freely and abundantly throughout the body. If Qi is stuck in one place, unable to move easily around the body, it will cause illness. If there is too little Qi in the body, a person will be weak and tired. If too much Qi rises to the head, headaches or dizziness occur.

■ **Organs**
The organs of the body are understood as having slightly different functions to their role in western medicine.

The Heart is seen as the organ which makes blood from Qi. The Lungs are the organs which take in air, a form of Qi, and distribute it to be used by the rest of the body.

The Spleen is the part of the digestive system that allows food to be converted into Qi. If

the Spleen is working well and the diet is appropriate, a person will feel full of energy. Stomach Qi should descend to allow food to be properly digested.

Environment

In TCM, environmental factors are referred to as pathogenic influences. These include:
■ Wind – associated with head colds, pain in the joints and skin complaints
■ Dryness – associated with dry skin, irritation of the eyes, dry throat and mouth, chest problems and constipation
■ Cold – associated with abdominal pain, period pains in women, painful joints and cold hands and feet
■ Heat – associated with inflammation, and excessive bleeding
■ Dampness – associated with headaches, skin problems, feeling bloated, stiff limbs, vaginal discharge, and fatigue.

Causes of disease

TCM places emphasis on understanding the cause of disease, so that, if necessary, the patient can make changes to their lifestyle or diet to prevent the disease recurring or becoming worse.

SHORT-TERM PROBLEMS
The role of the Chinese herbalist is to find the underlying cause of the illness. Some problems may be caused by trauma or an invasion by a pathogen, such as:

Examining the tongue is a vital part of making a diagnosis in Chinese herbal medicine. The tongue is thought to reveal much about the patient's health.

Herbs are dispensed as part of a regime to treat the whole person, rather than just the symptoms. The treatment aims to tackle the causes of illness.

■ Wind-heat, which causes fever or flulike symptoms
■ Bad food, which causes an invasion of damp-heat in the Stomach and Intestines, leading to abdominal pain and diarrhoea
■ Excessive antibiotics, locking heat into the body.

LONG-TERM PROBLEMS
Problems that develop gradually may be attributed to an unhealthy lifestyle. Factors that can lead to poor health include:
■ Excessive work or activity of one particular type
■ Emotional problems, such as excessive worry or frustration
■ Diet that is unsuitable for the individual.

CHINESE APPROACH
Chinese herbal medicine aims to treat not just the symptoms, but also to tackle their underlying causes. This is called a holistic approach to patient care, meaning that the patient's physical and mental state as well lifestyle factors are all taken into account when diagnosing and treating an illness.

'HOT' DISEASES
An example of a recipient of the holistic approach might be the person who is always hot, has eczema and eats a lot of 'hot' foods such as curry, red wine

and coffee; all these make the skin condition worse. In addition, the patient may develop another 'hot' disease, such as the burning discomfort of indigestion, or cystitis.

Chinese herbs can be given to treat the indigestion, burning urination and eczema, but the patient will also be advised to cut down on their intake of hot foods, thus treating the underlying cause.

EASTERN MODEL
In some ways, the objectives of TCM are similar to those of Western medicine, and many of the differences are simply in the terminology and language of Chinese medicine.

In the long-term, the proof of the system must be judged on its results; clinical trials have shown that Chinese herbal medicine can improve certain conditions.

Common problems treated with Chinese herbalism

By virtue of its unique basis, TCM can potentially treat almost any symptom.

Today in China, herbalism is used alongside conventional medicine because it is recognized that certain problems are best treated with one or the other.

Herbalism in the West
These days, people in the west visit Chinese herbalists with a wide variety of health problems.

Many patients choose Chinese herbal medicine because Western medicine has not found a cure for their symptoms; others cannot tolerate Western drug therapy or would like to try a gentler option before going ahead with surgery.

Skin conditions, such as eczema, can be treated with Chinese herbs. Affected children can benefit, although they receive smaller doses.

Babies and children, the elderly and very weak patients can benefit just as much from treatment with herbs but are given smaller doses.

Patients who are taking conventional drugs should seek advice from the Chinese herbalist about whether the herbs suggested are compatible.

Treatable conditions
Areas in which Chinese herbs are well known to have particularly good results include:
■ Skin diseases, such as eczema, psoriasis and acne
■ Gynaecological conditions – for example, dysmenorrhoea, menopausal symptoms and infertility
■ Respiratory conditions including asthma and rhinitis (inflammation of the lining of the nose)
■ Digestive complaints.

Chiropractic

Chiropractic is a method of treating disorders of the musculo-skeletal system. The treatment uses a series of manipulative techniques, focusing particularly on the spine and nervous system.

Chiropractic specializes in the diagnosis, treatment and management of conditions that are due to mechanical dysfunction of the joints and muscles, particularly those of the spine. Chiropractors are also concerned with the effects that such dysfunction can have on the nervous system.

MANIPULATION
The word chiropractic is derived from the Greek words, *cheiro* (meaning 'hand') and *praktos*

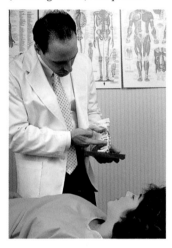

(meaning 'to use') and therefore means 'done by hand', or 'manipulation'. Although chiropractic is a comparatively new type of treatment, bodily manipulation was performed by both the early Greek and Chinese civilizations.

TECHNIQUES
Chiropractic treatment consists of a range of techniques involving specific hand movements, known as adjustments, designed to restore normal alignment and motion to the muscles and joints. The treatment relieves pain and discomfort and improves mobility. Drugs and surgical procedures are not a part of chiropractic care.

Chiropractic involves treatment to the musculo-skeletal system of the body. The treatment focuses particularly on the spine and nervous system.

The theory behind chiropractic is that most disorders can be traced to incorrect functioning of the joints. This can, in turn, cause nerve interference.

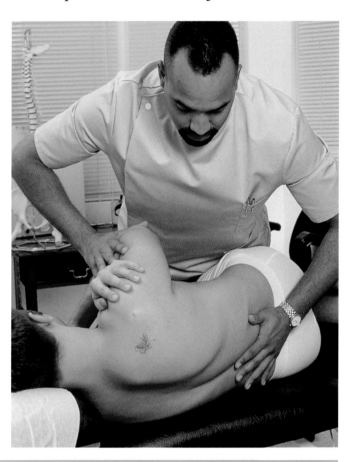

The principles of chiropractic

SPINAL NERVES (ANTERIOR VIEW)

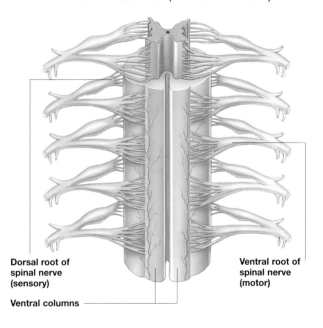

Dorsal root of
spinal nerve
(sensory)

Ventral root of
spinal nerve
(motor)

Ventral columns

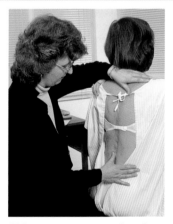

Chiropractors use a series of manipulative techniques to treat musculo-skeletal disorders. Normal mobility is gradually restored over time.

There are 31 pairs of spinal nerves, arranged on either side of the spinal cord. Chiropractic treatment focuses on the spine and nervous system.

Chiropractic treatment focuses on the spine and nervous system. The spinal cord runs down from the brain within the spinal column. A total of 31 pairs of nerves arise from the spinal cord and pass out through the spaces between the vertebrae. These nerves form a complex network that runs through the joints, muscles and skin, affecting all body tissue.

LOSS OF FUNCTION
A joint or vertebra may lose its normal motion or function as a result of accidents, stresses, over-exertion or general lifestyle factors. Areas of the nervous system, often the spinal nerve roots themselves, may be irritated, which causes pain or discomfort.

Chiropractors use their manipulation skills and techniques to remove nerve interference and thereby restore normal mobility.

What problems can chiropractic help?

Chiropractic is generally similar to osteopathy. However, chiropractic differs in that it focuses on the manipulation of one joint at a time, whereas osteopathy works on several joints at once.

SUITABILITY

Chiropractic practitioners decide which techniques to use according to each patient's individual condition and circumstances. This means that chiropractic treatment is suitable for people of any age, including babies, pregnant women and the elderly. The only groups of people for whom it is not suitable are those with damaged bones, or with bone disease, for example bone cancer.

Generally, a chiropractic adjustment is not painful. There may be some minor short-term discomfort, but this quickly passes for most patients.

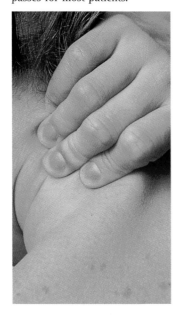

Neck pain is one of many problems that responds to chiropractic treatment. Pain may be caused by muscle spasm or injury.

DISORDERS

Chiropractic can be used to treat a range of problems, including:

■ Back pain
■ Sciatica
■ Tension headaches
■ Migraine
■ Neck, shoulder and arm pain
■ Knee, ankle and foot pain
■ Sports injuries
■ Repetitive strain injury (RSI)
■ Osteoporosis
■ Arthritis
■ Miscellaneous joint and muscle disorders.

OTHER CONDITIONS

Patients who have had chiropractic treatment for one or more of these conditions often find that, because of the direct connection between the nervous system and all the organs and tissues of the body, they also see improvements in other unrelated conditions.

As a result, a growing number of patients visit their chiropractors for treatment to alleviate problems other than 'orthopaedic' ones. Chiropractic treatment has been found to give relief to problems such as:

■ Asthma
■ Irritable bowel syndrome
■ Painful menstrual periods
■ Indigestion
■ Constipation.

There is also evidence to suggest that chiropractic treatment can be effective in relieving colic in babies.

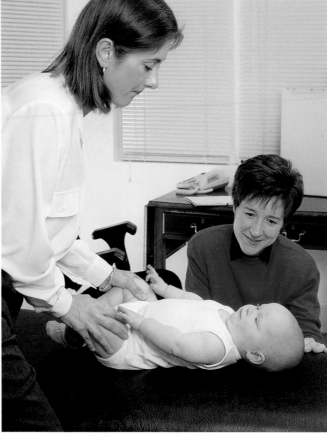

REFERRAL

While some people are referred for chiropractic treatment by their doctors, many others refer themselves directly to a chiropractor. A doctor's referral is not necessary, unless the patient's private medical insurance company requires it.

REGULATION

Chiropractors are now recognized as primary health care professionals by the medical establishment. A recent report on complementary and

Chiropractic can alleviate colic in babies. This is just one of several conditions not thought of as strictly 'orthopaedic' which can benefit from this treatment.

alternative medicine categorized chiropractic as one of the principal medical disciplines that is regulated by law. Doctors have now been issued with guidelines recommending manipulative treatment within the first six weeks after a patient presents to their GP with low back pain.

Training

Only chiropractors trained to an internationally accredited standard can become members of the British Chiropractic Association (BCA), the largest association for the profession in the UK.

The BCA has been established since 1925, and now represents over 800 chiropractors in the UK. As chiropractors can carry out their own X-rays, the BCA issues strict guidelines for the use of

Chiropractors undergo several years of study. They then work under supervision in a chiropractic clinic before being allowed to practise.

ionising radiation, and employs a Radiation Protection Advisor to inspect the X-ray installations of all its members on a regular basis.

In the UK, a number of colleges run BCA-approved four-year full-time chiropractic degree courses. At the end of this training, graduates are required to spend a further year on a postgraduate vocational training scheme, working in a chiropractic clinic under the supervision of a qualified trainer, before they receive their Diploma in Chiropractic (DC).

There is also a two-year MSc course for those who already have a medical qualification.

Visiting a chiropractic practitioner

The first consultation with a chiropractor takes the form of an assessment and examination. The number of subsequent treatments depends on the nature of the problem, and risks are minimal.

On average, the initial consultation with a chiropractor lasts for about forty minutes. A chiropractor always commences the consultation with a discussion of the patient's symptoms, past medical history, lifestyle and problems with posture. The chiropractor records these details, which are considered confidential; no-one is given access to medical notes without the patient's prior permission.

PHYSICAL EXAMINATION
After the case history has been obtained, the chiropractor performs an examination, using standard neurological and orthopaedic tests, to confirm any early ideas he or she may have about the patient's problem. The patient is asked to undress as far as the underwear, and female patients are always offered a back-opening gown to wear for this part of the consultation, and for any subsequent treatment.

RADIOGRAPHY
X-rays may also need to be taken, but decisions will be made in consultation with the patient before any such procedure is undertaken. Those

patients who may, typically, require an X-ray include those who have had recent injuries, older patients with bone density problems or those with unusual examination findings or a history of other serious diseases.

If the examination identifies any underlying disease or, alternatively, a condition for which chiropractic is inappropriate, the chiropractor will then immediately refer the patient to either their general practitioner or to a hospital consultant.

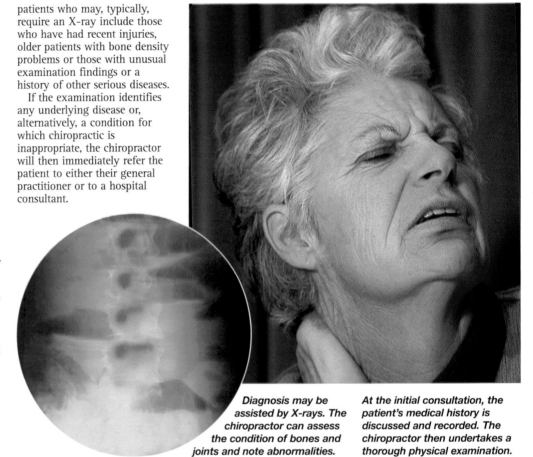

Diagnosis may be assisted by X-rays. The chiropractor can assess the condition of bones and joints and note abnormalities.

At the initial consultation, the patient's medical history is discussed and recorded. The chiropractor then undertakes a thorough physical examination.

Treatment

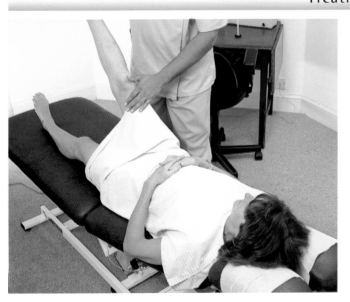

Chiropractors diagnose problems by observation and examination. Any of around 150 different chiropractic techniques are used in a treatment.

Before treatment commences, the chiropractor discusses in full detail the findings of the initial consultation, and will also address any concerns that the patient may have regarding treatment.

ADJUSTMENT
The patient is asked to lie on a specially designed treatment table. The chiropractor then begins the adjustment – a very specific manipulation of a vertebra or joint that is not functioning normally.

There are over 100 different chiropractic techniques. The most common are:
■ Thrusting techniques – these move the two surfaces of a joint apart. This causes a change of pressure within the joint space, and sometimes patients report a noise. This is the sound of a bubble of gas popping and is not painful or significant
■ Soft tissue techniques – these are often performed before a manipulation in order to relax the joints and reduce muscle spasms.

As well as using a range of different techniques, chiropractors frequently offer self-help advice to patients, on matters such as posture, diet and other lifestyle changes.

How many treatments are needed?

A chiropractic treatment lasts, on average, around 15 minutes. The number of chiropractic treatments necessary varies considerably, and depends upon the patient, the particular condition and the length of time since the problem first appeared.

Some patients feel immediate relief, while others need several treatments before they start to feel better. Once the condition has improved, many people do not need to visit a chiropractor again. Others are advised to return for regular check-ups to ensure that they remain well.

LIFESTYLE
Some people, especially those whose conditions are caused by their lifestyle, may have to continue regular chiropractic treatment in order to remain symptom-free and fully fit. These people include sportsmen and women, who are prone to injury and strain, and those with sedentary occupations, whose posture can be poor.

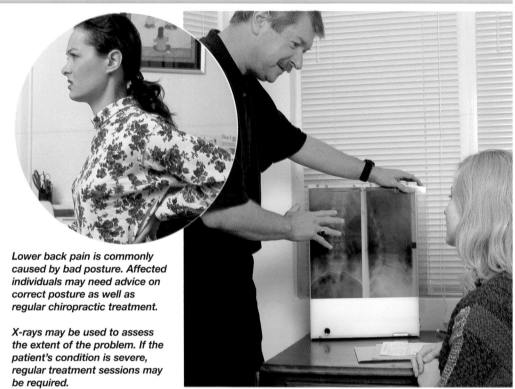

Lower back pain is commonly caused by bad posture. Affected individuals may need advice on correct posture as well as regular chiropractic treatment.

X-rays may be used to assess the extent of the problem. If the patient's condition is severe, regular treatment sessions may be required.

Reactions to treatment

The risks associated with chiropractic treatment are, in general, much lower than those related to other treatment options (such as non-steroidal anti-inflammatory drugs) for joint and muscle disorders.

Some patients may experience temporary soreness over the areas being treated, with redness or even bruising of the skin if deep-tissue massage has been administered.

SPINAL DISCS
Spinal disc problems may appear to flare up in the early stages of treatment and, where an underlying inflammation is already present, the condition may seem to worsen initially.

HEADACHES
Treatment to the neck may cause a temporary feeling of light-headedness; rarely, the patient may experience a short-lived headache.

Neck manipulation is often performed to treat joint dysfunction in the neck. People occasionally experience light-headedness after treatment.

Serious side effects are extremely uncommon. Very rarely, manipulation of the neck has been linked with strokes – although research shows that chiropractic is one of the safest and most effective forms of treatment available for a wide array of nerve, spine and muscle associated problems throughout the body.

A temporary headache is an occasional side effect of chiropractic treatment. In general, this therapy is extremely safe and effective.

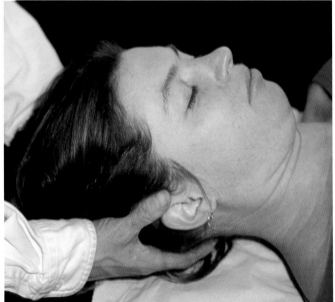

McTimoney chiropractic

This form of chiropractic was developed by John McTimoney (1914–1980). He originally qualified in chiropractic and then went on to devise a new technique known as the toggle recoil technique.

Toggle recoil technique
The techniques used in McTimoney chiropractic are very similar to straight chiropractic. One particular movement used in this speciality is the toggle recoil thrust.

This technique involves a swift thrust to a joint using one hand as a 'hammer' and the other as a 'nail'. The aim is to 'free' the joint so that it becomes more mobile.

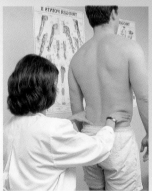

McTimoney chiropractic uses many of the same techniques as the original treatment. An assessment is always carried out prior to treatment.

Homeopathy

Homeopathy is a holistic discipline, which means it aims to treat the whole person. It relies on the principle of treating like with like, using dilute preparations of animal, vegetable and mineral extracts.

Homeopathy is based upon a principle known as the 'law of similars': that the best treatment for any set of symptoms is ingestion of a substance that can cause the same symptoms in a healthy person. This principle contrasts with 'allopathy' (which underlies orthodox medicine), in which medicines cause different or opposite symptoms to those of the illness. For example, a GP might use a sedative to treat insomnia, whereas a homeopath might use a stimulant.

Although this approach may seem illogical, the homeopath's aim is to exaggerate the symptoms temporarily, in order to encourage the body to recognize and then correct the disturbance.

INVENTION OF HOMEOPATHY

The 'law of similars' theory was first applied in earnest by a German physician, Samuel Hahnemann, in the eighteenth century. He was disillusioned by the medicine of his time, which was still based on ancient theories. Although drugs such as morphine existed, they were present in crude mixtures containing many substances. Out of curiosity, while studying the use of quinine in malaria, Hahnemann took quinine and developed a malaria-like fever. He realized that this might be explained in terms of the 'law of similars', and set about testing other substances.

After much experimentation, he began to apply the principle

Homeopathists prescribe remedies that are personalized for the patient's specific needs. Practitioners may operate privately or within the NHS.

to his medical practice. For instance, the effect of a bee sting is very similar to urticaria, a common inflammatory skin condition characterized by swelling and itching. Hahnemann decided that a solution derived from bee venom would be a suitable homeopathic remedy for urticaria.

Hahnemann insisted that only a single medicine be prescribed at each visit, to enable the

prescriber to determine which remedies had been effective and to prevent interactions. This is an important principle, although in practice certain remedies are helpful for one symptom only.

The principle of homeopathy is that small doses of a drug cure symptoms that larger amounts can cause. This even applies to poisons such as arsenic (above).

Personalizing homeopathic treatments

Homeopaths have developed a large number of stock remedies. The most suitable one can be chosen by assessing the patient.

As clinical experience grew, it became apparent that certain patients responded better than others to particular remedies. This information was incorporated into homeopathic practice, along with features such as a person's physique, their reaction to environmental factors (weather, for example) and their temperament. Homeopathy is therefore a 'holistic' discipline, seeking the image of the illness at all levels (physical, emotional and mental).

For success in homeopathic prescribing, it is important to mimic the symptoms of the illness as closely as possible. In addition, the total number of remedies is well over 3000, many of which share the same features. In order to use the correct one, it is important to uncover the unique features of an individual's illness. It is this information that interests the homeopath, who must 'individualize' the illness.

Homeopathic remedies

Repeatedly diluting the active agent of the remedy limits its ability to cause side-effects. Homeopaths believe that this action also increases its potency.

A characteristic, and somewhat controversial, feature of homeopathy is its use of very low doses of active ingredients. Hahnemann was forced to dilute substances such as belladonna (deadly nightshade), which is poisonous and can cause harmful side effects. He found that by shaking the medicine vigorously ('succussion') in between repeated dilutions, there was no apparent loss of effect. If anything, the effect of the remedy seemed more powerful. This was the case even for very high dilutions.

ACCEPTING HOMEOPATHY

As knowledge of chemistry developed, it became apparent that these high dilutions did not contain any molecules of the original substance at all. Not surprisingly, this has proved a barrier to the general acceptance of homeopathy within mainstream medicine, which explains the action of medicines in terms of chemical molecules acting on cell receptors.

Homeopaths, on the other hand, claim that the succussions give the remedy a physical 'memory' of the original substance even after it has been diluted out, which makes it different from pure water. However, exactly how the remedies act is not understood as yet, and research is still at an early stage.

HOW REMEDIES ARE MADE

A homeopathic remedy such as belladonna is prepared as follows: the whole plant is chopped up and steeped in a solution containing 70 per cent alcohol to produce a 'mother tincture'. For the most common potency scale – the centesimal scale – one drop of the resulting mother tincture is added to 99 drops of alcohol and shaken

vigorously to produce the 'first centesimal' potency. This process is repeated five more times to produce the sixth centesimal, or '6c' potency, which has a dilution of 10 million million to one of the mother tincture. This is the potency available over the counter in pharmacies.

Most homeopaths use much higher (more dilute) potencies, generally '30c' or above. Any potency higher than a '12c' theoretically contains no

Homeopathy relies on highly dilute quantities of active ingredients. This means a tiny amount of the remedy must be very carefully diluted in alcohol.

molecules of the original substance. However, because they have been succussed a greater number of times and are therefore more 'energized', the higher potencies are thought by some homeopaths to have a stronger effect.

Preparing a remedy

1 *Homeopathic remedies are derived from plant, mineral and animal sources. The homeopath will initially chop up the substance.*

2 *Material is then extracted by soaking the substance in a concentrated solution of alcohol. This is left to soak for two to four weeks.*

3 *The mixture is sealed in an container and periodically shaken to further dissolve the material. Modern remedies are usually shaken by machine.*

4 *The infusion is strained into a dark glass bottle. This is now the 'mother tincture' from which all subsequent dilutions are based.*

5 *Samples of tincture are further diluted in alcohol, by a ratio of 1:100. The solution is shaken vigorously – this is known as succussion and is believed to increase potency.*

6 *The sample may be diluted and succussed many more times, until the required dilution (level of potency) has been achieved. Drops are then added to lactose (milk sugar) tablets.*

7 *The jar containing the remedy and the tablets is gently agitated in order to coat each tablet with a sufficient quantity of the potentized remedy.*

8 *The resulting tablets are stored in an airtight bottle, made of dark glass. The container must subsequently be stored away from direct sunlight.*

Hypnotherapy

Hypnosis is a means of inducing a relaxed state in an individual to enable them to confront problems. Hypnotherapy involves using hypnosis to treat a variety of physical and emotional conditions.

Hypnotherapy is a form of treatment in which patients are encouraged to face their problems under the conditions of relaxation. The therapist and patient work together towards a solution to the present problem.

There are two schools of thought about the nature of hypnosis. On the one hand, there are people who consider that there is a definite state of hypnosis, involving an alteration of the level of consciousness. The alternative view is that hypnosis simply involves focusing attention.

Whatever the persuasion of the therapist, there is general agreement that hypnosis is a pleasant, interesting experience.

WHO CAN BE HYPNOTIZED?
Patients vary as regards their ability to achieve hypnosis. Some are excellent subjects, while others find hypnosis more difficult. There are a number of factors that influence the depth of hypnosis, including fear, prejudice and religious objections. On the whole, people with highly obsessional personalities, such as those with obsessive-compulsive disorder, find it almost impossible to co-operate with hypnotherapy.

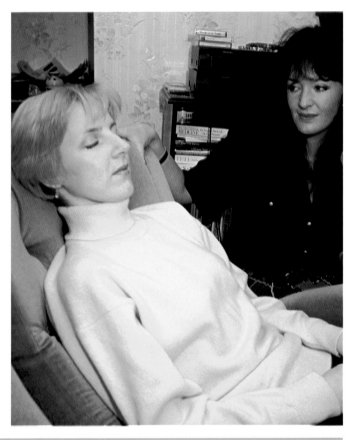

Among the many problems which can be helped with hypnotherapy are a variety of addictions, such as smoking and alcohol abuse.

Hypnotherapy may be used in the treatment of a wide range of emotional disorders. Examples of these include phobias and stuttering.

Misconceptions about hypnotherapy

Hypnotherapy does not provide a magical cure for patients' problems, nor does it involve forcing people to carry out activities they do not wish to do, or to make fools of themselves. Hypnotized people are neither asleep nor unconscious, but are pleasantly relaxed.

SUITABLE THERAPISTS
Learning the technique of inducing hypnosis is a relatively simple matter. However, this alone does not equip a person to become a hypnotherapist.

People wishing to be treated by hypnosis should choose their therapist with care. It is best to go to doctors, dentists or clinical psychologists who have accreditation certificates.

The popular image of hypnosis is of the subject being put into a trance. However, this is not an accurate reflection of what hypnotherapy involves.

Hypnotherapy should only be carried out by suitably qualified healthcare professionals, such as doctors, dentists and clinical psychologists, working within their own sphere of practice. This is particularly important, as there are occasions when patients have unexpected reactions to hypnosis, and only an experienced qualified therapist will know how to deal with these situations competently.

Uses of hypnotherapy

Hypnosis can be used in the treatment of many medical and emotional disorders, as well as for the control of pain and for improving athletic performance.

Hypnosis enables patients to imagine a scene that is stressful to them with vivid clarity in the setting of a quiet, calm, comfortable environment. If stress is experienced at any stage, the scene can be 'frozen' at this point, and a relief response introduced.

A relief response is a pattern of thought that does not cause the patient any anxiety. It has the effect of reducing the anxiety about the fear situation. As a result, when the scene is re-introduced the patient will find that it has become less stressful.

Hypnotherapy can help people to overcome specific phobias. For example, it may help to conquer arachnophobia (fear of spiders).

Hypnosis is often believed to be able to treat conditions that drugs have failed to cure. As it is a natural form of treatment, it does not produce the side effects commonly found with conventional medication.

Hypnotherapy may be employed in the treatment of:
■ Emotional disorders
■ Physical disorders
■ Athletic performance.

TREATING CONDITIONS
One condition that responds particularly well to treatment with hypnosis is excessive sweating. This condition is one of the physical manifestations of anxiety. In order to treat this problem, patients are guided under hypnosis through a graded series of fearful situations of increasing difficulty (referred to as a hierarchy), alternating with a relief response, until they are anxiety-free in all these situations. This technique can be used for a variety of problems, including impotence, travel phobias and post-traumatic stress disorder.

Hypnosis can be used in a number of ways to help patients with cancer. For instance, it can be used to:

Hypnosis can lower the blood pressure of patients who have hypertension. It is also helpful for treating skin irritation.

One of the distressing features of anxiety is insomnia. Patients who suffer from insomnia and do not respond to sleeping tablets can learn self-hypnosis in order to get to sleep.

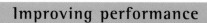

■ Reduce pain
■ Help people who suffer from nausea and vomiting before chemotherapy
■ Improve mobility
■ Improve appetite.

Hypnosis is helpful in the treatment of many other conditions. These include:
■ Anxiety states (such as that caused by taking examinations)
■ Migraine
■ Skin disorders.

There are many other instances besides cancer where the level of pain associated with physical illness can be reduced using hypnotherapy. This is especially the case in dentistry. Hypnosis has been used to replace a general anaesthetic for major surgery, although an anaesthetist is always present too.

Improving performance

Hypnosis is thought to be valuable for enhancing and improving physical performance and personal achievement. For instance, hypnotherapy has been found to be helpful for participants in sports such as golf, football, archery and skiing.

Some Olympic gymnasts have used hypnotherapy to improve their routines, and professional singers have been trained to use it to improve their singing method. It has also been used to improve performance in martial arts.

Some experts believe that hypnosis helps people to perform better and improves stamina. It has proved to be useful in sports such as golf.

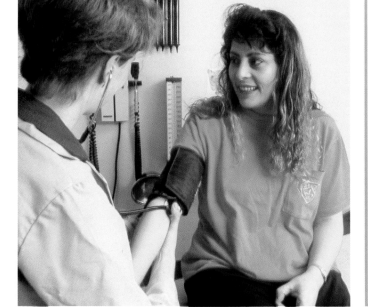

Indian head massage

Indian head massage brings both physical and emotional benefits, relieving stress and promoting well-being. A series of techniques are used by practitioners, each one offering distinctive benefits.

Indian head massage is a safe, gentle, de-stressing therapy. Its effects are not only physical but also work on an emotional level, promoting relaxation and a feeling of well-being.

Indian head massage involves applying a sequence of massage techniques to the upper back, shoulders, neck, arms, head, face and ears. It is non-invasive, the client can remain fully clothed and all groups can benefit from its application, including pregnant women and the infirm.

ORIGINS

Indian head massage has been practised in India for more than 1000 years. It has been performed mainly by women, in the belief that massaging the head with pure vegetable oils helps to keep long hair in healthy condition.

Mothers would massage their children from birth on a regular basis and thus the technique was passed down from generation to generation and became an integral part of family life.

This form of massage was introduced into the West in the early 1980s, the usual area of massage (the head and hair) being extended to include that of the upper back and shoulders.

TENSION RELIEF

Stress cannot be avoided, as it is one of the key elements of life. It is when it becomes extreme, and a person feels unable to cope, that tension builds and depletes the immune system. Muscles tense up and individuals develop tight necks and shoulders, and suffer headaches, for example.

Indian head massage helps to alleviate blockages and relieves this build-up of tension. It also stimulates the supply of nutrients to the hair root, which encourages strong, healthy hair growth.

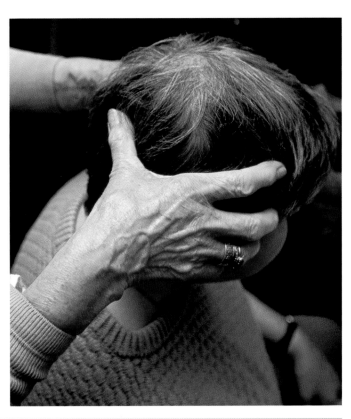

Indian head massage is a traditional therapy that has been performed in India for over 1000 years. It alleviates tension and increases circulation to the scalp.

Benefits

Stress-related conditions, such as headaches and eye strain, can benefit from head massage. Effects can be felt almost immediately, as tension is eased.

Indian head massage is a holistic therapy that treats the whole person, and which aims to integrate mental, physical and spiritual concerns.

HOW IT WORKS

Practitioners believe that the benefits of Indian head massage are achieved by:
- Stimulating circulation and enhancing the supply of oxygen to the brain
- Stimulating the lymphatic system so that toxins can be released more effectively
- Stimulating the immune system
- Assisting the respiratory system as deep breathing is encouraged
- Rebalancing the energy flow in the body
- Improving muscle tone and revitalizing the body

- Relieving tiredness and promoting alertness by improving circulation of cerebrospinal fluid around the brain
- Stimulating the body's self-healing abilities, by providing an antidote to stress, anxiety and mental tension
- Promoting hair growth and helping to improve the strength and condition of the hair and scalp.

WHAT IT TREATS

Indian head massage offers an instant de-stressing programme for the entire body, and physical benefits can be obtained immediately, with the relaxation of the muscles and the easing of tension.

Many conditions are often stress-related and these may benefit from treatment. They include insomnia, anxiety, depression, eye strain, hair and scalp problems, headaches, sinusitis, tinnitus, stiff neck and shoulders, migraine, nightmares, and muscular and respiratory problems.

Visiting a therapist

The only equipment that is needed for Indian head massage is an upright chair that is comfortable for both the client and practitioner. The therapy room can be made serene, for example by the use of soft lighting and soothing music.

MEDICAL HISTORY

The practitioner begins by checking with the client whether any conditions that might indicate that treatment is inadvisable are present. These include a recent head injury, scalp or eye infections, a history of thrombosis, epilepsy or skin disorders such as psoriasis.

The client is asked if they would like oils to be used during the massage; coconut oil is generally used because it is particularly good for the condition of the hair and scalp, but it is not essential. Necklaces and ear-rings should be removed.

BREATHING

The client sits down with legs uncrossed, hands on lap, with soles of the feet on the ground. The practitioner stands behind the client and lays their hands on the client's shoulders, asking them to take three deep breaths.

The practitioner then places their hands lightly on top of the

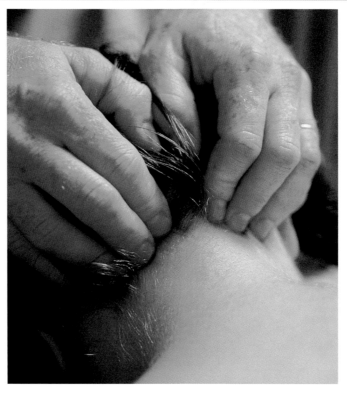

client's head and takes three deep breaths. This exercise centres and grounds both the client and the practitioner and allows the client to relax and connect with the practitioner's touch.

The massage then begins and usually lasts for 30 minutes, ending by working on the higher chakras (energy gates) – the throat, brow and the crown. It is believed that the chakras (of which there are seven) govern

▼ Practitioners always take a medical history before commencing the massage. This helps to assess a person's suitability for treatment.

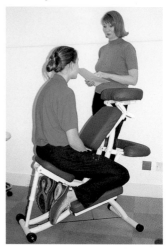

◀ Pressure points all over the head and neck are massaged. Sometimes, oils (such as coconut oil) may be used, although these are not mandatory.

the energy needed for bodily health, and that working on the higher three alone can bring the energy of the body back into balance. After the massage, the client should drink water to flush out any toxins released.

Techniques

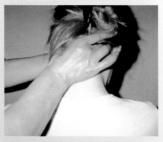

Pressure – deep-tissue massage clears nerve pathways and increases circulation. It is applied to pressure points at the base of the skull, head and face.

The techniques used in Indian head massage are simple and effective. Both hands are utilized by the therapist; if only one hand is used for the massage, the other supports the client. This maintains continual contact between client and practitioner.

A variety of massage techniques are used. These may be applied with the palm, thumbs or fingers, either singly or in combination.

Different effects

Some massage techniques gently increase the blood circulation to

the area being massaged, whereas others have a calming effect. Some techniques create warmth, which helps muscle tissue to become more pliable; and others help to drain away toxins and relax muscle, being used generally on the neck, shoulders and arms.

Number of sessions

A head massage can be enjoyed at any time. If it is being given for a specific problem, the number of sessions given will depend upon the severity of the condition.

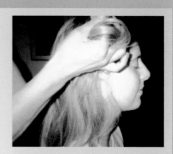

Hair tugging – this is achieved by taking handfuls of hair and tugging gently. Tugging stimulates the blood circulation to the scalp area.

Hacking – the edges of the hands apply quick, light, striking movements across the shoulders. This stimulates blood circulation and eases tension.

Rubbing – the flat palm of the hand is used to lightly rub the sides of the head. This warms and stimulates the scalp, improving its overall condition.

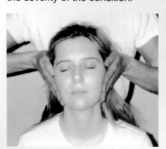

Gentle hand placing – this is a soothing, uplifting massage technique. Therapists use it on the head, face and throat areas.

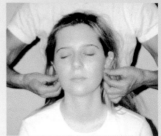

Squeezing and circling – the outer ears are squeezed between thumb and forefinger. This regulates the digestive system and boosts immunity.

Massage

Massage uses a variety of techniques to manipulate the soft tissues of the body. It is a safe and effective form of therapy that can treat certain conditions and also promotes health and well-being.

Massage therapy involves the safe, non-invasive, systematic manipulation of the body's soft tissues. Therapists are able to locate any problems in the body's muscles, tendons and ligaments, and treat them using a variety of techniques.

HOW MASSAGE EVOLVED
Everyone practises massage instinctively. At times of emotional upset, stroking actions are often used to give comfort, particularly when children are involved. This is probably the reason why massage is one of the most enduring physical therapies; its use is documented as far back as 3000 BC in the medical systems of ancient China, Egypt and India.

All the major civilizations, in particular the Greeks and Persians, made many references to the benefits of massage and frequently integrated it into their medical practices.

SWEDISH MASSAGE
Massage as we know it today in the West (or Swedish massage as it is often called), was introduced by a Swedish gymnast called Per Henrik Ling (1776–1839). On his travels to China, he learned some remarkably effective techniques. On returning to Sweden, he assembled what he had learned into a routine of strokes that are now very well known and which have become the basis for many other styles of massage therapy.

HOLISTIC THERAPY
In the USA in the 1960s and 1970s, Per Ling's knowledge was applied at the Esalen Institute in California. There, therapists realized that massage could be used in a holistic way – in other words, it could help to promote balanced health by bringing about the connection of mind, body and spirit.

OTHER THERAPIES
Massage may be used in conjunction with other therapies, such as aromatherapy. Massage is just one of the methods used to introduce the properties of essential oils to the body.

Massage is the manipulation of the soft tissue in the body to promote health. Therapists use their skills to find and treat problems within the tissues.

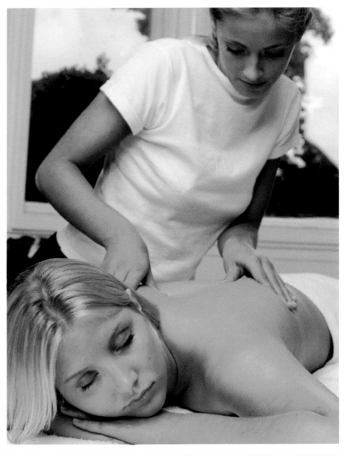

How does massage work?

Massage works on physical, mental and emotional levels to promote relaxation. It helps the body to help itself by encouraging homeostasis (the physiological process by which internal bodily systems are kept in balance, despite variations in external conditions).

Massage techniques remain an art, although research has highlighted the physiological mechanisms underpinning the therapeutic effects. It is believed that massage has a number of effects on the major systems of the body:

Circulatory system
■ Encourages blood circulation
■ Stimulates lymphatic system
■ Strengthens immune system
■ Increases blood and nutrient flow to the cells.

Digestive system
■ Can relieve irritable bowel syndrome and spastic colon
■ Reduces oedema (swelling in the tissues)
■ Cleanses blood by toning kidneys
■ Helps with constipation and waste elimination.

Massage helps reduce pain and restore normal muscle activity. A neck massage, for example, stretches hard or contracted muscles, aiding relaxation.

Muscular system
■ Relieves muscle tension
■ Eliminates waste, for example lactic acid
■ Helps to restore muscle tone
■ Helps to increase joint flexibility
■ Stimulates blood and nutrient supply.

Nervous system
■ Relaxes and calms
■ Helps insomnia and headaches
■ Raises endorphin (natural pain-reliever) levels
■ Releases withheld emotions.

Respiratory system
■ Helps to improve breathing patterns
■ Can help coughs and asthma.

Skeletal system
■ Increases nutrient flow to bones
■ Reduces muscular tension
■ Helps correction of body posture and balance.

Massage techniques

There are three main 'mother' strokes of massage. These are defined as effleurage (stroking), petrissage (kneading) and tapotement (heavy pummelling or light tapping movements).

EFFLEURAGE

This is a gliding stroke, using the whole palm of each hand, with pressure on the upward strokes.

Effleurage is used as an introductory stroke, to set the tone for the treatment, while applying oil or cream and so warming the skin and muscles in preparation for deeper work. It encourages the receiver to relax, and is also used as a 'finishing-off' stroke.

PETRISSAGE

This is the general name for any stroke that presses, squeezes or rolls the muscles under the skin. It can be performed with both hands, or using one hand or the pads of thumbs or fingers on smaller areas.

Petrissage is used to 'milk' the muscles of any waste products and, literally, to squeeze tension, toxins and tiredness out of the body. This, in turn, loosens and stretches muscle fibres and fascia (connective tissue) and prepares the body for deeper friction work.

TAPOTEMENT

This is a general term for a variety of manipulations with different pressures. It includes:
- Light pressure – pincement (pinching), tapping, and point hacking (tapping with the fingertips)

- Moderate pressure – clapping, cupping, light and heavy hacking (tapping with the sides of the hands)
- Heavy pressure – beating, pounding.

ADVANCED METHODS

More advanced techniques are used in cases where a local increase in circulation or stimulation is considered desirable. Such techniques, however, require the in-depth knowledge of a fully trained massage therapist.

Other advanced manipulations may be used, including shaking, vibration and frictions.

Petrissage is a basic massage technique. This therapist is pressing and squeezing the muscles under the skin to release tension and stiffness.

Hacking involves striking the skin with the outside edge of the hand in a chopping motion. It is used to stimulate fleshy, muscular areas of the body.

Cautionary advice

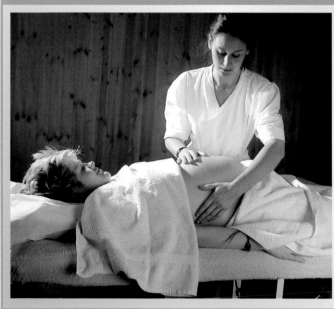

In general, massage is safe and relaxing, but there are some common-sense guidelines to follow. Those who are unsure about whether it is safe to have a massage should consult their doctor before booking.

A massage should not be given:
- Within two hours of eating a heavy meal or if an individual has not eaten for a considerable time
- In cases of weakness or clinical exhaustion. This includes those who are recovering from influenza or other viral infections

Pregnant women should not have a massage in the first trimester. After this time, any massage should avoid areas such as the lower back.

- Within 12 months of major surgery, or six months of minor surgery
- In those with serious medical conditions, without the GP's approval
- On the site of a recent fracture, strain or sprain, although work can be done above the area concerned
- During the first trimester of pregnancy; thereafter deep pressure on the lower back and inside leg areas should be avoided
- If the individual is receiving radiotherapy or chemotherapy treatment for cancer
- If the individual has an infectious skin disease
- Immediately before or after consuming alcohol or taking non-prescription drugs.

Nutritional therapy

Nutritional therapy uses dietary and supplementary methods
to balance the body and treat a range of disorders. The therapy is
one of the safest types of complementary medicine available.

A holistic method of improving health, nutritional therapy makes use of dietary and supplementary interventions to achieve optimum health and body functioning.

AIMS OF THERAPY
Nutritional therapy looks at all aspects of a person's health and lifestyle. It then aims to improve any areas that are causing problems by:
- Detoxifying the body
- Improving nutrient levels
- Imparting dietary knowledge
- Improving mental attitude to diet.

ORIGINS
It is hard to say when nutritional therapy first began because food has been used as a medicine for hundreds of years. In AD 390, Hippocrates was reputed to have said, 'Let food be your medicine and medicine your food.' In Hippocrates' time, there were no modern-style antibiotics or medicines, so people had to rely on the available herbs and foods; garlic, for example, was commonly used as an antibiotic.

Taking folic acid prior to, and in the early stages of, pregnancy protects the baby against spina bifida. This is just one example of how diet can influence health.

Nutritional therapy uses diet to treat illness and balance the body. A healthy diet is one that comprises all the necessary nutrients for the body to exist.

Today, researchers have been able to demonstrate that garlic contains around 100 active agents that may improve a number of problems, ranging from high cholesterol to poor immune function.

Every year, more is discovered about the way in which nutrition affects health. Some years ago, researchers discovered that folic acid supplements, taken both before and during the first three months of pregnancy, can reduce the risk of conditions such as spina bifida. New research shows that taking vitamins C and E in the second half of pregnancy reduces the occurrence of pre-eclampsia (high blood pressure).

Benefits of nutritional therapy

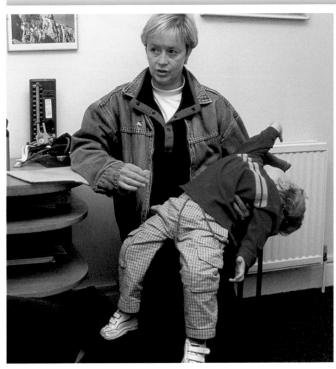

It is well recognized that nutrients are vital to health and well-being. Some people, however, disagree with the use of supplements because they feel that they should obtain everything they need by eating a well-balanced diet.

SPECIFIC KNOWLEDGE
It is important to acknowledge, however, that nutritionists have acquired specific knowledge and training. They can use their expertise to help answer certain dietary questions.

They can advise, for example, on the levels of nutrients contained in certain foods. For example, some foods may be deficient in important nutrients, or the nutritional content of the

It is well known that nutritional therapy can help to improve disorders such as hyperactivity. The avoidance of certain foods can be very beneficial.

food may be destroyed by cooking it. Moreover, people are individuals and therefore vary in their need for different dietary factors in their daily food intake.

DISORDERS
A nutritional therapist can be invaluable in helping people in their choice of a correct diet. The therapy can be effective in treating:
- Fatigue
- Headaches and migraines
- Depression
- Digestive disorders
- Hormone problems
- Skin disorders, such as eczema
- Arthritis
- Weight problems
- Diabetes
- Coeliac disease
- Allergies
- High blood pressure
- Candidiasis
- Irritable bowel syndrome
- Hyperactivity and learning disorders, such as autism.

The initial consultation

Before the nutritional therapist puts forward any dietary changes, he or she may suggest that the client's GP is consulted. This is a precautionary measure because therapists are not medically trained.

CLIENT DETAILS
Once the therapist is happy with the client's medical status, questions will be asked about lifestyle, medical history, family history, moods, digestive health, dietary history and, in women, any menstrual problems.

Some of the questions may seem very personal, but it is imperative to answer honestly because the aim of the therapist is to obtain a clear picture of their client's health and body function. The answers given during this questioning often signify to the therapist that the client may have a dietary deficiency, an allergy or a build-up of toxins in the body.

TESTS
If the therapist wants to determine mineral or toxin levels, they may suggest a hair mineral analysis; hair often provides more information on mineral levels than blood. The procedure involves cutting a tablespoon of hair from the back of the head and sending this

Hair samples can be sent to a laboratory for analysis. Levels of different minerals in the body can be determined, and the diet adapted accordingly.

The first consultation with the nutritional therapist takes about an hour. The therapist asks a series of questions about the client's health and background.

sample to a laboratory to undergo testing.

If a woman is having menstrual or fertility problems, the therapist may recommend a hormone saliva test. This gives detailed information about hormone levels and may identify the cause of the problem.

Towards the end of the initial consultation, the therapist will suggest dietary changes and may give advice on suitable supplements. The client will be given a review date for the next session and a contact number in case they have any concerns between consultations. Most problems can be dealt with successfully over the telephone.

Treatment examples

There are many conditions that benefit from dietary changes and a nutritional therapist often works alongside conventional medicine.

ARTHRITIS
A person with arthritis may benefit from a low toxin diet, a reduction in the consumption of red meat and an increase in oily fish, vegetables, grains and rice. Wheat and dairy products should be considerably reduced

Arthritis can sometimes be helped by following a wholefood diet and avoiding artificial foodstuffs. A nutritional therapist can provide advice.

and may need to be eliminated at a later date.

RESPIRATORY PROBLEMS
Nasal congestion or lung conditions such as asthma may benefit from the removal of dairy products for a trial period. Dairy products can cause a build-up of mucus in the body, worsening symptoms. Garlic can be used to help reduce and eliminate the mucus.

ECZEMA
Eczema can be a sign of increased toxicity, a sluggish bowel, and a possible fatty acid deficiency. A person with eczema often has a wheat or dairy allergy, so this needs to be addressed and the offending food removed from the diet. *Acidophilus* may help to improve bowel functioning and essential fatty acid supplements can correct deficiencies.

Is it risk-free?

Although nutritional therapy carries very little risk, it is important to bear in mind that supplements can interact with medication.

For example, if the client is taking warfarin (an anticoagulant) or aspirin, they should avoid taking vitamin E or high-dose fish oils (unless directed by the therapist), as these all act to thin the blood. Pregnant women and breastfeeding mothers also need to be careful about the supplements they take.

Breast feeding mothers should take specialist advice about supplements. Some substances can be present in the breast milk.

Choosing a therapist
When choosing a therapist, it is important to make sure that they are registered. Only therapists who have completed recognized courses and received recognized qualifications can register for practice. They are bound by a strict code of conduct that protects them and their clients.

Osteopathy

Osteopathy is a system of gentle manipulation of the body that aims to rectify musculoskeletal imbalances. An increasingly popular discipline, it is used to treat many conditions, such as back pain.

WHAT IS OSTEOPATHY?

The founder of osteopathy, Andrew Taylor Still (1828–1917), believed that 'structure governs function'; that is, if the anatomy of the body is disturbed in some way, the body will no longer function as well as it should.

Osteopaths aim to treat their patients using an extensive knowledge of human anatomy and well-developed palpatory skills. Such treatment not only has an effect on patients' musculo-skeletal systems but also has far-reaching effects on their physiology. This relies on the belief that the body has the potential to heal itself through its own self-regulatory mechanisms, and that these sometimes need to be activated and assisted.

OSTEOPATHY IN THE UK

The first osteopaths to practise in Britain arrived from the United States of America about 100 years ago and the British School of Osteopathy was founded in 1917. The popularity of osteopathy has now grown to the extent that in 1997, 23,000 patients consulted osteopaths every day – about six million consultations a year. Its growing acceptability led to the 1993 Osteopaths Act, and since the year 2000, all osteopaths working in Britain must be

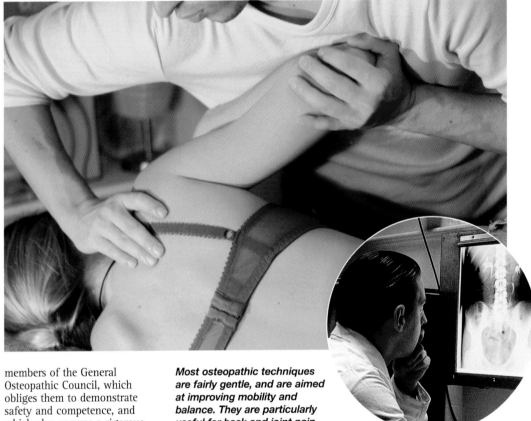

members of the General Osteopathic Council, which obliges them to demonstrate safety and competence, and which also ensures a rigorous code of practice.

Craniosacral osteopathy is based on the work of William Sutherland, who published much of his work in the 1930s. In the last 15 years, this approach has

Most osteopathic techniques are fairly gentle, and are aimed at improving mobility and balance. They are particularly useful for back and joint pain.

undergone an enormous growth in popularity, not least for its gentle nature, which lends itself to the treatment of delicate patients, such as children.

Some osteopaths are also medically qualified. Here, a practitioner studies an X-ray of the spine and pelvis, in order to determine the best treatment.

Visiting an osteopath

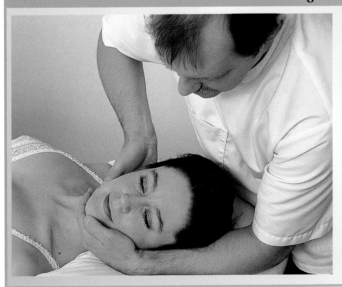

A consultation begins with the osteopath taking a detailed medical history from the patient, to determine their general state of health and the source of the pain. The osteopath will also carefully examine the patient's body structure.

Many people may be put off going to see an osteopath by the concept of joint manipulation with its infamous, occasionally loud, click of the joints. The noise is caused by the formation of a

Osteopathy is often associated with physical manipulation. While this can bring about a dramatic improvement in terms of relieving pain, the discipline is more complex than this implies.

slight vacuum as the articular surfaces of the joint (commonly, but not always, the vertebrae) are 'gapped' rapidly, much like taking a sucker off a smooth surface. It should be noted that this technique (often called a 'high velocity thrust') is only one of many practised by osteopaths.

Most techniques, such as soft tissue work (massage), articulation, muscle energy work and a variety of techniques working with the involuntary mechanism of the body, such as craniosacral osteopathy and functional and fascial unwinding, are extremely gentle. In a recent survey, less than half the patients treated said that they had received the high velocity thrust.

Cranial and craniosacral osteopathy

Cranial and craniosacral osteopathy are both increasingly popular techniques. Cranial osteopathy treats the bones of the skull, while craniosacral osteopathy treats the joints in the skull, spine and pelvis.

Osteopathy relies on the fact that the central nervous system is bathed in cerebrospinal fluid, which undergoes a rhythmic, pumping, pressure change. The tidal effect of these fluctuations can be felt throughout the body, but it is especially palpable as movement between the bones of the skull, and movement of the sacrum within the pelvis. Although the effects are small, it is vital that this system works well.

Craniosacral osteopathy attempts to treats distortions caused by restrictions of movement between and within the bones of the skull and of the pelvis. Such distortions may also be caused by contractions of connective tissues.

BIRTH PROBLEMS

Osteopaths believe that children are prone to bony distortions, particularly newborns delivered by forceps. On testing, about 80 per cent of babies are found to have some imbalances. Often the symptoms heal themselves; however, in an appreciable number of cases, comparatively minor mechanical distortions of the body will lead to a range of problems, such as colic, feeding problems, other digestive conditions, distress, fretful behaviour and sleep disturbance.

Bones and joints of the cranium

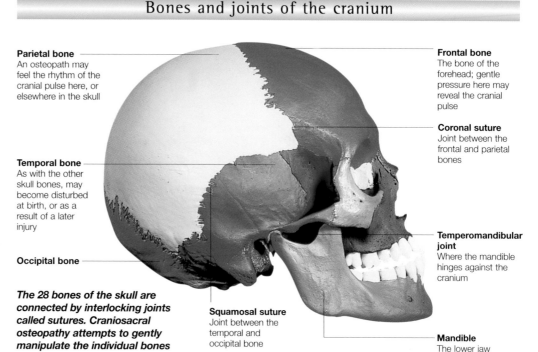

Parietal bone
An osteopath may feel the rhythm of the cranial pulse here, or elsewhere in the skull

Temporal bone
As with the other skull bones, may become disturbed at birth, or as a result of a later injury

Occipital bone

Frontal bone
The bone of the forehead; gentle pressure here may reveal the cranial pulse

Coronal suture
Joint between the frontal and parietal bones

Temperomandibular joint
Where the mandible hinges against the cranium

Squamosal suture
Joint between the temporal and occipital bone

Mandible
The lower jaw

The 28 bones of the skull are connected by interlocking joints called sutures. Craniosacral osteopathy attempts to gently manipulate the individual bones along these sutures.

Caesarean births are a little better for the baby in terms of stresses and strains, but they lack the 'kickstart' to life, which is given by the sudden decompression of the birth process. It is thought that these problems can lead to failure of the sinuses to drain, recurrent ear infections, headaches, behavioural problems and many other conditions.

OSTEOPATHY AND CHILDREN

When a child is brought for treatment, the diagnostic processes are the same as those used for adults, but when treating with craniosacral work, the osteopath uses very small forces to encourage the child's body to heal itself. Although some children dislike anyone holding their head, it is not unusual for a baby to sleep during treatment.

Craniosacral techniques

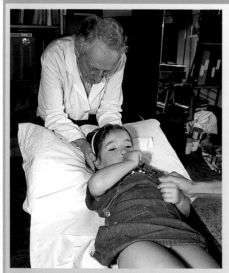

By exerting very gentle pressure on the skull, the practitioner is able to feel the rhythm of the cranial pulse. Irregularities can be resolved by gentle manipulation.

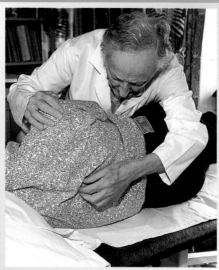

The practitioner progresses to manipulation of the patient's back to correct imbalances in the vertebrae of the spine, where cerebrospinal fluid also circulates.

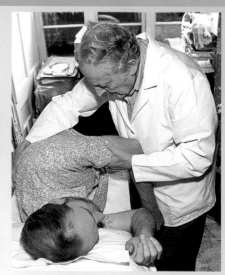

Finally, the practitioner works to correct the sacrum. The sacrum lies at the base of the lower vertebrae, and forms part of the pelvis (hence craniosacral therapy).

Shiatsu massage

Shiatsu, meaning 'finger pressure', is an ancient healing practice that originated in Japan. The principles of this type of massage are similar to those used in acupuncture.

Shiatsu massage grew from earlier forms of massage, Anma massage from Japan and Tuina from China. Like acupuncture and other oriental therapies, it works upon the body's energy system, using the network of meridians (energy pathways) that relate to the functioning of the internal organs as well as to our physical, emotional and spiritual well-being.

HOW SHIATSU WORKS

Shiatsu works by stimulating the body's vital energy flow (Ki) in order to promote good health. Ki is thought to flow through the body, via the meridians, which resemble a system of canals.

It is when the smooth flow of the Ki is disrupted that disharmony occurs, manifesting as physical symptoms or spiritual or emotional disturbance. Shiatsu uses physical pressure, gentle holding, rotations, stretches and other techniques to restore harmony to the Ki in the body.

EFFECTS

Physically, Shiatsu has the effect of stimulating both the circulation of blood and the flow of lymphatic fluid around the body. This helps to release toxins and deep-seated tension from the muscles, and it also stimulates the hormone system.

On a more subtle level, Shiatsu allows the receiver to relax deeply and get in touch with each part of their body, thus utilizing the body's own healing abilities.

POWER OF TOUCH

Although many forms of massage can fulfil the basic human need for touch, Shiatsu is particularly effective in harnessing the power of touch in an accessible and practical way. There are three reasons for this:
- The recipient remains clothed during treatment and therefore feels less vulnerable and inhibited about fully accepting the touch given
- The slow and sustained holding nature of the pressure applied differentiates Shiatsu from other forms of massage. This allows the physiological mechanisms governing muscle tone to release tension more efficiently than with other forms of body work
- Shiatsu is very practical and requires no special equipment, just a blanket or mat on the floor, a quiet peaceful space and the right intention.

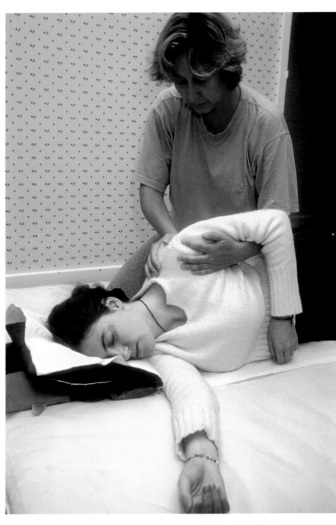

Shiatsu is a type of massage that involves using physical pressure on key points of the body. This acts to stimulate energy flow (Ki) in the body.

Uses of Shiatsu

Shiatsu can be used to treat people with health problems. Releasing muscle tension can relieve common ailments such as headaches.

Regular Shiatsu can be used as a preventative measure to keep the body healthy and in balance. In addition, Shiatsu helps the recipient become more in touch with spiritual, physical and emotional needs.

PHYSICAL DISORDERS

For people who already have health problems, Shiatsu can be used as a treatment in its own right or to complement other treatments. Many conditions respond well to treatment with Shiatsu. As Shiatsu moves joints and stretches muscles and ligaments, it can be used to treat musculo-skeletal disorders, such as back pain and arthritis.

The treatment also affects the movement of body fluids (blood, lymph and intra-cellular fluid) so that internal tissues and their functions are affected. Shiatsu is often effective in the treatment of intestinal, circulatory and respiratory disorders and hormonal problems.

EMOTIONAL PROBLEMS

The ability of Shiatsu to relax the body at a deep level and work with the subtle energy aspects of the body makes it a useful tool in the treatment of anxiety, tension, depression and emotional instability.

What happens during a treatment?

At the beginning of a first treatment, the practitioner will take a history, including details of previous health problems and current medication being taken and questions about general lifestyle, diet and exercise. A practitioner may also examine the tongue, a method of diagnosis in oriental medicine.

Clothes are worn during treatment, preferably light cotton clothing covering the arms and legs. The treatment generally takes place on a Shiatsu futon (thin mattress) on the floor.

HARA DIAGNOSIS
It is usual to start treatment with a hara diagnosis. The hara is the area of the abdomen that stretches from below the ribs to above the pelvic bone on the front of the body.

By palpating the hara, the practitioner can identify the meridians that are blocked and those that seem weak or empty. At this point, the practitioner will normally choose two or three meridians to work on during the session. As the meridians run all over the body, no two sessions will be the same, but they will follow a similar format.

TECHNIQUES
The practitioner uses different techniques, depending on the energy state of the person and the part of the meridian being worked on. Dynamic moves such as rocking, stretching and rotating help disperse blocked Ki. Long, deep thumb pressure on specific points, and holding and palming a meridian helps draw Ki to areas of weakness.

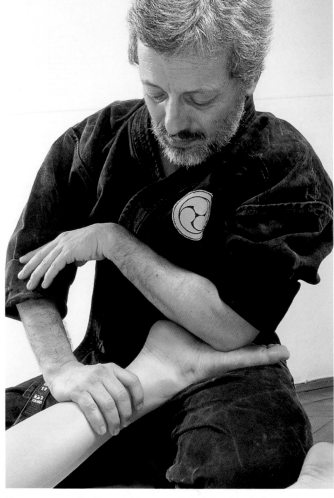

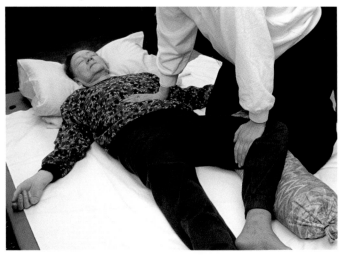

To assess a patient's condition, a Shiatsu practitioner palpates the abdomen (hara). This diagnostic technique reveals any problems in the body.

A variety of techniques are used in Shiatsu to stimulate the flow of energy along the meridians. These include applying pressure to the soles of the feet.

After a treatment

At the end of the treatment, the recipient is allowed time to rest. People who have fallen asleep are given time to wake up.

Sensations
After treatment, people often report feelings of relaxation, well-being and peace. Some people feel invigorated, ready to 'get up and go' and some feel like going to sleep. This often depends on the energy state of the patient before treatment and the type of treatment given.

Healing reaction
Occasionally, a new patient may experience a temporary 'healing reaction' as toxins and negative

At the end of a treatment people are usually given some time in which to relax. A patient may feel after effects, known as a 'healing reaction'.

emotions are released; this takes the form of a headache or flulike symptoms for 24 hours.

If there are any worrying symptoms following a Shiatsu massage, the practitioner should be contacted for reassurance and advice.

Recommendations
The practitioner may make recommendations about diet, exercise and lifestyle, encouraging patients to reach a deeper understanding of themselves and greater independence in health matters.

Practitioner

People wishing to receive Shiatsu massage should seek treatment from a practitioner who is on the list of Registered Practitioners compiled by the Shiatsu Society.

REGISTERED PRACTITIONERS
The Shiatsu Society was first established in 1981 and is an umbrella organization for Shiatsu in Britain.

Registered practitioners will have the initials MRSS after their names, indicating that they have all achieved an approved standard of training as established by the Shiatsu Society Assessment Panel.

As members of the Shiatsu Society, they are considered competent to practise Shiatsu safely. In addition, they are bound by a code of ethics and they have professional indemnity insurance.

Ayurvedic medicine

Ayurvedic medicine is a traditional medicine, practised widely in India and Sri Lanka. Practitioners concentrate on detoxification, herbs, diet and exercise to address imbalances in an individual's health.

Ayurveda is an ancient holistic system of medicine that is practised widely in Sri Lanka and India. In Sanskrit, 'Ayurveda' means the science or wisdom (veda) of life (ayur).

TRADITIONAL MEDICINE

Ayurvedic medicine is a complex system of healthcare, which takes into account factors such as detoxification, meditation, exercise and dietary advice in order to encourage physical, emotional, spiritual and mental health. It is based on advice formulated by a group of holy men, written down in an ancient Indian text believed to date back to before 3000 BC, making Ayurveda probably the most ancient of all medical systems.

Practitioners believe that all living things are made up of five elements: fire, water, earth, air and ether. These are converted by the 'agni' (digestive fire) into three doshas, vital energies that exist throughout nature as well

In Ayurvedic practice, the doctor checks the patients pulse at three different points on the wrist. Each point corresponds to one of the three vital energies.

as in the human race, and influence our physical and mental well being.

The doshas are fluctuating centres of energy, each of which is made up of two of the five elements. Air and ether form vata; pitta is produced from

fire and water; kapha is water and earth.

CONSTITUTION

Each person has a dominant dosha that determines their temperament and constitution. An individual is born in the

'prakruthi' state, which means that they are born with the correct dosha levels for them as an individual.

Ayurvedic practitioners believe that illness is caused by an imbalance in the doshas, brought about by a poor diet, stress, injury or trauma. These imbalances are thought to impede the flow of 'prana', the breath of life. Ayurvedic practitioners treat people to restore them to their correct 'prakruthi' state.

Ancient Ayurvedic textbooks were written on bamboo wood (shown) or palm leaves. This system of medicine dates back to before 3000 BC.

Three doshas

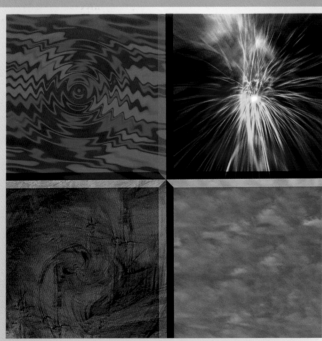

The four elements of water, fire, air and earth (plus a fifth, ether) are integral to Ayurveda. Each dosha is a combination of two of the five elements.

Every living body possesses three vital energies, or doshas, in unique individual proportions. The three doshas are known as vata, pitta and kapha.

■ Vata

This is the driving force within the body, and its functions are similar to those of the nervous system.

When balanced, a person has plenty of energy and happiness. When vata is low, it leads to an accumulation of fluids, bowel infections, tiredness and poor circulation. When vata is in excess, it causes dry skin, brittle hair, bone problems, bowel disorders, worry, anxiety, insomnia and depression.

■ Pitta

This is the metabolic force or fire in the body. It controls factors such as the appetite, warmth and digestion.

When balanced, people can eat and drink well without becoming overweight or underweight, and can hold bodily energy. When pitta is low, it can cause indigestion, poor appetite, weight loss and lethargy. When it is high, it can cause acidity, stomach ulcers, inflammation, skin disorders, irritability and anger.

■ Kapha

This is linked to water in the phlegm, fat and bodily fluids.

Low kapha leads to weight loss, dry chest, dehydration and thirst. Excess of kapha leads to asthma, sinus problems, fluid retention, obesity and high cholesterol disorders.

Treatment

Treatment begins with an initial consultation which lasts for about one hour. During this consultation, the Ayurvedic practitioner questions the individual about their health, and asks about factors such as lifestyle, occupation, diet and appetite. The practitioner will then conduct a physical examination, noting any particular problems.

DETOXIFICATION
Before treatment commences, it is essential to detoxify the body. Depending on an individual's health, they may undergo a seven-day detoxification (panchakarma), which involves a range of therapies. These include enemas, purgatives, laxatives and nasal therapy or steam inhalation to clear the lungs and upper body. Practitioners say that such

strong measures are needed for long-standing complaints.

HERBAL REMEDIES
After detoxification, herbal or mineral remedies may be prescribed to address imbalances in an individual's doshas. Pills, remedies and tonics are prepared from plants, minerals, sea shells, and metals. Herbal remedies might include hot spices such as coriander for fever, diarrhoea and influenza, and ginger for asthma and vomiting. Aloe vera is an important Ayurvedic plant, used to treat bowel disorders and skin problems.

Enjoyable treatments may be recommended: for example, marma massage is a therapeutic massage with oils; rasayana is a rejuvenation regime that incorporates yoga, chanting, meditation and sunbathing.

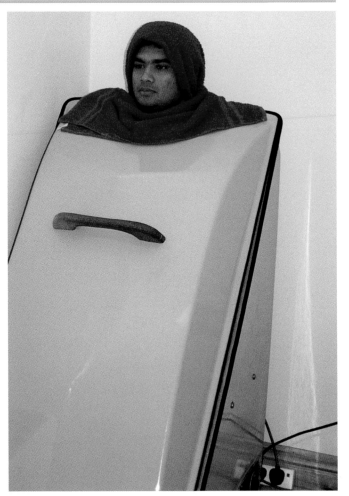

Oil therapy, or shirodhara, can be effective in treating insomnia or migraine, for example. Oil is poured onto the forehead and then stroked down the hair.

Sweat therapy enables patients to eliminate waste products. The steambath always follows a massage with oil, which causes toxins to rise to the skin surface.

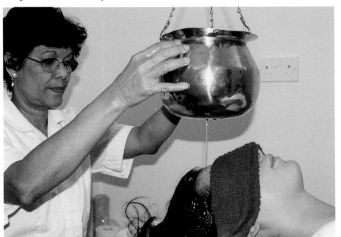

Treatable conditions

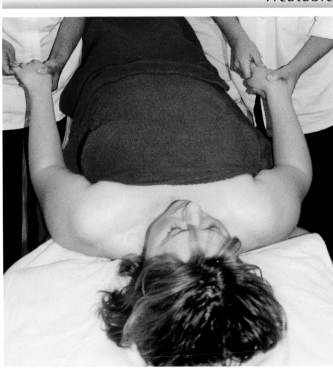

Ayurveda is beneficial for conditions such as eczema, acne and psoriasis and stress-related conditions such as migraine, insomnia and irritable bowel syndrome. Chronic joint disorders such as arthritis and rheumatism, and sexual problems such as premature ejaculation and infertility, can also benefit.

ROLE OF DIGESTION
In Ayurveda, good digestion is considered the key to good health. Poor digestion produces 'ama', a toxic substance believed to cause illness. 'Ama' occurs when the metabolism is impaired due to an imbalance of 'agni'. Agni is the fire which, when working normally, maintains all functions. Imbalanced agni is

Ayurvedic oil massage aims to improve circulation, eliminate waste and relax muscles. The patient usually follows the massage with a steambath.

caused by irregularity in the doshas, eating and drinking too much of the wrong food and liquid, and repressing emotions.

Agni affected by too much kapha can slow the digestive process, making a person feel heavy and sluggish. Too much vata can cause wind, cramps and alternating periods of constipation and diarrhoea.

EMOTIONAL HEALTH
Toxins that cause illness can be produced by emotional as well as physical factors. For example, fear and anxiety relate to vata and the large intestine; when held inside, these emotions can cause bloating and intestinal pain.

Food allergies can also develop because of poor emotional heath. Failing to express the emotions can start cravings for food likely to cause imbalance. Yoga and meditation can help people to understand and deal with negative emotions.

Biofeedback training

Biofeedback training enables individuals to use information from their bodies to learn to control certain processes. Heartbeat, blood pressure and temperature can all be regulated in this way.

Biofeedback training is a therapeutic and meditative tool by which individuals learn to control certain physiological processes such as heartbeat, body temperature and blood pressure.

Physiological processes are not normally under conscious control, at least partly because they cannot normally be consciously sensed. Biofeedback makes the individual aware of such processes by monitoring them and presenting the information to the person being treated in the form of a visual or auditory readout.

LEARNING BIOFEEDBACK

A typical example of biofeedback might involve a trainee whose heart rate is monitored and presented back to them as a series of beeps. The trainee attempts to speed up or slow down the beeping through concentration.

When the biofeedback skill is learned, the trainee can exercise it at will, without the use of biofeedback. Exactly how this is achieved is still not understood, but it does seem to work.

Biofeedback training monitors certain bodily processes, such as pulse rate. The information is fed back to the individual, enabling them to affect the process.

Biofeedback training can help to treat persistent headaches. Electrodes attached to the forehead monitor the electrical activity in the muscles.

HISTORY

Conventional medical wisdom holds that physiological processes, such as heart rate and blood pressure, are governed by the autonomic nervous system and that, therefore, they cannot be consciously controlled.

This view has long been contradicted by the claims of many Indian yogis, however, and was further challenged by the experiments of Neal Miller in the late 1960s. Miller showed that rats could be trained to increase blood flow to one ear at a time. If rats could do it, the theory went, then why not human?

In the early 1970s, trials of applied biofeedback training to treat chronic tension headaches seemed successful and, since then, many other types of biofeedback training have been tried.

Yogi power

Yogis are yoga/meditation adepts who can slow their heart rate and breathing at will, enabling them to survive for long periods without air. They can also control their circulation and pain responses to withstand burning or piercing.

Nobody knows exactly how the process works, except that yogis obtain their powers through relaxing the body to achieve deeper meditative states, while keeping the mind alert.

Brain wave rhythms
Biofeedback training can be used to the same end, by providing feedback on brain wave rhythms and learning to induce key rhythms. Alpha (relaxing) and theta (sleeping) rhythms relax mind and body; by adding beta (concentrating) rhythms, the relaxed body/alert mind state can be achieved.

▶ *Masters of yoga, known as yogis, are able to control bodily functions such as heart rate. It is not fully understood how they achieve this.*

◀ *Meditation involves deep contemplation and relaxation techniques. Biofeedback produces similar effects while the mind remains alert.*

Using biofeedback

With today's sophisticated equipment, most physiological systems can be monitored in real time, and the information obtained can be converted into a visual or auditory form.

TECHNIQUES

The most common types of monitoring used in biofeedback training are:

■ Electrical skin resistance (ESR) meter – ESR is a measure of the conductivity of the skin, determined by sweating, determined in turn by levels of physiological arousal. This makes ESR a measure of stress

■ Electromyography (EMG) – measures muscle activity, including those muscles of which an individual might not normally be aware

■ Electro-encephalography (EEG) – measures patterns of electrical activity in the brain (brain waves) using a series of electrodes attached to the scalp. Certain brain wave rhythms are associated with specific states of consciousness; for example, alpha rhythms are typical of a relaxed state

■ Measures of heart rate, blood pressure and other processes – apart from being markers of physiological arousal and therefore stress, these measures are also important biomedical indicators in their own right.

USES

A surprising range of conditions has been successfully treated with biofeedback training. Some of the more important ones include:

■ Tension and migraine headache – tension in the frontalis muscle (a band of muscle around the head, of which a person is not normally conscious) is thought to play a part in some chronic headache problems. EMG monitoring of the frontalis muscle was presented to sufferers in the form of clicks through headphones. By learning to slow the rate of clicks, sufferers learned to relax their frontalis muscle and relieve the headaches

■ Insomnia, pain and epilepsy – using an EEG to monitor brain waves, with feedback in the form of tones or patterns on a visual display, sufferers can be taught to induce patterns of waves associated with sleep, relaxation, pain relief or even immobility, helping them to drift off to sleep, block pain or calm an epileptic attack

■ Heart arrhythmias – a cardio-tachometer is a type of EMG, specialized for heart monitoring. People at risk of dangerous heart arrhythmias can use one to learn to regulate their heartbeat, and even to recognize the onset of arrhythmia without use of a monitor

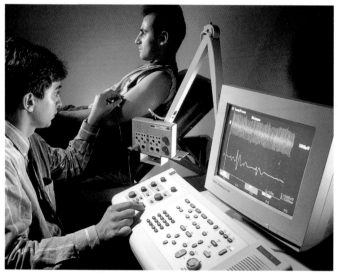

Electromyography measures muscle activity, such as the contraction of a biceps muscle. Information on the muscle is relayed to a screen.

Headaches can be treated with biofeedback training. Affected individuals learn how to relax the muscle around the head, and so relieve the headache.

■ Asthma and anxiety – using measures of stress, such as ESR, EMG and respiration monitoring, sufferers can learn to relax, reduce their level of physiological arousal, maintain normal respiration and cope with an asthma or anxiety attack

■ Blood pressure problems – using biofeedback from blood pressure monitors, trainees learn to control their blood pressure. Hence, people with hypertension can reduce their blood pressure.

In people with certain spinal injuries, a sudden drop in blood pressure on standing can cause loss of consciousness; the use of biofeedback training can help injured patients to overcome this problem by boosting their blood pressure at will.

Success rate of biofeedback training

In most trials of applied biofeedback training, the therapy appears to have been highly successful. However, proper controlled trials have not been performed, partly because no-one understands exactly how the biofeedback element works, making it hard to control for this variable.

SCEPTICISM

Considerable doubt still remains over the issue of whether trainees are genuinely learning to control their autonomic processes. As a result, the mainstream medical profession is still sceptical about the efficacy of biofeedback training, and it is often dismissed as a form of psychotherapy, effective mainly because it offers a placebo effect.

PATIENT INVOLVEMENT

Irrespective of how it works, biofeedback training has several positive therapeutic aspects. It puts the patient in control, involving them at every stage of the process, so that they are proactive in their own therapy. Studies show that these factors have a great impact on the outcome of therapy, making biofeedback training a valuable therapeutic tool.

Although the mechanisms of biofeedback training are not fully understood, the technique has successfully resolved a range of conditions.

Index